DO YOU SOLEMNLY SWEAR?

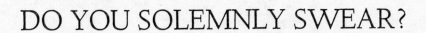

DO YOU SOLEMNLY SWEAR?

LOUIS B. HELLER
*Justice of the Supreme Court
of the State of New York*

Foreword by
ABE FORTAS
United States Supreme Court Justice

Doubleday & Company, Inc.
Garden City, New York
1968

Library of Congress Catalog Card Number 67-20910
Copyright © 1968 by Louis B. Heller

To my wife, Ruth, who, although she failed to produce a promised dowry, nevertheless by her devotion made it possible for me to spend many years in the rough-and-tumble of political life and the law, and who encouraged me to write this book; to my daughter, Marcia, who was most helpful and cheerful in assisting me; and to my son, Robert, to whom, while he was at law school, I tried to communicate the message of this book. At the time he was always "too busy," as most sons are, to listen. Perhaps now that he is a lawyer himself, I may hope that, after reading what I have written here, he will find himself concurring in the views of Mark Twain expressed in these words:

> When I was a boy of fourteen, my father was so ignorant that I could hardly stand to have the old man around. But when I got to be twenty-one, I was astonished at how much he had learned in seven years.

It did not take me seven years to learn what I have set forth in this book. It took me twenty-seven years at the bar and fourteen years on the bench.

Foreword

Judge Heller's life has been rich and packed with much more than the usual quota of color and excitement. Trial lawyer, state senator, United States Congressman, trial judge—he has been each of these. And he has now produced a book whose pages are replete with the humor and knowledge and wisdom a perceptive man extracts from careers such as these. This kind of book needs no external justification.

But Judge Heller put his thoughts and experience to paper for rather special reasons. His first love has always been the trial court—the lawyers and judges who devote their lives to that wood-paneled jousting place; the people—significant and unknown to the world—whose lives and fortunes provide the stakes; and the sometimes innocent bystanders who get caught up in the web of the trial court because they happened to see the defendant's car strike the plaintiff, because they witnessed the robbery with which the accused is charged, because they were the cause of the marital discord at issue. These people, enmeshed in what must appear unbelievable circumstances were we to read about them in another medium, are the staple of everyday life in the trial courts of the Nation, and particularly in those of a great city like the City of New York which is Judge Heller's scene.

Judge Heller is a man with a mission. That mission is to assist young men to carve lives for themselves in the trial courts, professional lives in which their craftsmanship and artistry will help to assure that justice gets done, and is seen to be done. That mission led the Judge to lecture embryo lawyers at the New York Law School on the art of courtroom advocacy. It led him to fashion interesting proposals for the training of young lawyers so that the present-day shortage of skilled courtroom hands may be remedied. And it led him to write this book, which is a guide to the perplexed law student or member of the bar setting out to become a trial lawyer.

No one knows better than the Judge, of course, that one does not become a craftsman at the law, and still less an artist at it, from the pages of a book, or even of a library. Lawyers have to be tempered in the furnace of experience. No book or collection of them can fully prepare a young man to cope with the always changing, ever variegated life of the law. One cannot master the art of defending a murder case, or of marshaling the materials needed to resist an antitrust prosecution, by reading about it.

But when they are close enough to life, to the real thing, books can be of significant didactic value. For life is not long enough to acquire at first hand the experience which living demands, and we must look to literature as experience's surrogate. We must learn from experience. But those experiences need not always be our own. The pages of this book, with their genuine "feel" for the trial court and what happens there, should prove of value to anyone embarking—or already well embarked, for that matter—on a career in the trial courts.

Judge Heller's book has another value. I have long thought that Americans, and particularly those concerned with the quality of our national life and the integrity of our national institutions, have too much neglected the trial court. This is where the citizen comes face to face with "the law." Whether the matter concerns liability for a traffic violation, the dissolution of a marriage, a dispute over property or commercial affairs, or the accusation of crime, it is in the trial court that one experiences the quality, good or bad, of the ultimate institution of his society, short of its armed force. There, too often, one personally experiences the strange phenomenon that an affluent and a sensitive society can neglect a vital institution. There it is that one too frequently witnesses shabby, inhuman, medieval facilities, insufficient or inadequate personnel, insufferable procedures, an atmosphere which is reminiscent of Hogarth instead of the Ivy League. And this totality frequently adds up to justice denied and the law brought into disrepute.

But the world of the trial court is not all bleak, as many of the pages of this book illustrate. Indeed, no one can read a book like this without acquiring an appetite for more. Hopefully, those who learn to share the excitement and color of these courts will stay to assist in their improvement. That was the response of a generation of Englishmen who read with mingled fascination and horror of their Courts of Chancery in Charles Dickens' *Bleak House,* and eventually pruned the system of the grosser evils which Dickens had portrayed. Hopefully, a new generation of Americans, informed and stimulated by books like Judge Heller's, and brought into the trial courts in rapidly increasing numbers

by the new demand for appointed counsel in criminal cases and for
Neighborhood Legal Services on behalf of the poor, will achieve a similar refashioning.

Judge Heller's book serves these dual functions: as a Baedeker to the
aspiring trial lawyer who needs a wise and trustworthy guide to the
art of trial advocacy, and as a summons to all of us to examine our local
trial courts and to raise sharply the quality of justice there administered.

Abe Fortas

Contents

VI. CROSS-EXAMINATION

VII. CLOSING TO THE JURY

VIII. IMAGE OF A PROFESSION

I

PREPARATION

1

The Readiness Is All

It is not hard to understand why trials and courtroom scenes have long been and still remain among the favorite subjects of writers for the stage, screen, and television. Whether in fact or in fiction, there is hardly a trial at law without at least some of the elements that make for dramatic interest and excitement. There is, for one thing, the suspense about the outcome, as well as the emotional tension that inevitably accompanies any conflict between unyielding antagonists. And what trial is altogether lacking in some moments of sentiment, pathos, or even humor? If we add to these the ever-present possibility of a surprise confrontation or a sudden, unexpected turn of fortune for either side, it is no wonder that we are perennially fascinated with the way in which lawsuits are prosecuted.

The crossing of swords in the verbal duels between opposing lawyers, the cautious sparring of witness with cross-examiner, the baited traps into which the unsuspecting are artfully lured, the fatally incriminating off-guard admission, the telltale evidence of a document, a fingerprint, an instrument, or a weapon, the moving eloquence of counsels' summations—all these have become part of the familiar repertory, even the stock-in-trade, of our writers of melodrama. Indeed, it is probably not too much to say that the prevailing conception of a trial owes much to the view that sees it as a kind of combat in which the adversaries' lawyers, acting as the champions of their clients, enter the lists to do valiant battle on their behalf. No doubt many an idealistic young person has first been attracted to the prospect of a career as a trial lawyer because he liked to envision himself in precisely such a role. I confess that I was.

Yet this dramatic—or, rather, melodramatic—view of the work of our profession is incomplete. It is, in fact, much like the view of the members of the audience attending a performance at the theater, for whom the play begins when the curtain goes up. The actors on the stage, already in costume, setting, and character, are seen from the outset solely as participants in the drama that proceeds to unfold before the eyes of the spectators. So skillfully has the spell been woven that the illusion is complete. In reality, of course, long before the curtain rose, weeks, even months, may have been spent in such arduous and undramatic activities as casting, rehearsing, designing costumes and scenery, and reviewing the script. The actual performance is but the result of all this prior labor.

It is no less an illusion to suppose that the work of a trial lawyer begins when, after the judge has mounted the bench, and the court clerk has intoned the traditional "Hear ye! Hear ye! All persons having business before this court draw near. Give your attention, and ye shall be heard," the moment comes for counsel to present his opening statement to the jury. Just as the audience sees and hears only the actors on the stage, but is unaware of the technicians and assistants behind the scenes, so too the jury sees and hears only the witnesses and the lawyers, but is not directly aware of that important intangible which underlies all the questions and answers, all the preliminary and incidental trial motions, namely, pretrial preparation. Actually, the trial itself is—or properly should be—only the culmination of a lengthy period of intensive preparatory activity on the part of the lawyers on both sides.

If, as I have suggested, a trial may also be likened in many respects to a battle, then victory or defeat may well depend on the extent to which the opposing forces have been equipped and marshaled for combat readiness. In a military engagement, before the first shots are fired, the generals on both sides map their strategy. They reconnoiter the terrain. They gather intelligence concerning the character and composition of the troops of the enemy. They collect ammunition. They anticipate traps and ambushes. They decide at what point to concentrate their attack and attempt to strengthen the places at which they consider their own defenses to be most vulnerable. They take pains to deploy their troops in battle array. And they do not forget to prepare alternate lines of defense to fall back upon in case of necessity. Each of these activities has its counterpart in the work that a lawyer does in preparing his case for trial.

Obviously the outcome of the ensuing contest is, in great measure, dependent on the thoroughness and care with which this strategic and tactical planning is carried out. In fact, I should say that ninety per cent of a lawyer's case is won long before he ever sets foot in a courtroom. In the professional life of a lawyer, it is preparation that makes the difference between top-flight success and mediocrity. The rewards of exhaustive planning are, as we shall see, indeed great, but the penalties of inadequate or careless preparation are equally considerable. Any lawyer so foolhardy as to neglect or skimp this essential part of his professional duty, in the hope of depending on the inspiration of the moment in the heat of combat, does a distinct disservice to both his client and himself. For this reason, the preparation of a case cannot begin too early or be too thorough. The more comprehensive and detailed the planning, the less is left to chance; and thus the greater the confidence with which counsel can present his arguments to judge and jury, the more assured he can be in examining and cross-examining witnesses. In these respects, at least, "the readiness," as Hamlet says, "is all."

The advantages of taking pains to lay the groundwork of a case solidly in advance of trial are strikingly illustrated by an experience I had as counsel in a matrimonial matter on behalf of a gentleman whom I shall call Mr. Daniel Adams. He suspected that, during the hours when he was employed in the conduct of his business, his wife was carrying on an affair at their home with the physician who had been professionally engaged to treat her infirm, eighty-year-old mother, bedridden in their apartment, and requiring a visit from him at least twice a week.

To obtain evidence of his wife's infidelity, Mr. Adams hired a private detective. It was not long before Mr. Adams' suspicions were confirmed. The detective submitted reports concerning the length of time the doctor stayed at the house during each of his visits, the fixing of the blinds in the couple's bedroom, and other circumstances equally suspicious. However, the investigator insisted that he could not possibly make a successful raid unless Mr. Adams was prepared to engage another detective to help him, and to pay an additional fee, which Mr. Adams considered prohibitive. Besides, Mr. Adams, who was by no means a fool, foresaw a further problem. As he put it, "Suppose a raid does take place. How could I get away from the doctor's plea that he was only treating my mother-in-law?"

The problem, therefore, was how to obtain additional evidence that would definitely tie the doctor to Mr. Adams' wife and untie him from the mother-in-law.

In questioning Mr. Adams, I learned that for at least six months prior to their matrimonial difficulties his wife had denied him marital relations, and that, when they had had relations, she was in the habit of using vaginal jelly. I asked him whether he knew where she kept it, and he said that he did. I thereupon instructed him to buy a torsion scale of the kind used by pharmacists to weigh drugs, capsules, and powders from one-eighth of a grain up. I further instructed him to weigh the tube of vaginal jelly each midnight for at least a month and to keep a precise record of his findings.

At the end of that period, the record definitely indicated a diminution in the amount of vaginal jelly in certain proportions on every occasion that the doctor visited the house. It was clear that the vaginal jelly was being used on the days when he came to examine the mother-in-law.

With this record neatly tucked away in my files, arrangements were made for a raid. But by the time the raiders managed to reach the couple's bedroom, the agile doctor was almost fully dressed. Only his necktie remained to be knotted. As a detective was recouping a soiled towel from underneath a disarrayed bed, the doctor, before he had even been accused of anything, shouted, "I was only examining the old lady!"

A week or two later, at a conference attended by the couple, the co-respondent, and their respective attorneys, the doctor continued to insist stoutly that he had done nothing wrong, that he had simply been examining the mother-in-law. However, when he was confronted with our chart, in which the date of every one of his visits was precisely correlated with a definite decrease in the supply of Mrs. Adams' vaginal jelly, he almost jumped out of the window of my office—without a parachute!

Of course, the question may be raised whether such a chart would be, as lawyers say, "admissible in evidence" in a court of law. I doubt it. The judge would probably have excluded it, as a matter of law, and the jury would not have been permitted to take it into consideration in reaching a verdict. Fortunately, however, this legal question was never presented for adjudication, since the matter never came to trial. Whatever a court might have done, it was enough that the doctor himself accepted the evidence—because he knew it was true, and he was, apparently, not inclined to take the risk of public exposure. After all, as a practicing physician, he had his reputation to consider, and, even if he were completely exonerated at a trial, he could hardly expect to emerge unscathed by the sensational manner in which his role in the case would undoubtedly have been portrayed in the press. In my opinion, he was smart to capitulate. At any rate, my client had the additional proof he needed, though he had been told in advance that it might be inadmissible.

As we can see, a lawyer needs to be something of a sleuth. To be successful, he has to have in him a bit of the spirit of Sherlock Holmes. After all, a trial is, strictly speaking, a search for truth as rigorous and demanding as any that takes place in the laboratory of a scientist, and the truth is not likely to be brought out in court if counsel has not first patiently investigated and thoroughly sifted all the facts of the case beforehand. No matter how conversant he may be with the law as expounded in the books, if he is not in a position to apply this knowledge to the facts, he will find himself seriously handicapped in presenting his case when it comes to trial. Besides, I think it is safe to say that the law seldom resolves the issue; more often than not, the facts do. The facts of a case remain the decisive forces that shape the rules of law.

For this reason, a case cannot be adequately prepared for trial simply by sitting in an office or a library poring over law books. Nor, in most cases, and especially in those involving alleged negligence or crime, is a lawyer likely to do a professional job of preparation if he contents himself with merely interviewing his client and his witnesses without stirring from his office. Facts are his ammunition, and, if he is to be sure of obtaining all that he needs, he must be willing to take an active and personal role in gathering them. Even if he can afford to hire someone else to do the job for him, it would be most unwise for any lawyer to forego making an independent investigation of his own concerning dates, persons, places, events, and other data relevant to his case. To this end, he should not hesitate to get out of his office and take the pains to familiarize himself at first hand with the scene of the accident or crime, the neighborhood, and the people living and working in it.

In a criminal case especially, no rumor is too insignificant to be investigated, no conjecture too wild to be considered, no "lead" too far afield to be followed up. No lawyer can afford to be indolent or indifferent in this respect. For sometimes he may have to do the work that should have been done by the detectives on the police force. I recall a case in which I was engaged to defend a client against a charge of murder. In talking to all of the people I could find in the neighborhood where the killing had occurred, I heard a rumor that one of the men working on a nearby subway excavation and construction project had witnessed the stabbing. For over a week I clambered over steel girders, gingerly picked my way along narrow boards stretched shakily over yawning, debris-filled chasms of reinforced concrete, and squeezed myself between churning cement-mixers and clattering compressed-air pumps as I proceeded from one worker to another, trying to find my witness. At last I located him. Overlooked by the official investigative forces, he gave testimony that helped to save a man from the electric chair.

The importance of bestirring oneself to obtain direct knowledge of pertinent physical details by personal investigation in advance of trial is also well illustrated by an accident case that was tried in one of our courts. The plaintiff was injured when she missed her step on the stairs leading to the porch of a belvedere at a summer resort. Her lawyer took the trouble to make the trip to the scene of the accident, a mountain hotel, which was about one hundred miles from his office. There he found, just as the management had boasted in its advertising brochure, one of the hotel's prime attractions, the breath-taking beauty of the view of the surrounding countryside to be had from the porch of what it called its "Panorama" building, where the plaintiff had been injured. In the course of his examination of this site, he noticed that the floor of the porch was painted the same shade of battleship gray as the landing that led down from it to the stairs. This identity in color gave rise to the optical illusion that there was no gradation between the plane of the porch and that of the landing. They both seemed to be on the same level. Accordingly, as a consequence of counsel's preliminary reconnaissance of the terrain, he was able to adduce evidence at the trial tending to show that his client, while lawfully using the steps and casting her gaze outward to catch a view of the lovely scenery, which she had been told by the defendant to look for, could not observe, under the circumstances, the drop in the level between the porch and the landing.

The effect of this testimony may be seen in the ruling of the Court that the question whether there was contributory negligence—i.e., negligence on the plaintiff's part which, if established, would nullify any liability of the defendant—was one for the jury to determine in the light of the evidence. In other words, it was a question of fact, to be decided by the jury, not a question of law, to be decided by the judge. Had the Court treated it as a question of law, and found the plaintiff guilty of contributory negligence, the judge could not have permitted the jury to pass on this issue and would have dismissed the plaintiff's case. However, the thorough preparation of the case on the part of the plaintiff's lawyer enabled him to adduce evidence that raised a question of fact, which the Court was required to and did submit to the jury. The jury held for the plaintiff.

A further illustration of the value of personal investigation on the part of a lawyer in advance of trial is a case recounted to me by a friend of mine. He was engaged as counsel for the plaintiff, a house painter, in a suit against the owner of a building for the balance of a bill for services rendered in painting an apartment. In response to the suit, the landlord interposed a counterclaim for an even greater amount than he was being sued for, alleging that the work had been so poorly performed that the new tenant, who had taken possession of the apartment, had complained vehemently about the paint job, and another painter had to be called in to do it all over again.

Before the trial, counsel for the plaintiff went to the premises and spoke to the tenant, who denied having ever complained about the quality of the painting and stated that no one had repainted the apartment. The tenant was accordingly subpoenaed to appear at the trial.

After the plaintiff had testified to having performed the work, the landlord took the stand. He swore that the apartment had needed repainting, and he even mentioned the name of the painter he had hired for the job. This painter was not present in court.

When the landlord had completed his testimony, the tenant was called to the stand. At the sight of this wholly unexpected witness, the landlord's face turned a fiery red.

The tenant testified that the apartment had never been repainted. The first question asked of the tenant by the attorney for the landlord on cross-examination was: "What is your business or occupation?"

The answer was: "I am the sexton of _____ Church."

There was no further cross-examination.

Just one personal visit by plaintiff's attorney did the trick!

The average person who engages the services of a trial lawyer is hardly in a position to appreciate the many hours of toil or the extent of the investigations that go into the planning of what may appear to be a rather simple and even routine case. Still fewer are the laymen who can adequately appraise what we lawyers call the legal craftsmanship that every well-planned case exemplifies. The fact is that, for the conscientious advocate, there are no routine cases. Each presents a special and perhaps a unique problem and a fresh challenge to his resourcefulness and imagination. Though he cannot, of course, anticipate every contingency that may arise when his case comes to trial, he tries to leave as little as possible to chance. His problem is to elaborate a well-coordinated plan of action that will serve him as a blueprint in constructing the edifice of legal and factual evidence to be presented to judge and jury. When he comes to court, he may have to deviate a little from his plan on occasion, but by and large he will, if it has been properly conceived, follow it closely. Accordingly, he cannot afford to consider any detail too small to be overlooked. And when the whole plan is completed, it constitutes, in the truest sense of the word, a work of art, in which every element has its appropriate place. Thus, a lawyer must have something of the instinct and pride of workmanship of an architect or a master builder as he painstakingly goes about the task of laying each piece of evidence in the right place to sustain the solid structure of proof he seeks to erect. Indeed, members of the legal profession derive a certain esthetic satisfaction from the contemplation of a carefully thought-out pretrial plan.

To be really thorough, preparation before trial must anticipate the needs not only of direct examination but of cross-examination as well. As an illustration of the extent to which pretrial investigation may have to go if it is to meet these exacting standards, I may cite a closely contested election case in which I was personally involved some years ago. In advance of the primary election, which is in many States the vehicle for designating candidates, my opponent had filed with the Board of Elections of the City of New York a petition purporting to designate him as a candidate for an important position in the Democratic Party. The only issue to be decided by the Court was whether he was, in the year mentioned in his petition, a bona fide resident of a certain Assembly District in Brooklyn. If he was, he was entitled to have his name placed on the ballot as a candidate. If he was not, his petition would have to be invalidated, and his name stricken.

In his nominating petition he gave as his residence an address in Brooklyn which, on investigation, proved to be that of his mother and other members of her family. I suspected that he himself did not actually live there, although his name did appear on the nameplate in the house letterbox. At first I had nothing more to work on than a mere suspicion. However, the fact that for some years previously he had used this address in obtaining important political posts did not deter me from undertaking, in the short time allotted to me, a far-reaching investigation based on that suspicion. As a result, I discovered that at the time mentioned in his petition he had not been living in Brooklyn, but had been residing with his wife in a Manhattan apartment which he had rented under her maiden name.

I planned my strategy for this case on the theory that I had to produce irrefutable affirmative testimony so overpowering in its cumulative impact that my opponent and his wife, after hearing my witnesses, would not even attempt a reply. And, in fact, by the time the case was called for trial, I had under subpoena over twenty-five witnesses armed with documents and data, ready to testify and expose the falsity of my opponent's claim. The voluminous minutes of the trial refresh my recollection that I actually put on the stand twenty-three witnesses, each of whom formed an essential part of a thoroughly prepared attack on the point at issue, namely, my opponent's allegation concerning his place of residence. Among these witnesses were such varied personalities as an employee of the Board of Elections, an officer of the real estate company that had leased a Manhattan apartment to him, the superintendent of the building in Manhattan, the day and night elevator operators employed there, a representative of the New York Telephone Company, an employee of the electric company, various long-time residents of the Brooklyn Assembly District which, my opponent contended, encompassed his place of residence, and several prominent attorneys, including an Assistant District Attorney.

Here is how I went about setting up my roadblock. Armed with the information that my opponent was actually occupying the Manhattan apartment, I visited a number of tailor shops and valet establishments in the neighborhood until I came upon one that he and his wife regularly patronized. From the proprietor of this shop I ascertained that it was his practice to place a certain identification mark on the inside of every garment accepted for cleaning and to keep a book in which he recorded, opposite each customer's name, the number of the ticket issued to the customer for reclaiming his garments. Careful preliminary investigation demonstrated conclusively that my opponent and his wife were regular customers of this valet shop in Manhattan at the very time when he was steadfastly maintaining that he was a resident of Brooklyn. To show how the owner of the valet shop closed the roadblock with finality, here is some of the actual testimony from the original record of his direct examination, changed only with regard to names, addresses, and other identifying details:

Q. Mr. Taylor, you have a business you call John's Valet Service, is that right?
A. Yes.
Q. And this valet service is at No. 283 West 55th Street?
A. Yes.
Q. In Manhattan?
A. That is right.

Q. That is about directly across the street from the apartment house at 280 West 55th Street, Manhattan, is that correct?

A. Yes.

Q. And how long have you been doing business at John's Valet Service at that address?

A. For over the last five years.

Q. And you are still in business there at that place?

A. That is right.

Q. Now, do you know Mr. X [naming my opponent]?

A. Yes.

Q. Did you ever see him with his wife?

A. Yes.

Q. You saw them together?

A. Yes.

Q. Do you know where they lived during the entire year 1950 [the year of the dispute]?

A. 280 West 55th Street, Manhattan.

Q. Now, when, for about the first time, did you see either Mr. X or his wife?

A. It was more than a year ago.

Q. Where did you see them?

A. In my store.

Q. Did they do any business with you?

A. They brought me cleaning.

Q. Garments, wearing apparel?

A. Yes.

Q. Did they leave the garments with you?

A. Yes.

Q. About how often did you see them in your store on business?

A. Well, sometimes once a month, once in two months, sometimes once in three months.

Q. And did you give them any kind of identification number?

A. They never accepted a ticket, but I had to have a number on it when I take it in to clean.

Q. You have a book, haven't you?

A. Yes.

Q. Will you look at your book, please?

A. (Witness looks at book.)

Q. May I direct your attention to ticket No. 4226, December, 1949. Have you got that?

A. Yes.

Q. Is that made out to Mr. X?

A. Yes.

Q. Did you write that name?

A. Yes.

At this point, a photostat of the entry was offered and was, as we lawyers say, "received in evidence," that is, it was duly shown to my adversary, who raised no objection to its acceptance, and was ordered marked
by the Court as part of the record of evidence presented on my behalf
which the Court could then take into account in resolving the issue.

Q. Now, Mr. Witness, may I direct your attention to ticket No. 4326,
   dated December 31, 1949. Is that ticket made out to Mr. X?
A. Yes, that is right.
Q. Now, will you please look at ticket No. 1867, dated May 1, 1950.
   Is that in the name of Mr. X?
A. Yes.
Q. And ticket No. 18, dated January 31, 1950, is that in the name of
   Mr. X?
A. Yes.
Q. Now, please look at ticket No. 403, dated March 31, 1950; ticket
   No. 367, undated; ticket No. 573, dated April 5, 1950; and ticket
   No. 4509, dated January 25, 1950. Are all of these tickets in the
   name of Mr. X or his wife?
A. Yes, they are, all of them.

All of these tickets were offered and received in evidence. So too was
the daily record book of the proprietor of the valet establishment, showing his business transactions with my opponent and his wife during
the period in question.

The clincher came when the Court was asked and granted permission
for my opponent to be interrogated in chambers. (As he was a lawyer,
I made this request in the hope that he would see the utter futility of
his claim and abandon it.) There he was asked to remove his trousers
and read the identification number on the inside, where the owner of
the valet shop had inscribed it. As I expected, the identification mark
made by the Manhattan cleaner matched perfectly the number that he
had mentioned in his testimony. This information was duly read into
the record. Similarly, a laundryman, who testified that Mr. X brought
his shirts and undergarments to his laundry, identified from his records
the markings he had assigned to them. When my opponent's shirt and
shorts were exposed to the judge's view, the identification marks on
them likewise matched those recorded by the laundryman, and this evidence too was added to the record. If there was any scintilla of a doubt
in my opponent's mind by this time about the hopelessness of his contention, it must have evaporated completely when he heard the following testimony from the lips of the local letter carrier, who attested to

the fact that no mail had been delivered to Mr. X at the address in Brooklyn where he alleged he resided during the period in question:

Q. Are you employed in the Post Office Department of the United States Government?
A. That is correct.
Q. You are what is known as a mail carrier, is that correct?
A. That is right.
Q. Do you carry the mails in the vicinity of 15 R Avenue [Mr. X's alleged Brooklyn residence]?
A. That is correct.
Q. And do you deliver mail, should there be any, to 15 R Avenue?
A. That is correct.
Q. How long have you been delivering mail to that address?
A. Approximately a year and a half.
Q. Well, does that period cover the full year 1950?
A. That is right.
Q. Now, do you know this gentleman [indicating my opponent]?
A. No.
Q. How often have you been to 15 R Avenue?
A. Five days a week.
Q. Did you ever, during the one year and a half that you have been delivering mail to 15 R Avenue, Brooklyn, see Mr. X or bring him any mail?
A. No, I haven't.

Earlier in the trial my opponent had seen witness after witness take the stand, including the landlord of the Manhattan apartment where he and his wife lived, the night and day elevator operators there, and the representatives of the utility companies, all of whom pinpointed his address as identical with the one on my prepared blueprint, which was not the address in Brooklyn alleged by him to be his residence. A man of less audacity than my opponent would long since have given up.

In the light of such compelling proof, he was unable to call as a witness a single neighbor or shopkeeper or tradesman in the neighborhood to try to break through my roadblock. So successfully was he hemmed in that even his wife, who had been in the courtroom throughout the trial, was not called to the witness stand. The Court, offended by the fraud, had no difficulty in deciding that my opponent's actual residence was in Manhattan, and not in Brooklyn. In fact, the Court stated in its decision that the alleged residence of my opponent "was false and made for the purpose of deception and to gain whatever personal advantage could be derived therefrom." His petition was accordingly invalidated, his purported enrollment was canceled, and his attempt to be designated as a candidate for political office was thwarted.

2

"Gingering Up" the Witness

Generally, the first information that a lawyer is likely to receive concerning the facts of a case will come from the lips of his client and his witnesses. They supply him with the raw data, and, if he knows how to interpret what they say, the clues they give him may lead him to the means of establishing the facts to the satisfaction of the jury.

But he cannot make any evaluation of what is communicated to him in these interviews unless he has first patiently heard his informants to the end. A lawyer must therefore learn to be a good listener, rather like a psychiatrist. However tempted he may be to interrupt, to ask a question, to brush aside an apparent irrelevancy, or to make a comment that may be crossing his mind, he should restrain himself and resolve to hear the entire recital, rambling and incoherent though it may be. There will be time enough later to sift the details, to winnow the chaff from the grains of truth, and to assemble and organize the facts coherently. For the moment, before he can give any advice at all, an attorney's primary task is simply to listen closely and to remain alert to the slightest hint or suggestion of something that may later need further inquiry or precise scrutiny. To this end, during the interview, I used to conceal a small pencil in the palm of my hand and make a few furtive notations of a word or two as reminders to myself, but I would always allow the narrator to go on with his story.

Attentive listening of this kind can be most fruitful. In the first place, it permits counsel the opportunity to assess the personality of his informant and to observe and take due account of the feelings and emotions—fear, worry, excitement, bitterness, nightmare memories, etc.—that may be affecting the witness as he recounts his version of the facts. Indeed, the very act of telling one's story to a sympathetic listener is a form of emotional catharsis and often has, for a client, the same salutary therapeutic effect that the soothing bedside manner of a doctor has in relieving a sick patient of anxiety or distress. No lawyer can afford to neglect this aspect of his professional duty. An interested and understanding approach on his part in the preliminary interview helps to place both client and witnesses at their ease and to inspire them with the necessary feelings of confidence.

Such conferences thus serve a double function. They not only provide counsel with the information he needs to lay the groundwork of his case, but, at the same time, if they are managed rightly, they present opportunities for preparing the witnesses, most of whom are generally inexperienced and often unsure of themselves, for their role in the trial. Just as the commander of an army has to have regard for the morale of his troops before sending them into battle, so an essential element of a lawyer's preparation of a case consists in putting those on whose testimony he must rely for his evidence in a frame of mind in which they will appear to best advantage when they take the stand. Accordingly, each witness must be helped to overcome whatever faulty preconceptions or fears he may have about the way he is to conduct himself when he testifies.

For example, if a witness tends to freeze up and become inarticulate, he should be urged to relate his story as best he can in his own words. He should be assured that the judge and the jury will understand him even if he does not use elegant language, since they are interested in "nothing but the truth."

On this subject, David Wise, Washington Bureau Chief of the New York *Herald-Tribune,* had some cogent observations in an article entitled "Words of Witness Ringing Terribly True," which appeared on November 29, 1964, commenting on the testimony given before the Warren Commission concerning President Kennedy's assassination:

> For the actual words of the participants in the tragedy at Dallas a year ago, released—almost as an afterthought—nearly eight weeks after the report of the commission, are in the end more persuasive than that impressive document itself.
>
> There is something about the real language of real people that carries with it a litmus-like quality of truth or falsity.
>
> Jack Ruby, solicitously asking the Chief Justice of the United States, "Do you follow that?" and Earl Warren solemnly assuring the witness that he did indeed—somehow the official transcript means more than the thousands of words that have been written anywhere else. Listen:
>
> Ruby: "And I went home that weekend, the Sunday morning, and saw a letter to Caroline. . . . Someone had written a letter to Caroline. The most heartbreaking letter. . . . And alongside that letter . . . was a small comment in the newspaper that . . . Mrs. Kennedy may have to come back for the trial of Lee Harvey Oswald. That caused me to go like I did; that caused me to go like I did.
>
> "I don't know, Chief Justice, but I got so carried away. . . . And

I don't know what bug got hold of me. I don't know what it is, but I
am going to tell you the truth word for word. . . .

"I realize it is a terrible thing I have done, and it was a stupid thing,
but I just was carried away emotionally. Do you follow that?"

Chief Justice Warren: "Yes, I do indeed, every word."

There are some witnesses who look with such dread upon the whole
ordeal of testifying in open court before judge and jury that they would
like to write down their answers in advance, just to be sure of not forgetting any essential detail. They may even go so far as to ask counsel
for a copy of their statement of the facts so that they can memorize
their testimony before the trial and rehearse their performance until
they are letter perfect.

Under no circumstances should a lawyer permit this. An overpre-
pared witness can be just as much of a liability to him as one who is
underprepared. Once opposing counsel senses that he is confronted
with memorized testimony, he can easily make the witness the target
of a withering cross-examination by pounding him repeatedly with the
same question and getting from his lips the identical verbatim answer
over and over again, until his credibility is completely undermined. If
this happens, the consequences can be disastrous for even the strongest
and best-prepared case.

That memorized testimony is a boomerang which can be most damaging to the witness who resorts to it is well illustrated by what happened in a famous criminal case, The People vs. Harris and Blanck, reported in a fascinating book entitled *The Triangle Fire* by Leon Stein,
published in 1962 by J. B. Lippincott Co.

This case grew out of a fire that occurred many years ago at the
Triangle Shirtwaist Company, at Washington Place and Greene Street,
New York City, at the edge of what is now the campus of New York
University, in which 146 persons died. The factory owners were prosecuted for misdemeanor-manslaughter on the ground that they had, it
was alleged, unlawfully kept an exit door locked through which many
employees could otherwise have fled to safety. However, as the door itself had been consumed in the blaze, the State, in order to prove its
case, had to call witnesses to establish both that the door had been
locked at the time of the fire and that the victim named in the indictment had tried to escape through the door.

The State's chief witness was a friend of a girl whose body had been
found near where the door in question had been. The witness testified
that she and her friend had rushed to the door, tried it every which

way, but could not open it, and that "a red curtain of flames" had wrapped itself around her friend.

During cross-examination, Max D. Steuer, the defense attorney and an outstanding cross-examiner, twice asked this witness to repeat her story. Each time she did so, her account was a verbatim repetition of her original testimony. The Court then adjourned for lunch. After lunch, Steuer again asked for her story, and again she repeated it in virtually identical terms. As she testified, Steuer even prompted her with such questions as, "Wasn't it like a wall of flame?" But the witness insisted on sticking tenaciously to the very same words she had already used three times before in describing the flames; they were, she maintained, "like a red curtain of flames."

In this way, the witness was completely discredited. The jury refused to believe her.

A lawyer would be well advised to tell this story, if circumstances warrant, to any of his witnesses who may be tempted to memorize testimony.

But the timid or inarticulate witness is not the only type that needs friendly counsel and guidance before he can safely be trusted to take the stand. Although witnesses may have many characteristics in common, it is their individual differences in temperament, personality, and background that have to be carefully observed and taken into account in preparing them for their role in the trial. Just as a physician has to adapt his therapy not simply to the disease but to the particular patient he is treating, so a lawyer must learn to vary his pretrial approach according to the character and caliber of each of his witnesses. If the client or witness is nervous, he needs to be encouraged and reassured. If he is excitable, he has to be calmed. If he is eccentric, his idiosyncrasies require study so that he will not get out of hand when he is questioned on direct examination. And if he is inclined to be garrulous, he must be gently but firmly restrained. An overtalkative witness can prove quite as much of a problem to a lawyer as one who is tongue-tied when he takes the stand. Long experience with witnesses who talk out of turn amply bears out the truth of the oft-repeated statement of Jerry Geisler, the renowned trial lawyer, that ninety-five per cent of the people who are in prison are there because they talked too much. As one murderer is reported to have said just before his execution, "You know, Warden, shootin' off a gun ain't dangerous. It's shootin' off your mouth."

Equally troublesome is the dull, lackluster individual, withdrawn into himself, who testifies in a flat monotone without any trace of apparent interest or feeling, as if he couldn't care less. It takes a good deal of tact and skill on the part of an advocate to prevent such a witness from hurting the case by his gray outlook. An effective way of handling this type of person is to humor him a little and make him feel how important he is to the case. Here again, the preparation of the witness before trial may mean the difference between success and failure.

A special problem is raised by the witness whose conception of a trial is based exclusively on movies or television programs. Unless counsel thoroughly dispels these prepossessions in advance of trial, the results can sometimes be startling and even ludicrous. This is what actually happened to one lawyer I know. After his client took the witness stand and gave her name and address, counsel asked her, "Are you the plaintiff in this case?" At this, the witness suddenly rose, stepped off the stand, bowed ceremoniously to the jury, and, beginning with "Ladies and gentlemen of the jury," forthwith launched into an oration! The astonished judge had all he could do to maintain decorum in a courtroom convulsed with laughter. He declared a recess, called counsel into his chambers, and said, "This is crazy. You fellows better settle this case, or we'll all wind up in the nuthouse." After a settlement had been reached, the young lady was asked what had impelled her to act the way she did. She naïvely replied, "I thought that is what I had to do because I see it on television."

Even the way a witness dresses when he or she appears in court is, or should be, a matter of concern to counsel. To be sure, a lawyer cannot change an individual's personality, nor would I suggest that he even try to do so; but he can see to it that the person who dresses loudly or in slovenly fashion comes to court properly attired, and that the colorless, nondescript witness, normally given to somber shades, brightens up and adds a little life to his appearance when he takes the stand.

The dress of female witnesses in particular poses a number of delicate questions. A litigant who wants to wear a daring gown that accentuates a plunging neckline may be courting trouble. While some male jurors may not protest, there is always the risk that a female member of the jury may not like it. On the other hand, a lawyer who represents a woman in a contested matrimonial action has to be careful not to overplay his part in suggesting her attire. If, for example, she has been publicly photographed in a way that sets off her feminine charms to best advantage, as illustrated in Exhibit 1, and if there is any likelihood that such a photograph will be brought to the jury's attention, it would be the height of folly to let her appear in court in the modest garb also depicted on that page. A lawyer would do well never to underestimate the intelligence of a jury. In such a case, they would have no difficulty in seeing through the pretense and exaggeration.

Indeed, in preparing a client to take the stand in a matrimonial action, in which there are sharply disputed questions of fact, and most notably in a suit for a separation brought on the ground of cruel and inhuman treatment, counsel may find it necessary to give advice that goes beyond matters of appropriate attire; he may have to provide his client with guidance on the proper way to behave in giving testimony. For in such actions the demeanor of the litigants on the stand has a vital bearing not only on the question of their credibility but on the very issue that is being tried. In this respect, matrimonial cases are different from most lawsuits. In a personal injury case, for example, the plaintiff may conduct himself in a most disorderly manner on the witness stand, shouting at and insulting cross-examining counsel and even so far losing his temper with the Court as to be held in contempt, without in any way forfeiting his legal right to recovery as long as he can show that he suffered injury as a result of the defendant's negligence and that he himself was not guilty of any contributory negligence. But the same is not true at all in a matrimonial action. If, in such a case, the plaintiff's wife excoriates her cross-examiner, she is doing more than raising a serious question as to her reliability as a witness; she is disclosing to the Court the type of woman she is and revealing in the most graphic manner what actually must have gone on in the privacy of the litigants' home. She is, in fact, confirming by her behavior on the stand the very charge brought against her by her husband. Observing such demeanor, a judge could very well conclude: "What a shrew she is! I couldn't live with her myself." In a case such as this, the actual behavior of the witness on the stand is, in itself, more compelling evidence on the very issue of cruelty than even a tape recording.

It is therefore essential, in preparing a client for this kind of action, that counsel impress upon him or her the critical—nay, the imperative —importance of orderly deportment at all times. Indeed, any provocative thrusts by opposing counsel, who, in the zeal of advocacy, may raise his voice or otherwise behave in an unseemly manner, should be welcomed as opportunities for demonstrating the client's sweet composure under attack. If the witness answers under offensive or hostile cross-examination with the same civility and self-control manifested under direct examination, it is only reasonable for the trial judge to conclude: "This is really a nice person. I can't believe the complaint that this party is violent and bad-tempered."

When the ability to pay alimony is an issue in a matrimonial action, a defendant husband should be very carefully examined by his lawyer before being allowed to testify concerning his income. If there is any doubt about whether he can withstand cross-examination on this point, the problems involved should be brought to his attention. In particular, he should be made aware of the difficulty of concealing assets, earnings, and sources of income, especially when his station in life and his standard of living are known or can easily be verified by inquiry.

It is always wise for counsel to point these facts out to his client in advance of trial in order to avoid the kind of situation that occurred in a case for separation tried before me when the question arose of the amount of alimony to be paid to the wife. On direct examination, the husband had testified that he earned $12,500 a year. Cross-examined as to his standard of living, he admitted that he maintained a $45,000 home and paid all the charges on it; that he was in the habit of giving his wife $150 a week for food for a household consisting of the couple, their two children, a sleep-in maid, and his mother-in-law; that he bought his wife's and children's clothes, as well as his own, never paying under $185 for a suit and $10.50 for a shirt; that every year he bought a new Cadillac, which he garaged at $65 a month; that he sent both children to camp each summer at a cost of about $2000; that he paid the maid $60 a week; and that he carried $175,000 in insurance.

At this point I stopped him and asked, "How do you do all these things on an income of $12,500?"

"Your Honor," he replied, "it's not easy."

It was, however, easy enough for me to judge whether he was telling the truth about his income.

But even more likely to prove embarrassing to a witness than understatement is any kind of exaggeration. A client or a witness, especially if he displays a disposition toward extravagance in his speech or behavior, needs to be cautioned against the all too common tendency to overstate one's case, to stretch a point, to embroider the details, to add a touch of extra color to the picture in an effort to make it look more convincing. If opposing counsel can expose even the slightest hint of hyperbole in a witness' testimony, its credibility is undermined.

And one can never tell just what point in a story will be selected for testing. A lawyer, in trying a case before judge and jury in the early years of his practice, had an experience that could well be cited to any witness who might be inclined to use his fancy in building up his story. His client, on direct examination, had carried his tale to the point at which his doctor had given him a prescription for some drugs, which he had filled in a drugstore. At this point, the judge stopped the trial, sent for his secretary, and directed him, in front of the jury, to telephone the pharmacist in order to determine whether he had in fact filled the prescription for the plaintiff.

To be sure, if counsel had objected to what the Court did and had been overruled, there is no doubt in my mind that counsel would have prevailed on appeal.

No doubt this incident is an altogether unpredictable eventuality. But it did happen, and it does show how essential it is for a witness to hew to the thin straight line of truth.

A most informative and thought-provoking treatment of this whole subject may be found in a very scholarly article entitled "Swearing on the Bible" by Jack Brandfon which appeared in *News and Notes of the Supreme Court*, Kings County, New York, on January 20, 1961. When a witness swears to tell "the truth, the whole truth, and nothing but the truth," the oath means just what it says. It is derived from the Hebrew word *emes*, meaning "truth," spelled with the three letters Aleph, Mem, and Soth. Aleph is the first letter of the Hebrew alphabet; Soth is the last; and Mem is in the middle. Hence, when a witness swears to tell the *emes*, he is promising, in effect, to tell the truth from A to Z. The moment he starts to lie, the Aleph falls, and the word that is left is *mes*, the Hebrew word for "death." In other words, the moment a witness who takes the oath deviates from the truth, he is in a mess. Or, as Sir Walter Scott wrote,

> Oh, what a tangled web we weave,
> When first we practice to deceive.

But just how sure can a lawyer be that his client is telling him the truth, the whole truth, and nothing but the truth? Can he rely implicitly on the veracity of anyone and everyone who comes into his office seeking his professional counsel? May not his client be exaggerating, distorting, or concealing some of the facts?

Surely this is a possibility that no attorney can afford to disregard. It would hardly be safe for him to assume that his client is telling him everything. Yet it is reasonable for him to expect that his client's testimony will be subjected in court to the most rigorous scrutiny by opposing counsel, in an effort to bring out discrepancies and contradictions. Therefore, a lawyer can scarcely do less himself in preparing his case for trial. The same skepticism with which he expects to confront the witnesses of the opposing party should be brought to bear on his client's story in the pretrial conference between counsel and his client. Without revealing his suspicions, counsel should probe for inconsistencies and consult with his client to resolve them. Certainly it is far better for a lawyer to make this kind of investigation before trial than for him to discover only in the courtroom, with his witnesses on the stand, that he has not been given a true or complete picture of the facts.

Sometimes he may not make such a discovery until after he has sufficiently looked into his case on his own and the truth manifests itself. This is precisely what happened to me in one of my earliest cases at the bar. A doctor called me to his office and asked me to initiate proceedings for the recovery of five thousand dollars on a promissory note. When I inquired into the circumstances of the loan, he told me that he had lent the money to a friend of his, a businessman who had been having trouble with creditors and was in need of immediate cash to stave off bankruptcy. The doctor was prepared to defray the expenses of the litigation and promised me, as my fee, twenty-five per cent of the amount recovered. The whole arrangement seemed to me to be most promising. I was quick to envision earning over a thousand dollars, certainly a mighty pleasing prospect for a young lawyer, in my circumstances, to have dangled before him.

I at once returned to my office, dictated a summons and a complaint, and had the defendant served in due course. When he failed to interpose an answer, I filed a judgment against him on default. A few days later, I communicated with him and suggested that we have a conference concerning the judgment. On receiving no reply to my letter, I served him with what is known as a "subpoena in supplementary proceedings." This required him to appear in court to be examined concerning his assets.

He came to court without an attorney and showed no sign of being in any way worried or concerned. He readily submitted to examination, conceded that he had received the five thousand dollars, and admitted that he had not answered the complaint because he had no defense.

However, he testified that he had no assets. What few assets I suspected he had were all in his wife's name.

In the early afternoon, as I was finishing my examination, a strikingly attractive woman came into the courtroom and sat down beside him. She was his wife. In the course of our conversation, it occurred to me that I might be more successful in reasoning with her about coming to a satisfactory settlement than I had been with her husband. Accordingly, I suggested to her that perhaps I might be able to induce my client to agree to some compromise that would be within their means and thus satisfy the judgment.

But my efforts proved unavailing. Finally, the husband turned to his wife and said, "Why don't you tell the counsellor the truth about this matter?"

Thereupon, this ravishingly beautiful creature turned her lovely gaze upon me and said, "I am surprised that the doctor had the nerve to sue my husband on this note. I was the doctor's mistress for about seven years. During all that time my husband knew what was going on, and certainly when the doctor gave him the money, it was understood by all concerned that my husband would never have to return it."

Her husband then added, "That doctor must be an idiot. I knew all along that he was having an affair with my wife and this was simply a pay-off."

I did not believe a word of this. But, before I left, the wife said, "If he insists on holding this judgment against my husband, I intend to see his wife and explain to her just what I told you."

That evening I related to the doctor what I had heard. He pleaded "not guilty" to what he was accused of and used some rather uncomplimentary language in characterizing the woman. When I asked him whether he had ever had any contact with her, his answer was, "Why, yes. She used to like taking automobile rides, and from time to time she would accompany me on my house calls."

Finally, however, he said, "Well, let's forget the whole thing. Send him a satisfaction of judgment, and send me a bill for your services."

I did so. The secret remained the doctor's and mine. The wife never learned what had happened.

Not surprisingly, it is the prospect of being subjected to cross-examination that makes many a witness nervously apprehensive about taking the stand. Even those who are most confident of their facts tend to quail at the thought of having their veracity more or less openly questioned, if not actually attacked. Then too, there is always the fear that one may, through a lapse of memory or some other inadvertency, be caught in a humiliating contradiction or put in a ridiculous light by some trick question or cunning stratagem. Few people are so sure of themselves that they feel up to matching wits with an experienced lawyer.

Pretrial preparation of each witness for cross-examination can do much to allay these fears and to forestall embarrassment. In the first place, a witness must be made to realize that not every question put to him by opposing counsel is to be looked upon with suspicion, as if it were a booby trap for the unwary. He should be counseled to behave under cross-examination no differently from the way he did under direct examination. He must be given to understand that what most persuades a jury is naturalness, sincerity, truthfulness, and knowledge of the facts of the case.

On the other hand, a witness is most likely to comport himself well under cross-examination if he has some appreciation of what opposing counsel will be aiming at in his questioning. In general, the purpose of cross-examination is to dilute, contradict, disprove, neutralize, or completely destroy the story the witness told on direct examination. Accordingly, the cross-examiner can be expected to try, with all the skill at his command, to lure or beguile the witness into giving answers that may make him lose his temper, overtalk, look foolish, or exaggerate. These, then, are precisely the pitfalls against which the witness must be forewarned. He should be reminded that his conduct on the stand will be closely observed by the jury, that his demeanor will be quite as important as his spoken words, and that he must be ever watchful lest, like a fish, he bite at the bait. He must learn to be on guard and circumspect in his answers, without being evasive or untruthful. Under no circumstances should he allow himself to be provoked into demonstrations of anger, belligerency, sarcasm, or even discourtesy. No matter how bitterly he may feel toward the person against whom he is testifying, he must control his emotions and give no outward sign of the hatred, contempt, or righteous indignation that may be welling up within him. Even if he is prodded by the cross-examiner on a sore point, he must be careful not to display any feelings or express any sentiment that might suggest or betray bias, because such conduct could have the effect of nullifying the impact of his testimony.

But it is not enough for a lawyer just to caution a witness in general terms about the way he is to conduct himself under cross-examination.

Really thorough preparation should include a dry run, in which he is put to the test by his own attorney or by an assistant. A trial lawyer's faith in the ability of his witnesses to emerge unscathed from cross-examination depends, to a considerable extent, on their own confidence in themselves, and there is nothing like a little pretrial drill to infuse courage into the faltering. It can also serve, as I often discovered, to reveal points of weakness and potential danger. Whenever I examined a witness in advance of trial, I used to have one of my associates in the office with me. After I had finished the direct examination, I would turn the witness over to him for cross-examination. By the time we were through with the witness, he had received a good going over. This practice paid dividends. On many occasions the case was lost in our conference room—a far better place to lose it than in court.

Many laymen have the mistaken idea that there is something unethical about a lawyer's going over testimony with a witness in advance of trial—a practice that in England is called "gingering up" a witness. Understandably, therefore, a question very often asked of witnesses under cross-examination is: "Have you discussed this case with anyone? Your lawyer? Your wife? Other witnesses?" etc. A client who has not been warned in advance and who is unprepared for the question may say no. It is therefore one of the duties of counsel, in preparing a witness for cross-examination, to point out how such an answer can adversely affect a jury's appraisal of his veracity.

I used to say to my clients, "If you didn't talk to me, how did I learn about the facts of your case? It is my job to discuss your case with you; otherwise, I wouldn't be worthy of being a lawyer. And wouldn't it be foolish to say that you didn't discuss this case with your wife—or, for that matter, with anyone else who has knowledge of the facts, such as your witnesses?" I would follow through by asking my client to recall the questions I had put to him when we first met, and then I would repeat these questions, by way of reminder: "Tell me the facts of the case." Then, if asked by opposing counsel during cross-examination, "Did your lawyer tell you what to say?" the witness, recalling our first conference, could truthfully answer, "No, he didn't tell me what to say. I told him the facts just as I have related them on the witness stand."

Of course, no self-respecting attorney will ever, either directly or indirectly, encourage or permit a client or a witness to tailor his testimony. It is the solemn duty of a lawyer, as an arm of the Court, to insist that every witness, his own as well as those he confronts as a cross-examiner, stick to the truth without any deviation. The oath administered to each witness, binding him to tell "the truth, the whole truth, and nothing but the truth," is not one to be taken lightly. Too many young advocates, in their zeal to win a case, make the mistake of relaxing this principle in preparing their witnesses for trial. It never pays to do so. No lawyer who values his reputation for professional integrity and the esteem of bench, bar, and public can afford to settle for anything less than the strictest adherence to the highest standards of honor in all his dealings with clients, witnesses, opposing counsel, judge, and jury.

The same scrupulous regard for the truth should extend as well to those areas of a witness' knowledge or recollection which are hazy, confused, or altogether blank. Any reluctance on the part of a witness to appear unsure of himself when testifying under oath makes him an easy mark for a cross-examiner bent on leading him into making positive statements that later turn out to be completely wrong. A witness should be advised in advance of trial that if he is asked a question he cannot answer, he should have no hesitation in saying, "I do not know." For example, if opposing counsel asks, "How many feet were you from the scene of the accident?" a witness who is not reasonably sure of the distance should say so. If he takes a guess, and says twenty feet, and the distance proves to have been twenty yards, his credibility will be undermined, and the case may be seriously weakened.

Finally, a witness needs to be told that when the cross-examination is completed, and he is excused from the stand, he is to leave the courtroom. If he remains to watch the rest of the trial, opposing counsel may, in his summation, attempt to capitalize on this fact by drawing the inference that the witness must have had some personal interest in the litigation and was therefore not altogether unbiased in his testimony.

However, the same rule should not be applied to the parties to the controversy. A lawyer should be sure to instruct his client to remain in court throughout the duration of the trial. Any litigant who fails to stay with the trial to the end runs a certain risk. A lawyer once told me of an occasion when he represented an automobile owner who was suing the City of New York for property damage caused by its negligence. After his client had testified, he left the courtroom and never came back. He was just too busy to take the time to stay in court for the remainder of the trial. Counsel proceeded with other witnesses; the defense, which was very feeble, was duly presented; and the jury retired, only to return within a few minutes with a verdict for the defendant. The attorney for the plaintiff was stunned, because he was sure that he had presented a good case. Later, he caught up with the members of the jury in the hallway and questioned them about their verdict. This, in substance, is what they told him: "If your client isn't interested enough in his own case to wait around and hear what we have to say, we're not interested either."

As Congressman Adam Clayton Powell discovered when he was sued for defamation of character, a litigant's failure to appear in court during the trial of his case can prove very costly indeed. The plaintiff attended the four-day trial; Representative Powell did not. After the jury had found him guilty and ordered him to pay a judgment of $211,500 (an amount subsequently reduced on appeal), several jurors, on being questioned, stated that the defendant's absence from court was one of the factors that had influenced them in arriving at their verdict. As one of them said, noting that defense counsel had promised that Mr. Powell would testify, "She [the plaintiff] was here. We had to be here. So why wasn't Powell?" A lawyer would be well advised to tell this story to any client who considers his business or personal affairs to be so pressing that he cannot afford to take the time to attend the trial of his own case.

The resolution of the issues involved in a case may sometimes require the testimony of an expert in some field of specialized knowledge—a doctor, an engineer, an architect, etc. Such testimony, if it is properly prepared and presented, can carry great weight with a jury. Albert S. Osborn, himself an eminent handwriting expert, makes the cogent observation that what we in the legal profession call the "expert witness" occupies an unusual position, that his testimony often decides the case, and that he should be carefully selected with regard to his technical qualifications, character, and reliability. Whereas the ordinary witness is obliged to confine his testimony to what he knows from his direct experience—what he saw, heard, smelled, tasted, or felt—the expert witness may testify to his inferences or the conclusions he drew from the facts or would draw from a hypothetical set of facts.

However, the fact that a man is an expert in his field does not mean that he is necessarily an expert in presenting or explaining his conclusions in terms understandable to the layman. It is all too common for the great scholar to be a poor teacher. He may be so accustomed to using technical terminology in writing for or talking to his fellow specialists and academic colleagues that he has lost the ability to communicate his ideas clearly to those unfamiliar with his field. This is one reason why an expert witness, like any other, needs to be interviewed personally by counsel in advance of trial.

Besides, even if an expert has had experience in testifying in similar trials, he still has to be prepared for the particular questions he is going to be asked when he takes the stand in the pending case. He must know what points are in dispute, what kind of information he will be called upon to supply, and what documents or books he will have to be ready to cite in support of his conclusions.

Moreover, a pretrial conference with an expert witness is instructive for counsel as well. A trial lawyer is just as much in need of orientation from an expert concerning the technical details to be brought out in court as the expert may be in regard to the precise issues involved in the case. Each has something to learn from the other.

For all these reasons, questions for the expert must be resolved and gone over with him in person before the trial begins. A lawyer would be well advised never to allow himself to be put off with the excuse that the expert is too busy to see him in his office in advance of trial. Sometimes the expert may try to induce him to be satisfied with a brief telephone conversation about the case or a hasty conference in court just before taking the stand. This simply will not do. There is no adequate substitute for thorough preparation. Questions for the expert just do not pop into counsel's head at the moment when they are needed, phrased precisely in the form that will make them most effective, and arranged to achieve their greatest possible impact. Any lawyer who asks an expert questions in direct examination that have not been previously prepared in consultation with him is risking a most dangerous and frustrating experience. For one thing, counsel must have the opportunity to understand the technical terms used by the expert, as well as the contents of any books or pamphlets he may refer to and the reasons underlying his conclusions; otherwise, it will be impossible to rehabilitate him in case he is shown to disadvantage under cross-examination. In addition, as we shall see, he can be helpful in preparing questions for counsel's use in cross-examining any expert called to the stand by the other side. When experts disagree, a jury is likely to be confused, unless one of them clearly has the edge over the other.

Accordingly, before interviewing an expert, a lawyer should read some of the literature on the problem involved in order to familiarize himself in advance with the technical terms in common use. In the course of such research, he would do well to make a note of any matters which he finds perplexing and which he would like the expert to explain.

The importance of this kind of preparation and the danger of neglecting it were well demonstrated in a negligence case tried before me some time ago. The plaintiff alleged that she had sustained severe personal injuries because of defects in a stepladder that broke while she was standing on it. On her behalf, an expert witness testified for several hours, stressing in detail all the specifications which ladders of this type were required to meet. Referring from time to time to a pamphlet published by the American Institute of Architects in which these specifications were set forth, he testified in such a convincing manner concerning the failure of the ladder in question to conform to them that I began to wonder what, if anything, the defendant's counsel would be able to cross-examine him on in order to weaken the favorable impression created by his knowledgeable presentation.

Defense counsel began his cross-examination by requesting the expert to hand him the pamphlet. After a quick glance at it and a few harmless questions, counsel asked the witness to look at the pamphlet again and tell the Court and the jury the year of its publication. The mortified expert sheepishly read from the pamphlet a date two years *after* that of the accident. This wholly unexpected setback was enough to shake the expert's confidence. He suddenly lost his aplomb and appeared to be deeply embarrassed and chagrined at the realization that he had been caught in such an elementary and glaring mistake. The shock treatment administered by defense counsel made the witness thereafter easily amenable to further successful cross-examination.

But it was not until about a year after the trial, when the counsel for the defendant recalled this incident to me, that its full significance became clear. He told me that he had prepared for the cross-examination of the expert by studying the pamphlet of the American Institute of Architects, but the copy which he had used was one published a few years before the date of the accident. However, a comparison between the relevant specifications contained in the copy he had consulted and those printed in the later edition of the same pamphlet brought to court by the expert indicated that the date of publication made no difference whatsoever in respect to any of the points he had made in his testimony; the specifications for the particular type of ladder involved in the accident were *identical* in every respect in both editions, the later as well as the earlier. Unfortunately for the plaintiff, neither his counsel nor his expert witness had taken the trouble to examine and discuss the pamphlet during the preparation of the case.

We know from Shakespeare that even in his time there were bitter complaints about what Hamlet called "the law's delay." Since then, of course, conditions have become much worse. An ever-increasing press of litigation continues to crowd the dockets of our courts with a backlog that has lengthened considerably the waiting period before trial.

Under these circumstances, even the most dilatory lawyer, it would seem, can count on plenty of time to prepare his case. But the long weeks, months, and even years that may intervene between the day a lawsuit is instituted and the day the parties to the controversy finally appear in court for the trial present counsel with problems as well as opportunities.

For one thing, as time elapses, witnesses may become unavailable. They may die, or they may travel to parts unknown or far from the jurisdiction of the Court. And if they do appear to testify, they may find that their recollection has dimmed appreciably in the interval. Time may have either completely erased from their memories or greatly dulled the vividness of most of the details whose recall would give significance and point to their testimony. Finally, a lawyer may discover, when the case comes to trial, that the lively sympathy his witnesses once evinced for his client, in the days when their sense of the justice of his cause was still fresh in their minds, has lapsed, with the passage of time, into indifference or even worse. This is especially likely to happen if, in the meanwhile, opposing counsel has had the opportunity to interview the witnesses, win them over to his side, and obtain statements from them.

There are two possible ways of dealing with such problems. One is to adopt the attitude of the soldier who, when asked whether he wasn't afraid to stand up in a battlefield with bullets and shells whizzing all around him, replied that he felt protected by the law of probabilities. A lawyer might likewise console himself with the thought that whatever may happen to his own witnesses—death, removal, lapse of memory, or disaffection—is just as likely to happen to those of his adversary. The other way is to take a few reasonable precautions to insure that, in any event, there will be testimony to present and the case will not become altogether stale while he holds it ready for trial.

Certainly one of the first things he should do is to see his witnesses promptly—the sooner, the better. In particular, he must make every effort to interview them before his adversary sees them and while their recollection of events is still clear and fresh. The first lawyer to interview a witness and to obtain a statement from him enjoys an obvious advantage right from the outset. He can immediately take steps to put the witness on his own team and to win him over to a sympathetic attitude toward the party counsel represents.

In fact, even if opposing counsel has already seen the witness, and obtained a statement from him, a lawyer should not be deterred from making an attempt to obtain another statement from him. Experience shows that in most instances the subsequent statement will not dovetail with the first. If there is any discrepancy between them, no matter how slight, it may provide a basis for raising a doubt concerning the witness' version of the event and for destroying, minimizing, or diluting the effect of his testimony. Therefore, in taking a statement from a witness, a lawyer should, before coming to the issue in which he is really interested, ask about such matters as the witness' occupation, place of employment, employer's name, past employment, age, the names of members of his family, the ages of his children, etc. This information, though apparently irrelevant, can prove very useful in case the witness denies having said in the pretrial interview anything crucial or important set forth in his signed statement. For then he can be cross-examined in some such fashion as the following:

Q. Now, do you say that you did not tell me that the accident happened in broad daylight?
A. Yes.
Q. And do you now say that you did not tell me that the child ran across the street?
A. Yes.
Q. Well, did you tell me your wife's name is Pauline?
A. Yes.
Q. That in 1960 you were a plumber's helper employed by Ace Plumbing Company?
A. Yes.
Q. That since 1962 you have been president of Dixon & Company, Inc.?
A. Yes.
Q. That you have three children: John, six years of age; Paul, eight years of age; and Marie, twelve years of age?
A. Yes.
Q. That these children attend St. Augustine's Parochial School in Brooklyn, New York?
A. Yes.

The cross-examination can continue with questions about other personal information that the witness gave counsel about himself, concluding with:

Q. Did I correctly state these things which you told me?
A. Yes.

This kind of interrogation lays the groundwork for remarks in summation, in which counsel can point out that he took a true and correct statement from the witness, as indicated by the verified accuracy of all the personal details reported in it.

Thus, the signed statement of a witness interviewed before trial can be a very valuable asset which every lawyer should treasure highly. It deserves, therefore, to be drawn up with the greatest care. Failure to do so can be costly. If a lawyer is very busy, or if his stenographer is ill or otherwise occupied, he may be tempted, after talking to a witness for a few minutes, to skip the chore of dictating the witness' verbatim statement, and, as an alternative, ask him to sign a piece of paper in blank, intending to fill it in later when time permits. The peril of resorting to such makeshifts is illustrated by the following incident, which was reported to me by a friend:

In a negligence case, the defendant's attorney called his witness to the stand and began to ask his prepared questions, only to find that the answers he was receiving were altogether different from what he had been led to expect from the statement before him. Finally, the exasperated attorney, showing a copy of the statement to the witness, asked him whether he recognized his own signature at the bottom of it.

"Yes," the witness readily replied, "that is my signature all right. But when I signed it, the paper was blank."

If there is anything worse than getting a witness to put his signature to a blank piece of paper, it's obtaining from the other party to the controversy, or from one of his witnesses, in what we lawyers call an examination before trial, a lengthy statement, containing a beautiful collection of implicit contradictions, evasions, and absurdities that could be brought out to devastating effect in cross-examination, and then forgetting or neglecting to have the statement signed!

An examination before trial is a means by which a lawyer can require the opposing party, and witnesses under certain circumstances, to appear in his office or in court before the trial in order to answer, under oath, questions in regard to their knowledge of the pertinent facts of the case. In fact, an examination before trial can give both sides a clearer picture of the testimony that will be presented and pinpoint the areas in dispute.]

But eliminating a great deal of the element of surprise in the court-room is not the only end served by the examination before trial. Any discrepancies between the testimony of a witness on the stand and the testimony he gave under oath when he was examined before the trial can be brought to the attention of the jury in an effort to impeach the witness' credibility. And since all answers given in the examination before trial are reduced to writing, in what is called a "deposition," the testimony of witnesses who may not be called or are unavailable to testify at the trial is thereby perpetuated.]

A deposition does not necessarily have to be signed by the person examined. If he fails to sign it, the officer before whom the deposition was taken (any person authorized to administer an oath, such as a notary) may sign it and state on the record the fact of the witness' failure or refusal to sign, together with any reason given. The deposition may then be used as fully as though signed.

In preparing to conduct a cross-examination, an attorney will find few weapons more potent than the signed depositions he obtains in a prop-erly conducted pretrial examination of the opposing party. But even when the depositions have been signed by the persons examined, there are pitfalls for the unwary. Naturally, the witness who is examined should be asked to read the transcript of his statement carefully, and, by way of precaution, a sentence indicating that he has done so should, as a matter of course, be included at the end of it. But before allowing the witness to sign the transcript of his pretrial statement, an attorney should take the precaution of first checking it himself for accuracy. He should satisfy himself that the answers reflect exactly what the witness said. Unless he does so, he runs the risk of finding himself, on the day of the trial, with something really fantastic. Here is what happened in a case in which a deposition of an orthopedic surgeon was taken, in the presence of opposing counsel, by a shorthand reporter in a pretrial examination. Reduced to a transcript, it was duly sub-mitted to the doctor for corrections, signed by him, evidently without a careful reading on his part or the lawyer's, and returned to the re-porter, who thereupon mailed a copy to the attorneys for the respective parties.

A part of the record of this examination before trial is quoted below. Had it not been furnished to me by Mr. John M. Braisted, Jr., District

Attorney of Staten Island, I should have thought of it as something out of Mr. Ripley's "Believe It or Not":

Q. You could see that the bone was protruding without X-rays? Is that correct?

A. No. The bone was not protruding at the time I saw him, but the bone protruded, causing this compound injury.

Q. And had the bone protruded the outer skin?

A. It cut through all the soft tissue, muscles, and outer skin.

Q. Would you continue, Doctor, please?

A. This is another X-ray, the number 1 B 28971, of the left femur. It also shows a displacement and comminution. That is, it's in several places with displacements and the incision of the so-called Kirschner wire.

Q. And the purpose of this *wife* was what, Doctor?

A. To try to manipulate the fragments and position and maintain them.

Q. At some time subsequent to this X-ray, was this *wife* removed from this man's body?

A. Yes.

Q. And how did you remove that *wife*, Doctor?

A. Just by cutting one end and pulling out the other.

A neat trick indeed!

It is safe to say that most witnesses are not likely to have had much experience in a court of law. In fact, chances are that their day in court will be not only their first, but their last. They therefore need all the friendly help and guidance they can get if their performance on the stand is to be anything but a dismal fiasco. Even the few who are experienced and think they know just what to do and say can usually profit from a little refresher course in the ways of the law and trial procedures. As we have seen, it is not advisable for a lawyer to take anything for granted.

Thus, witnesses should be warned not to be confused or agitated if, just as they are in the midst of answering or are about to answer a question, the opposing lawyer rises and cries out, "I object!" These words can have a shattering effect on the morale of a witness who has not previously been made to understand that they are not addressed to him, but to the Court, and that he is not permitted to respond to the question objected to until the judge sustains or overrules the objection. If the objection is sustained, the witness will not be required to answer the question. If he has already done so in whole or in part, what he has said will be stricken from the record, and the jury will be instructed to disregard it. If, on the other hand, the objection is over-ruled, the witness may proceed with his answer. Since these rulings re-late only to matters of law and reflect in no way on the witness himself, there is no reason for him to lose his composure, and he should not allow them to affect his equanimity. But this must be explained to him in advance.

Of course, a lawyer can never quite predict what the effect of his words of advice may be on a witness, especially one disposed to follow them to the letter, like the injured client who telephoned his attorney immediately on arriving at the hospital and asked for instructions. He was given the usual admonition against making any statement or giv-ing out any information. Thirty minutes later the client telephoned again. "Couldn't I at least give them my Blue Cross number?" he pleaded. "They won't admit me to the hospital without it."

Direct, personal contact between lawyer and witness in advance of trial takes on particular importance when the witness is the client himself, and especially if he is the plaintiff in the case. There just isn't any more reliable source of information about a case than the plaintiff —not even the most articulate and voluble eyewitness, be he relative or stranger.

Perhaps the best way I can illustrate the importance of careful, pa-tient, personal preparation of a client and the responsibility of a lawyer to devote himself to this task in disregard of his own convenience is to recount an experience I had many years ago before I became a judge. My client, the plaintiff in the case, on alighting from a bus, had begun to walk in front of it, with the intention of crossing the street to a building on the opposite side. Just at that moment, the driver of the bus, without actually putting the vehicle in motion, turned on the ig-nition and started up the motor. The sudden roar of the engine so startled my client that she accelerated her pace. In attempting to get out of the way of what she thought would be the moving bus, she ran into the roadway in front of an oncoming automobile, which was proceeding in the same direction as the bus. The automobile, whose driver carried no liability insurance, struck her, causing severe injuries.

On several occasions the plaintiff had visited my office with one of her sons, but she had spoken very little. Because her son, who had been with her at the time of the accident, was so much more articulate than she, I relied on him to supply me with all the relevant informa-tion. I therefore failed to elicit from the plaintiff herself her own recital of the circumstances under which she was injured. This proved to be a serious mistake on my part. Fortunately, I discovered it in time, practically on the eve of trial.

I had planned to take my family to Florida for the Christmas holidays. The case was scheduled for trial the first Monday in January. A week before my planned departure, I had the plaintiff come to the office to complete the final preparations before trial. I shall never forget how shocked I was to discover for the first time, when I talked to her at length alone, how completely ignorant she was. She did not know the difference between a bus, a car, a mule, and a load of hay.

For example, I asked her, "Were you riding in a bus on the 15th day of June, 1938?" From the expression on her face I could tell that she didn't have the slightest idea what I meant by "bus."

I tried a different tack. I asked her whether she had been struck by an automobile. Again that blank expression. When I finally got her to tell me that she had been struck by a car, I asked her, "Weren't you struck by a mule?"

"Yes," she said, with the same uncomprehending look on her face.

Then I asked her, "Weren't you hit by a bale of hay?"

Again she answered, "Yes."

It soon became apparent that she thought I expected her to say yes in answer to every question.

I promptly canceled my trip to Florida. I knew that my work was cut out for me.

I need not, of course, go into further details. Suffice it to say that in about two or three days I arranged to meet with her and her son at the scene of the accident. Then I had an engineer build a replica of the street and a miniature scale model of the bus and the automobile. My assistant and I spent the Christmas holidays lying on the floor of my office preparing the case, with the aid of my client and her son.

I had no cause to regret the extra effort I had made. It paid a handsome dividend. The verdict was substantial.

But if the inadequately prepared witness is a liability to a lawyer, the one who has received too much advice can be just as damaging to his case. No matter how long and tirelessly he may have worked to instruct a witness about how to behave on the stand, there comes a time when counsel must be resigned to let well enough alone, lest he spoil everything by overzealousness. A mistake often made by inexperienced lawyers is to get so carried away with the idea of anticipating everything that might happen in the courtroom that they lie awake nights thinking of ways to make sure their witnesses are ready for any and every conceivable contingency. Like the student who stays up late the night before the examination desperately trying to cram facts into his aching head so as to be able to answer every possible question that may be asked, a lawyer may try to advise a client or a witness beyond the point of diminishing returns—and perhaps even beyond the point of no return. After all, there is just so much that can be squeezed out of even the best witness, and unless counsel can learn to sense just how far to go in pressing his case, he may find, when it comes to trial, that in his oversolicitude he has succeeded only in "painting the lily."

Charles H. Tuttle, one of the most respected and talented leaders of the bar, recounts an experience of this kind which he had as a fledgling advocate. Here it is in his own words:

> Shortly after I was admitted to the bar, there came my way an accident case, which to a young lawyer seemed like a heavenly dream.
>
> The client was a sweet, old widowed lady who resembled Whistler's "Mother." She had been knocked down in the street by a delivery truck operated by a large department store, and she had sustained various injuries for which a gallant jury could be expected to be handsomely sympathetic monetarily. One of these injuries was an increase in her deafness as a result of the shock.
>
> Before she took the witness stand, I had warned her that the wily cross-examiner would begin by shouting his questions directly in front of her and then backing further and further away and gradually dropping his voice; and that, if there came a moment when she did not hear him clearly, it would be quite appropriate for her to say so.
>
> What I foretold happened exactly. Gradually the cross-examiner backed almost to the rear of the small courtroom and then put a question in a distinctly low voice. The trap was obvious. Whistler's Mother gazed at him with the sweetest of blank expressions, and time passed with no reply. When her silence reached an obviousness sufficiently significant, I hopped up and said: "Your Honor, my learned brother asked that question in so low a voice that quite evidently my client did not hear him."
>
> Whereupon Whistler's Mother turned her sweet face to me and graciously said: "Oh, yes, I heard him. I was thinking of the answer."

One of the services a lawyer can perform for every witness he puts on the stand—and indirectly for his client as well—is to provide him with a certain amount of general advice concerning his deportment in court, the procedures to be followed when the oath is administered, and expressions he might use in certain types of common situations. I used to keep a set of these suggestions handy, and I made sure to go over them with my witnesses. They knew that they had to speak up, to be brief, to think before answering a question, to avoid volunteering any information, to wait until the entire question was asked before answering, and to admit errors or slips rather than try to cover them up. They were told, also, that if they found they could not truthfully answer with a yes or a no, they should say so frankly and qualify their responses. My witnesses were warned not to carry on conversations, during the recess, with other witnesses or parties to the case, to arrive in court early, and to avoid looking at me while being cross-examined. Finally, when they had finished testifying, they knew enough to ask to be excused and to leave the courtroom without delay.

All this formed a part of my regular pretrial "training course" for witnesses, and I made sure to include it in my interviews with them. Though I cannot say that they all remembered what I taught them, at least I knew that I had done the best I could to ensure a creditable performance from them on the witness stand. Indeed, I consider this kind of instruction necessary in preparing most witnesses for their appearance in court, and I found that most of them appreciated the assistance and profited from it.

3

The Silent Witness

There is one kind of "witness" that every litigant and every lawyer would like to have on his side. That is the mute witness represented by a document, a picture, a map, etc. A photograph, an official record, a weapon, or an instrument doesn't need to be drilled on how to behave on the stand. There is no danger that it will forget or change its testimony with the passage of time while awaiting trial or, once it is safely in counsel's possession, that it may disappear to parts unknown. It always remains fresh and available.

Moreover, it enjoys one other inestimable advantage over even the best witnesses. It has a kind of objectivity that no human being can ever hope to duplicate. It is there for all to see, just as it is. Even if it has been tampered with in some way, there are generally scientific means of detecting and exposing the fraud. When the members of the jury can see for themselves the evidence presented—photographs taken before and after the accident, the hospital record, the police blotter, the canceled checks, or whatever it may be—the effect often far exceeds that of anything a witness, no matter how convincing, can say on the subject. One such exhibit is worth a thousand words of oral testimony.

For these reasons, a very important part of a lawyer's preparation of a case consists in finding as many relevant documents, diagrams, sketches, plans, charts, pictures, and other examples of what is called "real and demonstrative" evidence as possible, examining them carefully for the light they may shed on the facts, and deciding on the use to be made of them. For such evidence speaks for itself, and with a certitude that could not possibly come from oral testimony.

When, for example, he is trying a negligence case, a lawyer has to learn how to construe the various forms and reports that are usually filled out by the parties involved when an accident occurs. The most common type of accident case today is that involving motor vehicles. Although the forms for reporting such an accident vary in the different States, the information called for in the New York State Report of

Motor Vehicle Accident filed by those directly involved in it, the Police Accident Report of the Department of Motor Vehicles of the State of New York, and the Detailed Vehicle Accident Report is fairly representative of the kind of data that can be found in such documents.

Aside from identifying the persons and automobiles or other vehicles involved, these reports call for information concerning the persons injured, the nature and extent of their injuries, the time of the accident, the direction of moving traffic, the positions of the vehicles, the nature of traffic controls, if any, the positions of injured persons, witnesses, apparent condition of the drivers, the extent and nature of the damages to the vehicles, the hospital to which the injured persons were taken, road and weather conditions, actions of the vehicles before the accident, and apparent contributing circumstances. In addition to describing the accident verbally and diagramming it, the person filling out the report has an opportunity to check off the relevant data from among a number of alternative possibilities listed under each of the above headings.

Properly read and understood, such forms are full of valuable clues for the resourceful lawyer, and many cases could be cited in which the data so provided proved to be of crucial significance.

For example, a case was recently tried before me in which the plaintiff alleged that, as he approached a certain street intersection, the traffic light turned red. According to his testimony, he duly stopped his car and did not proceed until the light had turned green. The defendant's story was to the contrary, namely, that the plaintiff had failed to stop when the light turned red and had gone right through the intersection, thereby causing the accident.

The plaintiff's attorney, in his opening remarks to the jury, stated that, aside from the parties to the controversy, no witnesses would be called in the case by either side. It would be up to the jury to decide the issue of liability solely on the word of the plaintiff as against that of the defendant.

However, the attorney for the defendant, in opening to the jury, said, "Even though you have been told that there was no other witness to the accident, please reserve judgment on that point until you have heard my case. There may be a witness, after all."

Later, during the discussions carried on while the parties were seeking to negotiate a settlement, the attorney for the plaintiff asked opposing counsel, "What do you mean by saying that there may be a witness? There was no witness. No witness is named in the police blotter."

But the defendant's attorney kept on insisting, "There is a witness, and he will be produced."

When the case was finally settled, he called the attention of the plaintiff's attorney to the Detailed Vehicle Accident Report, a document which that gentleman either did not know existed or did not know how to interpret. The witness that the defense had expected to call was none other than the police officer who had filled out the report. For the report indicated that the plaintiff had apparently told the police officer he had failed to stop his car on signal.

From my observation of the look on the face of the plaintiff's attorney when he saw the police report, I was convinced that if he had known of its existence or had read it carefully, he would never have told the jury in his opening remarks that no witness would be called for either side.

Another instance in which careful pretrial examination of the pertinent documents led to the obtaining of a good settlement was a recent case in which a woman was suing to recover damages for serious personal injuries sustained as a result of an accident involving the collision of two automobiles. Both vehicles mounted the sidewalk, where she had been standing, struck her, and threw her to the ground.

It happened that the owners of both automobiles were covered by casualty insurance policies issued by the same company. Each policy was in the amount of $10,000. Apparently, the strategy employed by the company was to try to exonerate one of the defendants and to place the blame entirely on the other, thereby saving itself $10,000, and depriving the plaintiff of a like amount in damages.

However, in the course of his very diligent preparation, the attorney for the plaintiff turned up two very interesting facts. First, in examining the motor vehicle accident report filed by each of the defendants, he noticed that the handwriting in both reports was identical in numerous places. Furthermore, in digging deeply into the facts and circumstances during his preparation for trial, he found that each of the defendants had submitted a written statement concerning the accident, and that each of these statements had been witnessed by the same employee of the insurance company.

As the trial progressed, the tactics of the insurance company became clearer. One defendant—whom we shall call Jones—threw the entire blame for the accident on the other defendant, Smith, and Smith's lawyer, employed by the same insurance company that was representing Jones, did little or nothing to blame Jones. In other words, in the defendants' preparation of their case, Smith was to be cast as the villain, with his lawyer not lifting a finger to rehabilitate him in the eyes of the jury.

When this became clear, the plaintiff's attorney asked that the jury be excused, and, during their absence, he brought to the attention of the Court all the details he had discovered about the identity of the handwriting in the motor vehicle reports and of the employee of the insurance company who had prepared and witnessed the statements of both defendants. Pointing out the obvious effort on the part of the company to bail out one of the defendants, to the detriment of the plaintiff's rights, he exposed the whole shabby scheme.

The trial came to an abrupt conclusion. Rather than risk being forced to pay $20,000 and subjecting each of the defendants personally to a possible additional liability for a substantial amount above the $10,000 limit set in each policy, the company settled the case for the sum of $17,000. Its plan had backfired because of the alertness of the plaintiff's attorney and the thoroughness of his examination of the documents in the case.

In another case it was only the alertness of the judge that—unfortunately for the defendant—brought to light a significant fact that neither side had noticed in a crucial document which had been received in evidence. The accused, an attendant in a parking lot, was charged with accepting "policy" bets. On his person at the time of his arrest was found a slip of paper with many numerals written on it, one below the other, each consisting of three digits followed by a dash and two digits. This became People's Exhibit 1. Neither the District Attorney nor defense counsel paid any particular attention to it. The police officer who made the arrest, testifying as an expert, asserted that in his opinion the first three digits represented the number selected by the player, and the last two digits represented the amount paid on the number.

The defendant then took the stand. He admitted readily enough that he had written the numerals on the slip, but he contended that they represented the license plates of cars that were placed in the parking lot.

After both sides had rested, the judge restudied the slip. He then proceeded to question the accused further:

Q. You say that these are all the numerals of license plates of cars in the parking lot?

A. Yes, Your Honor.

Q. And you say that you made these notations to remind you as to which cars were in the lot?

A. That's exactly it, Judge.

Q. If that is so, why did you find it necessary to add up the sum of the last two digits of every "license plate"?

A. Well—Your Honor—you see—.

Here the witness just stopped. He looked at the judge and then burst into an embarrassed laugh.

Q. Do you have anything further to say?

A. Your Honor, I just throw myself on the mercy of the Court.

Needless to say, the defendant was convicted, but the judge, who had a keen sense of humor, told me he gave the man a light sentence for having provided "the best chuckle of my judicial career."

The introduction of an exhibit in evidence also offers special problems. Any carelessness on the part of counsel in preparing it for use may prove disastrous. This is especially true if the jury is expected to handle and inspect it. In such a case, it is wise to have an expert examine the exhibit thoroughly in advance of trial.

Writing on this subject, Samuel Levitt, Associate Professor at the New York Law School, says, "Time and again I have seen a physical exhibit offered in evidence which destroys the offerer."

As an example, he cites a case in which the plaintiff alleged that the clamp of a roller skate had become loose and caused serious injury. In order to show that the alleged occurrence was simply impossible, counsel for the defendant offered a skate and a clamp in evidence. But just as he handed the skate to the reporter, the clamp fell off!

In another case described by Professor Levitt, the issue revolved around the height that water had risen in a cellar. If it had risen to five inches, the plaintiff would recover, but if it had risen to three feet, the defendant was entitled to recover.

A photograph of the cellar, taken the day after the occurrence of the flood, was introduced into evidence by the defendant in order to substantiate his argument. However, when the photograph was being passed around among the jurors during their deliberations, one of them discovered that it included a picture of a cardboard box lying on the floor in the corner. On it he noticed what appeared to be a mark left by the water, five inches above the bottom of the box. He therefore reasoned that the plaintiff was correct in his contention. Neither counsel had observed this evidence, which determined the issue in the case. The jury's verdict was for the plaintiff.

Unfortunately for the defendant, it later turned out that this box had been on a two-foot-high shelf during the flood and had been taken off the shelf, together with other things, and placed on the floor after the flood, shortly before the photograph had been taken.

Professor Levitt concludes: "You cannot examine exhibits too carefully or prepare yourself too exactingly in their use. Their effect is frequently more devastating than oral testimony."

Sometimes a case depends on proving the durability, soundness, or strength of some article or product. Of course, a lawyer can call expert witnesses to testify to its conformity to standards and specifications in the industry or to describe the exacting procedures used to ensure product control in its manufacture. But counsel may consider that he could present an even more readily understandable and convincing case if he just brought the product to court and allowed the jury to judge for itself how good it is. This is an excellent procedure, no doubt, but it does involve risks unless counsel has first, in preparing his case, satisfied himself that the article in question has the ability to withstand whatever tests he expects to put it to in open court. On such an important question it is not advisable to take anybody's word, least of all that of the client. It pays to check everything personally in advance.

This point is strikingly illustrated by the following incident. Counsel represented the defendant, who was a partner of the plaintiff in the manufacture of novelty items made out of plastic. His client contended that the accounts should have shown substantial losses resulting from the breakage of samples and in handling and shipping the various products of the firm. This the plaintiff disputed.

During the trial, in order to controvert the defendant's contention that the product was fragile and easily broken, the plaintiff's attorney picked up a sample of the product and, in a surprise move, pitched it across the room, intending to demonstrate the durability of the plastic. To his astonishment, and to the amusement of everyone else, it broke into many pieces. Apparently, he was overoptimistic, or, relying on information provided by his client, he had failed to test it himself before the demonstration. It proved, of course, conclusive in deciding the issue.

In another negligence case, the plaintiff contended that while driving along a highway, he was forced to proceed into an allegedly unlighted and unguarded excavation. At the time of the accident there was a heavy rain, with winds of over thirty-five miles an hour. The defendant produced a foreman who testified that there were lanterns at the scene of the accident known as "hurricane lamps" which could not be affected by the elements. The lights in these lanterns, he said, could not be blown out. A lantern of exactly the same type as was allegedly lit at the time of the accident was produced in court and marked in evidence. Then, in the presence of the jury, the attorney for the defendant struck a match, lit the lantern, and invited the foreman to step up and try to put the light out in any way he wanted. Whereupon the foreman picked up the lantern and raised and lowered it just once. The light promptly went out, and with it the defense.

Scars or other signs of disfigurement on the body of the plaintiff are, of course, eloquent evidence if they can be shown to be the result of the defendant's negligence, and lawyers for the plaintiff are naturally eager for the jury to see the injuries for themselves. But propriety and good taste require that certain limits be observed in adducing this kind of evidence and sometimes may be the determining factors in the Court's decision on whether or not to admit it. In preparing a plaintiff for trial, counsel has to take such considerations into account.

The problem may become particularly serious if the plaintiff has a poor understanding of English and fails to comprehend the meaning of the Court's ruling on this point. The results can sometimes be most embarrassing for all concerned. A young lady of foreign background once sued a doctor for malpractice. He had allegedly injected silicone directly into her breasts, with the object of making them less pendulous. But instead of lifting them up, the operation only deformed them, producing large, painful lumps. When these symptoms developed, the doctor suggested that she undergo another operation to remove the silicone and eliminate the lumps and the pain. Incisions were made over the nipples for this purpose, but they left very ugly postoperative scars.

There were adequate graphic photographs showing the condition of the breasts before and after surgery. Nevertheless, plaintiff's counsel kept insisting that his client be permitted to exhibit her breasts to the jury while she was on the stand. On each occasion when he made this request, the Court denied it on the ground that it would be inappropriate, immodest, and unnecessary for the lady to expose her breasts, since the photographs were already in evidence.

Later, after the defense attorney had summed up to the jury, and while her attorney was in the middle of his summation, the plaintiff suddenly jumped up from her seat in the front row of the courtroom, said something rapidly that neither judge nor jury understood, slipped off her light coat, and, before anyone knew what was happening, opened her blouse and paraded up and down in front of the all-male jury, holding up first one breast and then the other, to show the ugly scars which were the result of the doctor's alleged malpractice. What she was saying all the while in a foreign language was: "With your permission, Your Honor, and with your permission, members of the jury, I want to show you what this doctor did to me."

Everybody was taken aback, and for a moment not a word was uttered. Finally the judge turned to counsel for the defendant and asked, "Do you have any motion to make?"

"Yes, Your Honor," he replied. "I move for a mistrial."

The motion was granted, and the case was set down for trial at a later date and before another judge. The judge reprimanded the plaintiff and said she was very fortunate that she wasn't being held in contempt of court.

4

"Legwork" and Brainwork

So far, we have seen the trial lawyer in a number of different capacities: as a detective patiently tracking down clues and piecing the evidence together; as a confidant and therapist of the insecure, the inarticulate, the withdrawn, the overemotional, and the garrulous; as an architect and master builder, blueprinting his plans for the construction of the edifice of proof on which his case will rest; as a military commander marshaling his forces and mapping out a battle strategy; as a psychologist probing into the hearts and minds of litigants, witnesses, and jury; and as a stage manager and director arranging the props and rehearsing the members of the cast for their roles in the drama to be enacted in the courtroom.

A trial lawyer is, or must be, all these, to be sure. But must he not be something more besides? From what has been said up to now, it would seem as if anyone who managed to combine these varied talents could very well do the job of getting a case ready for trial. But of what value, then, are legal scholarship and the knowledge so painstakingly acquired in years of study at law school? Do they count for nothing in the preparation of a case?

Of course they count. The truth is that they are indispensable. But they come into play only by being applied to the concrete facts of each case. The legal question that a lawyer has to concern himself with is always basically this: Even if the testimony and exhibits to be presented at the trial could convince a jury of the truth of the allegations made in the complaint, would the facts so established be sufficient to justify the recovery of damages (in a civil suit) or an acquittal (in a criminal prosecution)? In other words, granted the truth of the allegations, was a wrong committed, in the legal sense, against a person or society in general? Since the answer to this question depends on what the law is, it is not one that a jury is empowered to decide. It is solely an issue for the Court to resolve. It is the Court, too, that will have to determine whether or not to sustain or overrule objections to the introduction of testimony or exhibits on the various grounds that may be raised as to their relevance, competence, or materiality. The only arguments that can be presented for this purpose are those taken from the vast body of law and precedent that may govern the case in question.

Of course, no attorney can be expected to know all the law, nor can any judge, for that matter. But certainly no trial lawyer can afford to appear in court without having at his fingertips all the law applicable to the case he is trying. For he will find that there is always a dispute about the law. Leonard Lyons, a columnist of the New York *Post*, tells the following story:

> Justice William O. Douglas was halted by a traffic cop while he was driving on the outskirts of Washington.
> The cop began, "Hey, you _____, don't you know the law?"
> Douglas, the Supreme Court's dissenter, replied, "You can get a hell of an argument on that either way."

A lawyer cannot count on his general background of legal knowledge to provide him with the appropriate citations when he needs them. For this kind of information, he has to do a good deal of research in advance of trial. What he learns in the silence and solitude of the library he puts to use in the heat of battle in the courtroom. Let us, therefore, quietly open the door of his study, peep in, and observe him at work as a scholar. His legal education did not stop after he left law school. Here he is, continuing his pursuit of legal knowledge in the service of his client.

The first thing he will want to do is to find out what laws and judicial precedents are relevant to the facts he has gathered, and how cases like his have fared in the courts.

To this end, even before drawing up a complaint, I made it a practice to go to the law library to look up the record of similar actions. There I spent many an evening over the years poring over the transcripts of the minutes of cases like the one I was preparing for trial. In fact, I worked there so frequently that the law librarian and I became fast friends. He was extremely helpful and cooperative. I remember that on many evenings he would walk over quietly to the table at which I was working and almost apologetically say, "You're the only one left in the library. Have a heart. I've got a dinner to attend." Sometimes he would mention that he had promised to take his wife to the movies that evening or that friends were coming to his home for a visit. One day we talked over the whole problem, and, as a result, we entered into a secret agreement. Now it can be told. It was understood between us that he would leave whenever he pleased, and I would be in charge of putting the books away, closing the windows, turning out the lights, and locking up the library with his key, which he entrusted to me. I promised to leave it for him in a nearby hiding place known only to the two of us. Little did he know, though, of the occasions when I "extended" the closing hours of that library from 5 P.M. to the early hours of the morning. Alas, this agreeable arrangement came to an abrupt end one day when I forgot to leave the key in the usual place!

It was hard work going over all those old cases night after night, but it was worth every minute I devoted to it. By reading countless records, I became familiar with the skills and techniques of experienced and able advocates. I learned to distinguish between good and bad questioning in both direct examinations and cross-examinations. I became acquainted with the work of trial lawyers whom I later personally observed in court and, still later, encountered as my adversaries. Some of these distinguished lawyers are now trying cases before me. As my revered friend and colleague, the Honorable Albert Conway, formerly Chief Judge of the Court of Appeals, said in addressing newly admitted members of the New York Bar on December 27, 1952: "You have to learn from the experience of others, as there is not enough time in one's life to learn everything by personal experience."

This was precisely the procedure I followed. Having satisfied myself that the complaint had already survived scrutiny by a higher court, I would extract from it the pertinent paragraphs and adapt them to the facts of my case, on the basis of my file of statements made to me previously by my client and witnesses. Next, reviewing the questions in the transcript, I would arrange them in the order that suited my case, deleting those that did not apply to it, and retaining only those that were vital to the issue. With these models, it was easy for me to frame my questions for direct examination in such a way as to establish what we lawyers call a prima facie case, that is, proof, on the basis of direct testimony, at least sufficient to prevent the complaint from being dismissed, as a matter of law, by the Court. For if a plaintiff cannot produce sufficient evidence to convince the Court that he has a prima facie case, there is no requirement for the defendant even to offer any evidence, and the Court, in such an event, will dismiss the case.

Let us, therefore, examine more closely each of these related steps in the preparation of a case: the drawing up of the complaint and the framing of questions for direct examination.

Long before a case is called for trial, what is called a "bill of particulars" must be prepared by counsel for the plaintiff, amplifying the complaint, so that the defendant may know just what accusations he must meet and what facts are alleged in support of them. It is essential that the bill of particulars, besides being clear and responsive to the demand of the defendant, be so drawn up as to give counsel for the plaintiff all the latitude necessary to present his proof from the lips of his client and witnesses. Each of the allegations in the bill of particulars should be prepared with a view of being supported by the testimony of one or more witnesses at the trial. Counsel can do this by drawing upon the results of his interviews with his client and witnesses, including expert witnesses, technicians, and doctors, and his own reading of the pertinent literature on the injuries involved.

Each item in a bill of particulars must be complete, truthful, relevant, and free from exaggeration. A judge once had a case before him in which the plaintiff, in her bill of particulars, alleged that as a result of an injury to her neck she could not move her head up or down or from side to side. During the course of the trial, it appeared to the judge that she was exaggerating the extent of her injury. When she was off guard, he suddenly called out to the court attendant, "Quick! Bring in a fire extinguisher. The ceiling is on fire up there." The witness immediately moved her head back without any apparent difficulty to look up to the place to which the judge was pointing. After that she changed her testimony and tried to ease her predicament by saying that once in a while she could move her head, although she had previously testified that she could not move it at any time. But she was stuck with her allegation in the bill of particulars, and she paid the penalty of exaggerating.

A classic example of carelessness in preparing a bill of particulars was brought to my attention by an attorney for an insurance company. The defendants were two owners of taxicabs insured by the company. The plaintiff was a fairly attractive woman, a passenger in one of the cabs, who had sustained various facial injuries as a result of negligence on the part of the defendants. Counsel were unable to settle the case because of the excessive demands made by the plaintiff.

In opening to the jury, counsel for one of the defendants admitted liability but expressed his confidence that the jurors would be able to

reach a reasonable and just decision as to the amount of damages to
be awarded.

The bill of particulars alleged, among other things, that one of the
consequences of the accident was that the plaintiff had lost her tolerance for alcohol. But during the entire course of the direct examination, her attorney never once referred to this allegation. The cross-
examination, on the other hand, was devoted chiefly to this point, and
the plaintiff proved to be a most responsive witness. She freely stated
that before the accident she had been in the habit of imbibing between seven and eight martinis during the day, but, alas, after the accident, her daily intake had to be considerably reduced. She just
couldn't take as much as she used to.

The plaintiff received a verdict in her favor, but the amount of the
judgment was relatively small. Could it be that one of the jurors was
a teetotaler? Could that juror have succeeded in convincing the other
members of the panel that the accident had done the plaintiff some
good after all, since, as she herself had conceded, she drank less after
it? Surely it was unnecessary, in the first place, to allege, in the bill of
particulars, a loss of tolerance for alcohol, and then make no further
reference to it on direct examination.

As we can see, the questions asked on direct examination should be
closely connected with the allegations in the bill of particulars. For a
lawyer to leave the framing of these questions to chance or to momentary inspiration is to risk the possibility of having the entire action
dismissed and losing not only his case but his client. I have seen too
many blunders made in court by the "busy" lawyer who just couldn't
take the time to formulate his questions for direct examination well
before the trial or to arrange them in the most effective sequence or
to review them carefully to make sure that he could prove a prima
facie case.

Sometimes lawyers feel embarrassed about bringing their written
questions to court. I have often heard them say that it doesn't look
good for counsel to read questions from a paper or a set of cards in
front of a jury. It might seem as if he hadn't fully mastered all the
details of the case. In fact, the contrary is true. Written questions are
a sure sign of preparation, and the better the questions and the more
effectively organized they are, the more obviously thorough the preliminary work of the lawyer has been. Ideally, of course, he should have
such a complete grasp of the facts that he does not appear to be reading his questions word for word, even though this practice is not, in

my opinion, to be feared or condemned. If a lawyer has gone over his questions often enough in advance, as an actor does his script, he will find, after a while, that he needs to consult them only occasionally to prompt himself; he will be referring to them as a guide rather than leaning upon them as a crutch. I believe that when a trial lawyer comes to court with prepared questions for conducting his examination of his own witnesses and, for that matter, even questions anticipated for cross-examination, he is fulfilling to a very high degree his solemn obligation to his client to be ready for trial in every respect.

To a witness on the stand, it may seem as if the questions he is asked under cross-examination must have been made up on the spur of the moment, or at least that they could not possibly have been prepared before he testified, for how could opposing counsel have known in advance what the direct testimony would be? It is, of course, true, as we shall see, that a lawyer has to take his cue for cross-examination from the testimony and behavior of the witness under direct examination, and that it is impossible to anticipate everything that is going to be said. But this does not mean that an experienced attorney cannot make a rather accurate conjecture of the substance and character of the testimony he is going to have to refute or that he cannot lay his plans accordingly.

Suppose, for example, that, in a matrimonial action for separation on grounds of cruel and inhuman treatment, he is to defend the husband. Let us assume, further, that counsel has reason to believe that the testimony to be given by the wife is likely to be grossly exaggerated in the narration of certain incidents because of bias instilled in her as a result of pressure from others. What can he do to prepare himself to expose the forces underlying her testimony?

In the course of his preparation for trial, he might make notes of details concerning the place or places where the parties to the controversy lived; who, if anyone, lived with them; who visited them; who went out with them socially; and how both of them spent their days and weekends during the period of time involved in their dispute. Armed with this specific information, he may be able to establish the fact that the plaintiff's parents had never approved of the marriage, had no respect for their son-in-law, and, filled with a venomous hostility toward him, succeeded in poisoning their daughter's mind against her husband and browbeating her into giving false testimony.

Now counsel is in a position to break down the plaintiff's exaggerations. He can cross-examine her concerning conversations which her parents had with her about her husband. He can elicit testimony showing that they had manifested ill-will toward him even before the marriage, and that their actions indicated a studied effort to break it up by imbuing their daughter with bias against him.

To be sure, the plaintiff's attorney might object to this line of inquiry on the ground that the attitude of her parents is irrelevant, since the controversy is between husband and wife, and not between the husband and his "in-laws." However, such an objection would have to be overruled, because the proof to be adduced touches directly on the plaintiff's veracity. To insure success in this phase of the trial, the counsel for the defendant would have to be prepared to call witnesses who would testify to the conversations with the plaintiff's parents, to outbursts or other demonstrations by them against the defendant, and to other incidents indicating their calculated attempts to destroy the marriage. In this way, the credibility of the plaintiff's testimony concerning her husband's alleged cruelty to her would be undermined, because it would be shown to have been affected by the prejudice instilled in her by her parents.

Thus, if enough forethought is given to the kind of opposition to be expected, even the questions to be asked in cross-examination can be prepared in advance and brought to court for use when they are needed.

But the legal research which a lawyer engages in while getting his case ready for trial is not performed solely for his own benefit. The judge, too, appreciates guidance from counsel on the law of the case and often will ask for it. Since no judge can possibly be familiar with all the statutes and other authorities that may be relevant to the legal questions raised by the case, the Court is very much in the hands of counsel in this regard and naturally expects the lawyers on both sides to bring to its attention whatever laws and precedents bear in one way or another on the matters at issue. After all, the lawyers have lived with the case for some time before coming to court, whereas the judge knows nothing about it until they appear before him. If they have done their homework, they should bring to court the citations they need in order to justify their objections to the introduction of certain testimony or exhibits and to support their judgment of the law of the case. They should be able to give the judge a ready answer to any legal question he may pose.

It is therefore not sufficient for a trial lawyer to have signed statements, pleadings, and pertinent exhibits before him as he tries a case.

He needs, besides, what we in the legal profession call a "trial brief," that is, a memorandum setting forth the law and the facts. This should be divided into logically arranged sections and furnished with tabular indices to enable counsel to find easily any point he may be looking for. I can remember few instances when I entered a court to try a case without having in my possession a memorandum of this kind. It was my practice to hand this document up to the judge at the very outset, whether the legal questions presented by the case were simple or complicated.

Usually the judge reads the memorandum in his chambers while the jury is being selected.

Justice Brandeis once said, "A judge rarely performs his functions adequately unless the case before him is adequately presented." A clear, concise trial memorandum, briefly stating the facts and expounding the pertinent law with appropriate citations, goes a long way in helping a judge to follow the reasoning of counsel and in winning acceptance for it.

Indeed, a thorough knowledge of the law applicable to the case can make it possible for an attorney to forestall his opponent by requesting the Court to exclude his adversary's testimony even before it is given or offered. In a negligence case once tried before me, in which one of the major issues was the point of original impact in a collision between two automobiles, the plaintiff's lawyer knew that the defendant planned to call to the stand the police officers who had conducted an investigation after the accident. They were to testify concerning skid marks, the position of the cars, etc. He suspected that the experienced attorney for the insurance company would attempt to use the police officers as experts and would ask them where, in their opinion, the point of impact was.

Therefore, as soon as counsel for the plaintiff had completed the presentation of his case, he asked permission to approach the bench and addressed the Court substantially as follows: "I know that counsel for the defendant will call certain police officers who investigated the accident, and I have a feeling that they will be asked to give expert testimony concerning the point of impact. Now, Your Honor, I have prepared a memorandum of law touching upon this very question. It shows that such testimony is inadmissible. May I suggest a short recess at this time to give Your Honor an opportunity to read my memorandum and the three or four cases cited in it?"

I thereupon excused the jury, retired to my chambers with counsel for both sides, and read the memorandum and the cases cited by the plaintiff's attorney. After listening to the arguments presented by both attorneys. I told the counsel for the defendant that I had been persuaded by the precedents cited in the memorandum to sustain an objection to the line of questioning that the plaintiff's attorney had expected would be pursued. Of course, to preserve the record in case of an appeal, I told the defendant's attorney that, if he so desired, he could ask the question, and I would then rule it inadmissible.

A judge has a high regard for a trial lawyer who goes about his work in the way that the counsel for the plaintiff did in this case. Not only was his procedure helpful to the Court in preventing an erroneous ruling that might have led to a reversal on appeal, but it saved time by eliminating a good deal of wrangling between counsel in front of the jury. But for a lawyer to be able to secure a ruling of this kind, he must first have done a thorough job of legal research.

This is especially important in the preparation of a criminal case. The responsibility of the lawyer who undertakes to defend a person charged with a crime is indeed onerous. So many new decisions have been handed down and so many dramatic changes have recently been made in this branch of the law that no attorney should try a criminal case unless he is thoroughly familiar with the latest rulings of the courts and understands fully the implications of the new concepts they involve. For these have a direct bearing on the many problems that arise not only in the conduct of the trial itself but also in the investigation preceding it. In this connection, counsel must pay particular attention to possible violations of the accused's constitutional rights as a result of the methods employed by the police in gathering the evidence to be presented at the trial.

For example, among the questions to which careful consideration must be given are the following:

Was there probable cause to arrest the accused?

Was he, immediately following his arrest, apprised of his right to remain silent and to have the advice of counsel?

Was any inculpatory statement made by the accused? If so, was it made voluntarily, without intimidation, coercion, or promise of leniency, and in full knowledge that it could be used against him? Was the accused trapped into making such a statement to a professional police informer disguised as a cellmate?

Does any of the evidence to be presented at the trial consist of or depend on statements made by the accused against his interest and recorded without his knowledge or consent by a concealed electronic listening device?

Were any incriminating documents, weapons, or instruments taken from the accused? If so, was the search that led to their discovery a lawful one?

To what extent was the accused's right to a fair trial prejudiced by adverse publicity in the press or on the radio or television?

How long was the accused detained for interrogation without counsel?

What facts about the reputation or circumstances of the accused might warrant a request to reduce his bail or to eliminate it entirely?

It goes without saying that the use which counsel makes of this kind of information requires a thorough grounding in the most recent decisions in the field of criminal law.

So now counsel has personally interviewed all his witnesses, including the experts. He has gone to the trouble of holding a pretrial examination of the opposing party and has obtained and reviewed statements from witnesses. He has taken the pains to make an on-the-spot investigation of conditions and places to be referred to in court. He has had all his exhibits carefully tested and has checked all his documents. He has spent many hours looking up the law in the case. He has drawn up a detailed bill of particulars, if he is representing the plaintiff. He has prepared his questions for direct examination and cross-examination. And he has written a learned and scholarly legal memorandum for the judge.

Hasn't he done enough? Isn't he ready for trial at last?

By no means. There is still more to be done. For not only is the lawyer the stage manager and director of the drama to be enacted in the courtroom; he will himself be one of the principal actors in it, and for the role he has to play he will need to prepare his own script. How does he do it?

He will first want to go over all the statements, documents, and exhibits in his file at his leisure in his office in order to determine where to lay the emphasis, where to be brief, where to enlarge, in what order to call his witnesses, and when to introduce each document and exhibit. For this purpose, he must learn to separate the important facts from the unimportant, to concentrate on the most convincing evidence in his own favor, and to bear down hard on the most damaging admissions, contradictions, confusions, and weaknesses on the other side. He will thus be prepared to concede, without hesitation, if called upon to do so, the inessential facts, thereby winning the respect of the judge and the confidence of the jury. Instead of scratching all over and drawing no blood, he will strike at the jugular vein.

He will also need to prepare himself well in any specialized field of knowledge which the case may call for. For example, he may find it necessary to become conversant with the practices, procedures, and techniques of a particular industry. Unless he takes as much care in acquainting himself with such technicalities, which have nothing directly to do with the law, he may find that all his painstaking preparation of witnesses, documents, exhibits, and legal memoranda will go for naught.

This is what happened in a recent case in which a worker whose occupation required him to walk on structural steel beams hundreds of feet above the ground was being cross-examined as to the manner in which he performed his job. Annoyed by the failure of the cross-examiner to understand his verbal explanations of his technique, the witness suddenly darted from the stand, jumped on the rail in front of the jury box, and paraded back and forth on it with the greatest of ease, saying, "This is the way I walk a beam."

The cross-examiner, although a seasoned lawyer, forgot for the moment to think out the questions which he next put to the witness. He first asked, "How wide is the rail on which you are now standing?"

"I guess about eight to ten inches," the witness replied, all the while maintaining his upright position on the rail.

Then came the question that counsel later wished he had never asked: "Do you mean to say that you walk on beams that are only about eight inches wide?"

Whereupon the witness shot back the devastating answer: "Mister, this is a boardwalk to me. The beams I work on are two inches wide, hundreds of feet in the air."

Of course, counsel should have known this. The time when he should have learned all about the skills required of such workers, about the shape, dimensions, height, and position of the steel beams they walk on, about safety devices and practices and accident statistics in the industry, and about the specifications and standards which the equipment has to meet, was the period during which counsel prepared the case for trial. He paid the penalty of his inadequate technical knowledge.

Finally, a lawyer should be looked upon—and should look upon himself—not only as the commander of a troop of witnesses whom he has to assemble, train, and deploy to best advantage, but as himself a soldier fighting side by side with them on the field of battle. He too, then, will need to be equipped to meet his adversary face to face. To that end he must know his adversary—not just his name, address, and telephone number, but his personality and his technique of offense and defense. After all, in every arena of combat, a thorough knowledge of the opposition is a *sine qua non* of success. Debaters study their antagonists' style of delivery; baseball and football teams employ scouts to observe and report on the strengths and weaknesses of opposing players; and military intelligence constantly strives to learn as much as possible about the intentions and tactics of the enemy. A trial lawyer can do no less in familiarizing himself with the character and methods of opposing counsel.

For this kind of information, it is not enough to rely on newspaper accounts or on what his friends and associates may say about him. In the last analysis there is nothing like firsthand observation for filling in the picture. Before a boxing match, a prizefighter will often study the pugilistic style of his opponent by observing him in the ring in an effort to discover when, if ever, he is off balance or lets down his guard and lays himself open to a knockout blow. In the same way, before his case comes to trial, a lawyer would do well to make it his business, as part of his combat training, to take a good look—and, if possible, several looks—at his adversary in action in the courtroom.

There is much to be learned from such pretrial reconnaissance. The perceptive observer watches how opposing counsel opens to the jury, notes his method of putting questions on direct examination as well as in cross-examination, marks the manner in which he conducts himself before the jury, gives heed to the way he addresses the Court, takes cognizance of his conduct in objecting to testimony, and even checks on his behavior during recesses while he is in the court corridors. I have been told of one instance in which an attorney was in the habit of frightening witnesses who were waiting in the corridor to testify against his client. Approaching each one menacingly, he would wave a finger under the witness' nose and growl, "Just wait until I get you under cross-examination!" Of course, such crude attempts at intimidation are rendered quite futile if the witnesses have been warned against them in advance by a lawyer who knows what to expect. Although tactics of this kind are rarely employed, a lawyer has to be constantly vigilant lest his adversary be tempted to resort to them.

Indeed, to the knowing eye, a lawyer's behavior in court can reveal a great deal. But one must know what to look for. Is he a judge-baiter? Does he have certain mannerisms that are likely to annoy the Court? Is he irascible? Does he like to jump up with endless objections? Is he given to making side remarks for the benefit of the jury? Does he follow a set pattern when summing up? Does he always tell the same stories? Does he have certain favorite quotations that he is fond of citing? Is he unprepared on the facts or the law? Does he like to indulge in flights of oratory? What is his attitude toward opposing counsel? Does he change his style from case to case, or does he follow a formula? Does he appear to be sincere, or is his manner cold and calculating? Does he stick to the issues, or does he go off on sidetracks? Is he the tenacious, aggressive, "bulldog" type of cross-examiner, who refuses to let a witness go until his testimony has been thoroughly demolished? Is he the kind who cajoles, mocks, jokes, or tries to laugh his opponent's case out of court? Is he the erudite, reserved type, who submits a comprehensive trial brief bristling with citations and refers to them again and again in objecting to testimony?

The answers to questions like these about opposing counsel can be of inestimable value to a lawyer who knows how to make use of such information in advance of trial.

Recently I noticed a young attorney sitting all day in my court and busily taking notes as he watched the trial of a case. At the end of the day I called him to the bench and asked him what he had been doing. He explained that he was getting ready to try a similar case against one of the lawyers engaged in the trial before me. He told me that this lawyer was reputed to have unusual talents. He had, it seems, a way with juries. In particular, he was known to have a fund of anecdotes which he used with telling effect in summing up. These had produced for him an unbroken string of victories. He was likewise known in the courts for having a unique knack of laughing away his opponents' cases. Juries evidently enjoyed his antics.

The young lawyer said that he wanted to watch his prospective adversary and learn all he could about the man's style, technique, stories, and mannerisms. Accordingly, for several days he continued to sit in my court observing his quarry most carefully.

A few weeks later I happened to meet the young man, and I asked him how he had fared with his case. He told me that he had watched the same lawyer in a few more trials, studied his characteristics, and even stalked him to his law office in order to observe the contrast between his behavior there and his manner in court. With the voluminous notes accumulated during this extensive period of surveillance, the young attorney knew, when his case came to trial, just when to use the "Emily Post" approach and when and how to "get tough" and hit his adversary with everything that weeks of scouting had revealed.

Among the discoveries made in the process of this persistent reconnoitering was the fact that opposing counsel was in the habit of using the same stories and analogies in practically all of his trials. All that was needed, then, was a little time to find an appropriate, dignified answer for each anecdote and to prepare a sober comment on every analogy. In this way the young man was able to convince the jury, as others before him had failed to do, that his case was to be taken seriously and not to be laughed out of court. The reward of his concentrated effort, careful preparation, and hard work came when the jury returned a verdict in favor of his client for a substantial amount —the largest he had obtained in his ten years of practice.

American business enterprise and the progress of technology have accustomed us to an economy that places virtually every commodity at the disposal of the consumer in a form in which it can be put to use immediately, with a minimum of preparation. Houses today can be put together in record time from prefabricated materials and standardized parts; housewives now rely, as a matter of course, on quick-frozen foods that need only to be taken out of the freezer, thawed, and heated for a few minutes to be ready for eating; and "instant" coffee, soapsuds, shaving cream, and a host of other ever-ready conveniences are now taken for granted as a part of our everyday lives. Gone are the days when bread was laboriously baked at home in the oven from dough prepared in the kitchen; today it comes sliced and packaged in the supermarket. The whole toilsome process of getting things ready for use has been enormously simplified and facilitated.

By contrast, the lengthy investigations, interrogations, and research required of a lawyer in the preparation of his case may seem like an anachronism in today's busy world. The kind of thoroughness, patience, and perseverance I have described here may have been all right for the leisurely days of the horse and buggy, but at the pace at which things are done nowadays, is there time for all that?

Unfortunately too many lawyers seem to think that there isn't. After they are retained in a case, they take a legal folder, affix on it a label on which the title of the action has been typed, place in it a few statements, affidavits, and documents, and then "put it on ice" in a filing cabinet. When the case comes to trial, they expect to remove the file folder from the cabinet and find everything instantly ready for use, just as the housewife does when she removes frozen food from the freezer. But the housewife is able to prepare an "instantaneous" and palatable meal from the frozen food only because it was processed and properly prepared long in advance of her purchase. Woe to the lawyer who expects to find a processed and carefully prepared case in his "frozen" file! Any lawyer who tries to work in this "instant" fashion will find himself serving his client a most unpalatable dish.

Some things just can't be hurried: the birth of a baby, the maturation of a tree from its seed, the healing of a wound, and, I may add, the preparation of a case for trial.

What is more, the work of preparation is never-ending, because each trial must be prepared anew, as if it were the first. It is said that Dickens, during his readings in America, although he had thirteen years of experience behind him in these wonderful performances, never came before his audience without freshly going over, for hours on end, every piece he was to read. He studied each point he was to make with the anxiety of a novice. Indeed, it is the mark of the master in every profession that his life is one of perpetual study and preparation. This is what Michelangelo meant when, in his old age, he said, "I carry my satchel still!"

As Lloyd Paul Stryker, a brilliant trial lawyer, says in his instructive book *The Art of Advocacy:*

> The conduct of a trial is likened to a game of chess, and the two have many similarities, but there is a great difference . . . Chess is . . . pure skill, without any element of chance. But in war and litigation, chance plays an enormous, incalculable part. Advocacy without the most minute study and patient preparation is nothing. Without these it is a snare and a delusion. No eloquence, no quickness of wit, no knowledge of the law can be a substitute for mastery of the facts.

As the day of the trial nears—a trial of and for the lawyer as much as it is a trial of the case itself—he may well wonder what more he can possibly do to prepare himself for it. Even though he may have satisfied himself that he has done everything he could, he may yet feel vaguely unready and uneasy.

For there is one other essential ingredient in his preparation that has not so far been mentioned. There is a sense in which, on the day he appears in court to try his case, everything that he has ever done in his whole life has contributed toward putting him in a state of readiness for that moment: everything he has ever read, everyone he has ever met, everywhere he has ever been. We may call this indispensable element "experience" if we like, provided that we do not understand the term in the narrow sense that denotes only his accomplishments in the practice of law. In the sense in which I am using the word here, it may be said that even the fledgling advocate trying his first case might have a rich treasury of experience in other fields to draw upon, while one long seasoned in the ways of the courts could have a relatively impoverished background. The element I am referring to is what distinguishes the master lawyer—a Clarence Darrow, a Max D. Steuer, a Louis Nizer, a Samuel S. Leibowitz (now my learned colleague on the bench)—who takes a broad view of his profession, from the ordinary yet capable trial lawyer. Unfortunately I can think of only a few outstanding trial lawyers whom I can compare with this select group. I could include Harry Gair, Edward Bennett Williams, Percy Foreman, Jacob W. Ehrlich, Perry Nichols, F. Lee Bailey, and William F. X. Geoghan, Jr., in this illustrious category.

The truth is that the effectiveness of an attorney in the courtroom is only partly dependent on his legal knowledge and attainments and the length of time he has been trying cases. What counts just as much, in the end, is the kind of man he is, or rather the kind of man he has made himself in his leisure time, when he wanted to be concerned with anything but legal problems, by the literature he has chosen to read, the range of humanity that has come within his ken, the places he has visited, the philosophy of life he has developed. For it is ultimately out of the depth and the breadth of his cultural, social, moral, political, and religious commitments that a successful lawyer draws the spiritual sustenance and strength needed to give conviction to his pleadings before judge and jury. Insight into the human heart, sympathy with the human condition, compassion for human frailty—these are not products of research in a law library; yet they are essential requirements of the trial lawyer. By consciously making himself the heir to what Matthew Arnold called "the best that has been thought and said in the world"; by immersing himself in the great humanistic tradition of moral idealism that stretches back through the centuries to the Romans, the Greeks, and the Hebrews; by drawing on the inspiration of the prophets, saints, and heroes of the past; by identifying himself actively with the institutions and movements of his own age that are carrying on the grand work of mankind's progressive improvement in all spheres of human endeavor—in short, by trying to live the sort of life that exemplifies all that is best in the spiritual heritage of civilized man—a lawyer molds himself into the kind of person whose judgment is respected, whose words are listened to with approbation, and whose moral fervor in a righteous cause carries conviction because it is weighted with the solid substance of accumulated wisdom and truth. True eloquence is not just a matter of rhetoric or art; its roots lie deep within the soul of the orator.

Fortunate indeed is the client who can find a lawyer with this breadth of culture and human understanding!

But the day of the trial has come at last. Lawyer, client, and witnesses are as ready for it as they'll ever be. Let us follow them into court and see what awaits them there.

II

SELECTING THE JURY

5

"Twelve Good Men and True"

I have often wondered why the scriptwriters for Hollywood and tele-vision hardly ever depict for their mass audience the fascinating proc-ess by which the lawyers on both sides of a case go about screening and selecting the members of a jury. Although this is one of the most in-tensely absorbing and important preliminaries of the trial itself, it has been virtually neglected as a subject for popular drama.

In the usual play or movie dealing with a trial, the jury is given the center of the stage only after all the evidence has been presented and the panel has retired to deliberate upon a verdict. Then we are treated to the spectacle of the conflicts and passions that erupt in the privacy of the jury room. There, as each embattled juror seeks agreement on his own terms, the controversy heats up into a prolonged war of at-trition that may culminate in deadlock or compromise. Many an en-thralling tale has been spun around the smoldering resentments and bitter outbursts of conscious or unconscious prejudice that mark these hostilities.

In such narratives the wheels of justice seem to make a terrible grinding noise, as if they did not mesh together very well. In any properly constructed machine, of course, the parts are all standardized to ensure a perfect fit. But how can we expect to put a jury together so that it will function with the smooth efficiency of a well-oiled mechanism? What possible assurance can we have beforehand that its members, gathered from here and there, will adjust to one another like ball and socket or gear and ratchet?

There is a story here, but it has hardly been noticed. Yet it is no less charged with its own excitement and tension. It is the story of how this strange assortment of a dozen human beings was brought together in the first place, from their diverse daily occupations and pursuits, to judge the facts of the case.

Nor, for that matter, has much attention been paid to the role of the lawyers on each side in selecting just these and no others to hear the evidence and decide the issues. A surprising oversight, indeed, in view of the crucial importance of obtaining just the right "mix"!

Perhaps the explanation is to be found in the notorious unpredictability of juries. They conform to no known pattern or formula. Each panel is absolutely individual and unique. It is impossible for even the most experienced attorney to be certain of the way the members of a jury are going to react to the evidence. One can never be sure what the verdict is going to be until the jurors file back into the courtroom, and the foreman announces the outcome of their deliberations. Under the circumstances, the whole procedure of questioning and screening prospective jurors does appear to the layman at least, and even to some lawyers, as rather pointless. Consider all the chance factors, all the personal quirks and idiosyncrasies, that enter into the thinking and feeling of each juror. Does it not seem as if no precaution that a lawyer can take could possibly affect the outcome to any significant extent?

Indeed, some lawyers are convinced that it is utterly futile to try to probe into the soul, heart, and mind of each prospective juror in the effort to ferret out every last trace of prejudice. They have told me quite frankly that they are satisfied to take their chances with any twelve people who are willing to listen. For these lawyers there is nothing especially challenging about the selection of a jury. As far as they are concerned, the whole panel could just as well be chosen by tossing a coin or drawing the names of the jurors blindly out of a hat. Everyone, they say, has some prejudice, whether he is aware of it or not, and, of course, no one is ever going to admit it. So why indulge in an exercise in futility? As Henry Luce, of Time, Inc., observed, "Show me a man who claims he's completely objective, and I'll show you a man with illusions."

It cannot be denied that there is some justification for the attitudes of such lawyers. Certainly plenty of cases could be cited in which the decision of the jury could hardly be said to have been the result of a dispassionate, objective search for truth. Nor would it be difficult to find many others in which the decisive role was played by factors that no lawyer could reasonably have been expected to take into account in selecting the members of the jury.

A particularly apt illustration is provided by a case tried some years ago, in which the plaintiff was a gracefully curvaceous young woman with the kind of physique that would have made her an ideal "sweater girl." Unmarried at the time of the incident described in her complaint, she had attended, attired in a décolleté dress, a gay party given at the apartment of some newly married friends. During the course of the festivities she had gone to the bathroom, which was situated at the end of a long, narrow hallway at a considerable distance from the living room where the party was going on. As she emerged, she encountered her host. Attracted by her womanly charms, he took advantage of her close proximity as she brushed by him in the intimate confines of the corridor to give her a pinch in the breast.

According to her testimony, the pinched area immediately turned black and blue and subsequently required surgery because of a suspected malignancy. She was suing to recover damages for the personal injuries she had sustained. The medical evidence she adduced was overwhelming, and hardly a spectator in the crowded courtroom had any doubt that the defendant had actually committed the act complained of. A verdict for the plaintiff seemed like a foregone conclusion.

And yet, surprisingly, the jury found for the defendant. When questioned later by several of the interested parties, the members of the all-male panel were quite frank in disclosing the reason for their decision. If the defendant had indeed committed the alleged act, they said, it was no more than what every one of them had done, in like circumstances and under similar temptation, many times. They reasoned that each one of them, then, must have caused many a breast cancer. Not a man among them could bring himself to require the defendant to pay out money for an act like that.

Now, can we imagine any lawyer, even if he could have anticipated such a reaction on the part of a prospective juror, asking him, "Have you ever given a woman an unsolicited pinch in the breast?"

It must be admitted that what goes on in the minds of some jurors as they reach a verdict can hardly be dignified with the name of "reasoning." Their thought processes often follow a roundabout course that begins, meanders, and ends very far indeed from any of the evidence presented at the trial. Even the selection of jurors whose training and background might lead one to expect from them at least some regard for the elementary rules of logic scarcely provides a guarantee of straight or pertinent thinking.

A case in point is one in which Mr. Denis M. Hurley, former Corporation Counsel of the City of New York, and once President of the Brooklyn Bar Association, appeared recently in defense of a contested will. One of Mr. Hurley's partners had not only drawn the document but had subscribed his name to it as a witness of the testator's signature, and another partner was also a subscribing witness. Both therefore appeared in court with him.

A jury was selected, and the lawyers on both sides presented their opening statements. At the end of the second day, before the contestant had quite completed the presentation of her case, a settlement was reached out of court, and the jury was accordingly discharged. To satisfy the curiosity of the jurors, who asked Mr. Hurley's associate what had happened, he explained the situation to them and then inquired of them how they stood.

At that time, eight were definitely in favor of the proponent, Mr. Hurley's client. Of the other four, three said that they wanted further clarification before finally making up their minds. Only one juror—a college graduate and a technician in a biology laboratory—said that she had already definitely decided in favor of the contestant. This scientific observer, concentrating her attention on the clothing of the attorneys in the case, had noticed a sharp contrast in their appearance, which seemed to her to be very significant. The three attorneys for the proponent were well dressed, while the lone attorney for the contestant was wearing a shabby suit of clothes. It was clearly, she concluded, a case of three prosperous lawyers "ganging up" on the poor counsel for the contestant. Therefore, the contestant must have been in the right!

Sometimes it is only sheer luck that saves a lawyer from having on the jury someone who can nullify all his efforts. In another case, also involving a contested will, a friend of mine selected a jury that seemed altogether satisfactory to both sides. Suddenly one of the women jurors jumped up and asked to be excused, saying:

> My own father died two weeks ago, and I must run home and tell my husband to tear up the will, or we will be in court like tigers and lions. Such a terrible thing for brothers and sisters to fight over—money! [Pause.] Unless, of course, there is a lot of money.

Needless to say, she was excused.

A particularly insidious source of bias is the often unconsciously accepted racial, national, or religious stereotype. Even when this kind of prejudice is suspected, it is very difficult for counsel to bring it out into the open in the preliminary screening of prospective jurors. As we shall see, it takes a skillful lawyer indeed to pick a jury for any case in which there is the slightest possibility that such deeply rooted preconceptions may be given opportunity to flourish. It is not enough for him to satisfy himself, if he can, that at least the members of the panel are not prejudiced against the particular group with which his client may be identified in their minds. The very acceptance of the stereotype, even without any feelings of disrespect or hostility, can color the whole process of a jury's thinking.

For example, I was told of a case in which a rabbi was sued by a corporation (let us call it here Cohen's Coal and Ice Company) for the value of the coal it had delivered to a certain building. The rabbi's defense was that the building was actually owned by a corporation, of which he was only an officer, and it was solely in that capacity, on behalf of the corporation, that he had ordered the coal.

One would have supposed that the word of a member of the clergy would not be questioned by a jury. Nevertheless, in this case a verdict was returned in favor of the plaintiff. Afterwards, counsel asked the foreman of the jury, who was a Christian, why the decision had gone against the rabbi.

He answered, "Let's face it. Cohen is a Jew. The rabbi is a Jew. Cohen would never have sued the rabbi unless he was convinced that the rabbi had personally ordered the coal on his own behalf."

Unfortunately it is impossible for even the most skillful attorney to be sure that he has detected, in questioning veniremen, every faulty prepossession that might later prove fatal to his case. And once jurors with erroneous views of this kind have slipped through his net, he is powerless to protect his client. Indeed, it needs only one such mistaken assumption, one fixed idea on the part of a single juror, to confound a lawyer's best efforts, as is shown by a case tried by a friend of mine in the early days of his practice. The plaintiff, while driving a truck along a cobblestone street on which trolley tracks had been laid, lost control of the steering wheel and was injured when one of the front wheels hit a rut where several cobblestones were missing. The railroad law at that time required the trolley company to keep the roadway in repair up to three feet on each side of the tracks. Every indication pointed to a verdict in favor of the plaintiff.

And yet, the jury found for the defendant. When questioned by counsel after the trial, the members of the jury said that if there had been any truth to the plaintiff's allegation about the missing cobblestones, counsel would have placed photographs in evidence to prove it.

It so happened that the missing cobblestones were replaced a day or two after the accident, and several months before counsel had been retained to handle the case. However, the law prohibits the introduction of testimony or evidence concerning repairs made *after* an accident, except in cases where the defendant has denied ownership, operation, and control.

Apparently one or more of the jurors had received the impression from a movie, a play, or previous experience on a jury that photographic evidence forms an indispensable part of the proof in a negligence case.

Now, how could any lawyer possibly anticipate such thinking on the part of the jury?

Many other examples could be cited of the unpredictable behavior of jurors. Their bias or irrationality can upset a lawyer's best-laid plans. In this connection I like the following quotation from "Mr. Dooley in Peace and War" by the humorist Finley Peter Dunne:

> Whin th' case is all over, the jury'll pitch th' tistimony out iv th' window, an' consider three questions: Did Lootgert look as though he'd kill his wife? Did his wife look as though she ought to be kilt? Isn't it time we wint to supper?

On the same subject Charles Dickens, too, who had himself served as a clerk to a Gray's Inn solicitor and had observed many a trial at Old Bailey as a newspaper reporter, had this to say in his *Pickwick Papers:*

> "I wonder what the foreman of the jury, whoever he'll be, has got for breakfast," said Mr. Snodgrass . . .
> "Ah!" said Perker, "I hope he's got a good one."
> "Why so?" inquired Mr. Pickwick.
> "Highly important—very important, my dear sir," replied Perker. "A good, contented, well-breakfasted juryman is a capital thing to get hold of. Discontented or hungry jurymen, my dear sir, always find for the plaintiff."

Perhaps it was similar considerations that led H. L. Mencken, in a characteristically cynical vein, to remark to a friend that, next to throwing dice, he regarded trial by jury as the best method of ascertaining guilt thus far devised.

Undoubtedly, human nature being what it is, the selection of a jury is very far from being an exact science. But then, neither is anything else that a trial lawyer does. At best he is practicing an art, and, like every other artist, he has to reconcile himself to the unforeseen and the unpredictable. After all, the material with which he works is man himself, in all his variability, contrariety, and peculiarity. Consequently there can be no hard-and-fast rules to guide an attorney in culling out a panel to judge his case. In the end he has to rely on his common sense, his knowledge of men and women, and his skill in judging people. There is no denying that it is extremely difficult for even a seasoned lawyer to decide who will be a suitable juror. Even at best, it's a guess, and no bets should be taken on what a jury will do. Until someone invents an electronic machine that could, as it were, write out the total equation of a human being and punch out his predicted reaction to the evidence to be presented, lawyers are going to have to content themselves with making the best possible conjecture about each prospective juror.

I cannot, however, agree with those members of the legal profession, although few in number, who contend that there is really nothing at all that a lawyer can do to protect his client against impaneling biased jurors. True, no system of screening can guarantee the selection of an impartial panel of clear-thinking individuals. Of course, there are many cases like the ones just described in which a lawyer could hardly have been able to anticipate the prejudices later manifested by the jury. No doubt, too, it is impossible to devise questions that will bring every prejudice to the surface before the trial. Nevertheless, in most instances juries, if carefully selected, perform their duties conscientiously and intelligently. The verdict rendered by the average jury is, in the main, reasonable and just in terms of the evidence.

In a column entitled "Watching the Jury," which appeared in the New York *World-Telegram and Sun* on January 19, 1966, Murray Kempton aptly expresses the judgment of a perceptive observer of the process of selecting jurors for a murder trial he was attending:

> There can hardly be a lawyer alive who has solved the riddle of jurors; and most of the damage to defendants has been done by lawyers who thought they had. . . .
> Nothing more than a guess is provided in the lottery of this process. . . .
> Still, it is the only process we have to find out the truth about the murder. . . .
> And . . . oddly enough, the ideal does rather often get served by persons who seem, at first, especially unqualified to serve it. We shall sit for weeks with these jurors, and in the end they will make a judgment, and we shall be surprised at how close it is to our own, assuming we have paid attention. The process attempts the impossible, and somehow it manages quite often to achieve the terribly difficult.

Over the years the jury, as an institution, has won the respect it deserves. It is now generally recognized that, ordinarily, jurors do a good job. But their function has not always been understood, nor have their services always been appreciated, as the following story shows. When the West was still very wild, a suspected horse thief was arrested and tried. After lengthy deliberation, the jury found him innocent. But when the foreman delivered this verdict, the judge stared at him incredulously and bellowed, "You fellows'll have to go back into that jury room and reconsider. The defendant was hanged two hours ago."

We've come a long way from those days!

At any rate, in spite of its faults, the jury system will have to be accepted, because nobody has succeeded in devising any better way of deciding the facts when they are in dispute. As the late Robert von Moschzisker, Chief Justice of the Pennsylvania Supreme Court, said:

> Considering the fact that it must be administered by human beings, and therefore subject to the frailties which we all share in common, it is, to my mind, about the most perfect instrument which can be devised as an aid to organized society in administering justice between the State and its citizens and between man and man.

I fully concur with this opinion and with that of Carroll C. Moreland, who says, in his *Equal Justice Under Law* (New York: Oceana Publications, Inc., 1957), that the jury system has withstood the test of experience:

> Twelve men, from all walks of life, bring to the deliberations of the jury more experience and insight, more understanding of the motives and outlook of mankind, than can any judge, no matter how learned he may be. And the secrecy of the deliberations of the jury assures the juror freedom to vote for the plaintiff or the defendant, as he chooses, without fear of retaliation.

Indeed, Lord Devlin, the eminent English jurist, goes so far as to say that the jury is "the lamp that shows that freedom lives."

I am aware, of course, that this opinion is by no means unanimous. A number of learned men have sharply dissented. Herbert Spencer, for one, described a jury as "twelve people of average ignorance." Dr. Harry Elmer Barnes, in his book on *The Repression of Crime*, has made what is probably the most sustained and scholarly critique of the jury system, which he considers to be an obstacle to "scientific" —and presumably more effective—procedures for arriving at justice. No doubt a good many lawyers, psychiatrists, criminologists, and members of the lay public would agree with him.

However, the most authoritative and up-to-date appraisal of the virtues and shortcomings of the jury system in the United States that I know of is a book entitled *The American Jury* published by Little, Brown and Co. in 1966. The result of a ten-year study financed by the Ford Foundation, this prodigious work by Harry Kalven, Jr., Hans Zeisel, and others of the faculty of the University of Chicago Law School, is based on an examination of over three thousand criminal trials in the 1950s, selected so as to constitute a representative sampling of all types of crimes and all areas of the country. In each instance, the authors questioned the presiding judge in the case in order to learn what he thought of the jury's verdict.

The results are most revealing.

In the first place, these investigators found complete agreement between judge and jury in over seventy per cent of the cases. In those in which there was disagreement, the judge was only rarely less severe than the jury. The study showed that, on the whole, juries tended to be more lenient toward the accused than the judge and to interpret "reasonable doubt" in the defendant's favor. In any case, the difference in leniency or severity between judge and jury proved to be relatively small.

Moreover, it was found that most judges, even when they considered themselves bound by law to be somewhat harsher in their judgment than the jury, felt grateful to the jury for being less inclined to adhere strictly to the letter of the law and to take a more compassionate and indulgent view of the defendant's situation.

True, juries did tend to be more sympathetic than judges toward pretty women—especially mothers—and young defendants, but not to any significant extent. It was also discovered that juries reflect public sentiment in their reluctance to enforce laws against gambling, drunken driving, killing game out of season or without a license, and "moonshining."

As for the ignorance and incompetence often alleged against juries, it was found that, although individual jurors might be forgetful or confused about particular details, their combined recollection proved to be phenomenal, and their "net intelligence," as the authors put it, turned out to be "miraculous." The fact that in all but a few cases the presiding judge fully agreed with the jury's verdict would seem to indicate that a group of persons untrained in the law, when instructed by a wise and impartial judge, can reach a decision on the facts that will withstand the test of knowledgeable scrutiny.

Then, too, the popular idea that a jury is often "hung" by a lone hold-out proved to be mistaken. According to the authors, what happened in *Twelve Angry Men* just does not take place, or, at least, the chances of its occurring are extremely small. Deadlocked juries usually begin by having at least four dissenters from the majority view.

In short, what this study shows is that, in criminal trials at least, our American juries, by and large, are performing their duties conscientiously and creditably. They follow and understand the evidence, review the case thoroughly in the jury room, and arrive at a sensible verdict that most judges would approve, though tempering the rigidity of the law with a good measure of mercy. The authors, who began, as good scientists should, without any preconceptions, conclude their survey by expressing their admiration for the American jury.

I hope a similar study is made soon of the conduct of juries in civil trials. Without wishing to prejudge its outcome, I should be inclined to predict, on the basis of my own experience, that the results would not be much different, on the whole, from those reached by Kalven and Zeisel.

To be sure, if one has been the victim of a biased verdict, it is very easy to become cynical about juries. In fact, however, the cases in which such verdicts are returned are the exception rather than the rule. Moreover, it is possible that even their number could be reduced, at least to some extent, by appropriate precautions on the part of the lawyers in selecting the members of the panel. As we shall see, it is not only jurors, witnesses, and clients who sometimes make snap judgments and unwarranted generalizations. Lawyers too are human, and occasionally, in selecting jurors, they are culpable of the very sins they are inclined to impute to others.

At all events, the very fact that a jury can behave in an irrational or prejudiced way is all the more reason why a lawyer is obliged to do everything he can to try to eliminate the wrong kind of people from the panel. In fact, he owes it to his client, whose fate is ultimately going to be decided by the jury he accepts, to draw upon all his intellectual resources and powers of intuition in selecting the ablest group he can get under the circumstances. For if there are no certainties about human nature that a lawyer can rely on, there are still probabilities which he is morally obligated at least not to ignore.

Let us, then, accompany the lawyer and his client into the jury room and observe the process called the *voir dire*. This is an Old French expression that means "to speak the truth." In many States, in fact, the examination of the panel of prospective jurors is made under oath. But the term is employed not only in reference to the examination of jurors, but also to the questioning of witnesses, particularly when exhibits are being offered in evidence.

The purpose of the *voir dire* is to inquire into the qualifications, competence, and possible bias of the prospective jurors and to assure, so far as possible, that only qualified and unprejudiced persons sit in judgment on the case. Through questioning or independent inquiry, the lawyers on each side seek to ascertain who can listen intelligently to the evidence and render a fair and impartial verdict.

The conditions governing the selection of a jury are prescribed by law in the various States. In small communities, the *voir dire* is generally conducted in the same courtroom in which the case itself is to be tried. In large counties, on the other hand, such as there are in New York City, there may be a single, central jury room, divided into a number of sections, each with its own jury box. This is an enclosure, open at one end, with two rows of six or seven chairs to accommodate the members of the panel and any alternates selected by the lawyers on both sides. Alternates are frequently selected in cases expected to be protracted to take the place, if necessary, of any regular juror who may become ill or prove otherwise unable to serve after the trial begins.

What role, if any, the judge plays in the *voir dire* is likewise prescribed by law. In most State courts, the examination of prospective jurors is conducted by the lawyers in the absence of the judge. In front of each jury box tables and chairs are placed for them and their clients. Technically the lawyers are under the jurisdiction of the Court at all times, even if the judge is not actually in attendance during this phase of the trial. Accordingly, a lawyer can always appeal to the judge to protect the rights of his client against any prejudicial remarks that opposing counsel may be injecting into his questions. If, for example, an attorney has reason to believe that his adversary is resorting to dilatory tactics or referring to extrinsic matters that could not legally be received in evidence, he has the right and the duty to bring such practices to the attention of the judge and to request the latter's presence or intervention during the *voir dire*.

In a criminal case the jury *must* be selected in the presence of the judge as well as the defendant. Moreover, in the Federal courts the right of either the prosecutor or the attorney for the defendant to question the jurors personally rests in the sole discretion of the Court before whom the jurors are selected. If the Court does not permit the attorneys to examine each of the jurors personally, counsel may submit proposed questions in writing for the judge himself to ask.

But where did the people who sit in the jury room awaiting interrogation and impaneling come from in the first place? How did just these and no other persons come to be there? On what principle, if any, were they chosen? Even before the lawyers have a chance to interview them, have they been put through a preliminary screening to eliminate those obviously unfit for service? If so, on what basis was this accomplished? Does everybody in the community get a chance, sooner or later, to serve on a jury? To what extent do the prospective jurors constitute a random and representative cross-section of the people in the community?

In order to answer these questions, we shall have to go back in time before the day of the *voir dire* and review the process by which the prospective jurors came to be chosen. For they did not just voluntarily walk into the jury room from the street.

A clue to their status may be gleaned from the technical name under which they are commonly known. They are called, in legal parlance, *veniremen*, from the Latin word commanding the one to whom it is addressed to "come." The veniremen were summoned to appear for jury duty by a process strictly prescribed by law. Although the statutory requirements differ in the various States, they are generally designed to exclude, from the very outset, certain classes of persons deemed to be unfit by virtue of occupation, criminal record, physical incapacity, or educational background.

The procedure followed in New York is fairly typical. The first step is for the county clerk to compile, from voting lists, tax rolls, and various street directories, a roster of names of those presumably eligible for jury service. He then mails to each person on his list an Examination Summons (see Exhibit 2). This directs him to appear in person at the office of the Division of Jurors to complete a questionnaire bearing on his competency and qualifications (see Exhibit 3).

Under New York law, however, certain categories of persons may claim automatic exemption from jury duty. They need not, therefore, appear at the county clerk's office to complete the questionnaire. All they have to do is to fill out the Certificate of Exemption (see Exhibit 4) that is attached to the Examination Summons.

Among those who do not have to serve, if they do not want to, are clergymen, physicians, dentists, pharmacists, embalmers, optometrists, attorneys, members of the armed forces, firemen, policemen, teachers, officers of vessels or pilots making regular trips, newspaper editors, reporters, and women. In most State courts and in the Federal courts, women are now permitted to serve on juries. In New York and in several other States, a woman may not only claim exemption and be excused solely by reason of her sex, but, if she requests it, the judge must order her name stricken from the jury rolls, so that she will not be summoned again. Most women, however, are eager to serve.

To judge from the list of exemptions, it may seem as if the very people whose educational background might best fit them to render intelligent verdicts are precisely the ones who are excluded from being even considered as jurors. Under the circumstances, there appears to be some justice in the remark that the typical jury panel can hardly be said to reflect the entire intellectual and educational gamut represented in most communities of heterogeneous character. But this criticism, although it may be factually correct, is really beside the point. The essential qualities required of a juror are impartiality, intelligence, and common sense. These are by no means limited to persons of any particular experience or education. Hence, the exemption of certain professional people need have no adverse effect on the quality of the judgment rendered by a panel of jurors.

Besides, there is another reason for exempting them, which Gilbert K. Chesterton has very aptly stated:

> Our civilization has decided, and very justly decided, that determining the guilt or innocence of men is a thing too important to be trusted to trained men. When it wishes for light upon that awful matter, it asks men who know no more law than I know, but who can feel the things that I felt in the jury box. When it wants a library catalogued, or the solar system discovered, or any trifle of that kind, it uses up its specialists. But when it wishes anything done which is really serious, it collects twelve of the ordinary men standing round. The same thing was done, if I remember right, by the Founder of Christianity.

Those who cannot or do not claim exemption appear in person at the office of the Division of Jurors or some similar bureau to fill out the questionnaire. Although the form shown (see Exhibit 3) is that used for male jurors, the inquiries are substantially the same for both sexes, and the questions are representative of the type asked in other jurisdictions as well. Particularly significant are those touching on physical or mental incapacities, criminal record, prior involvement in litigation, and possible grounds of bias.

Obviously, much of the information called for in the questionnaire would be useful to the attorneys for both sides in determining whether or not to retain a prospective juror on the panel. For example, the answer to the question regarding marital status might be relevant in deciding his or her fitness to serve as a juror in a matrimonial case. Data on disabilities could be pertinent in a suit involving a claim for injuries sustained as a result of negligence on the part of the defendant. However, under New York law, all answers to this questionnaire are confidential, and the completed document may be obtained only on order of the Appellate Division. Consequently, all such information must be freshly elicited during the *voir dire*.

After completion of the questionnaire, the prospective juror is interviewed by an examiner of the county clerk's office and is preliminarily qualified or disqualified, as the case may be. Surprisingly, only about twenty-eight per cent of the persons so examined prove to be qualified.

Next, for each person accepted, the Division of Jurors prepares an index card with his name, address, occupation, date of birth, former or other names, former addresses, and height. This is sent to the Police Department to be checked against its records. If the prospective juror has been convicted of a crime involving moral turpitude, he is disqualified. For those who finally qualify, a card called a ballot is then prepared (see Exhibit 5).

New York law permits a prospective juror to select any two months between September 30 and June 30 in which he finds it most convenient to serve. If he indicates such a preference, it is marked on the ballot, together with his name, address, occupation, and date of birth, and he is so accommodated.

So far, the process of selection has been based on certain qualifications and exemptions provided by law. But at this point an element of chance enters. The ballots, arranged according to month of preference, are placed in drums, with a separate drum for those indicating no preference at all. Then, in the presence of at least one judge and the county clerk, names are drawn, to the desired number, from the drum containing ballots showing a preference for the month in question. If these do not suffice to make up the quota, ballots are drawn next from the drum containing those on which no preference has been shown. Quotas are set each month by the clerks of the several courts according to their respective needs.

After the names are drawn, a jury subpoena (see Exhibit 6) is mailed to each venireman, as he is now called, at least nine days before he is supposed to appear for service. This normally lasts for a minimum of twelve days. However, on the very first day of his appearance at the courthouse, a venireman may apply to the judge for a postponement of jury duty or even ask to be excused from it entirely. In support of his application, he may present such reasons as hardship, bias, recent service, etc. By law, a person may not be called to serve more than once every two years. The judge, at his discretion, may or may not grant the application for delay or excuse.

To be sure, some people welcome the summons to jury duty. Retired persons and those with a certain amount of leisure are more likely to be willing to serve than busy executives or men of affairs, who may feel that they can ill afford to take so much time from their work. When a plea is made that service at a particular time would work a hardship on an individual, judges generally try to be reasonable and accommodating. However, the venireman, in turn, is expected to understand that if our courts are to function properly, he must accept his share of civic responsibility, even though this may mean an occasional sacrifice on his part. The right we all have, under our Constitution, to a jury trial carries with it the reciprocal obligation to serve as jurors, if we are qualified, at reasonable intervals when called upon to do so.

Nevertheless, the fact must be recognized that at least some of the veniremen who await screening in the jury room may be there against their will, only because the judge refused to excuse them or to postpone the date of their service. A lawyer can hardly afford to ignore the effect that this fact may have upon their whole attitude toward the proceedings.

It is obviously desirable for all concerned that the veniremen be not only able but ready and willing to serve. It should be a matter of vital concern to the Court as well as the litigants and their lawyers that all the prospective jurors be in the right frame of mind—instructed in their responsibilities and disposed to perform their duties conscientiously. In fact, however, the steps taken, if any, to achieve this eminently worthwhile goal vary considerably in different jurisdictions. Whatever is done to prepare the jurors for their task depends chiefly on the attitude of the local judge or court clerk. As a result, there is no uniform practice or set rule in orienting veniremen when they assemble in the jury room to await impaneling.

What do they do during this time, which may sometimes last for several days? In New York City the courts are empowered to permit them to be excused from continuous attendance for periods of a day or a number of days until they are needed. Elsewhere, they may just be left to sit and wait their turn to be called for interrogation, meanwhile passing their time in reading or chatting. A splendid opportunity for strengthening the whole jury system and improving the functioning of our courts is thus allowed to pass unused. In other jurisdictions, on the contrary, every effort is put forth to make the veniremen physically comfortable while they await screening and to provide them with at least some understanding of their duties.

A shining example of intelligent and enlightened treatment of prospective jurors is that provided by the Honorable James V. Mangano, administrative director and general clerk of the Supreme Court of the State of New York, County of Kings. He does everything he can to make the waiting period both pleasant and instructive for the veniremen. Music from an FM radio is piped into the central jury room, which is also furnished with comfortable chairs, pay telephones, and writing tables for their convenience. He has even arranged to have educational films, such as travelogues and historical pictures, presented for their entertainment. But, in addition, every Monday morning he seizes the occasion to address the assembled veniremen. In his talk he emphasizes the importance of jury duty and expresses appreciation, on behalf of the Court, for their service. At the same time he urges them to speak to their friends and neighbors about their experiences as jurors. In this way he tries to encourage a more positive, wholesome attitude toward jury service in general.

If more of our courts sought to improve their public relations by such means, there might be less misunderstanding of what jury service entails and a readier and more widespread acceptance of it as a civic obligation.

In the Supreme Court of Queens County the veniremen are likewise shown documentary films in an effort to break the monotony of sitting around until they are called for actual service. In fact, the Honorable Joseph M. Conroy, the senior justice of that court, provides them with live entertainment, in the form of instrumentalists, singers, and even a professional magician!

A recent innovation in the Central Jury Room of New York County Supreme Court is the presentation of an educational film entitled *The True and the Just*, which informs the talesmen of their responsibilities.

Conceived by Justice Bernard Botein of the Appellate Division, First Department, the script was prepared under the supervision of the New York judiciary. After a brief historical survey of the jury system, the film portrays the typical reactions of the average citizen on receiving his notice to serve and follows him through the various stages of his experience in court, including the selection of the jury, the challenges by counsel for each side, the trial of a fictitious negligence case, the testimony of witnesses, the rulings and charge by the Court, and the deliberations in the jury room.

The narrator, a movie and television actor, explains the reasons for calling more veniremen than may be immediately needed and answers typical questions asked by prospective jurors. Although acknowledging that jury service has its inconveniences, the film reminds its audience that "but for the grace of God, any one of you might be either plaintiff or defendant in this case."

This film, so far as I know, is a pioneer effort in the right direction. It helps jurors to know in advance what attitudes and behavior are expected of them, what goes on at a trial, and what duties they are called upon to perform. It should go far toward promoting better public understanding of our jury system and of its importance in the administration of justice. It is indeed heartening to know that it will be available for distribution all over the United States for showing in jury rooms as well as by educational, legal, and civic groups.

Meanwhile, however, there is a wide disparity in the pretrial instruction provided prospective jurors even in different jurisdictions in the same State. There was a time when, in some counties of New York State, a venireman would be handed a primer designed to inform him of his duties. Unfortunately it was couched in rather general terms. Nevertheless, it did attempt to provide some guidance for the jurors concerning the circumstances in which inferences might be drawn, the weight to be given to the testimony of interested witnesses, and suggestions for determining the credibility of testimony in civil cases. Nothing, however, was included in such primers to guide a juror in criminal cases. In these, he needs a clear understanding of what is meant by "beyond a reasonable doubt." This is something very different from a "clear preponderance of the evidence," which is the standard of proof employed in civil suits.

Because of their manifest insufficiency in these respects, such primers have been discontinued. In their stead, the adoption of a revised, uniform primer is now under consideration. Meanwhile, in certain courts in New York State, judges address the assembled veniremen in an effort to provide them with some orientation. But what they are told in these speeches varies from one court to the other. One judge may launch into a real "Fourth of July" oration, glowing with inspirational sentiment and lofty flights of rhetoric, but singularly devoid of any clear guidance concerning the way in which a juror is supposed to apply the law to the facts of a case. Others may content themselves with routinely following a formula patterned along the lines set forth in the now discarded primer.

The result is a lamentable lack of uniformity in the instruction given to veniremen. No lawyer can really be sure what a prospective juror may have been told concerning his responsibilities and the manner in which he is to go about fulfilling them. Consequently, during the *voir dire,* counsel has to be circumspect in his inquiries. He must make certain that when the jurors are impaneled, they completely lay aside any fixed ideas they may have formed as a result of these well-intentioned attempts at instructing them in their duties.

The ignorance of some jurors concerning even the most elementary procedures to be followed in discharging their responsibilities is well illustrated by the following incident, which was reported to me by a woman who had served on a panel in a negligence case. When she and her colleagues retired to the jury room after hearing the evidence, the foreman promptly began by saying, quite decisively, "Well, I guess we're all for the defendant, and that's it."

Nobody in the room had ever served on a jury before. It did not at first occur to anyone to challenge the statement of the foreman, and it seemed for a moment as if everything had been conclusively settled by his announcement. But somehow this way of doing things did not seem right to the lady. She began to wonder why they had all been so carefully selected and then made to listen to both sides of the case if it rested with the foreman alone to decide the outcome. So, somewhat timidly, she rose and said, "I can't see by what right you tell us we're all for the defendant. How do you know that? Maybe some of us aren't so sure. Don't you think we ought to discuss it and take a vote?" It was not long before the others followed her lead. A discussion ensued, and eventually a verdict for the plaintiff was returned.

Juries need to be told—and I think this ought to be the responsibility of the judge—that the foreman is merely the chairman of the group, and that his vote counts for no more than that of anyone else on the panel. Obviously, knowledge of this fact cannot simply be taken for granted in every instance.

The problem of selecting jurors with a correct understanding of their duties has been further complicated by the fact that our mass media of entertainment often give people a lopsided view of what goes on at a trial. Judge Paul Kelly, of Nassau County, New York, has expressed his amazement at the number of people on juries who say, in effect, "That's not the way they do it on television." And his colleague on the bench, Judge Harold Strohson, is quoted in a recent issue of *Trial* (published by the American Trial Lawyers Association) as saying, "Jurors and many other citizens have accepted as gospel truth the things they see on TV. The same problems, I guess, exist on programs depicting doctors and medicine." In the absence of any effective educational plan for counteracting such misimpressions, the task of counsel during the *voir dire* becomes all the more difficult.

An element of chance is likewise involved in the next stage of the process of jury selection. In the jury room, in the presence of the lawyers on both sides, the clerk draws a card out of the drum containing the names and addresses of the veniremen. As his name is called, each takes his place in the jury box, until twelve have been seated, though additional jurors may be impaneled as alternates if the case is likely to be a protracted one.

The cards bearing the names and addresses of the prospective jurors are then inserted by the clerk into the slots in what is called a panel board (see Exhibit 7), and this is handed to the lawyers. A glance at the address shown on each card should suffice to indicate to a perceptive attorney the probable economic status of the prospective juror. Thus, counsel is not likely to be wrong in assuming that anyone living in the fashionable part of town is a person of means, and that someone with an address in the slums or "on the other side of the railroad tracks" is probably in the lower income brackets.

Reading the names on the cards, we find that our panel consists of the following:

1. Mr. Boris Implacable. Office Manager.
2. Mr. Hate Light. Post Office Clerk.
3. Mrs. Vera Cruelty. Housewife.
4. Mrs. Leila Lyar. Housewife.
5. Mrs. Faith Enmity. Housewife.

6. Mr. High Mind. Auditor.
7. Mrs. Eudora Heady. Bookkeeper.
8. Mr. Live Loose. Engineer.
9. Mr. Love Lust. Insurance Agent.
10. Miss Cleo Malice. Comptometer Operator.
11. Mr. No Good. Maintenance Man.
12. Mr. Blind Man. Retired.

A likely lot, indeed! And do not the names I have given to this sup-posedly random sample of the population suggest the very attitude of cynicism on the subject of juries that I have explicitly disclaimed? Not at all. It must be remembered that this is not yet a panel of jurors. They have still to be sifted and examined. In borrowing some of these names from those given by John Bunyan to some of the characters in his *Pilgrim's Progress,* I do not at all intend to reflect adversely on the intelligence or character of the average juror. Still less do I seek to suggest that our juries are composed for the most part of fools or knaves. Rather, I wish to emphasize the problem that faces the lawyers who will have to select a satisfactory panel of jurors from among the veniremen in the jury room. It is not cynical, but simply realistic, to recognize that people with the traits of character suggested by such names could very well appear among the veniremen summoned to fill a panel. Surely it is important for the litigants and their lawyers to be aware of the possible range of human types that might be represented among those from whom the jury is to be picked.

Or would I, perhaps, have been more realistic if I had chosen the following names and occupations for the members of the panel?

1. Miss Honor Bright. Private Secretary.
2. Mr. Able Reasoner. Research Scientist.
3. Mr. Benedict Benevolent. Welfare Worker.
4. Mr. Christian Charity. Philanthropist.
5. Miss Constance Proper. Governess.
6. Miss Innocent Trueheart. Hospital Receptionist.
7. Mr. Justus Noble. Securities Analyst.
8. Miss Faith Loving. Author of Children's Books.
9. Mrs. Grace Fairplay. Librarian.
10. Miss Angelica Goodwill. Practical Nurse.
11. Mr. Fidel Kindman. A.S.P.C.A. Worker.
12. Mr. Clement Trusty. Accountant.
   Alternate: Mr. Frank Wellwisher. Gardener.

Doubtless it will be said that this panel is no more representative than the first. Granted. Neither is a fair sample of mankind, and chances are that most panels would include a mixture of both in varied proportions, some with more of one, and some with more of the other. This is no doubt what Sir Geoffrey Lawrence had in mind when he said, in his article entitled "The Art of Advocacy," which appeared in the December 1964 issue of the *American Bar Association Journal:*

> After all, every one of us has his own prejudices, but a jury goes into the box with twelve sets of prejudices. In the end they cancel out and result in a corporate wisdom that produces perhaps not the perfect result, because nothing in life is perfect, but the best we can hope to get.

In any event, the question still remains: How does a lawyer weed out the Lyars, No Goods, Cruelties, and Lusts, and get a jury with a reasonably fair number of Wellwishers, Truehearts, and Fairplays? This is the essential problem with which we must now be concerned.

6

The Voir Dire

It would be naïve to suppose that a lawyer's foremost objective in selecting a jury is to secure the kind of impartial panel that the interests of even-handed justice would require. After all, he wants to win his case, and he would naturally like to have a jury as favorably disposed to his client as he can get. But he has to reckon with opposing counsel, who, of course, is seeking to tip the scales in the opposite direction. In the end, then, if the lawyers on both sides are more or less evenly matched, each will have to settle for a panel that is, at least in his opinion, not prejudiced against his own client. Thus, the ends of justice, which require an unbiased jury, prove ultimately to be quite compatible with the conflicting aims of the opposing lawyers.

It is indeed an awesome responsibility for a lawyer to pick a jury that he can safely trust to sit in judgment on his client's case. In fact, the task may at first seem hopeless. Faced with a panel of veniremen whom he has never seen before, he is obliged, after questioning each one for a few minutes, to make a fateful decision. But on what grounds? Is it really possible to learn enough about anyone during that brief encounter to establish a reasonable expectation about the way he is likely to react to the evidence in the case? I believe that, in the main, it is.

In the first place, I assume that counsel does not come to the *voir dire* altogether unprepared. If he has done his homework as he should, he already knows what the sensitive issues are likely to be. He has a pretty good idea of the areas in which prejudice could affect the verdict one way or the other, and he plans to probe carefully for any signs of bias along these lines.

To be sure, an interrogation with this object in view could be extended indefinitely. No doubt if the lawyers on both sides could have their way, each would like nothing better than to have a limitless number of opportunities to pick over the veniremen, rejecting those he does not want, and retaining only the ones that seem the most suitable.

However, there never would be enough time for such an interminable procedure. Nor, I may add, would there ever be enough veniremen to satisfy requirements so exacting.

Therefore, some curbs have to be imposed on the otherwise natural disposition of counsel to go on endlessly comparing one prospective juror with another. To this end, the law in each State places a limit on the number of chances a lawyer is given to reject a venireman "peremptorily," that is, to challenge or excuse him without being required to give any reason whatsoever. Thus, a lawyer has to hoard his peremptory challenges carefully. If he uses too many of them at the beginning, in accepting only a few jurors, he runs the risk of later needing more peremptory challenges than he has left. As his supply of them continues to diminish, a certain amount of suspense and even tension may begin to build up. For one can never know in advance what kind of person may take the seat on the panel left vacant by the challenged or excused venireman.

Consequently, counsel has to have regard for tactical considerations even in challenging those he does not want on the panel. For one thing, he must choose his words carefully in order to soften the psychological impact of his rejection. So he makes it a point never to "challenge" anyone. Rather, he "excuses" a venireman from the panel. Moreover, as we have seen, he must give careful thought to the timing of each challenge. Before considering the kinds of questions he might ask to determine a prospective juror's suitability, let us see how a lawyer might handle a typical situation in which he chooses to exercise a peremptory challenge.

As he selects the jury, he keeps before him a diagram arranged in block form (see Exhibit 8) with spaces to correspond with those on the panel board. In these spaces he enters the names of the individual prospective jurors and records such information about them as he considers significant. Of course, he tries to make these notations out of the view of the panel. Keeping his eyes focused on each venireman as he is called, counsel watches him as he leaves his seat to enter the jurors' box. In that brief moment an observant lawyer may make a meaningful appraisal from the prospective juror's walk, dress, or general demeanor.

Suppose, for example, that in questioning Mrs. Faith Enmity, No. 5 on the panel, he decides, on the basis of her responses to one of his questions, that she is not the type of juror he would want in the case. If he exercises this peremptory challenge immediately after hearing her answer to his question, the other members of the panel will know what motivated his rejection of her. Accordingly, they might be tempted to tailor their own responses in order to remain on the jury. They may conceal or disguise their true feelings on any points that they think will displease counsel. For there are many people who, for one reason or another, enjoy serving on a jury. Among them are women, retired individuals, and employees who suffer no financial loss while on jury duty. Once they know the basis on which counsel has objected to a prospective juror, they may shape their answers to his questions so as to avoid being excused.

Then too, as soon as opposing counsel learns that a particular juror is not welcome to the other side, he will bend every effort to keep the juror on the panel. On the other hand, if opposing counsel is ignorant of any intention on the part of his adversary to exclude a juror, he himself may very well excuse the same individual for reasons of his own. Thus, the poker-faced attorney is saved a valuable peremptory challenge. In this little tug-of-war between the opposing lawyers, the odds favor the one who knows how to bide his time.

The strategy, then, is not to allow the rest of the panel to know what answer prompted Mrs. Enmity's rejection or to "tip one's hand" to one's adversary. The experienced lawyer will simply go on asking her a few more questions, chiefly of a perfunctory nature, and then proceed to another member of the panel. Meanwhile, he will slide her card about halfway to one side on his panel board (see Exhibit 9) as a reminder to himself to excuse her later, after he has examined a number, and perhaps all, of the other prospective jurors. Then, smiling amiably, he will say simply, as he takes her card out of its slot on the panel board, "Mrs. Enmity, I believe I will excuse you," without giving any reason, for he will be exercising one of his peremptory challenges. He will follow the same procedure with each of the other members of the panel (Nos. 8 and 10 on the panel board in Exhibit 9) whom he decides to excuse. In this way, too, before exercising any peremptory challenges, he can see how many of them he might want to retain, and adjust his standards accordingly.

Failure to take this factor of timing into account when excusing a venireman from the panel can sometimes prove costly. Once, in an action for breach of contract, the plaintiff's counsel, during the *voir dire*, asked the members of the panel whether they believed that a contract should be performed and whether they would award damages for nonperformance. All said yes. Later, while the defendant's counsel was examining the panel, one of the prospective jurors made the unsolicited statement that he believed in "the sanctity of a contract." Defense counsel immediately excused him. Thereupon, the very first question put to the next member of the panel by counsel for the plaintiff was, "Do you believe in the sanctity of a contract?"

Thus, by his precipitate conduct, counsel for the defendant made this phrase the issue in the trial. He could easily have avoided becoming embroiled in this fashion if he had simply ignored the remark made by the venireman and not excused him right away. The proper procedure would have been to have kept him in the jury box for some time further, answering some innocuous and inconspicuous questions, and thereby taking the spotlight off his gratuitous statement. Then, after counsel had completed his examination of the remaining members of the panel, he could have excused the venireman. By that time neither he nor any other prospective juror would have been able to suspect what had motivated counsel to excuse him.

Of course, if a prospective juror's answers to counsel's questions reveal an obvious bias, he can and should be excused forthwith "for cause," as the law puts it. In every State the law specifies the precise grounds on which challenges for cause may be permitted. There are certain responses which are sufficient, under the law, to disqualify a prospective juror from serving. He will, for example, be excused for cause if he says that he knows one of the parties or lawyers, or that he would favor the plaintiff because he himself was once involved in the same kind of case. The same is true if a venireman says that he is in sympathy with anyone in the defendant's position and cannot divest himself of that sympathy and decide the case purely on the facts. When responses such as these are given, the reason for excusing the venireman is quite clear, and no peremptory challenge need be used.

Obviously, then, a lawyer's knowledge of the statutory grounds on which he may excuse a juror will guide him in framing a number of broad questions designed to sweep a wide area that will include all the types of bias recognized in the law. He will thus be in a position, at the outset, even before touching on the substantive issues in the case, to determine whether each venireman is legally qualified to serve.

On the other hand, if counsel, in questioning a venireman, elicits responses suggesting any disposition favorable to his client's cause, he would do well to conceal his elation over such a fortunate discovery, lest opposing counsel be moved to raise some objection to the juror.

Naturally, rather than use up a peremptory challenge, a lawyer would prefer to find, if he can, some statutory ground for excusing a particular individual that he does not want on the panel. There are any number of such grounds on which he can base his challenge. As we have seen, a juror may be discharged for cause if he does not possess the qualifications required by the laws of his State. For example, in New York a juror must be a citizen of the United States and a resident of the county in which the trial takes place. Moreover, he must be between the ages of twenty-one and seventy. He must be the owner or spouse of the owner of property worth at least $250. The law also requires that he be in possession of his "natural faculties" and not infirm or decrepit. He must not have been convicted of a felony or misdemeanor involving moral turpitude. Finally, he is required to be "intelligent," of "sound mind," and good character, well informed, and able to read English with understanding and to write it understandably.

It is normally the task of the county clerk, in examining those summoned for jury duty, to satisfy himself, in the first instance, that they meet these qualifications, and the courts of New York State have generally been disposed to accept his judgment in this regard. A recent case in which it was challenged was that of a professor of political science whom the county clerk denied the opportunity to qualify as a juror on the ground that the gentleman was totally blind. Contending that his affliction had not prevented him from earning a doctorate at Columbia University or carrying on his professional work as author and scholar, the professor argued that, like many blind people, he had compensated for his handicap by keenly developing his other senses. Indeed, he maintained, the absence of visual distractions enabled him to concentrate better than a sighted person. He therefore contended that, in every relevant sense, he was in full possession of his "natural faculties" and no more handicapped, as a potential juror, by his blindness than a person with only one arm or one leg.

However, the Court, while commending the petitioner's exemplary and even inspiring desire to participate actively in civic affairs, held that qualifying a totally blind person for jury service, only to subject him to later challenge and examination, would unnecessarily impede the already slow administration of justice. The ruling of the county clerk was therefore upheld.

Provisions more or less similar to those in New York are to be found in the laws of other States. Although the prospective jurors were supposedly screened to determine whether they met these qualifications, some who lack one or more of them may have slipped through, either because circumstances may have changed since they were last examined, or because they failed to make a full disclosure of the facts. Consequently, it is a good idea for counsel to make a preliminary check on the qualifications of each juror.

It is not generally difficult to carry out this test. But it does take a certain amount of tact to phrase questions that touch on a venireman's competence to serve, without at the same time offending him. The mere asking of a tactless question in this regard may make an otherwise fully qualified juror unfriendly to a lawyer.

Just how "intelligent" is a juror expected to be in order to qualify? An attorney is certainly not helped by the fact that the law specifies no particular degree of intelligence or grade of educational attainment. No intelligence test is administered to prospective jurors in New York State. In the one case that I know of in which such a test was given, the Court of Appeals stated that the practice is not to be encouraged. The statute has been interpreted to mean that a juror must "be possessed of ordinary information and reasoning faculties." His very ability to answer the questions put to him on the *voir dire* should help to indicate whether he meets this standard of intelligence.

Then, too, a juror must be able to hear all the testimony. This ability is a "natural faculty," as the law calls it, which he is supposed to possess. If he cannot hear, then a challenge on this ground is proper. In some situations good eyesight may likewise be essential. For example, if a case involves the examination of documents or the comparison of signatures, the juror has to be able to see all that there is to be seen in the evidence. Thus, eyesight or hearing that might be good enough for other cases may not be sufficiently sharp for the case at hand. A lawyer has to be alert to impress this point on the Court, since all challenges for cause are subject to the discretionary power of the judge. If the facts are proved, the judge will uphold the challenge and excuse the prospective juror for what is called "principal cause."

There are, besides, a number of other grounds on which a lawyer can ask to have a venireman excused "for cause," without having to exercise a peremptory challenge. In the first place, the law infers bias if a prospective juror is too closely related to either of the parties to the controversy. In New York, for example, kinship "within the ninth degree" is enough to constitute a basis for excluding a juror in a criminal case, and consanguinity "within the sixth degree" in civil proceedings. In the latter case, the party related to the juror must raise the objection before the trial begins. Any other party may object up to six months after the verdict is rendered. So it behooves a lawyer to make sure that none of the members of the panel is related too closely to either party in the case. Hence, a question to this effect should be included, as a matter of course, among those asked of all veniremen.

Moreover, an individual may be legally disqualified from serving as a juror in a criminal case if he has certain business or other connections with either the complainant or the defendant. These include the relationships of guardian or ward, attorney or client, master or servant, landlord or tenant, and employer or employee. If the prospective juror was or is involved in any litigation with the defendant, he is likewise to be excused. Here too, then, the law provides counsel with a guide that he can use in framing questions designed to determine each venireman's fitness to serve.

In civil suits the rights of litigants are protected by a statute permitting the disqualification of any prospective juror who is a stockholder in a corporation that is a party to the case. Indeed, the law goes even further in restricting the jurors who are qualified to serve in actions for recovery of damages to persons or property. In civil suits, any interest or connection whatsoever is sufficient to constitute a ground for challenge under New York law. This would exclude from the jury officers, employees, or shareholders in any insurance company that issues policies protecting against liability for such damages. These possibilities should not be overlooked during the *voir dire*. Questions touching on interests of this kind should be asked of all prospective jurors in any case in which damages to person or property are claimed.

Certain kinds of previous service on a jury will likewise constitute a cause for excusing a venireman. For example, it will not do, in a criminal case, to have on the panel anyone who has served on the grand jury that handed down the indictment. For the same reason, where the indictment is concerned with the death of a person, a venireman must be disqualified if he served on the coroner's jury that inquired into it. Similarly, a prospective juror is to be excused if he was a member of a jury that tried another person for the crime charged in the indictment. Nor should counsel ignore the possibility, in a criminal case that is being retried for one reason or another, that one or more of the veniremen may have sat on a jury sworn to try the defendant on the same charge. Such a situation is possible if the original verdict was set aside, or if the jury was discharged without a verdict after the case was submitted to it. Nobody who was a member of the original jury would be qualified to sit on a panel retrying the case. A venireman may also be challenged for cause if he served as a juror in a civil action brought against the defendant for the act charged as a crime.

Evidently, then, the selection of a jury is not quite the blind "grab-bag" type of affair that some people imagine it to be. A lawyer does have some basis for deciding, at least at the outset, on the suitability of each of the prospective jurors on the panel. Carefully prepared questions by counsel during the *voir dire* can bring the relevant facts to light in time to avoid later problems.

The conscience of each venireman, especially as it may affect the issues in the case, deserves the most careful examination. Where, for example, the crime charged is punishable by death, a prospective juror must be excluded from the panel if he entertains such conscientious objections to the death penalty as would preclude his finding the defendant guilty. For similar reasons, a person who honestly believed that no circumstances whatever could morally justify the legal dissolution of a marriage would be unfit to serve on a jury in a divorce action.

In criminal cases, New York State law leaves the judge no discretion at all in excusing jurors for cause. If he fails to disqualify a prospective juror who comes within the degree of relationship to the defendant specified in the law, the ruling of the Court may be reversed on appeal to a higher tribunal.

In civil suits it is left to the discretion of the judge whether or not to disqualify a prospective juror if his relationship to one of the litigants or his possible interest in the case is within the limits interdicted by law. Accordingly, opposing counsel may raise other considerations to induce the judge to exercise his discretion against disqualifying the venireman. Then, if the judge refuses to excuse him, any appeal to a higher court would have to be based on the allegation that there had been an abuse of discretion. This is a ground on which it is generally very difficult to secure a reversal.

For example, suppose the prospective juror is a tenant of the defendant. In a criminal case, he would have to be excused. But if a landlord-tenant relationship between a litigant and a juror is shown in a civil case, the judge need not disqualify the juror. However, the attorney seeking the disqualification is free to adduce other facts that might persuade the Court to excuse the venireman. Thus, he might be able to show that the tenant does chores about the apartment building for which he receives a credit against his rent. From this fact it might be inferred that he would be afraid to antagonize the landlord.

In the case of family relationship, however, the venireman must be excused not only in criminal cases but in civil actions as well. The same is true if the prospective juror lacks any of the qualifications for jury service specified by law. He may also be challenged for what the law calls "actual bias" if he reveals on the *voir dire* that he cannot try the issues impartially and without prejudice to the substantial rights of the challenging party.

A final, but rarely used, type of challenge based on statutory grounds is that directed against the entire panel or "array," as it is called. Such a challenge raises fundamental questions about the legality of the procedure by which the veniremen on the panel were selected in the first place. Although not often resorted to, it has played a significant role in civil rights litigation, notably in the Scottsboro case of 1935. In that case, the systematic exclusion of the names of Negroes from the jury lists led to a reversal of the conviction. A basis for this type of challenge is made possible if there has been any substantial departure from the provisions of the law in selecting the panel or any intentional failure to summon one or more of the veniremen whose names are drawn from the drum. A challenge of this kind must be made in writing and submitted before any juror is sworn. Then the issue is tried by the judge. Court personnel charged with irregular conduct may be called and examined to prove or disprove the allegations.

Thus, the law itself provides counsel with a number of different grounds for requesting that jurors be excused. But it is his responsibility, not the Court's, to frame the questions that will bring the pertinent facts to light during the *voir dire*. It is up to him to probe for the attitudes or conditions which the law recognizes as presumably or actually prejudicial to the interests of his client. He has no one to blame but himself if his negligence in the examination of veniremen results in the impaneling of a biased juror who could have been disqualified or excused for cause. A lawyer cannot, under the circumstances, take refuge in the excuse that picking a jury is a hit-or-miss affair in which blind chance is the ultimate determining factor. If counsel takes the trouble to question the veniremen at all, instead of just accepting the first twelve who present themselves, he has an obligation, in conducting the *voir dire*, not to leave unexplored any possibilities which the law itself, in its wisdom, has foreseen. It is only after he has exhausted all of these that he can, in good conscience, fall back on his own personal assessment of each juror's suitability and assume the risk of an error of judgment in the exercise of a peremptory challenge.

The procedure is for the attorney for the plaintiff to examine the prospective jurors first. When he says, "No challenge for cause," it then becomes the turn of the defendant's attorney to conduct his examination. Only after defense counsel says, "No challenge for cause," may counsel for the plaintiff have his opportunity to exercise his peremptory challenges. The last to do so is the attorney for the defendant.

As we have seen, aside from citing some statutory ground for excusing a juror, the only other method a lawyer has of eliminating a member of the panel is to use up one of his limited supply of peremptory challenges. For these he needs to give no reason. The total number of them allotted to each side differs in the various States and according to the type of case being tried.

In New York, for example, the number of peremptory challenges permitted in criminal cases depends on the severity of the punishment for the crime. If the penalty is imprisonment for more than ten years, twenty peremptory challenges are allowed for the jury and two for each alternate. In all other criminal cases, there are five peremptory challenges for the jury and one for each alternate. But when several defendants are all on trial for the same crime, their counsel cannot exercise collectively on their behalf more peremptory challenges than would be permitted to a single defendant. In other words, they must all share in every such challenge.

In civil suits, on the other hand, each party has six peremptory challenges under New York law and one peremptory challenge for each alternate. This applies to each litigant if there is more than one on either side. However, in cases where a party is involved in litigation with more than one opponent, the Court may, in its discretion, grant additional peremptory challenges to the side with the smaller number, in the interests of justice. Thus, before selecting a jury, the attorneys on each side should know how many peremptory challenges they have, so as to use them to best advantage.

Counsel can find in the law a helpful guide not only to the scope and content but also to the arrangement of the questions to be put to the veniremen during the *voir dire*.

In criminal prosecutions, the State presents its challenges first, but in civil proceedings the plaintiff has priority. In both types of cases, a challenge directed against the entire panel must precede all the others.

In civil suits, a challenge "for principal cause" would include family relationship within the prohibited degree or lack of any of the qualifications set forth in the law. Then counsel should follow up with challenges based on presumable bias arising out of the prospective juror's business relations.

On the other hand, in a criminal case, after challenges founded on disqualification under the law should come those for implied bias. These should be followed by challenges for actual bias, revealed, for example, in the *voir dire*.

In both civil and criminal cases, the peremptory challenge is, of course, the one that needs to be most carefully and judiciously used. It is, in fact, in the exercise of this challenge that most of a lawyer's skill in picking a jury will be put to the test. Ordinarily, as previously stated, it is wise for counsel to retain a peremptory challenge in reserve in order to guard against the ever-present danger that, in replacement of some excused juror, another may be called who is even more objectionable.

For obvious reasons, a challenge based on statutory grounds should be presented out of hearing of the jury. If the judge is present during the *voir dire*, counsel would do well to ask permission of the Court to "approach the bench." This would allow him to confer with the judge in subdued tones in the presence of opposing counsel, who, of course, has the right to object to the challenge. But if there is any chance that the jury may overhear the discussion, a lawyer would be wise to ask that the hearing on the challenge be held in chambers.

At all events, a reporter should be present to transcribe the proceedings if the merits of the challenge are argued before the judge. Otherwise, there will be no record for appellate review in case counsel takes exception to the judge's ruling. In order to prove or disprove the basis of the challenge, the venireman in question, as well as other witnesses, may be examined. The rules that ordinarily apply to the conduct of all trials govern the admission or exclusion of evidence in the hearing of a challenge. At the hearing, as well as in the *voir dire* itself, a prospective juror is bound by law to answer truthfully all questions put to him that touch on his qualifications. He may not suppress any facts which he has reason to believe would render him unacceptable as a juror.

If counsel fails to persuade the judge to excuse a prospective juror, he may, to be sure, use one of his peremptory challenges to do so. But he will naturally want to preserve his supply of these, so far as possible. He will therefore seek, wherever he can, to find statutory grounds for disqualifying any prospective juror he does not want, and he will have to frame his questions accordingly. This, too, of course, will put a lawyer's knowledge, judgment, tact, and skill to a severe test, as we shall shortly see. Only after he has no other recourse will he resort to a peremptory challenge to exclude a juror who fails to meet his standards of acceptance.

But even before he reaches this point in his examination of a venireman, counsel may have to face a crucial decision. Suppose that he discovers or suspects the existence of some fact about a prospective juror which, if brought to light, might disqualify him. Does a lawyer run any risk in failing to make an issue of a juror's known or suspected bias as long as it is not considered prejudicial to the interests of his own client? If opposing counsel sees no objection to impaneling the juror, does he thereby forever waive the right to raise any question of that juror's competence or qualifications?

Under the law, all challenges are supposed to be presented before the jury is sworn. If a lawyer discovers later that there is a statutory basis for challenging a juror who has already been sworn, it may or may not be possible to have him removed or to have the entire trial invalidated on that account, depending on the circumstances and the laws of the State.

Normally, after returning a verdict, a jury is not required to reveal the process of its deliberations; the arguments and votes of the jurors are protected from disclosure unless the privilege is waived. However, this privilege is itself based on the presumption that all the jurors were, in fact, impartial arbiters from the very outset. If, after the trial, this presumption is brought into question by one of the parties, a Court may conduct a hearing into the circumstances of the *voir dire*, the jury's deliberations, and the alleged misconduct of a juror. After all, a talesman who conceals his bias and carries it into the jury room not only violates his oath of office but taints the jury of which he becomes a part. Hence, if it is discovered that a juror deliberately concealed or misstated, during the *voir dire*, facts which he had reason to believe would disqualify him from service, and which counsel had sought to elicit from him during questioning, the verdict may, under certain circumstances, be set aside.

This is precisely what happened in a case tried before Justice Crisona. Suit was brought against a trucking concern on behalf of a child to recover damages for very serious personal injuries sustained when the plaintiff was struck and knocked down by the defendant's truck. At the *voir dire* (at which the judge was not present), plaintiff's counsel, after briefly explaining the nature of the suit and the need for an impartial jury, inquired of the panel as a group whether any of them or any members of their family were at the time or had ever been truck drivers or employees, officers, directors, or stockholders in any transportation, delivery, or trucking company or allied field. Only one member of the panel held up his hand; and when it was established that he was a chauffeur for a utility company, he was excused, with the explanation that, in the opinion of plaintiff's counsel, anybody who operated a truck would tend to be sympathetic toward other truck drivers or to trucking companies. Each juror was then individually asked to state his occupation. No one indicated any connection, present or past, with trucking or transportation.

However, after the case had been tried and a verdict had been brought in against the plaintiff, it was learned that one juror, who had said at the *voir dire* that he was a salesman, was a member of a trucking union and for eight or nine hours each day drove a truck of almost the same type as the one involved in the accident. Under later examination before the Court, he admitted that he had understood the purpose of the inquiries made by plaintiff's counsel at the *voir dire*. Moreover, he acknowledged having brought his experience as a truck driver into the jury room and having used it in his discussions with other jurors. He also confessed that he was sympathetic to the problems of truck drivers and that this sympathy impelled him to seek to influence the judgment of his fellow jurors against the plaintiff.

Furthermore, according to the testimony of other jurors, it became clear that another member of the panel, who had represented himself as a waiter when he was asked his occupation during the *voir dire*, had once driven a bakery truck but had failed to make any mention of this fact when the panel was asked whether any venireman had ever been a truck driver. Similarly, a third juror, although not himself a truck driver, had not disclosed at the *voir dire*, when the talesmen were asked whether they had relatives in the trucking industry, that his father, with whom he resided, had been a truck driver for more than thirty years. Finally, a fourth juror was found who did not tell counsel during the *voir dire* that his father-in-law was a truck driver.

Under the circumstances, the Court found that, in withholding from plaintiff's counsel at the *voir dire* information that was material and relevant to their qualifications to serve as impartial arbiters, these jurors had willfully and deliberately misled him and had, in effect, deprived the plaintiff of the right to excuse or challenge presumably biased members of the panel. "The cards," said the Court, "were stacked against the plaintiff . . . from the inception." The verdict was accordingly set aside, and a new trial ordered.

In criminal cases, too, the Court has inherent power, in the interests of justice, to conduct an examination on application to have the verdict of guilty set aside and to obtain a new trial if it is complained that the misconduct of a juror prejudiced the right of the accused to a fair and impartial trial. Trial before a biased jury constitutes a denial of due process. Thus, evidence indicating that one of the jurors showed racial prejudice against the accused was one of the grounds on which the Court set aside the verdict of guilty in the much-publicized Whitmore case in New York City.

But the New York State Court of Appeals has refused to uphold an objection to a juror made after he is sworn if the basis for it is a mere technicality. In one case, for example, a lawyer discovered after the trial that one of the jurors did not own the minimum of $250 worth of property required by law. However, this fact was held not to be a sufficient ground for invalidating the proceedings. On the other hand, if a lawyer knows some fact about a prospective juror's character that would disqualify him from serving, but fails to challenge him on this ground during the *voir dire*, it is too late to do so after the juror has been sworn. The right to challenge in such a case has been held to have been waived.

Although both of these decisions refer to criminal cases, it may be assumed that they are applicable to civil suits as well. Indeed, there is no certainty that even a challenge based on a juror's character will be upheld when raised after the trial, although counsel may have been ignorant of the facts when he selected the jury, as long as he could have elicited them at the time by questioning the venireman. This clearly demonstrates the crucial importance of formulating the right questions and putting them to the right people during the *voir dire*.

Let us see how this is done.

7

Choosing a Panel

As we have seen, there are definite rules under which counsel for both sides must operate in selecting a jury. Yet a knowledge of the law concerning the qualifications of jurors and the grounds for excusing them, although certainly necessary, is scarcely sufficient to ensure a satisfactory panel. The law may prescribe the rules governing this process, but its outcome depends on the power and skill of the respective antagonists. The technicalities of statutes and judicial precedents merely constitute the general framework within which counsel must employ his talents. His primary task is to search for the prejudices and predilections of each venireman in regard to any of the issues or persons (and, as we shall see, sometimes even animals!) that are likely to figure in the case.

To this end, he will have to draw chiefly upon his knowledge of human nature and his skill in questioning. Accordingly, the well-prepared lawyer comes to the *voir dire* with a plan already drawn up. In connection with each of the specific attitudes and qualities that he wants every venireman to reveal to him, his blueprint will indicate whether it is particularly favorable or unfavorable to his case. He should therefore have prepared a list of the questions designed to elicit the desired information.

This kind of planning is just as important as the pretrial preparation of witnesses, documents, and legal memoranda. Indeed, a failure to carry out the plan properly can have consequences quite as serious as any other error or omission on the part of counsel. He must make sure, in advance, to include in the questions he puts to the prospective jurors reference to all the factors that might presumably be pertinent to their reaction to the evidence in the case. Unless he takes this precaution, he runs the risk of later finding himself in trouble from which it may be difficult or impossible to extricate himself.

By way of illustration I may cite what happened in a personal injury case once tried before me. The plaintiff had been struck by a car while she was walking her dog in the gutter near the curb. As the animal had been injured too slightly to need treatment, no claim was made for damages to it. In opening his case to the jury at the outset of the trial, the defense counsel pressed the point that the injury to the plaintiff was, in fact, as slight and inconsequential as the dog's. Yet later, after the plaintiff's case had been presented, the attorney for the defendant, instead of trying to refute it, asked for a conference in chambers and sought a settlement out of court. His behavior was all the more surprising as negotiations prior to the trial had not brought even the semblance of an agreement between the parties. After a settlement had been reached, I was naturally eager to learn from the defense counsel what had prompted his rather abrupt change of heart.

He told me quite frankly. "I suddenly realized that I had forgotten to exclude dog lovers from the jury. I had never asked any of the prospective jurors whether they owned dogs. I was afraid that if, by any chance, there were some dog lovers on that jury, I might get clobbered."

On the other hand, an attorney who comes to court with a carefully formulated set of written questions must be on his guard against allowing opposing counsel to put him in the position of appearing as an oversuspicious Grand Inquisitor with a low opinion of the jurors' intelligence and sense of fair play. On many an occasion when I was counsel for a defendant in a civil or a criminal case, I would encounter an adversary who would resort to this stratagem. After asking the prospective jurors only a few cursory questions, he would unexpectedly turn away from them and say to me, in grandstand fashion, hoping no doubt to make an impression on the panel, something to this effect: "Mr. Heller, this jury is entirely satisfactory to me. I am confident that these jurors can be fair and impartial, and I accept them. Is this panel satisfactory to you?"

What does one do in a situation like this, especially if one has gone to the trouble of preparing a lengthy list of thoughtfully phrased questions to put to each venireman? To join in this play-acting would be, in effect, to forfeit one's right to a thorough *voir dire*. I would usually meet such a gambit with a response like the following:

"My distinguished and experienced adversary, Mr. _____, has just expressed the very feeling that I have about this jury. You all look like fine, intelligent, and fair jurors. For this reason, I want to be perfectly frank with you and give you some of the facts and tell you something about my client and his background, so that you can decide for yourselves whether you want to sit on this case."

I would then proceed with my inquiries. It was not long before I found my adversary joining me in detailed questioning.

But precisely what questions should each prospective juror be asked? And in what order should they be put?

Since, as we have seen, the law specifies the different kinds of challenges allowable, depending on the grounds on which each is based, it is only logical for a lawyer to arrange his questions accordingly. Consequently, he will begin his examination with a preliminary line of interrogation applicable to all the members of the panel. He can then proceed with the more specific probing that their answers may later make necessary.

First of all, he will want to know whether any of the veniremen are related or known to the litigants, counsel, or witnesses. If anything more than a passing acquaintance is acknowledged, opposing counsel should be asked to agree that the prospective juror be excused then and there by consent. For at least at this point in the proceedings, it is still in the interests of both parties that whatever verdict is ultimately reached be not set aside.

This is precisely what happened recently in a case in Tennessee. After a man had been tried for second-degree murder in connection with a hit-and-run traffic death, and while the jury was still out, it was learned that some members of the panel were related to two of the defense witnesses. By that time the jurors had deliberated for some hours and were reported to have actually voted to acquit the defendant. However, before the verdict was announced, the judge was apprised of the facts, and a motion for a mistrial was accordingly granted.

To be sure, family relationships are not the only kind that need to be looked for during the *voir dire*. A relationship of importance in negligence cases, which constitute more than half of those tried in New York, is that of a juror to a company issuing liability insurance.

Questions on this score can be made to serve a double purpose. In the first place, they may bring to light facts that could disqualify a prospective juror. But even when no such information is elicited, the very raising of the question is a means of implying, on behalf of the plaintiff in a suit for personal injuries or property damage, that the defendant carries liability insurance. This is a point that counsel is not permitted to make directly. If, for example, during the trial itself, the attorney for the plaintiff were to make this fact known to the jury, the judge could declare a mistrial. It would likewise be improper for counsel to disclose such information explicitly during the *voir dire*. In fact, his doing so could result in the replacement of the entire panel. Although this prohibition is a ridiculous anachronism in an age of mandatory liability insurance, it constitutes an impassable barrier to any direct mention by counsel for the plaintiff that the defendant is covered by this kind of protection.

Nevertheless, it is possible for a skillful lawyer, by the very manner in which he phrases his questions, to convey the same point indirectly to the prospective jurors. As we have seen, New York State law authorizes a challenge on the ground of presumed bias if the venireman has any interest whatsoever, whether as employee, officer, or shareholder, in any company that issues insurance "for protection against liability for damages for injury to persons or property." Accordingly, it is safe for counsel to use the very words of the statute to frame one or two questions that will give the members of the panel to understand that the defendant is insured.

These questions should be put to the panel as a whole. However, each prospective juror should be requested to give his answer separately. If the veniremen, by their appearance, occupation, and answers to other questions, strike counsel as being an intelligent group, a single question will suffice, which might be phrased substantially as follows:

Q. Are you a shareholder, a stockholder, director, officer, employee, or in any manner interested in any insurance company that issues policies to protect people against liability for damages for injury to persons or property?

Then, addressing each juror separately, counsel will ask, "Are you, sir? Are you, madam? Are you, sir?" until he has polled the entire panel. Asking each one the same question, rather than putting it in a form to which they might respond by a show of hands, may seem unnecessarily time-consuming and repetitious, but it generally serves a useful purpose. In this instance, the procedure of obtaining an answer from each prospective juror in turn simply has the effect of driving the point home all the more effectively, until even the dullest member of the panel understands it.

In fact, if counsel feels that the jury will not be so quick to grasp what he is driving at, he can put his inquiry in two questions:

Q. Are you a shareholder, stockholder, or director of any insurance company that issues policies for protection against liability for damages for injury to persons or property?

Q. Are you an officer or employee or in any manner interested in any insurance company that issues policies for protection against liability for damages for injuries to persons or property?

Some lawyers even go so far as to put the wording of the statute in six different questions, one for each type of interest described in it: shareholder, stockholder, director, officer, employee, or "any manner" of interest:

Q. Are you a *shareholder* in any insurance company issuing policies for protection against liability for damages for injury to persons or property?

Q. Are you a *stockholder* in any insurance company issuing policies for protection against liability for damages to persons or property?

Etc.

However, this procedure could too easily be interpreted as an affront to the panel's intelligence and may have the effect of antagonizing the members of the jury. One must at all times beware of underrating them, or even of seeming to do so.

In addition, the preliminary line of questioning should seek to determine what, if anything, each prospective juror already knows about the case that might influence him in deciding the issues. Questions touching on this point assume particular significance if the issues and persons involved in the trial have for any reason received publicity in the newspapers or other mass media.

In this connection, Mark Twain is said to have remarked:

We have a criminal jury system which is superior to any in the world, and its efficiency is marred only by the difficulty of finding twelve men every day who don't know anything and can't read.

Commenting on this observation, Justice Bernard S. Meyer, of the New York State Supreme Court, in an address delivered to the trial lawyers' section of the New York State Bar Association, February 2, 1966, declared:

As with most such devastating wit, it is achieved by a slight misstatement of the problem, for the difficulty that we face is more properly stated as that of "finding twelve men every day who don't know anything and haven't read, heard, or seen anything about the cases on which they will be called to sit." Ideally, jurors would begin their duties on a particular case with what the behavioral scientists like to call a "tabula rasa," a clean slate, a mind devoid of any prior impression concerning the case.

Of course, as the distinguished Justice recognizes, the conditions of modern society, especially in our big cities, make the attainment of such an ideal quite impossible. A heavy burden is therefore imposed on the trial lawyer in selecting the jury, particularly in a criminal case. For if he questions prospective jurors concerning pretrial publicity, he runs the risk of bringing it once more specifically to their attention.

No doubt they may assure him that, notwithstanding what they already know about the case from the mass media, they could render an impartial verdict according to the evidence. Certainly he should ask them for such assurances. But what are they really worth, when the damage may already have been done? Can a juror, even with the best of intentions and a strong will, control his subconscious and overcome the impression already formed there? And yet, how difficult it is to find a venireman, these days, who is altogether unfamiliar with the details of a case that has received widespread news coverage in the press and on radio and television!

Other questions should seek information concerning the jobs that each prospective juror has held, for it should not be assumed that his current job is the only one he has ever had. The possibility that he may have worked in an entirely different field should not be overlooked, since such experience may have resulted in the formation of attitudes that unfit him for service in the case. A picture of a venireman's entire occupational background should be a matter of especial interest in interrogating retired persons or housewives who appear on the panel. At the same time, inquiry should likewise be made into the experience each member of the panel may have had, whether as party or juror, in similar litigation.

For example, an attorney for a plaintiff who has been injured while using a defective stairway, and who is suing the owner of the building, would want to know whether any of the prospective jurors own or ever did own property and, if so, whether they have been involved in a similar lawsuit. He might begin by asking, "Do you own the house that you live in?" If the answer is no, the venireman might then be asked whether he or his wife or any member of his family owns any property. If the answer is yes, further inquiry could proceed as follows:

Q. Have you or any member of your family ever been sued by anyone to recover damages for personal injuries?

If the answer is yes, the details must be obtained:

Q. What type of action was it?
Q. Did the action go to trial?
Q. What was the outcome of the trial?

This is better than asking, "Was it settled?" Reference to settlement could very well provoke objection from the defense counsel and an unnecessary argument. If the judgment was against the venireman, an effort should be made to exclude him. Further inquiry to this end might proceed as follows:

Q. Has the experience of being sued soured or prejudiced you against people who bring this type of action?
Q. Do you have any feelings, as a matter of principle, against people who sue to recover damages in personal injury cases?

These questions clearly reveal that the attorney for the plaintiff wants a jury free of persons who have been sued for similar acts of negligence. By the same token, defense counsel wants a jury free of persons who, by reason of previous injuries sustained as a reult of negligence on the part of others, are likely to be prejudiced against the defendant, for he may have committed acts of negligence similar to those from which they suffered. Such possibilities should not be overlooked when a lawyer plans his line of questioning for the *voir dire*.

There are, of course, many other possible sources of bias besides those already mentioned. Perhaps the most insidious is racial and religious prejudice. Although clearly in conflict with the basic principles of democracy and with the moral code to which the vast majority of Americans subscribe, it is still, unfortunately, far too prevalent for counsel to ignore it.

Ideally, the race, religion, or nationality of a prospective juror, which his name or appearance may often reveal, ought to be altogether irrelevant to the question of his fitness to serve. Nevertheless, no lawyer can afford to overlook the fact, distasteful and saddening though it may be, that a Goldberg may tend to favor a Cohen, that a Reilly may be partial to an O'Casey, and that a Fiorenza may be inclined to be indulgent toward a Nitolo. Nor would it be prudent to close one's eyes to the possible antipathies that each of them might feel for persons of a different nationality or religion. As long as many prospective jurors do harbor some degree of bias stemming from this source, counsel must try the best way he can to ferret out such benighted souls.

Sometimes a member of a minority group may appear on the panel. If he is found to be acceptable, counsel should try to include at least one more juror from the same group to back him up. A lone individual may be hesitant to express or adhere to his opinion in the face of pressure from the rest of the jury if he believes that they think of him as "different" or even inferior.

By the same token, a lawyer whose client is a member of a minority group should be sure to ask each prospective juror whether he would allow that fact to influence him one way or the other. Although such a question may appear to be purely rhetorical, it nevertheless serves to remind jurors of their responsibility to be dispassionate. When a juror responds to the question, as he inevitably will, by disavowing any prejudice, he commits his honor to be fair.

On the other hand, a lawyer must be careful not to be guilty himself of jumping to conclusions about a venireman's bias simply on the basis of his name or nationality. After all, it is just as much a prejudice to attribute bias indiscriminately to every member of a particular group as it is to ascribe any other moral or intellectual failing to the group as a whole.

An apt illustration of the fallacy involved in such hasty preconceptions is a negligence case tried during the Second World War. It was a time when England was hard pressed, and when Italy was considered a potential enemy because of her alliance with Nazi Germany and her recent invasion of Ethiopia. Feelings ran high, and persons bearing Italian names were then no candidates for popularity contests.

It so happened that the plaintiff was of Italian extraction, as were her two witnesses and her attorney. Their names alone could have left no question in anyone's mind on this point. The plaintiff's attorney had exhausted the last of his peremptory challenges in the selection of the jury when a lady was called in to fill the seat vacated by the venireman who had just been excused. Obviously of Anglo-Saxon descent, she carried in her lapel one of the buttons calling for "All Aid to England" that thousands of people were wearing at that time. Counsel for the plaintiff tried in every way he could to find some ground to excuse her for cause, but without success, and she was sworn as a juror.

The accident complained of occurred at a station of the municipally owned subway line in New York City. According to the plaintiff, the stairway there was always wet and slippery with seepage from the walls. In rebuttal, the attorney for the City produced about eight persons, such as porters, change booth attendants, and maintenance engineers, who all testified that the stairs were always dry and safe.

After deliberating for about an hour, the jury returned a unanimous verdict in favor of the plaintiff. Walking through the hallway later, counsel for the plaintiff saw the lady juror whom he had tried so hard to challenge, and he thanked her for her part in the verdict. The lady waxed indignant in her denunciation of all the witnesses for the City as liars and perjurers. "Why," she exclaimed, "I use that station every day in the week, and it is always wet. I certainly told my fellow jurors what I thought of those City witnesses!"

In his concern over her possible bias on grounds of wartime hysteria, it had not occurred to the plaintiff's attorney to ask her about her possible familiarity with conditions at the station, nor, evidently, did opposing counsel raise the question either.

Another area of possible bias that may need to be explored is that arising from the tendency of many laymen to assume, in a criminal case, that where there is smoke, there must be fire. Defense counsel must make every effort to dispel the widespread illusion that "the People's cause," as it is technically called, is necessarily righteous. Jurors must be made to realize that an indictment is nothing more than an accusation, and not proof that the accused actually committed the crime he is charged with. They must also understand that the defense counsel is merely doing his duty in seeking to protect the rights of the accused, and that the prosecutor is only another lawyer fulfilling his obligation to present the case for the State.

It is therefore most important for the attorney for the defense in such cases to ask each venireman whether he will give greater weight to the testimony of public officials and policemen—or even, for that matter, ordinary citizens called by the prosecution—than to the testimony of the accused. Here too, this question and others put to the members of the panel may appear rhetorical, but they are designed to inform the jurors of the constitutional safeguards to which the defendant is entitled. At the same time, this line of interrogation serves to rebut the popular idea of the prosecution as being "on the side of the law" and to impress the jurors with their responsibility.

Questioning on these points might proceed as follows:

Q. Have you ever served as a juror in a criminal case?

(An affirmative answer would, of course, require further probing into details.)

Q. Would you entertain any prejudice against the defendant because of the nature of the charges against him?

Q. Have you read or heard about this case?

Q. Have you discussed this case with anyone who purports to know the facts and circumstances of the alleged crime the defendant is accused of?

Q. Have you formed or expressed any opinion as to the guilt or innocence of the defendant?

Q. Do you know the District Attorney or anyone in or connected with his office?

Q. Are any of your relatives or close friends connected in any way with the District Attorney's office?

Q. Are you acquainted with anyone in the Police Department, F.B.I., Justice Department, Sheriff's office, credit departments, or members of any society or organization for the enforcement of the law?

Q. Would you give greater credence to the testimony of a law enforcement officer merely because he is such an officer?

Q. Have you ever been the victim of a crime or a witness in a criminal case?

Q. Have you or any members of your family had any other unpleasant experience which, consciously or unconsciously, might make it difficult for you to render a fair verdict in this case?

Q. Do you have any feeling that there is any distinction between the prosecuting attorney and counsel for the defendant merely because one has an official title?

Q. Do you understand that we are both lawyers, one representing the State, and the other representing the defendant, and that both are entitled to an equal and respectful hearing from the jury?

Q. Will you give this case an impartial hearing and wait until you have heard both sides before forming an opinion?

Q. Will you follow the instruction of the Court that the indictment proves nothing and is merely a form of accusation?

Q. Will you follow the instruction of the Court that the defendant is presumed to be innocent, and that this presumption continues until the prosecution proves his guilt beyond a reasonable doubt?

Q. In other words, if the judge tells you, as I am sure he will, that the defendant, as he sits here at this moment, is presumed to be innocent, until proven guilty beyond a reasonable doubt, will you unhesitatingly accept this instruction from the Court?

Q. Will you follow the instruction of the Court that the prosecution must prove the guilt of the defendant beyond a reasonable doubt, and that the defendant does not have to establish his innocence?

Q. Will you follow the instruction of the Court that the burden of proof never shifts in a criminal case?

Q. Will you follow the instruction of the Court that the defendant may sit mute and say nothing, challenging the District Attorney to prove his guilt beyond a reasonable doubt?

Q. If the defendant testifies in his own defense, would you reject his testimony merely because he is the accused?

Q. Because you have been summoned here by the State and will be

paid your juror fees by the State or County, does this cause you to
believe that you are part of the prosecution?

Q. Do you know any of the following persons [naming the District
Attorney and his assistants trying the case and each person known
to be a prosecution witness]?

Q. Would you have any prejudice against the defendant because he is
represented by counsel from a neighboring county [if such is the
case]?

Q. Would you be prone to pull for the "home team," that is, the
prosecutor?

Q. Do you understand that you are the sole and exclusive judge of the
facts in this case, and that if you have a reasonable doubt as to the
guilt of the defendant, you should, under the law, acquit him?

Q. And, of course, do you understand that the Court is the sole and
exclusive judge of the law?

Q. Do you understand that the defendant is entitled to the individual
judgment of each juror?

Q. Would your judgment be affected merely because you may find
yourself in the minority at the time the jury begins its deliberations?

Q. Will you, if you are sworn as a member of the jury, decide this
case without prejudice, solely on the evidence presented before you
and on the law as the Court instructs you, and on nothing else?

Of course, these questions are very general and would be applicable
for use by defense counsel in virtually any criminal case. If a special
defense is to be offered at the trial—for example, an alibi, a plea of self-
defense, testimony that the confession was extorted under duress as a
result of police brutality, etc.—then counsel would, in addition, have
to frame relevant and material questions touching on these points too,
in order to explore the attitudes of the prospective jurors in respect to
them.

After he has completed his inquiries of all the jurors—and still before
exercising any challenges—counsel should ask whether any of them
know anyone else on the panel. If an affirmative answer refers to any
of the panelists whom counsel intends to challenge, he should inquire
further concerning the length and closeness of the acquaintance. A
prospective juror who is excused may sometimes feel that his intelligence has somehow thereby been questioned, and a similar resentment
on his behalf may be felt by any friend of his who remains behind on
the jury. Consequently, if "one of a pair" is excused, it may be necessary
to challenge the other one as well.

In this connection, I recall once questioning a panel and excusing a
prospective juror in a case that I subsequently lost. In later years,

after I had been initiated into a fraternal order, one of the members
approached me and reminded me that he had been a juror in the case.
It seems that the gentleman whom I had excused from the panel held,
at the time, the highest position in this order. He had been very active
in it and was regarded with great esteem by all the members. The
former juror related the incident with an injured air and told me that
I had offended his friend by excusing him from the panel.

The form in which a question is phrased can often be quite as
important as its content. This is true, as we shall see, in examining
witnesses, and it is equally true in interrogating prospective jurors. A
lawyer has to bear in mind that people in a group are reluctant to expose themselves. They need to be drawn out by appropriately stimulating questions. If the veniremen are simply asked, "Would you be
prejudiced against my client for bringing this type of action?" all counsel may get in reply is a collective no. Wherever possible, he should
seek to formulate his questions so as to avoid receiving a mere yes or
no in response. Every effort should be made to provoke an extended
answer. Thus, it would be preferable to ask, "How do you feel toward
a party who brings this type of action?" If this question is directed
toward each prospective juror individually, he will usually say enough
to allow counsel to judge whether there is any basis for challenging
him.

Ineptitude in the phrasing of even a single question can sometimes
lead to embarrassing consequences. In interrogating prospective jurors
in a case in which he was defending a man charged with armed robbery,
a very able lawyer was guilty of just such an unfortunate slip. He asked
the members of the panel, "Could you give this defendant the same
kind of fair trial that you would want for yourself if you were the
defendant?"

All but one of the veniremen replied in the affirmative. One lone
juror asked, "Where did I get the gun?" Pandemonium broke loose.

To be sure, not all the questions I have suggested as models lend
themselves, in the form in which I have phrased them, to extended
answers. But a lawyer can easily ask a juror to elaborate on any yes or
no given in response to them. For example, suppose one member of
the panel answers yes to the question whether he would follow the
instruction of the Court that the indictment is merely a form of accusation, and not a proof of guilt. Counsel can take this occasion to ask
each venireman in turn, "How do *you* feel about this?" and compare

their various reactions. From these he can begin, also, to decide whether the prospective jurors are intelligent, alert, and responsive. At the same time, their answers will enable him to form some judgment of their thinking processes, personalities, education, and character.

Or, to take another example, suppose one member of the panel answers yes, as he presumably will, to the question whether the defendant is entitled to the independent judgment of each individual juror. Every other prospective juror can then be asked, "How would *you* be affected if you found yourself in the minority during the deliberations?"

Follow-up questions of this kind help to educate jurors concerning their responsibilities. As they are induced to talk, their replies make it possible for counsel to judge whether they fit the pattern he is looking for.

As we have seen, certain kinds of witnesses offer an attorney special problems when he prepares his case for trial. For similar reasons, some types of prospective jurors require particular attention during the *voir dire*.

Of course, as soon as one thinks of human beings as belonging to "types," one has to be on one's guard against the all-too-common tendency to substitute prejudice for unbiased judgment. Obviously it is impermissible and even unfair to make sweeping generalizations about whole classes of individuals. Nevertheless, it is necessary for a lawyer at least to be aware of the possibility that people of a certain background or category may tend to think along particular lines that may or may not be favorable to his client or his case.

Consider, for example, the venireman—whatever his occupation may be—whose line of work brings him into frequent conflict with persons engaged in the same business as counsel's client. Other things being equal, it would be best if such an individual were not on the jury. Thus, if the client is a policeman, it would be well to avoid having any taxi drivers on the panel. If, on the other hand, one is representing a restaurant owner, then waiters, busboys, and bartenders should, if possible, be excluded from the jury. And if the client is a real estate operator, brokers dealing in the purchase and sale of property should be carefully screened out. In anticipation of problems like these, it is accordingly a good idea for counsel to give some thought, in planning the *voir dire*, to the kinds of work that are likely to lead to stereotyped attitudes prejudicial to the interests of his client. He can then seek to keep the jury free of anyone engaged in such occupations.

For the same reason, an attorney would be remiss in his duty to his client if he failed to take into account, in choosing jurors, the reluctance that an employee might quite naturally feel about saying or doing anything which could be interpreted as an act of disloyalty to his employer. This attitude assumes particular importance in cases where counsel is representing the plaintiff in a suit for negligence against the same type of company that a venireman is employed by. Anyone so employed may be unwilling to incur criticism for awarding a large sum of money to the plaintiff. Counsel should be especially wary of such prospective jurors.

Creative and performing artists, on the contrary—painters, writers, dancers, musicians, and bohemians—tend, for some reason or other, to be extremely generous in awards to claimants.

It would be equally short-sighted for a lawyer to fail to consider the effect that a prospective juror's financial situation or business may have on his attitude toward money and wealth. Certainly where substantial damages are being sought this is a matter that bears looking into.

Just as counsel for the plaintiff is prohibited from referring directly to the fact that the defendant carries liability insurance, so defense counsel is forbidden to make any mention, during either the *voir dire* or the trial itself, of the fact that his client is too poor to meet a judgment for the damages claimed. This is not properly the business of the members of the jury. Ideally, they are supposed to determine liability and fix damages independently of their estimate of the defendant's financial status. But it would be unrealistic for defense counsel to assume that such judgments on the part of the jurors will not affect their verdict. Since he can do little or nothing to apprise them directly of his client's limited financial resources, he must be all the more careful to select jurors likely to prove responsive to whatever indirect indications of the defendant's economic situation counsel plans to provide in the course of the trial.

Similar considerations must be taken into account by counsel for the plaintiff. Ordinarily, a poor man is the ideal juror for the plaintiff when the defendant is a big corporation, like a public utility or a nationally known company, or an individual of known wealth and position. However, a lawyer should not assume that a prospective juror is necessarily familiar with the financial standing of a wealthy defendant whose assets and income have been unpublicized, such as a closely held company.

By the same token, if a municipality is a defendant, it is a good idea for counsel to inquire of each prospective juror whether he owns any real estate. Property owners have a tendency to favor the city in negligence cases, evidently on the theory that their taxes will be increased if it has to pay out large sums of money to satisfy claims for damages.

If, on the other hand, a veteran is being represented, counsel will want to get on the panel one or more jurors of similar status. Hence he will need to elicit this information during the *voir dire*.

Obviously, too, there will be occasions—for example, cases in which a lawyer, an engineer, an architect, an accountant, or a doctor is suing for a substantial fee—when counsel would like to have on the jury at least a few individuals who are accustomed to dealing in large sums of money.

Like considerations should motivate counsel for a good-looking or otherwise attractive client to seek out jurors of the opposite sex who might be susceptible to such an influence. If, on the contrary, suit is being brought on behalf of a child, it would be well to fill the panel, so far as possible, with jurors who are married and have children of their own. In this case, too, counsel would have to be sure to include in his interrogation questions concerning the marital status and family of each prospective juror.

The basic idea underlying this approach to jury selection is, as it were, to fit the panel to the client and the case. Thus, in suits involving claims for personal injuries, a lawyer cannot afford to ignore the influence that a physical disability, whether congenital or acquired, may have on a juror's outlook. Disabled persons tend to be sympathetic toward an injured plaintiff and generous in their treatment of him. For this reason, counsel for the plaintiff should make every effort to keep a disabled individual on the jury against any attempts on the part of opposing counsel to exclude him. If he cannot be excused on statutory grounds, counsel for the defendant might well consider using a peremptory challenge to keep him off the panel.

In discussing this whole subject, the Honorable Bernard Botein, former presiding Justice in the First Department of the Appellate Division of the New York State Supreme Court, had this to say in an article entitled "A Judge Votes for the Jury":

> Indeed, a well-known trial lawyer who represents the plaintiffs in accident cases has written that married men and women favor plaintiffs; experts, professional people, nurses, and wives of professionals are to be avoided, because they are indifferent to pain and suffering and inclined

to rely on their own learning; and accountants are to be shunned, for they inform their fellow jurors that a plaintiff does not pay an income tax on any money he may recover for his personal injuries.

A famous prosecutor once told me he would never select a man with a beard as a juror; he had found they were nonconformists and would, in an open-and-shut case, hold out and hang a jury out of sheer cussedness. And so, ad infinitum, lawyers have their pet notions and techniques for excusing jurors, irrespective of their competence—in fact, frequently because of such competence . . .

Percy Foreman, for example, who is considered to be without a peer in the art of selecting jurors, makes it a rule to avoid seating Germans and Scandinavians whenever possible. "They're too severe and well disciplined," he maintains. "They have little understanding of mistakes." For similar reasons, he tries to eliminate jurors whose occupations demand great precision, like engineers, statisticians, accountants, bookkeepers, and draftsmen, for he finds them too exacting. He prefers Jews, Negroes, Irish Catholics, and others with backgrounds that tend to identify them with those who are persecuted or oppressed.

Yet, like every master of any art, Foreman knows intuitively just when it is safe to break the "rules" and make a bold move that seems to defy common sense. In questioning a prospective juror in a murder case, he asked, "Do you know me by reputation?"

"Oh, yes, I certainly do," the man replied.

"And would you be prejudiced against my client by what you know about me?" asked Foreman.

"I certainly would," the venireman promptly answered, "because I know what a shyster you are. Nobody would hire you unless he was guilty."

By all the rules, an answer like that should have immediately disqualified him. But Foreman, to everyone's amazement, declared, "I'll accept this juror. He's an honest man."

Nor did his judgment prove mistaken. As it happened, this was the juror who helped to persuade his colleagues on the panel that Foreman's client should be given the gentle treatment. In the end, the accused received a five-year suspended sentence.

As we can see, the reasoning by which lawyers conclude that a particular prospective juror is or is not acceptable is not always a model of strictly logical inference. Selecting a jury is an art, not a science. More often than not, what enters into the final decision to accept or reject a juror is a complex combination of hunches, more or less well-founded suppositions, time-honored traditions, questionable generalizations about human "types," and rule-of-thumb formulas. But these are, after all, about the best that a lawyer can hope to rely on in making this difficult choice.

Consider, for example, the problem confronting defense counsel in a recent case in which his client was charged with negligence leading to an automobile accident. Counsel asked one of the prospective jurors whether he knew much about the law.

"A little," the venireman responded, "but not more than the next man."

"But isn't your son a lawyer?" asked the attorney for the defendant.

The venireman said that he was.

"Isn't he, in fact, an administrative assistant to Senator Abraham Ribicoff?" defense counsel persisted.

"Yes, he is."

After a moment's reflection, counsel accepted the juror.

One can, of course, only speculate on the reasoning that led the defendant's attorney to make this decision. Senator Ribicoff, a famous champion of traffic safety, might be assumed to be on the side of the victims of traffic accidents, and his administrative assistant would presumably have been chosen for being, among other things, of like mind in this regard. But could it be reasonably inferred that the father would have the same bias as the son? Who knows? Evidently defense counsel in this case made no such assumption. He took a chance on the prospective juror's fair-mindedness.

Every attorney has his own idea of who makes a good juror. Some lawyers believe that retired policemen, bank clerks, subway guards, and utility company employees generally make good defendant's jurors. A distinguished and very able advocate of my acquaintance says that when he is representing the plaintiff, he acts on the following principle, which seems to have stood him in good stead over the years: "The more they have, the less they give; the less they have, the more they give." A very prominent lawyer active in matrimonial cases once told me that in suits for divorce tried before a jury, the defense counsel should attempt as far as possible to get older people into the box. Grandmothers and grandfathers, he said, are ideal jurors in such trials. They are understandably sentimental and reluctant to convict anyone, especially a wife who may also be a mother, of so serious an offense as adultery.

And what of women as jurors? According to the same authority, they react differently from men when the defendant in a divorce action is a man. Women jurors, especially if they are married, are more likely to be harsh in their judgment of a male defendant in such cases, not because of the difference in sex, but because of their natural antipathy toward the corespondent. If there is one thing that characterizes married women, my informant continued, it is their hostility—a manifestation of group bias—toward any woman who comes between husband and wife and breaks up a marriage.

In my experience I have found women to be extremely attentive and highly conscientious. They demonstrate a strong sense of the seriousness of their responsibility and seek to perform it with the utmost care. Generally they can be counted on to hew strictly to the rules of evidence and to the law as expounded in the judge's charge to the jury.

But, especially in suits involving claims for personal injury, most women do not think in terms of large sums of money. In their shopping, no doubt, they have been accustomed to dealing with limited allowances, based on a budget. They have become used to accounting for each dollar spent. As a result, they may consider reasonable claims for damages to be astronomically high, and they may be too insistent on finding a justification for each dollar claimed by the plaintiff. An exception, however, is the career woman. In the last few decades, she has equaled and, in many instances, surpassed men in many fields of business, industry, education, and the professions, and her financial outlook has been correspondingly broadened.

There is one other fact about women that must be taken into consideration in judging their fitness to serve as jurors.

It has been said that woman is man's best friend and her own worst enemy. Keeping this in mind, any lawyer who has a woman as his client would be well advised to keep other women off the jury so far as possible. If both litigants are women, then the attorney representing the one who is more attractive or more expensively outfitted with clothes and jewelry would do well to be wary of women jurors. On the other hand, women are very desirable to have on the panel in criminal cases or in those in which counsel is bringing suit on behalf of a child.

A lawyer runs a particular risk if he selects for the jury the wife of another member of the bar. Of course, the judge will admonish her, along with the rest of the jurors, not to discuss the case with anybody outside the panel. But does anyone really believe that she will be able to resist the temptation to talk to her husband about it and to consult his knowledgeable judgment? He, in turn, will no doubt be more than willing to instruct her in the law as he knows it. The only trouble is that his briefing, well-intentioned though it may be, might conflict with the instructions given to the jury by the judge—instructions which the lawyers on both sides of the case have some part in shaping.

Indeed, if a prospective juror's husband has been accustomed to appearing on behalf of the defendant in negligence actions, that fact alone could justify counsel for the plaintiff in keeping her off the panel. Certainly a relationship of this kind could well outweigh all other considerations. On the other hand, if her husband generally appears on the side of the plaintiff in such cases, then the attorney for the defendant would doubtless want her excluded from the jury. Almost inevitably, then, one side or the other in the case would seek to have her excused. In fact, she should be challenged peremptorily if no other grounds for removing her can be found.

Possibilities like these show how important it is, in general, for counsel to find out from a married woman, during the *voir dire*, what the occupation of her husband is. For one is usually safe in ascribing to the wife the same attitudes that her husband is likely to have as a result of the conflicts arising out of the nature of his work. For similar reasons, counsel should not neglect to probe the occupational history of housewives, who may have had some experience in the business world.

A special problem is raised by the person whom lawyers call "the professional juror." Actually, this term is used in two quite distinct senses. As it is most commonly understood, it means a person who has already served on so many panels that he is an old hand at the juror's game. He knows all the answers. What is more, he may really enjoy sitting in judgment on his fellow men. In this respect, he is unlike the active people who find the call to jury duty an unwelcome interruption in their busy lives. For them the performance of this civic obligation may involve a real personal sacrifice. Not so for the professional juror. With fewer responsibilities and more time on his hands, he is glad to have opportunities to hear cases and is more than willing to sit on a panel—perhaps, in some instances, even too willing.

In deciding on the suitability of this type of person for the jury, a lawyer has first to consider what may be motivating such eagerness to serve. Is it purely a disinterested love of seeing justice done? And what effect has long and varied experience in the jury box had on the professional juror's whole outlook? It will not do, of course, to put these questions directly to him. The way for a lawyer to get such information is to ask the professional juror about the nature of the cases he has heard and the verdicts rendered. Possibly he may have heard too many cases to be susceptible any longer—if, indeed, he ever was—to the kind of emotional appeal that counsel expects to rely on. Especially if an attorney is representing the plaintiff in a negligence case, he cannot safely ignore the possibility that the professional juror may have become calloused to the spectacle of pain and suffering presented by claimants for damages.

In the other sense of the term, a "professional juror" is simply one who has studied enough in a particular field, such as law, medicine, or architecture, to be knowledgeable on the subject. Anyone so well informed may tend to scrutinize the legal claims or the medical evidence too critically. For example, a person familiar with anatomy, such as a nurse, an intern, or a medical student, may be inclined to be skeptical of allegations that the injuries sustained were incapacitating or permanent in their effects. Obviously this kind of professional is not wanted on the panel by counsel for the plaintiff in negligence suits.

Where there is little room for dispute, however, a professional juror of this type is highly desirable, for he can guide the other members of the panel through the maze of legal, medical, or scientific technicalities involved. For a similar reason, when maps, blueprints, drawings, or the operation of certain equipment plays a role in a case, engineers, architects, and others with a knowledge of building construction or technology can provide a welcome guiding hand in the jury room.

Evidently, then, a prospective juror whose background, occupation, or specialized competence renders him quite acceptable to one side may, for that very reason, be unacceptable to the other. In short, the decision for or against letting a particular individual remain on the panel may very often depend on whether counsel is representing the plaintiff or the defendant. Indeed, in view of the inevitable opposition of one party or the other, it might seem as if a really knowledgeable person has virtually no chance of being selected as a juror in any case in which his special qualifications might be helpful.

However, the matter is not quite so simple. Paradoxically, a lawyer may sometimes serve his client's interests better by *not* challenging a prospective juror whose knowledge or experience in a given field may appear to him to be too formidable. For counsel has to consider not only the qualifications of the individual venireman, but also the possible psychological effect that excusing him may have on the remaining members of the panel. Failure to take this last point into account may prove to be a fateful mistake.

This is precisely what happened in a recent case involving a claim for damages caused by a fire in the incinerator of a factory building. In the course of selecting the jury, the attorney for the plaintiff came across a "maintenance man." Questioning him in detail, counsel discovered that this man had an expert knowledge of boilers and incinerators. Convinced that the rest of the jury would look to him for guidance in determining the cause of the fire, counsel was not at all happy about having such a well-informed person scrutinizing the evidence he intended to present. He was sorely tempted to excuse the man, but did not dare to do so because of the effect he thought this might have on the other veniremen. Consequently, the plaintiff's attorney felt greatly relieved when, to his surprise, opposing counsel challenged the man.

Later, plaintiff's counsel asked his adversary why he had done so and was told that such a juror would probably have been good for the plaintiff, and not for the defendant. Each of the lawyers in the case, it seems, lacked confidence that the evidence he proposed to rely on could withstand critical examination by such an expert. Whichever one of them may have been right on this point, the fact remains that defense counsel erred in excusing the maintenance man. He thereby revealed to the rest of the panel his apparent lack of faith in his own cause. After the trial it was learned that the other jurors had been alienated when they became convinced that he did not want anyone on the jury who understood the technicalities of the case.

Thus, it is not enough for counsel, in questioning prospective jurors, to consider how they strike him. He must also, as we have seen, take into account how his conduct may strike them. And, of course, he must conform his behavior accordingly. In practice this means applying a certain amount of psychology to winning the favor of the panel even in the process of selecting it. This is an art in itself that would undoubtedly be more widely practiced if it were better understood. Its principles deserve further, more extended examination.

8

Establishing Rapport

It should never be forgotten that the encounter between counsel and venireman during the *voir dire* is always a two-way affair. The impression made on the members of the panel by the lawyers on both sides is quite as important for their chances of eventual success as is the impression that each of the prospective jurors makes on them. The selection of the jury is not merely an occasion for an attorney to learn something about those who are to pass judgment on the evidence he proposes to present. The interrogation of the prospective jurors is also an opportunity for them to learn something about him and his cause.

Consciously or unconsciously, juries often decide cases on the basis of their attitude toward the lawyers on each side. That is why it is sometimes said that juries try lawyers (in more senses than one!) rather than cases. A lawyer may think of the veniremen as being on trial in his eyes, but he must always remember, at the same time, that he, too, is on trial in theirs. There is, after all, something peculiarly fitting—a kind of poetic justice, if you will—in the fact that, under our system of law, he who tests the fitness of others to judge his cause is, in the process, himself being tested by them. Their examination of him may be silent, but the judgment in which it culminates is no less decisive than his.

Indeed, everything counsel does or says during the *voir dire* is noted by the jurors and has its effect upon them: the pace and tone of his questioning, his respect for their intelligence, his regard for their sensibilities, even his way of treating his adversary. All his resources of tact, of courtesy, and of insight into human nature will therefore be needed during those crucial moments when he selects the men and women who are to serve as the judges of the facts in the case.

From the very outset, counsel must attempt, during the *voir dire*, to get the members of the panel to like him. The selection of the jury is his first opportunity to impress his personality on them and to give them an idea of what his case is about. The adage that first impressions are the most lasting is peculiarly relevant here. It is at this juncture that counsel has the chance to establish cordial relations and a rapport with the jury. He should try to win its acceptance of him as an earnest gentleman, sincerely dedicated to his cause and his client.

There are, in fact, a number of ways in which a lawyer can dispose the jury favorably toward him even in the process of selecting it.

First, he can use the occasion of identifying the litigants and their attorneys to explain the general nature of the case. To be sure, he cannot, in this explanation, give his version of the facts. This must be reserved until he presents his opening statement to the jury, after it has been selected and sworn. But he can set the prospective jurors straight on a number of essential points and correct possible misunderstandings. If, for example, he is representing the defendant, and opposing counsel has already given a fair statement of the facts in the case, there is no need to repeat them, but certainly the members of the panel should be made to realize that there is a defense to the action. In fact, the nature of the defense should be set forth in general terms at this time.

Counsel's introductory statement should also include a carefully phrased explanation of why he must, in the *voir dire*, inquire into certain matters that he feels compelled to question the prospective jurors about. Indeed, an astute lawyer will use this explanation as an opportunity to indulge in a certain amount of subtle flattery of the veniremen. He will dwell on the gravity of their responsibility and stress the significance of their role in seeing that justice is done. He may even go so far as to compare their importance to that of counsel and Court. Such a statement can do much to obviate the resentment which might otherwise result from the kind of probing that counsel may be forced, in the interests of his client, to perform in the selection of the jury. At the same time, he can foster an attitude favorable to himself and, indirectly, his client.

Accordingly, before asking the prospective jurors a single question, counsel might say something like this to the entire panel:

> The parties involved in this litigation have been waiting _____ years for a trial. Now, at last, they have an opportunity to be heard. You, as jurors, will be the sole judges of the facts and will resolve the issues between them.
>
> You will note that I have called you "judges." For that is exactly what you are. Each one of you is a judge of the facts, in the same sense that the Court is the judge of the law, and I am sure that the Court

will so instruct you, and I am equally confident that my friend [not, be it noted, "my adversary" or "my opponent"] here, Mr. _____, the attorney for the _____, will agree with me.

For this reason, you will, I am sure, understand why it is so important for us both, as lawyers, to inquire into your qualifications to discharge this grave responsibility. I, for my part, have no desire to pry into your personal affairs or to cause anyone embarrassment. But since each juror is a judge, I must be certain that each member of this panel is just as impartial, just as fair, just as unbiased, as the judge on the bench who will preside in this case. If, therefore, I ask you some questions that you may consider as personal, please understand that I do so only in the performance of my duty to insure a fair and unbiased set of judges for my client. This same duty I would owe to you if I were representing any one of you here in this jury box.

Now that you understand my position, as well as yours, may I put a number of questions to you? Incidentally, I am going to speak to you separately, but loudly enough so that all of you can hear me.

As counsel then proceeds with his preliminary examination of each prospective juror along the lines I have suggested, he should be careful to take his time. There is no good reason for being in a hurry, and there are many good reasons for adopting a deliberate, if not in fact a leisurely, pace. Any suggestion of haste, any manifestation of impatience, can have a most harmful effect on the members of the jury, especially if opposing counsel succeeds in conveying the impression of being very patient with them. But even aside from its impact on them, a desire to get the *voir dire* "over with" in a hurry could lead to costly mistakes in the selection of the panel. On the other hand, tactful and patient probing can often save a lawyer from misjudging a prospective juror.

An illustration of the value of these virtues in conducting the *voir dire* is an experience which a friend of mine, a talented trial lawyer, once had. In the course of examining an innocuous-looking gentleman of about sixty-five years of age, who gave the appearance of being anything but a rugged individualist, counsel asked whether he would accept the law as expounded by the Court. Politely but firmly the venireman answered, "No, sir." Since the man was of foreign extraction, counsel at first thought that perhaps some language difficulty had prompted the negative response. But instead of just assuming that he had inadvertently said no when in all probability he meant yes, counsel took the trouble to ask half a dozen or more specific questions touching on this point. The sum total of the replies elicited clearly indicated that this particular individual understood the questions and was insisting that he reserved unto himself the right to interpret the law without regard to any instructions from the Court. His last answer was, in substance, "I will not accept the law that any judge might give if I personally do not agree with it."

Of course, he was immediately excused. Yet later that week, at a nearby restaurant, counsel saw him sitting with a number of jurors in a case in which he apparently had been accepted. My friend is still wondering whether the attorneys in that case were in so great a hurry to select a jury that they did not know they had accepted at least one juror who would refuse to be bound by the Court's instructions on the law.

It is also a good idea for counsel to pay close attention to any questions that a perplexed venireman may raise during the *voir dire*. No matter how irrelevant or confused such questions may seem, they are important enough to be of concern to at least one member of the panel, and perhaps to others as well, who may be too shy or too inarticulate to ask them. If counsel is prepared to take the time to follow up these questions, he will often find in them clues to what may be going on in the minds of the prospective jurors. To brush a question aside suggests a lack of consideration for the person who asks it. What is more, a perfunctory, offhand, or evasive manner in answering a venireman's question may mean a lost opportunity to clarify a point that is troubling more than one of his colleagues on the panel.

Besides, a lawyer has to keep in mind that, in addition to being an advocate, he is also, in a sense, a teacher. Accordingly, he should welcome the chance provided by a question from a prospective juror to expound his ideas succinctly. He can thereby demonstrate to the panel his ability to convey technical information about legal matters in terms comprehensible to the layman. At the same time, he can use the occasion to instruct the entire jury concerning the exact scope of their responsibilities and to clear up misconceptions. A lawyer who can help to resolve a juror's difficulties wins his confidence. A lucid and concise exposition of some troublesome point can earn the gratitude of the whole panel, especially if the information is presented without condescension, as a helpful service gladly performed by an expert on the subject. If, on the other hand, the questions are sensible and pertinent, they offer counsel the opportunity to impress his point of view on an alert individual who may well prove later on to be the leader of the discussion in the jury room.

In fact, respect for each prospective juror's intelligence and regard for his sensitivities should be apparent in everything that counsel does from the beginning of the *voir dire*. A polite, dignified tone inspires respect in its turn. Nor should counsel allow his image as a scholar and a gentleman to be in any way tarnished by the slightest lapse of courtesy in referring to or dealing with his adversary. Before the jury, a lawyer loses nothing in referring to opposing counsel by name, and with some mark of esteem, such as "my learned adversary," "distinguished counsel for the plaintiff," or "learned counsel." Incidentally, in the process, he helps to set a tone of decorum conducive to orderly, judicial procedure. His adversary may, if he is astute, very well hesitate to be the first to lower this tone by any disparaging or uncomplimentary remark on his own part. But if opposing counsel does make the mistake of indulging in personalities while selecting the jury, the lawyer who is the object of such rudeness can emerge with dignity and honor if he can control his natural inclination to retort in kind. For in such encounters, the man who retains his composure is "one up" on his opponent in the eyes of the jury, and he should strive to stay that way.

For similar reasons, if opposing counsel puts a question to a venireman that an attorney considers improper, he would be wise not to attract attention to it by argument in the presence of the panel. It is better for him to draw his adversary out of hearing of the jury, suggest that the question is not appropriate, and try to come to an agreement on how to rephrase it. If no agreement can be reached, he should try to persuade his opponent to approach the panel to ask that both be excused for a few minutes without revealing the reason. Then the two of them can repair to the judge's chambers to argue the point in privacy. If the judge is present during the *voir dire*, counsel should ask his adversary to approach the bench, where, out of hearing of the jury, the argument can be presented to the Court. If there is any likelihood at all that the jury will understand or overhear what is being discussed, counsel should request the Court to permit the argument to be heard in chambers.

Then too, without in any way failing in zeal on his client's behalf, a lawyer should do everything he can to give the jury, during the *voir dire*, an impression of his fairness. While remaining vigilant to protect the interests entrusted to his care, he must always show a reluctance to take undue advantage of any situation. The image he should seek to project is that of a man eager to secure a truly impartial panel to hear his case.

In this connection I am reminded of an anecdote that was related to me by a court clerk. A noted trial lawyer, who was an amazingly keen student of human nature, and very quick to grasp any opportunity that looked favorable to him, was selecting a jury. One of the questions he asked was, "Do any of you know me?"

Immediately one of the prospective jurors smiled and replied, "Sure I know you, Tom. We went to Boys' High School together. I recognized you the minute I saw you."

Glancing hastily down at the ballots in the panel board, the lawyer took a quick look at the juror's name and said, returning the smile, "Why, Johnnie, old boy, how are you? I sure am glad to see you again after all these years."

Then he added, "Of course, it wouldn't be right for me to have an old chum of mine on my jury; so I will, rather reluctantly, have to excuse you."

With that, he shook hands with the gentleman, put his arm around his shoulders in comradely fashion, and, talking all the while in an animated, confidential way, led him back to the area where the venire-men sit while waiting to be called to occupy a seat in the jury box.

After the jury had been selected, the clerk said to Tom, the lawyer, "Isn't it wonderful meeting an old friend like that after so many years?"

Tom laughed and replied, "I never went to Boys' High School; I attended school in California—and I never saw this fellow before in my life."

However, by this gesture, he gave the remaining members of the panel an impression of his fairness, as well as his sharp, retentive memory.

A lawyer's concern for the feelings of the prospective jurors can be shown in many small ways, too. For example, he can try to be the first to suggest a break in the interrogation, so as to avoid continuing the selection of the jury past the lunch hour. He should also take pains, when addressing each venireman, to pronounce his name correctly. If necessary, counsel should ascertain beforehand how to do so, rather than risk an unfavorable reaction by mispronouncing it.

An amusing illustration of the value of paying attention to such niceties is the experience of a friend of mine (let us call him Mr. Dubroff), as a young lawyer, representing a man indicted for man-slaughter. The plea was self-defense. One of the witnesses he had to cross-examine was named Cipolla. The night before, Mr. Dubroff took the trouble to have an Italian neighbor instruct him in the correct pronunciation of this name—*chi pólla*, which means "onion" in Ital-ian—and so had no difficulty in this respect when he faced the witness the next day in court.

Later, in his summation, Mr. Dubroff, whose father was a renowned rabbi, quoted in Hebrew an expression from the Old Testament to the effect that "he who comes to kill may be killed." The jury acquitted his client.

Afterward, in leaving the courtroom, one of the jurors, who was of Italian extraction, approached defense counsel and confided, "I voted for you because any Italian who can speak Hebrew must be an honest scholar."

Apparently counsel's correct pronunciation of the witness' name was enough to lead the juror to believe that Mr. Dubroff was an Italian!

The same delicate regard for the sensitivities of the members of the panel should pervade all aspects of a lawyer's conduct during the *voir dire*. For example, a certain amount of tact is required, as we have seen, in challenging a prospective juror. One of the masters of this art is F. Lee Bailey. In selecting the jury for the trial of a case, he is very careful to avoid making any enemies. A venireman once asked to be excused because he was involved in an important business transaction. The judge declined to excuse him, and the gentleman was subsequently approved by both the Court and the prosecution. Mr. Bailey thereupon exercised one of his peremptory challenges to excuse the juror, saying, "I would not want him to serve if his mind is going to be on an important business deal."

Equally gracious and tactful was Mr. Bailey's way of excusing a venireman who did not appear to be intelligent enough for him. Before challenging the man, he went through the motions of conferring with his client, making it seem as if the latter were the one who desired the juror's elimination.

In general, Mr. Bailey lets it be known that he likes intelligent jurors. Accordingly, whoever is selected by him to serve on a panel is made to feel that his intellect has been appreciated, and this subtle form of flattery naturally disposes the jury favorably toward Mr. Bailey.

A lawyer should be especially careful not to say anything that could offend or embarrass any prospective juror. In view of the kind of information that a zealous advocate is obliged to probe for in selecting a jury, he has, in effect, to learn how to tread upon eggshells if he is to find out what he wants to know about each venireman without, in the process, alienating anybody on the panel. The pitfalls here are so numerous that it would be well for counsel to anticipate them and be ready to avoid them.

For example, it is not always advisable to mention the occupation

of a prospective juror, particularly if it is one that does not rank very
high in the social scale. Suppose his card in the slot of the panel board
lists it as "street cleaner," and counsel wants to learn whether he
changed his job since the card was last prepared. Without referring
specifically to the nature of the work, he should ask, "Are you still connected with the Sanitation Department?" Similarly, if the occupation
is "truck driver for the ABC Corporation," it is wise to inquire, "Are
you still connected with the ABC Corporation?" (Somehow people
seem to think it better to be "connected with" than "employed by" or
"working for" a firm or department.)

Nor should a question imply a lack of ordinary knowledge on the
part of a prospective juror. Thus, instead of asking, "Do you know what
a Picasso painting is?" counsel would do better to put the question in
a less offensive form, such as, "You are, of course, aware of the fact that
a Picasso painting is considered very valuable?" Besides allowing the
person to whom the question is addressed to appear knowledgeable,
the latter formulation actually conveys a piece of information that,
quite possibly, may not have been known to either him or other members of the panel, without exposing anyone's ignorance.

To the same end, counsel defending a husband in a matrimonial action on the issue of adultery will have to be careful in phrasing questions designed to elicit from the women on the panel information that
might indicate sympathy for the wife. He can hardly ask them bluntly,
"Are any of you ladies involved in any kind of matrimonial action
against your husband?" Yet with a few well-planned questions, he can
garner the same information by indirection:

Q. Mrs. _____, I see that your card indicates that you are a house-
    wife. Would you be good enough to give me the names of the mem-
    bers of your family who reside with you at 100 Main Street?

The juror will naturally give her husband's name first, thereby revealing
that they are living together. Counsel can then proceed:

Q. What is your husband's occupation?
Q. For how long have you resided with him at 100 Main Street?
Q. Would you [with hesitation, showing pain or reluctance at having
    to ask the question]—and, of course, this might sound like a ques-
    tion that may get my client and me into trouble, but lawyers un-
    fortunately, as I previously explained, have to make these inquiries,
    and there is nothing that we can do about it, so please forgive me
    if I ask the next question and perhaps similar ones—would you,
    because you are a woman, be more sympathetic to the plaintiff, who
    is a woman, than to the defendant?

Inevitably the answer will be no. Before proceeding, counsel should say, "Of course. I knew you wouldn't." Then he can continue with his questions:

Q. Would you be fair and impartial and come to no conclusions until you have heard both sides of the case?
Q. Have any of the members of your family or close relatives ever been involved in any kind of matrimonial suit?

The last question is, of course, applicable to both men and women jurors in this type of action. If the answer to it is yes, further inquiries will have to be made to learn the details, the nature of the litigation, the outcome, and its effect on the juror.

With appropriate adaptations to suit the nature of the case, a similar question must, as we have already noted, be asked of prospective jurors in other kinds of lawsuits as well.

It is a good idea, also, for counsel, if he foresees the possibility that he will be forced to make numerous objections to the evidence proffered by his opponent, to explain the need for this to the jury during the *voir dire*. He should receive assurances from the members of the panel that such conduct on his part would not be held against him or his client. A brief statement to this effect might be something like the following:

During the trial, my adversary may attempt to offer certain evidence which I consider inadmissible, and I may have to object. This simply means that the judge will decide whether or not the evidence is to be admitted. If I am sustained in my objection, the judge will exclude it. If I am overruled, the judge will allow it. Now, because of the nature of this case, I may very well be compelled to make many such objections. If I do, would you hold that against my client or me? Or would you rather take the position that a lawyer is within his rights and doing his duty in making such objections and that you will respect him for it?

An especially delicate problem of human relations is faced by the lawyer who is trying a case outside his own territory, particularly if his adversary is one of the "native sons" of the area. Some of the potential jurors may tend to favor home-grown talent. They may look upon "outsiders" with some suspicion or even, in places where feelings run high, with outright hostility.

If it seems as if community pride may play a role in the thinking of the jurors, it is generally advisable to blunt the edge of prejudice by retaining local counsel. But if a lawyer from outside the area does decide to try the case himself, he should at least avoid the mistake of making an issue of his "alien" status, as an attorney from New York City did once while he was examining prospective jurors in a case he was trying in Monticello. He prefaced his interrogation by saying, in effect, that when he had informed his associates of his intention to try a case in the Supreme Court of Sullivan County, they had warned him against doing so. He could not, they said, expect a fair verdict from a jury composed of residents of a rural area, because everybody there was too unsophisticated to be guided by a "city slicker." But, he continued, he had assured these skeptics that, in the true American tradition, he would receive fair and just treatment from the farmers of upstate New York.

Needless to say, the jury did not require much time to deliberate and return a verdict against this attorney's client.

For similar reasons, counsel should be careful to avoid creating the impression that he is a brilliant trial lawyer or a profound student of the law. The average person tends to sympathize with the underdog, and jurors are no exception. A dazzling display of oratorical pyrotechnics or of superior legal erudition may induce respect for counsel's abilities, but it may also spark undue sympathy for the other litigant, whose lawyer may appear less eloquent and scholarly. Modesty, simplicity, and naturalness are likely to yield greater dividends than a flamboyant exhibition of courtroom prowess. It is not always the worst thing to hide one's light under a bushel.

But what a lawyer does or says in selecting jurors can do more than just dispose them favorably toward him personally. Very often, he can profit from the occasion to plant the seeds of a favorable verdict for his client.

If, for example, he knows that his case is weak in some respects, it would be wise for him, during the *voir dire*, to make a frank admission of its shortcomings. He should seek to elicit from the prospective jurors assurances that they will not be unduly influenced by such facts in arriving at a fair verdict. If he fails to make a full disclosure in selecting the jury, his only other chance to do so is in his opening statement to the panel, after the jury has already been sworn and the trial has begun.

I recall a case in which the attorney for the plaintiff, during the *voir dire*, candidly described his client as a "dull-witted foreigner, unable to speak the English language." In fact, he told the panel that even the interpreter whom he expected to use when his client testified might have difficulty in understanding her "unintelligible gibberish." Then he asked each juror in turn whether he would be prejudiced against such a litigant. Each assured him he would not.

Later, in his opening remarks to the jury, counsel for the plaintiff referred again to her dull-wittedness and importuned them to ignore "glib and dovetailed testimony," to listen to the whole case before making up their minds, and to decide it solely on the basis of the credibility of the witnesses.

When counsel for the defendant, a man of many years of experience and a skillful trial lawyer, came to the cross-examination of the plaintiff, he asked her for so many details concerning the circumstances of the case that, unwittingly, he merely emphasized all the more everything that the plaintiff's counsel had previously said about her stupidity. This clinched the case for the plaintiff.

I would say that this was a case which the plaintiff's lawyer won during the *voir dire*—with a subsequent assist from his adversary.

Another case which was won, in my opinion, while the jury was being selected was tried by a young lawyer who was defending a department store in a negligence action. The plaintiff contended that while she had been standing erect on a descending escalator, it had suddenly jerked backward and caused her to fall.

Counsel for the defendant, who had thoroughly prepared his case, knew these details of the complaint from his pretrial examination of the plaintiff. He inquired of each prospective juror:

Q. Will you accept the law applicable to this case as the judge gives it
   to you?
Q. Will you accept the physical law of nature known as Newton's Law,
   should the judge so charge you?

When the time came for the judge to charge the jury, counsel asked the Court to take judicial notice of Newton's Law that a body in motion tends to remain in motion. The Court agreed to so charge the jury.

Then, in summing up his case, counsel pointed out to the members of the panel how "the escalator, in descending, transferred its momentum to the body of the plaintiff, causing her to be carried forward." Consequently, when the alleged backward movement of the escalator occurred, there would have to have been, according to Newton's Law, a lapse of time until the movement of the plaintiff's body in a forward direction could be counteracted by the backward momentum of the escalator. Thus, the body of the plaintiff would have fallen forward.

Yet, he reminded the jury, the plaintiff, on direct examination, had denied that her body, in falling, had at any time moved forward when the escalator allegedly stopped and jerked backward. Hence, her story was contrary to the laws of nature.

In another case, which arose out of an automobile accident, a friend of mine was defending the driver of the vehicle. During the *voir dire,* the plaintiff's attorney elicited from one of the prospective jurors the fact that he himself had once been in an accident, but not one involving automobiles. Hence, he said, he would have no prejudice or bias whatsoever in serving as a juror in this case. But counsel for the defendant refused to accept this statement at its face value. He suspected that something of significance was being held back, and he decided to leave nothing to chance. Accordingly, without antagonizing either the venireman or the other members of the panel, counsel proceeded to probe and prod until he was able to ferret out the nature of the accident. Then, by means of an artfully contrived series of questions, the attorney for the defense succeeded in bringing to light the fact that the juror had himself been the plaintiff in a poorly founded action for alleged negligence:

Q. You say that you were involved in an accident, but it was not an automobile accident. Could you tell us what kind of accident it was?

A. I was on a sled.

Q. You were on a sled when you got hurt? Where were you on the sled?

A. I was up in the Poconos.

Q. You mean you were at a resort?

A. Yes.

Q. Well, was this a toboggan type of sled?

A. No.

Q. Well, just what happened? Was it a regular sled?

A. Well, we were on a sled.

Q. A regular sled you mean? Like what we went belly-whopping on as kids?

A. Yes. We were going down a hill, and the sled was overturned when it hit a hole.

Q. What kind of hole was it?

A. I think a chuck hole.

Q. You mean a woodchuck hole?

A. Yes.

Q. Which was covered with snow?

A. Yes.

Q. And you were suing the hotel?

A. Yes.

These answers clearly indicated a lack of frankness on the part of the prospective juror in giving details about his own experience. But, aside from providing a ground for excusing him, the result of counsel's persistent interrogation was to give the rest of the panel the impression that this juror's lawsuit was a typical example of the sort of unjust claim that was also being put forward in the case at issue. Thus, adroit questioning in the selection of the jury served at the same time to lay the basis of a favorable verdict.

Probably every lawyer who has ever tried a case has his own stories to tell about juries and his own ideas on how to pick them. The fact is that this area of counsel's responsibility is a kind of no man's land stretching perilously between him and his adversary. It is a disputed domain, fraught with danger for all who tread upon it. From it men come back with all sorts of reports about what they encountered there and with all sorts of plans for its conquest, but with no clear maps of its topography, because conditions there are always subject to change. The practices and procedures that I have described here can be considered nothing more than rules of thumb or rough guidelines for finding one's way over this treacherous terrain. They can be neither exhaustive nor conclusive. Rather, they are intended as suggestive of the broad range of considerations that need to be taken into account during the *voir dire* in assessing prospective jurors. Perhaps, in the end, even more persuasive than any specific stratagem is the tone or attitude apparent from a venireman's response to the whole array of questions designed to probe into his outlook on the issues relevant to the case.

Certainly there is no system that I know of which will guarantee the right kind of panel. "There's no art to find the mind's construction in the face," says Shakespeare; nor, I may add, is there any science, either, that will enable one to judge character on the basis of a few minutes' conversation and observation. It is very easy for a lawyer to be misled by the juror who, as he is questioned, nods reassuringly and seems to agree wholeheartedly with everything that counsel says. The person who continually smiles ingratiatingly during the *voir dire* may very well act quite differently in the jury room.

A friend of mine had this interesting experience when he was trying a case on behalf of the defendant. After the jury had been out for about an hour, the jurors returned with a question for the judge. As they filed past the counsel table on their way back to the jury box, one of them winked at my friend and made the familiar Churchillian V for victory sign with his fingers. When the jury went back to deliberate further, defense counsel felt quite confident that it was only a matter of time before they would return with a verdict in favor of his client.

Twice the jury came back for further instructions, and each time the same juror telegraphed with a wink and a wordless sign of victory with his fingers a verdict for the defendant. Finally, when a verdict had been reached, the members of the panel filed back to the jury box, and the same wink and the same hand signal was once again flashed toward my friend. Then the foreman of the jury rose and announced a verdict in favor of the plaintiff.

Later, on being questioned about his conduct, the juror said simply that he thought it was a funny thing to do!

Even the most astute lawyers can be deceived by appearances. Bob Considine, the famous newspaper columnist, in an article entitled "My Son, the Law Student," relates the following incident:

> Mercurial Melvin Belli was asked, "Why are you so suspicious of these would-be Dallas jurors? Some of them look real friendly to you."
>
> "Tell you why, son," he said. "Just after I got in this business, I was summing up my case before a jury one day when I noticed that I had somehow gotten through to a nice fat lady in the box. She was beginning to cry.
>
> "Well, I lost by a hung jury, 11–1. And guess who was the lone juror who voted against me? The fat gal. I saw her later and asked her how come, for she obviously was touched by my plea.
>
> "'Not at all,' she said. 'I was just feeling sorry for you, as a young lawyer trying to get ahead in life. And I kept thinking of my poor son. He graduates from law school next month.'"

How completely deceptive appearances can be is illustrated by one of the most remarkable incidents that has ever been brought to my attention. It occurred to a friend of mine, Mr. George Wolf, one of the really great attorneys at the New York bar. His client, Jack Kearns, who had been Jack Dempsey's manager, was charged with using the mails to defraud.

In selecting the jury, Mr. Wolf naturally sought to obtain as many men as he possibly could, in the belief that his client's colorful career would be more likely to arouse nostalgic and sympathetic feelings in men than in women. However, he did make an exception in the case of one woman, who in the *voir dire* admitted to being a boxing fan.

No sooner had the trial begun than he bitterly regretted having selected her, all the more as he could have excused her with one of the peremptory challenges he still had left. He quickly became convinced that she was a decidedly cold, unsympathetic person. Every time he glanced in her direction, he felt a hostile rebuke. In her stern visage and forbidding mien he could see that she resented him and disliked his client intensely.

After the judge had charged the jury, counsel noted several exceptions. One in particular was based on his contention that the judge had erred in his recitation of the facts elicited from the chief witness for the Government. By way of proof, counsel attempted to cite specific passages from the transcript of the testimony, which he suggested that the Court read to the jury. This the judge refused to do, remarking that the panel was to be governed by its recollection of the witness' testimony, not by his or counsel's. However, Mr. Wolf persisted in asking for permission to read from the transcript, which he flourished before the jury as he made his plea. When he had prolonged the discussion of the point as much as he could, the judge at last admonished him to be seated.

Thereupon, to the astonishment of the judge, counsel, and a jammed courtroom, the lady rose and, dramatically pointing her finger at the judge, said in a loud and angry voice, "Why don't you let Mr. Wolf read the witness' testimony to us?"

The judge stared at the juror in utter amazement, but she did not flinch under his steady gaze. She was evidently not to be overawed by the majesty of the judge's position or by his austere, dignified appearance.

Finally, the spell was broken. The judge turned to counsel and said rather wearily, "All right, then, read the transcript, Mr. Wolf; please do."

To counsel's great surprise, the first person to reach him after the "not guilty" verdict was the lady. She gave him a hearty kiss of congratulations and told him that his opening statement to the jury had convinced her of the defendant's innocence.

Even a lawyer as perceptive and astute as F. Lee Bailey can occasionally be misled by what appear to be unmistakable signs of partiality on the part of a juror. When Dr. Carl Coppolino was on trial for the murder of his wife, one of the jurors, as they left for dinner on the evening before they handed down their verdict, nodded in apparently friendly fashion to Mr. Bailey on passing him as he sat at the defense counsel table. Later that night, when the jury retired, the same juror winked and smiled at him. At least one member of the panel, it seemed, was for acquittal.

When the jury returned to the courtroom the next day to announce its verdict, one of Mr. Bailey's assistants noted that there were tears in this juror's eyes. Evidently the "guilty" verdict was a compromise. The defense moved that it be set aside.

But when the juror was asked to explain his tears, he said, "Tears? Hell, I wasn't crying. I just had a bad cold. My decision was made up long before I ever went into that jury room. That's what I told the rest of the jurors."

Finally, counsel comes to his last question: "Does any juror know any reason why he cannot be fair and impartial in this case?" Counsel thus seeks to take care of possible causes of bias that he may have overlooked in the course of his inquiry. At the same time, he puts the members of the panel on their honor to come forward with anything that they think would debar them from conscientiously serving. The answers he receives to this question may yet give him a clue to the possible challenge of a juror.

Otherwise, he is ready to bring the *voir dire* to an end. Every member of the panel has passed his every test. All are qualified, under the law, to serve, and there are no statutory grounds for excusing any of them for actual or presumable bias. Counsel has been their patient teacher, explaining the essentials of his case, answering their questions, and instructing them in their responsibilities. He has probed, so to speak, into their hearts, prodded their consciences, and praised their virtue. He has explored their attitudes on the crucial issues in the case, and they have given him their solemn assurances of their absolute impartiality and lack of bias. Their backgrounds—occupational, marital, and educational—are unexceptionable, and their experience as jurors or litigants in other cases leaves nothing to be desired. They seem responsive, alert, and sincere.

And so, at last, counsel looks at the jury and says the fateful words, "This jury is satisfactory."

Let us hope that he will not have reason to regret this judgment.

III

OPENING TO THE JURY

9

Winning the Opening Round

Once both sides have signified to the presiding judge that the panel is satisfactory, the jury is sworn. The word "juror," in fact, is derived from a Latin expression which means "one who takes an oath." Usually administered by the clerk of the court, it binds the panel, as a body, to render a "true verdict according to the evidence."

The trial now begins in earnest.

"Counsellor," says the Court, "you may open to the jury."

If a civil suit is being tried, these words would first be addressed to the attorney for the plaintiff. They are the signal for starting the first round. From this point on, the struggle between the opposing lawyers is aimed primarily at winning the minds of the jurors.

Counsel approaches the jury box, bows respectfully to the judge, and says, "May it please the Court" or "If Your Honor pleases."

Having rendered this formal and traditional obeisance to the majesty of the law, he next turns to the panel and begins his opening statement:

"Mr. Foreman [or Madame Forelady] and members of the jury . . ." or simply, "Ladies and gentlemen of the jury . . ."

At the outset, he will want to identify his client, so that the jury may know who he is. Rather than just say, "My client, Mr. Jones, is in court," it is better to turn to him, ask him to rise, and, once again addressing the panel, introduce him: "The gentleman whom you see standing is my client, Mr. Jones, the plaintiff in this case."

Then, after requesting his client to be seated, counsel proceeds to state his case. His foremost objective, at this time, is to give the jury his client's version of the facts and to lay the foundations of the proof to be presented in substantiating the claim. A clear word-picture of the chief events and circumstances involved, narrated in the chronological sequence in which they occurred, will make it easy for both judge and jury to follow the main thread of the case through the maze of details to be brought out later in the testimony. At the same time, an attorney can use the occasion to strengthen his rapport with the members of the jury and to dispose them to be sympathetic toward his client.

This is the first of two opportunities that counsel will have during the trial to address the panel directly at some length. Later, after all the testimony has been heard, he will have another chance to plead his cause when he sums up his case and makes his final appeal to the jury.

Obviously, then, there should be some relation between the prologue to the drama and its epilogue. At least to a certain extent, and so far as possible, the two should be planned together and seen as complementary parts of a well-shaped whole.

The first step toward this end is for counsel to satisfy himself that his introductory statement to the jury sets forth what lawyers call a "prima facie case."

It will be recalled that in drawing up his complaint and his bill of particulars, counsel went to great pains to make sure that he had at least enough proof to justify his client's right to a trial of the issue. This is, of course, a matter of law, to be settled by a ruling of the Court, and therefore not properly within the province of the jury. But the opening statement, although addressed primarily to the jurors, is also heard by the judge and opposing counsel. Both will be listening attentively to it to see whether it presents a prima facie case. If it does not, defense counsel will move to "dismiss on the opening remarks," on the ground that the plaintiff has not demonstrated his right to be in court. Should the judge grant the motion, there is no need for the defendant even to offer a rebuttal of the plaintiff's allegations. The plaintiff will simply have been knocked out in the first round.

Although the appellate courts frown upon such technical "knockouts," they sometimes occur when plaintiff's counsel, in his opening statement, leads with his chin by failing to state facts sufficient to constitute a cause of action or by admitting some fact fatal to his case. The best way to insure against a humiliating defeat of this kind at the very outset is to leave nothing to chance. If the complaint and the bill of particulars have been properly drawn in the first place, they should be used as a guide in planning the content and arrangement of the opening statement.

This, as a rule, is not recorded by the court reporter in civil cases. But either counsel or both may request that the opening remarks to the jury be made a part of the trial record. Although these requests are generally made in advance, they may be made at any time during the course of the opening, and they are usually granted. The customary form is substantially as follows: "I respectfully request that the opening statement be taken down by the reporter." When such a request is made by defense counsel, it may be taken as an indication that he is laying the groundwork for a motion to "dismiss on the opening remarks." It is therefore a signal for special caution on the part of counsel for the plaintiff in this important and possibly even crucial phase of the trial.

For example, he has to be on his guard against inadvertently destroying his own case right at the start by making statements in his opening remarks which are at variance with those in the complaint and the bill of particulars. An alert adversary, noting the contradiction, may call it to the attention of the Court and move to have the entire case dismissed as soon as counsel for the plaintiff has completed his opening to the jury.

This is precisely what happened recently in a case of serious injury to a twelve-year-old girl. The child lost the sight in her left eye when she was struck by a ball while playing a game called "bombardment," "low ball," or "cannon ball" in a summer playground. In this game, the children were divided into two teams, with a line between them, and were given several balls. The object of the game was for each side to throw the balls at the opposing team so that its members would be struck below the waist. Those who failed in their aim were eliminated from their team until the game was completed. As the plaintiff was about to be eliminated, but before she could move off the play area, she was struck in the eye by a ball thrown at her head by one of the participants.

In the complaint and the bill of particulars, it was alleged that the children had been provided with *three hard balls*, smaller than volley balls. Accordingly, what the attorney for the plaintiff should have said, in his opening statement, following the allegations made in these documents, was, "The child was struck by one of three *hard* balls smaller than volley balls." Instead, he stated that the child had been struck by balls "the size of softballs or somewhat larger than baseballs." This, of course, put the case in an entirely different light and in contradiction with the complaint and the bill of particulars. Consequently, on motion of opposing counsel, the complaint was dismissed.

To be sure, the Appellate Division of New York State, in keeping with its liberal tradition, reversed the judgment of dismissal. Nevertheless, the fact remains that counsel lost his case in the court below. If he had not deviated, in his description of the balls, from that contained in the complaint and the bill of particulars, he could have spared his client the anxieties and expense attendant upon an appeal. How simple it would have been for counsel to have referred to the balls in precisely the terms in which they were described in his pleadings!

In requesting that the opening statement of the plaintiff's attorney be recorded by the court reporter, defense counsel may also intend to make other use of it. He may want to refer to it in his own summation by quoting parts of it verbatim. His purpose in doing so would be to compare the promises made or implied in the opening with the actual testimony and evidence presented, and to highlight the disparities. Hence the importance of correlating the opening statement not only with the complaint and the bill of particulars but with every document, deposition, and exhibit that counsel intends to place in evidence. He must make sure that from the beginning of the trial to its end, from his opening remarks to his final summation, his whole line of attack presents to his adversary a solid and unwavering front, without any logical gaps into which opposing counsel might drive the slightest wedge.

If any record of opening remarks is called for at all, the request for it is more likely to come from the defense counsel than from the attorney for the plaintiff. On rare occasions, however, plaintiff's counsel may ask that his adversary's opening be recorded in full. There can be no hard-and-fast rule as to when and under what circumstances such a request should be made. Only trial experience will enable a lawyer, when he is representing the plaintiff, to judge the possible effectiveness of this tactic. But unless he can clearly envision in advance the use that he might make of this record, he would be well advised not to ask for it, for he thereby puts his opponent on guard.

On the other hand, when a defense attorney knows that no record is being made of his opening remarks, he may become careless and make statements which he would otherwise avoid. For this reason, counsel for the plaintiff should listen very carefully to his opponent's opening to the jury. At the first sign of any statement prejudicial to the plaintiff, an objection should immediately be entered on the record. Since the court reporter did not record the objectionable language used by defense counsel, it should be repeated in full by plaintiff's counsel for the record, and a motion should be made for a mistrial. Should the Court deny the motion, at least a record for appeal will have been preserved.

For example, suppose that the plaintiff is suing to recover on a promissory note. If defense counsel speaks of him in disparaging terms, the objection may be formulated thus:

> Your Honor, I ask that the record show that the defendant's counsel just stated to the jury that my client, who is suing on a promissory note, is a "dead beat" and once filed a petition in bankruptcy. On the basis of that statement, I now move for the withdrawal of a juror and the declaration of a mistrial. ["Withdrawal of a juror" is legal jargon for "mistrial," to which a court may resort when it appears that a trial cannot proceed without injustice to a party.]

Naturally, the same form can be adapted to fit any type of case in which the opening remarks of defense counsel are objectionable.

There is probably no part of the trial in which a fledgling lawyer is likely to betray his inexperience more flagrantly than in opening to the jury on behalf of the plaintiff. For a beginner, the temptation is strong, now that he has the center of the stage for the first time, to use it as an opportunity to exhibit his own forensic prowess. It is, after all, somewhat intoxicating to exchange the rather colorless role of legal counsellor for the far more glamorous one of advocate and pleader at the bar. With the jury as his captive audience, he may find himself yielding, almost without realizing it, to the temptation to indulge in impassioned flights of eloquence in his client's cause. Enlarging on the injuries or damages suffered by the plaintiff, counsel may be moved to employ all his rhetorical resources in painting an unforgettable picture of the enormity of the wrong that he is calling upon the jury to set right. Before he knows it, he may allow himself to be carried away by the emotions of the moment and launch into a lengthy harangue.

Afterwards, as he returns to his seat beside his client, counsel may even congratulate himself on his performance. Did he not give everything he had in him in that glorious hour? Did he not work himself up into a fine fervor? Did he not go in fighting and swinging as hard as he could? Isn't that the way to win the opening round?

Definitely not!

The time has not yet come for such an approach—if, indeed, it is necessary at all. At this point in the trial, all that the jury wants and needs to hear from counsel for the plaintiff is a clear, forthright statement explaining:

What happened that caused the dispute between the parties?

How was the defendant to blame? What did he do that he should not have done, or what should he have done that he failed to do?

What injuries or damages did the plaintiff sustain as a result of the defendant's blameworthy conduct?

How is the dollar value of these damages to be calculated?

No display of histrionics or oratorical pyrotechnics is required to answer these questions. Indeed, anything more than a calm, factual presentation can seriously harm the plaintiff's case. A lawyer who indulges in a grandstand play when opening to the jury may impress his client, but, more often than not, he merely puts a noose of his own making around his neck.

For one thing, undue emotionalism on counsel's part suggests that he may be trying to cover up weaknesses or deficiencies in the complaint. His glittering verbal showmanship may do much to undermine the confidence of the jurors in his candor and integrity. What they want is something simple, natural, and, above all, sincere. A sincere speaker can overcome many obstacles. He can win a sympathetic hearing even from those inclined to be difficult to convince. On the other hand, the very suggestion of any affectation in speech or manner could be fatal to his cause. Ralph Waldo Emerson puts the matter thus:

> I have heard an experienced counsellor say that he never feared the effect upon a jury of a lawyer who does not believe in his heart that his client ought to have a verdict. If he does not believe it, his unbelief will appear to the jury, despite all his protestations, and will become their unbelief.

As he aptly remarks, "What you are stands over you and shouts so loud I cannot hear what you say to the contrary."

Moreover, high-pressure tactics lead almost inevitably to exaggerated claims that cannot later be substantiated by the evidence. Besides, if all the ammunition is used in the opening salvo, what will be left for the final assault?

Indeed, vanity on the part of counsel can prove very costly to his client. The self-centered attorney is generally too busy trying to sound like Cicero or Demosthenes to keep his mind on the business at hand. In the end, he risks jeopardizing his whole case by straining to make an impression on the courtroom spectators with his dazzling grandiloquence or by trying too hard to say something sensational that will make a big splash in the newspapers. He forgets that if the verdict is appealed to a higher tribunal, its judgment will be based on a review of the trial record, not on the press reports of his speeches to the jury.

In this regard, a lawyer can learn much from the observations made by Bob Considine, a veteran sports reporter, concerning the fatal deficiency that prevented Max Baer from becoming the outstanding heavyweight fighter that he could have been:

> Benny Leonard [former world lightweight champion] once told me that the reason Baer wasn't the greatest fighter of all time was because he recognized friends at the ringside while fighting. "He'll never be much," Leonard said, as the whole world hailed Max after he beat Primo Carnera for the title in a crazy and wonderful fight that sometimes resembled Graeco-Roman wrestling. "Just when Max gets a guy lined up and ready to take out, he sees Walter Winchell in the fourth row, drops his guard, and waves to him," Leonard said. "Soon as he does, he's no longer a killer. A fighter's got to stay a killer."

In like manner, counsel must be careful to keep his eyes at all times on the trial record rather than on the spectators or the press, or he may be knocked out while taking a mental bow.

Some lawyers think that this was the mistake made by the dynamic Melvin Belli in trying the Ruby case. Even a lay commentator, Max Lerner, observed in an article in the New York *Post* entitled "Ruby Tragedy":

> While I do not minimize Mr. Belli's talents and I consider him a talented trial lawyer doing a faithful job within the framework of his personality, there's no way to escape the fact that he tried to put a whole city on trial, and then asked twelve men and women from *that* city to acquit his client.
>
> The defense talked too big from the start, promised too much that it found it could not deliver later. Many were under the impression (I was one) that Belli had the testimony on Ruby's "psycho-motor epilepsy" all wrapped up and under lock and key, impregnable to attack. It seemed to be a three-layer defense-in-depth: a clinical psychologist who had given Ruby a battery of diagnostic tests, a psychiatrist who testified that his was the sort of sick mind that blacked out in rage, an expert on encephalograms, who could show the jury the tracings of Ruby's brain with the spiking bursts that showed organic brain damage. There was even talk that Belli would stage a psychological test right there in the courtroom.
>
> As it turned out, the experts for the defense were all but matched by experts for the prosecution. The jury was bewildered or bored; several of the women jurors are even rumored to have dozed during the technical testimony, and the whole process of presenting experts by both

sides (an "adversary" process that should have been outdated long ago) left the expert evidence pretty well canceled out.

Very different, and much more sensible, is the procedure followed by the less flamboyant type of trial lawyer. Disdaining all affectation, he addresses the jury in a quiet, conversational tone, as if he were telling a story to a congenial group of friends in his living room. Without straining after effects, he presents a temperate and dignified statement of the essential facts of the plaintiff's case. His tale is recounted in a plain, unvarnished style, with a restraint that suggests his complete belief in the righteousness of his client's cause. Whatever private doubts counsel may have he conceals in the secret recesses of his heart. Nobody listening to him could possibly suspect that he is anything but supremely assured.

One is not likely to hear an able and seasoned advocate bring the merits of his case into question by resorting to such clichés as, "We expect to prove . . . ," "We expect to show . . . ," "We hope to prove beyond a peradventure of a doubt . . . ," or "We expect to convince you that . . ." Rather, he says simply and positively, "The facts in this case are these . . ." and then proceeds, in a straightforward way, to set them forth affirmatively and without qualification. And, throughout, he keeps the emphasis on "facts," not surmises, promises, hopes, expectations, suppositions, inferences, or opinions. Instead of telling the jury that he has two witnesses who will testify "that they think that they saw the defendant go through the red light," he asserts flatly, "The defendant went through the red light." Even though counsel may be fully aware that the evidence favorable to his client may later be controverted, he interprets it at all times in a one-sided way, as if there could be no question about its probative value.

Indeed, far from overstating his case, an astute lawyer prefers to begin by understating it. He thereby avoids promising to prove more than he can. In this connection, he keeps in mind the sage advice that Abraham Lincoln once gave to one of his friends:

> In law it is good policy never to plead what you need not, lest you oblige yourself to prove what you cannot.

Mr. Clyde Woody, when he appeared recently as attorney for the defendant in a murder trial, after listening to the prosecutor's opening statement to the jury, characterized it as being "in the nature of a politician's promise." He thereby made implicit reference to the notorious fact that the platform planks and pledges of politicians are, as a rule, conveniently forgotten once the election is over, and he suggested that this prosecutor's promises would likewise not be redeemed.

However, the crucial difference between a politician's promise and a prosecutor's promise in his opening to the jury is that the former does not have to be redeemed until after the election, which itself takes place only after an intervening period of some two or three months, whereas the prosecutor must redeem his promises before the end of the trial. The politician has plenty of time before the next election in which to find excuses for his failure or to divert attention from it entirely, but the duration of the trial itself marks the limit of the time a lawyer is given in which to keep his promises before the jury passes judgment. In short, a lawyer has to be as good as his word before the trial ends and fulfill all his promises.

Hence, an attorney who starts his case by tying himself to commitments that he cannot subsequently meet may unwittingly be delivering his own and his client's requiem. For if he later fails to provide the proof he led the jury to expect, he will be giving his adversary ammunition for a devastating summation in which all the disparities between promise and performance are mercilessly exposed to view. It is better for the jury to be pleasantly surprised by the evidence than disappointed by its failure to fulfill the expectations raised in counsel's opening remarks.

For the same reason, he will do everything he can to curb the natural tendency toward verbosity that seems to be the besetting sin of our profession. More often than not, lawyers talk too long. They ramble on and on, without knowing when to stop. Many seem to have an irresistible impulse, once they stand before a jury, to indulge in an extended, disjointed monologue in which they unload everything on their minds. They scatter their fire in all directions at once, in the hope of somewhere hitting something.

But the only effect of such hit-or-miss tactics is to distract the members of the jury from the main line of the argument and to bog them down in a morass of irrelevant details. The ability to separate the wheat from the chaff is a skill that the trial lawyer has to master if he is to be successful in handling juries. He must learn how to hew to a clearly marked, straight line to his goal, through the mass of luxuriant undergrowth that tends to spring up in any disputed area. The course counsel maps in his opening remarks should lead the jury along a direct route, without any detours, twists, or turns. And the movement from each point to the next along the way should be lively and continuous, without lengthy stops to belabor every issue.

Diverging from the main road to enter into byways merely leaves the members of the jury confused about the direction in which counsel proposes to lead them. In fact, mingling important with unimportant and essentially irrelevant details can sometimes prove disastrous, as the following incident illustrates.

As a result of a fire and explosion, a mother and several of her children were burned to death. Her husband sued in his capacity as administrator of the estate. It seems that earlier in the evening he had left the house after a heated argument with his wife. Some time later, she went looking for him and found him in a bar and grill. There they soon came to blows and mauled each other so badly that they had to be taken first to a police station and then to a hospital for treatment. On returning home later that night, they went to bed, and the fire occurred shortly thereafter. The plaintiff alleged that a defective gas range had been so ineptly repaired by the utility company on the previous day that gas, escaping into the apartment, ignited and exploded.

In opening to the jury, the plaintiff's attorney chose to enter into all the foregoing facts, including the details relating to the altogether irrelevant fight between husband and wife earlier the same evening, their subsequent brawl in the bar and grill, the episode at the police station, and the treatment they received at the hospital. By injecting a recital of these immaterial details into a simple complaint of negligence on the part of the defendant, counsel merely provided his adversary with extraneous matter that eventually destroyed the plaintiff's case.

To be sure, there may be occasions when a rather circumstantial exposition is desirable in opening to the jury. If, for example, the issues involve a complicated set of facts, condensing or omitting any of them might tend to weaken the framework of the case. Similarly, a lawyer would be well advised to elaborate in his opening remarks if his witnesses speak a foreign language and require an interpreter, or if their English is so poor that it may be difficult to understand them. But even under such conditions, counsel must keep in mind that the purpose of extending his remarks is to facilitate comprehension. He should say no more than suits his purpose.

For the longer he speaks, the more he multiplies his chances of saying the wrong thing. The more he says, the more he risks. The greater the number of his words, the greater the number of possibilities of offending, boring, bragging, gossiping, misrepresenting, or at least of being misunderstood. For the inflated windbag who scatters his whirling words with abandon, the caution of Thomas à Kempis, "No man can safely speak but him who loves silence," is apropos, as is also the Biblical maxim (Prov. 10:19): "In the abundance of words there does not fail to be transgression, but the one keeping his lips in check is acting discreetly."

A clear, concise opening cannot fail to have a good effect on the jury. We often regard the person who does not say much with a great deal of respect. In appraising his intelligence, we tend to resolve every doubt in his favor. "He who spares his words has true wisdom. Even a fool when he holdeth his peace is counted wise, and he that shutteth his lips is esteemed a man of understanding" (Prov. 17:27, 28). All of us are inclined to say a hearty "Amen!" to George Eliot's beatitude: "Blessed are they who, having nothing to say, refrain from giving us wordy evidence of the fact."

Garrulousness, however, is not the only fault that can impair the effectiveness of counsel's opening to the jury. At the opposite extreme from the overexuberance of the verbose lawyer is the stammering diffidence of the panic-stricken advocate. Apprehensive about the merits of his case, he is assailed by doubts and misgivings even before he begins. His confidence may have begun to ooze out of him several days prior to the date of the trial, and by the time he faces the jury he is a pitiable spectacle to behold. Unsure of himself, and nervous at the very thought of the awesome responsibility that has been entrusted to his care, he feels drained of every emotion but fear. His voice quavers, his hand shakes, and the words stick in his throat, as if he were in the grip of some malevolent demon.

This kind of reaction is by no means confined to the neophyte trying his first case. It is natural for any sensitive and conscientious lawyer to feel somewhat shaky before starting a trial, and no amount of successful courtroom experience can altogether insure against the recurrence of such feelings each time a new trial is begun. In fact, they may well remain with him throughout his career. In this respect, the "stage fright" of a lawyer is much like that of any other performer, and he may learn how to deal with it by profiting from the experience of actors and concert artists who go through the same agonies.

An extreme case was recounted in an article by John Gruen entitled "Who's Nervous? Everybody!" which appeared in the magazine section of the New York *Herald Tribune* of January 12, 1964. He tells the story of "the fairly well-known young pianist who, a few seasons back, gave a recital at Town Hall."

He strode confidently enough across the stage, sat down at the piano, and began his first piece, Schumann's Sonata No. 3, a work that opens with a forceful G minor chord. He lifted both hands high above the keyboard and then struck the opening chord with such impact that he simultaneously struck his head on the piano lid board and knocked himself cold. It was the shortest concert in the annals of Town Hall. Later, it was learned that the young man had suffered only a minor injury, and the incident was attributed to a bad attack of nerves.

A lawyer, too, can knock himself out in the first round if he lets his emotions gather steam until he explodes before judge and jury. On the other hand, it may be reassuring to reflect that even the best-known and most accomplished artists are not immune to feelings of terror before each performance. Harold C. Schonberg, music critic of the New York *Times,* in an article entitled "The Rubinstein Touch, Untouched at 75," which appeared in its magazine section on January 26, 1964, reports that this great pianist, who has been appearing in concert halls all over the world for seventy-one years, terrifies his wife before every one of his recitals. Here is how she describes the tortures she goes through:

> On the way to the concert, in the taxi, Artur will say that his fingers are spaghetti, that he will have memory lapses, that he will disgrace himself, that he will never play again. He reduces me to absolute jelly. I understand, but when I sit in my box, I die a thousand deaths. Then he comes out and plays the first measures, and I know everything is going to be all right.

Schonberg then continues:

> Rubinstein nevertheless admits to butterflies before he walks out. "Fear before each concert is the price I pay for my superb life." His nervousness immediately disappears when he strikes the first note.

As a young trial lawyer, I too, when I started to try a case, would be nervous and unsteady. I used to feel a persistent, nagging pain in my stomach, and my knees would knock together like castanets. This feeling remained with me for some time. A lawyer who experiences it need not be ashamed of it. It is, after all, only normal to feel some fear when one considers that one's client may lose money or property or may be sentenced to prison if one mishandles the case. How can a lawyer be altogether imperturbable in the face of such a responsibility?

As proof that even the experienced attorney is filled with trepidation as he approaches the time of trial, I may cite a passage from a letter which John W. Davis, one of America's greatest lawyers and a candidate for the office of President of the United States, wrote to his mother before his first appearance as Solicitor-General:

> I write September 14th with a positive shudder, for it means that October 14th and the opening of the Supreme Court are but thirty days away. No school boy ever dreaded his commencement day oration more. As the work of this position opens up to me, and my own slender equipment becomes more evident, I have a positively smothering sense of my inadequacy, more than I have ever been sensible of before, and closely bordering on panic. I am conscious of the fact that I am letting my fears oppress me beyond reason, yet, try as I will, I cannot shake them off.

Yet these very qualms can have the effect of arousing in counsel a desire to give his cause the best there is in him. In reasonable doses, fear can even be useful. It somehow tends to put a higher value on our successes. Although public performers may, as we have seen, become fainthearted and tremulous before each appearance, the minute they begin, if they are really well-rehearsed and prepared, their fright itself acts as a stimulant. Similarly, if counsel has done his "homework" properly, the knowledge he has acquired in his days and weeks of preparation should carry him through the worst part of the momentary crisis at the outset and prove all his dreadful forebodings to have been delusive.

The same is true in any kind of combat—and, after all, a lawyer has to think of himself as a combatant as well as a performer. Some of our most highly decorated war heroes talk quite frankly of the sweating fear they experienced before battle, but they are unable to say at what point courage overcame fear. As a noted preacher once said, "Fear rightly used is the father of courage." That scared feeling at the start, which virtually every advocate worthy of the name experiences, is simply part of the excitement of the trial. The problem is only to rise to the level of the challenge. The seasoned fighter may even come to enjoy the feverish flush that accompanies every bout and look forward with eagerness to the fray itself.

Perhaps it is the fear of appearing tongue-tied or faltering that may tempt a lawyer to resort to reading his opening remarks to the jury from a prepared script. In this way he seeks to insure himself against any lapses in memory, awkward pauses for reflection, or irrelevant digressions. But the price he has to pay for this artificial prop to his own self-confidence generally proves far too high. For what he gains in fluency he loses in spontaneity. Especially at the outset of a trial, a direct man-to-man—or rather, eye-to-eye—contact with the members of the jury is indispensable for establishing the necessary rapport. Besides, the jurors are not likely to form a favorable impression of a lawyer who appears so unsure of his case that he has to depend, for every word, on a written account of the facts.

Rather, the story he has to tell should flow from his lips as if it were being recounted for the first time. It should carry the note of freshness and candor that betokens deep conviction and complete familiarity with every detail. If counsel has really mastered his case, he ought to be able to present it effectively without the aid of anything more than a few brief notes that he may occasionally consult inconspicuously to verify a date or a number or to cue his recollection.

Any doubts he may have about his ability to give this kind of performance can easily be put to rest by a pretrial "dry run" in the privacy of his office. A friend of mine who is a lawyer once told me that when he went to his office one Sunday morning to pick up his briefcase, which he had forgotten to take home, he was surprised to hear, in the adjoining room, an address to an invisible jury being delivered in the familiar voice of his associate. As my friend was sneaking out to the elevator, the "rehearsing" lawyer spied him and said, "I didn't know anyone was in the office. I've been preparing my opening statements to juries this way for over twenty-five years." The speaker was a well-known and highly respected member of the bar specializing in trial work.

Like the well-rehearsed actor or, for that matter, any thoroughly practiced performer, a lawyer should give a public appearance of artlessness, naturalness, and ease, no matter how hard he may have striven to achieve it. He has, in other words, to practice the "art that conceals art."

Contributing greatly to the total impression that counsel makes in his first formal appearance before the jurors is the language that he chooses in addressing them. Indeed, Sir Alfred Denning, in his book *The Road to Justice* (London: Stevens & Sons, Ltd., 1955), considers the proper choice of words the first virtue of a lawyer.

> He must have a command of the English language so as to put his client's case clearly and strongly. . . . I put this first because the very reason for employing an advocate is that he should present the case in the best possible light, and to do this he must have a command of the

language in which he speaks. The key to the correct presentation of a case is at the outset to state the point at issue and then to recount the facts simply and in good order, keeping to what matters and omitting the rest.

Particularly susceptible of abuse in this respect is that part of the opening in which the attorney for the plaintiff, in a case involving a claim for bodily injury, undertakes to describe its nature and extent. Too often, lawyers will use medical terms solely to make the injuries appear more serious than they really are. Black-and-blue marks will be direfully referred to as "ecchymosis"; loss of appetite assumes the horrendous name of "anorexia"; and an ordinary bruise is elevated to the status of a "contusion."

If such words are used at all, they should immediately thereafter be defined, so that the members of the jury will know exactly what they mean. Otherwise, counsel runs the risk of having his verbal balloon unceremoniously deflated by his adversary, and the jurors may very well think that they have been imposed upon.

The same procedure should be followed with any technical terms that may be employed in opening to the jury. For example, if it should become necessary to speak of a "transcervical fracture through the left femur," counsel should at once follow with an explanation: "This, in common parlance, means a fracture of the left thigh." Or he might simply say, "When the doctor takes the stand, he will undoubtedly use this medical term; but I will ask him to explain it to you in laymen's language and perhaps offer an illustration." Of course, if counsel has any doubt whatsoever about whether his expert witness will appear to testify, it is better to include the explanation of technical expressions in his opening remarks.

In fact, there are even times when it may pay to use language that is rather earthy. A touch of appropriate humor at the opening of the trial is often an effective means of thawing what may appear to be coldness on the part of the jury. It is amazing how much the right word will sometimes do to help counsel reach the jurors, especially when he finds it necessary to break through what may seem like a massive barrier erected by the opening remarks of his adversary.

Here is how one trial lawyer handled such a situation. He was appearing before an all-male jury as counsel for a defendant charged with concealing assets. The case against his client was a strong one, and the able prosecutor's opening was devastating. When it was defense coun-

sel's turn to open, he found himself facing twelve grim jurors, all obviously determined to mete out stern justice to the defendant.

Yet within minutes after beginning his remarks, he had the satisfaction of seeing a distinct change take place in their attitude. Thereafter,
they seemed to favor him with expressions of warm, human interest
and even sympathy.

This extraordinary transformation was accomplished simply by the
injection of a bit of earthy humor into what might otherwise have
been a colorless recital of facts. Counsel began by informing the jurors
that the case involved a pants-zipper manufacturing business which his
client was induced to enter because of his strong belief that it was a
"cocksure" venture. "After all," counsel continued, "my client is not the
only person who has been embarrassed—financially or otherwise—by a
zipper failure."

Even the judge and the prosecutor joined in the hearty laughter
of the jurors.

But the effects of this jocularity were apparently more far-reaching
than the momentary hilarity to which it gave rise. Although the trial was
broken off, because the defendant changed his plea to guilty, he received only a suspended sentence. Yet, before the trial, counsel's offers
to plead guilty, on condition that the Government recommend no
more than an eighteen-month sentence, were repeatedly rejected. Undoubtedly the good will and good humor that had affected the jury
proved to be infectious.

The whole subject of the language and form of address appropriate
for the opening statement has been well treated by Sir Geoffrey Lawrence, Q.C., of the English Bar, in his article entitled "The Art of
Advocacy," which appeared in the December 1964 issue of the *American
Bar Association Journal.*

> When you have to open a case—an ordinary one with no particular
> point of law in it—never forget that you have the advantage of having
> fresh hearers who are ready to give their attention to you. That advan-
> tage should never be wasted. The first sentences of your opening speech
> should reduce the issues to a few simple words, because those few simple
> words are among the most important that you will ever have to speak
> in the course of a case. They must be lucid, clear, and able to be under-
> stood by the jury or the judge. Of course, they must be impeccably ac-
> curate, because if they are not, your opponent has been presented a
> stick which he can pick up and beat you with when he hasn't got
> anything better to hit you with.
> Then comes the narrative of the facts based on the evidence to be

called. That narrative must immediately attract and compel attention; it must be so apparently convincing in its logical sequence and arresting in its story that the jury can be left themselves to supply the answers to the points that you know your opponent is going to rely on later.

Above all, avoid monotony of tone or manner. The right dramatic emphasis must be put in at the right moment: a slight change of intonation; a small variation of pace; a significant pause in delivery. All these should be used to help the jury receive what you want them to hear, but, above all, at this stage there should be an air of moderation, not only because it conveys an impression of absolute fairness, but because it leaves room for greater emphasis later on in the case. Your case will never stand so high as it does at the moment when you have finished opening it. . . .

No wonder that, over two thousand years ago, the elder Cato concluded, "The ideal orator of our quest is a good man skilled in the arts of speech."

In planning his opening remarks, counsel should also keep in mind what he may have learned, during the *voir dire*, concerning the background of each juror. It sometimes requires only a little imagination and resourcefulness to put this knowledge to effective use in winning the favor of a few members of the panel right at the outset.

This, for example, is the way in which one lawyer succeeded in immediately putting three jurors in his corner by his alertness in exploiting what he had learned about them when he interrogated them concerning their competence to serve. His case had substantial merit, but there were many small weaknesses in it, chiefly relating to the character of his client, the plaintiff. Remembering that three of the jurors had told him they were artists, counsel seized upon the idea of comparing the trial of a lawsuit to the painting of a canvas or the creation of a work of art.

And so he began by likening his work as a lawyer, in the accident case he was trying, to the painstaking labor of an artist as he seeks to translate into a visual image on canvas a general idea in his mind. Each detail in counsel's account of the accident, he said, was like a brushstroke applied by a painter in order to fill in the picture. How easy it would be, the plaintiff's attorney continued, for someone, after the painting had been completed, to come along with a pencil or other object and ruin the whole work by punching holes in the canvas! But, the jurors were reminded, in spite of the destruction of the painting, the original idea of the artist remained unchanged. In other words, nothing could alter or destroy the basic thought that he was trying to express in pictorial terms—in this case, the essential facts of the accident, as narrated by counsel for the plaintiff.

Evidently the use of this analogy had its intended effect. The jury was unalterably deadlocked, nine to three in favor of the defendant. Significantly, the three who voted for the plaintiff were none other than the artists on the panel. Later, when the case was being retried, a settlement was reached.

Incidentally, this lawyer's shrewd approach to the jury also illustrates another important principle that should be followed in planning an opening statement. The beginning of the trial is the appropriate time for plaintiff's counsel to be frank and to anticipate any weaknesses in his case that he knows his adversary may try to play upon. Suppose, for example, that the plaintiff in an accident case had a few cocktails before the occurrence of the incident which is the subject of the complaint. If counsel has good reason to believe that his opponent is likely to lay stress on this point, the best course to follow is to beat him to the punch. A good deal of the expected sting of this revelation can be taken out of it if, in opening to the jury, the attorney for the plaintiff mentions the fact and explains the occasion—perhaps attendance at a wedding or a party—during which his client had a few drinks.

Similarly, in a personal injury action, the attorney for the plaintiff loses nothing in bringing out, in his opening statement, a prior ailment or injury that his client may have suffered, if there is any likelihood at all that defense counsel will try to make capital of it. In that case, the opening for the plaintiff might include some remarks to this effect:

> Four or five years before this accident, my client suffered from dizzy spells on account of having high blood pressure. He was hospitalized and subsequently discharged as completely cured. Since that time he has enjoyed good health, and there has been no recurrence of this condition. In the case that you will now hear, the plaintiff will tell you that he fell over an obstruction on the sidewalk because of the defendant's carelessness and that he struck his head on the pavement and sustained, among other injuries, attacks of dizziness unrelated to the prior ailment.

Frankness may win friends among the jurors, whereas reticence regarding the revelation of some fact that is later brought out by one's adversary may cost valuable jury support.

But while it may be desirable for plaintiff's counsel to anticipate the weaknesses in his own case, and to prepare the jury for them, it is not generally advisable for him to try to forestall the tactics of the defense or to rebut his opponent's case in advance. The opportunity for refuting it is best taken in the closing argument, not in the opening statement to the jury.

Sometimes, indeed, in the effort to ward off an expected blow by defense counsel, a lawyer may swing so wildly as to expose himself to a crippling onslaught from his adversary. For example, in the trial of a certain case, the plaintiff's attorney, knowing that opposing counsel would call as a witness a surgeon who had treated the plaintiff, referred to the doctor, in his opening remarks, as a "snake in the grass." The surgeon, a gray-haired, distinguished-looking individual, made an excellent witness for the defense. In his summation, the attorney for the defendant commented substantially as follows:

> Counsel for the plaintiff has called this fine, dignified, and revered physician, who has trained almost all the orthopedic surgeons in this community, a "snake in the grass." How reprehensible! Will not my enthusiastic young opponent take time in his closing argument to apologize for his unseemly aspersion on the character of this deeply respected gentleman and scholar?

And so, in his closing argument, the attorney for the plaintiff found himself constrained to spend almost all his allotted time in apologizing for his rashness, leaving little opportunity to discuss the real issues in the case.

Only in exceptional circumstances is it wise for counsel to touch on the anticipated defense, and even then mention of it should be brief. For example, he might say something like this:

> The defendant has pleaded, in response to this action for the recovery of the value of goods sold and delivered, what is known in the law as "payment." It will be for you to determine, after you have heard the evidence, whether he has sustained this defense. Please watch this phase of the case very carefully.

Even this kind of statement should not be made unless counsel has documentary or other proof that will destroy the defense.

On the other hand, if he does have such proof—for example, in the form of a memorandum signed by the defendant that negates his defense—the opening statement should give no inkling of it. After all, there is no point in showing one's cards to one's adversary. The more effective procedure is to wait until the defendant has testified and then to confront him with the document he signed.

For a similar reason, it is not a good idea for counsel to name or enumerate the witnesses that he intends to call. Something may happen during the course of the trial that makes it imprudent to call a particular witness. It is also possible that a witness who has promised to attend may fail to appear in court. In either event, opposing counsel may make much of the failure to put a promised witness on the stand. Counsel must keep such possibilities in mind if he is to adhere consistently to the sound principle of not promising in his opening remarks more than he can perform.

Nor should an attorney take it upon himself to expound to the jury what he conceives to be the law of the case. This is solely within the province of the Court to determine, sometimes after consultation with the lawyers for both sides, and often in the light of their specific requests and suggestions. In any case, it will be covered later in the trial by the judge's charge to the jury.

A lawyer who does overstep his bounds by intruding into the domain reserved to the Court is almost certain to have his transgression quickly noted and called to his and the jury's attention. The judge himself may interrupt him and say something to this effect:

"Counsellor, please do not discuss the law of the case. I will tell the jury, at the proper time, what the law is."

Or opposing counsel may rise and address the Court in some such terms as these:

"Your Honor, I believe counsel is exceeding his proper bounds. He is discussing the law of the case."

In either event, the jury is likely to get the impression, at the very outset, that counsel is violating a rule of which he ought to be cognizant. The effect can only be to diminish the estimation in which the panel holds him.

Instead, once he has presented the essential facts of the case, he should bring his opening remarks to an end. It is best to conclude with an expression of confidence that the jury will have no hesitation whatsoever, after hearing all the testimony, in awarding a verdict favorable to his client. Accordingly, the last words the jury should hear from counsel for the complainant before he takes his seat should be to this effect:

"I feel confident that when you have heard all the testimony in this case, you will bring in a verdict for the plaintiff."

Having said this, he should stop speaking. He has said enough, and now it is his opponent's turn to take the floor.

More or less the same general principles that make for an effective introductory statement on the part of counsel for the plaintiff should be followed by the attorney for the defendant in his opening remarks to the jury. He too will have need of clarity, brevity, and naturalness if he is to be successful in offsetting the impression made by his adversary and in making some mark of his own on the minds of the members of the panel.

Certainly he should not allow this opportunity to go unused, as sometimes happens when defense counsel waives his right to open to the jury. The justification usually advanced for doing so is that the premature disclosure of certain facts might give the plaintiff a chance to obtain additional proof or to find rebuttal witnesses. In other words, the defense, in order to avoid "tipping its hand," holds in abeyance information that, it is supposed, might more effectively be revealed, by way of surprise, later in the trial. And so, for the time being, the jury hears no answer whatever to the statements made by counsel for the plaintiff.

Frankly, I do not subscribe to this strategy. In my opinion, the defendant's counsel should rarely, if ever, waive his right to open to the jury. I believe that the average juror wants to hear both sides. After all, he is told that he is a judge of the facts, and for the brief time that he has been elevated to that lofty position, he wants to enjoy its prerogatives. He naturally assumes that, in order to discharge his duties properly, he should have an opportunity to hear the answer to the complaint. If none is forthcoming, he may well conclude that he is being short-changed, snubbed, or bypassed. Sensing that important information is being deliberately withheld from him, he may feel slighted and resentful. It is surely most unwise and quite unnecessary for counsel to risk giving the members of the jury the impression that he is in any way minimizing their status in their new and responsible role.

But just how far should he go in answering opposing counsel's opening statement? Should his opening remarks consist of a point-by-point refutation of every single item? Or should counsel content himself with a general denial? Should he set forth at the outset the entire plan of defense, or should he hold back certain information, keeping it in reserve for the moment later in the trial when its introduction can have the greatest effect?

As we shall see, the answers to these questions will be determined, to some extent, by the particular circumstances of each case. But even if counsel decides, for strategic or other reasons, to confine himself to the most general and sketchy indication of his defense, he should still say something in his opening remarks that at least raises an issue or tends to cast doubt upon the plaintiff's claim.

For example, he might say something like this:

Ladies and gentlemen of the jury, the purpose of the opening is to acquaint a jury generally with the nature of the case, so that the Court and the jurors may intelligently follow the testimony as it comes from the lips of the witnesses. What counsel for the plaintiff has just told you is nothing more than what his client or someone else told him and what he expects to prove. But sometimes, you know, the things clients tell a lawyer are not supported by evidence. They tell you things they hope to prove. Therefore, I ask you to follow the testimony closely to see whether counsel for the plaintiff really proves his contention.

Here, nothing has been said to indicate what line of defense will be followed, what counterevidence is to be introduced, what means will be used to refute the claims of the plaintiff. Nevertheless, the jury has been alerted to the possibility that not everything they heard from counsel for the plaintiff may stand up, and they have been placed on their guard. This is certainly the least that defense counsel should do in his opening statement.

Of course, if he was alert when his adversary was addressing the jury, the attorney for the defendant no doubt noted any and all promises made in that statement, such as to produce named or even unnamed witnesses or specific evidence. But the opening statement for the defense is not the place to make any particular mention of these promises, even if counsel for the defendant is convinced that his adversary will fail to fulfill them. The time to call attention to discrepancies between promise and performance is at the end of the trial, during the summation. To refer, in the opening for the defense, to particular promises made by counsel for the plaintiff, or even to mention them during the trial itself, merely gives one's opponent an opportunity to mitigate, explain away, or alter his position.

However, this does not mean that no mention whatsoever should be made of such promises. Some general reference to them, such as the following, is in order in opening for the defense:

Members of the jury, the plaintiff's attorney has just made a number of statements that he promises to prove. Please bear them in mind throughout the trial. It will eventually be for you and you alone to decide whether he has fulfilled these promises by his "proof."

What has been said about the language to be used by counsel for the plaintiff in his opening remarks applies as well to those of defense counsel. There is no need for displays of high-flown oratory or fancy words.

Indeed, they prove to be more often an obstacle than an aid to understanding. I recall hearing a case in which the plaintiff was suing three defendants. The attorney for one of them, in opening to the jury, expressed himself thus:

> You have heard from the plaintiff's attorney and the two defendants' attorneys who preceded me what they intended to prove. As far as my client is concerned, and as far as I myself am concerned, all I wish to state to you at this time is that there is amphoreus liability in this case.

As soon as he used this phrase, six or seven of the jurors immediately turned to me, as if to ask, "Judge, what is he talking about? What does the word mean?"

I returned the look, without, of course, betraying any emotion, while I surreptitiously pulled a dictionary out of the drawer. There I found that the word "amphora" means "a jar with two handles." Evidently this was the lawyer's way of saying that there are two sides to every case!

Unless counsel is prepared to hand each juror a dictionary whenever he employs unfamiliar words, he is best advised to express himself in plain English.

I might add, incidentally, that a pocket dictionary would not have sufficed in this instance, because the Greek word "amphoreus" is not to be found in it. This particular advocate would have had to supply the jury with Webster's Third New International Dictionary of the English Language, a 2662-page volume. All things considered, it would seem to be cheaper and far more sensible to stick to the language of everyday usage.

One of the signs of the novice in opening for the defense is that he attempts to refute every single claim presented by counsel for the plaintiff. Listening to his adversary's introductory statement to the jury, the fledgling advocate busily takes note of each and every point made against his client, determined, when his turn comes, to leave none unchallenged or unrebutted. He considers it his duty not only to parry every blow but to return it with an even more forceful counterblow.

What he forgets, of course, is that it is the plaintiff who has the burden of the proof. Nor does it ever shift throughout the trial. Under this burden the plaintiff usually has a great deal to prove. Indeed, one of the chief dangers that counsel for the plaintiff runs is, as we have seen, that he may state more in his opening than he can demonstrate in the subsequent testimony. In taking upon himself a burden that he has no responsibility to assume, defense counsel is accepting the same risk, quite unnecessarily. There is no need for him to vie with his opponent in this respect.

The problem of the defense is not to match blow for blow, but to probe for weak spots and to hit hard at them. Instead of seeking to disprove all of his opponent's contentions, the attorney for the defendant will have done enough if, after presenting a clear, affirmative statement of his client's story, he succeeds in being persuasive in regard to just one major deficiency in the plaintiff's case. For example, if counsel is defending a client in a personal injury suit, anything that will show contributory negligence on the plaintiff's part will be sufficient to invalidate the entire claim. Therefore, the proper procedure is to look for the crucial issue on which the defeat of the plaintiff's case depends and to stress this and this alone. Then the jury can be asked to follow the testimony on this issue with particular attention.

Besides, there are circumstances in which counsel can best serve his client's interests by frankly conceding certain points, rather than entering a general denial or seeking to disprove every assertion made by his adversary. For instance, when liability in personal injury actions cannot reasonably be questioned, defense counsel may achieve very good results by honestly admitting it in his opening remarks and confining the dispute to the question of the extent of the injuries and damages. His candor in making such an admission may induce the jury to be more receptive to his appraisal of the seriousness of the injuries suffered and the amount of the damages sustained. If he seeks, on the contrary, to defend the indefensible, he may end by having to yield ground where he might have taken the offensive.

Finally, it is important for defense counsel to make clear to the jury that the statements made by his adversary are not evidence. It is worth pointing out, especially if counsel for the plaintiff has been eloquent and presumably persuasive in his opening remarks, that he has no more personal knowledge of his client's case than does the judge or the jury. The proof must come, if it comes at all, from witnesses, exhibits, or depositions. Having made this point, counsel can then appropriately conclude by expressing his confidence that, when the jury has heard all the testimony and examined all the evidence, the defense will prevail. At the same time, the members of the jury should be informed that, at the end of the entire case, he will speak to them again, at greater length, in his summation.

10

Lawyers in Action

The best way to appreciate the different possible approaches that lawyers can take in opening to the jury is to observe them in action. It may
therefore prove instructive to pay a visit to one of those large central
courthouses to be found today in the midst of almost any great American metropolis, so that we may look in on what is going on in each
of several courtrooms where different actions are being tried. If we time
our arrival right, we may come at the very moment when, in one of
these trials, counsel for the plaintiff is beginning his introductory remarks to the jury. Here we may see, if we are lucky, how an able and
experienced attorney puts into practice the basic principles that should
underlie a good opening statement.

Let us, then, go from one floor to the next, until we find what we
are looking for.

The first case of this kind that we come upon involves a claim for
personal injury. Counsel for the plaintiff steps up front and begins:

May it please the Court [making a little bow to the judge].

Mr. Foreman and members of the jury, this is my first opportunity to
talk to you about this case, and I want each of you to know at the very
outset that whatever I say—or, for that matter, whatever counsel for the
defense may say—is not to be considered as evidence. By now, from
the questioning you underwent before being sworn as jurors, you have a
fair idea of the nature of the case. At this time, I should like to tell
you the facts as the plaintiff told them to me and as I believe the evidence will disclose.

I should like to state that I represent Mr. Jones, the plaintiff, who
sits there at the counsel table [pointing him out and asking him to rise].
He is suing, and that is why he is called the plaintiff. Mr. Brown, the
defendant, is sitting next to his lawyer.

Mr. Jones is a schoolteacher and claims that on April 15, 1960,
while he was in his classroom engaged in instructing his pupils, Mr.
Brown, who is a plumber, came into the classroom and began to hammer
away at a radiator. On at least two or three occasions, Mr. Jones asked
Mr. Brown to leave the classroom. Mr. Brown said that he would be out

of the classroom in a few minutes. As he said this, he banged the radiator with such violence that chips flew off the radiator, and one of the fragments struck the plaintiff in his right eye. The plaintiff cried out something to the effect that his eye was injured. Later, on the witness stand, he will give you his own words.

Mr. Brown immediately helped Mr. Jones to the nurse's office, where first aid was administered. But Mr. Jones continued to complain of severe pain, and he was taken to the hospital for treatment.

Mr. Jones sustained an injury which the doctors called "dendritic keratitis." This is a medical term which the doctor will explain in lay language. It involves the cornea of the eye, which was scarred, as well as the nerve. At any rate, as a result, Mr. Jones has lost sixty-five per cent of the vision in his right eye.

The plaintiff will show that the defendant was careless and negligent in the work he was doing. He failed to use protective means of guarding against the possibility that the chipped fragments might fly into the air and strike the teacher's eye. As a result of the defendant's negligence, the teacher, Mr. Jones, sustained the following damages:

1. Loss of salary, amounting to approximately $1,000.00.
2. Doctors' bills, amounting to approximately $500.00.
3. Hospital bills, amounting to approximately $500.00.

Testimony to establish the exact amounts of the plaintiff's special damages, including loss of salary, will be offered. These are the things Mr. Jones will show you in his proof.

From what we have heard so far, it is obvious that the plaintiff in this case has a competent advocate. Note, for example, how careful counsel is to avoid exaggerating the amount of the damages. If an otherwise perfectly good claim is not to be altogether invalidated, any statement he makes about the length of time his client was incapacitated, or the extent of the medical expenses incurred, must not be contradicted later by payroll records or by the testimony of the attending physician.

But let us hear this attorney to the end:

After you have heard the plaintiff and his witnesses testify, if it appears that the facts as I have outlined them to you are different from what you hear from the witnesses, please disregard what I told you. The facts *as you hear them* recounted from the witness stand, and only the facts, speak for themselves. After all, facts are what count. At any rate, I am confident that after you hear and weigh the testimony on both sides, you will have no hesitation whatsoever in awarding a substantial verdict in favor of Mr. Jones, the plaintiff, to compensate him for the injuries and damages he sustained.

Short as this opening was, counsel managed to put into it all that he needed to say.

During the brief interval needed for us to reach the next courtroom, where a suit for breach of contract is being tried, counsel for the plaintiff has already begun and has introduced his client. We find him proceeding as follows:

In this case, the plaintiff is a druggist by the name of Mr. Pill. He is suing the defendant, a stockbroker, by the name of Mr. Moneybags. Mr. Pill will show that on the sixth day of January, 1964, Mr. Moneybags failed to execute an order to purchase, on the plaintiff's behalf, one hundred shares of stock of Universal Quicksand, traded on the New York Stock Exchange. Mr. Pill will testify that he gave Mr. Moneybags an order to purchase one hundred shares of this stock at twenty dollars a share, which was the market price on January 6, 1964. On January 13, Mr. Pill instructed Mr. Moneybags to sell the stock, which had, in seven days, risen to twenty-five dollars a share. On the day Mr. Pill sought to sell his stock, he learned for the first time that his order to purchase had never been executed on January 6, and hence, he was not the record owner of the stock.

Mr. Pill seeks to recover from Mr. Moneybags the profit of $500 less commissions which he would have realized.

Unfortunately, time does not permit us to listen to the complete opening statement presented in every one of the trials we visit. But even the few snatches that we do hear, as we look in briefly on each, prove to be, for the most part, rewarding.

Here, for example, is how one lawyer introduces his statement of the facts:

I will tell you what I intend to prove by giving you a sketchy preview of what happened in this case. I am confident my recital of the facts will be sustained by the testimony and the evidence. But, members of the jury, always bear in mind that what I say is not evidence. I do not intend it to be accepted as evidence. Evidence must come from the lips of the witnesses and from the exhibits. Please give this case your careful attention, as I know you will, and follow the evidence as it is presented. The facts in this case are . . .

Without waiting to hear more, we just have time to catch the following remarks of the lawyer in the next courtroom:

In my opening statement it is not my purpose to shape your judgment. It is just to give you a preview of what happened to the plaintiff as it was related to me. The facts are . . .

Upstairs, counsel for the plaintiff is equally modest and restrained in his opening statement, but he also uses the occasion to remind the jurors of the solemnity of their responsibility:

You are now entering upon a very serious duty. You are going to decide a law suit. I am going to ask you to decide it on your promise to do
justice.

I wasn't present nor was my adversary present when the accident
happened. I'm only repeating what I was told. Here is what I know
about the case . . .

Somewhat more formal is the introduction adopted by the plaintiff's attorney in another case:

It is my privilege to present my opening statement. An opening statement, members of the jury, has for its purpose to explain the plaintiff's
case. It is not my intention at this time to attempt to persuade you. I
am not a salesman. I am not here to sell you a case. I am a lawyer, and
I am here to present the facts. My function at this stage is simply to
help you to understand better the plaintiff's case by telling you what the
plaintiff and her witnesses expect to prove . . .

Elsewhere, counsel for the plaintiff is opening with a bold and possibly dangerous gambit:

While I might be content in this opening to speak to you in vague
generalities, and thereby obtain some minor advantage in not advising
my learned adversary of my proof, I think that that would be unfair to
you and to him. I intend to tell you now—though a bit sketchily—what
the plaintiff expects to establish during the trial, and I am sure that
my adversary, when he rises to speak, will be equally fair and precise
with you in discussing his proof. The facts are . . .

What is plaintiff's counsel trying to achieve by this type of opening?
The burden of proof, as we have seen, rests upon the plaintiff. If his
counsel cannot show, in this opening statement, that he has a prima
facie cause of action, his adversary may move to have the case dismissed
on the opening statement alone. Hence, no matter what plaintiff's
counsel may say here, he *cannot* be "content to speak . . . in vague
generalities," lest he lose his whole case. But he knows full well that
the same is not true of his opponent. In opening to the jury in a civil
action, defense counsel, as we know, will often give no indication of the
nature of his defense. He is permitted to be reserved on this point
precisely because the obligation to present proof falls exclusively on the
plaintiff. Here, however, plaintiff's counsel is evidently hoping to throw
his adversary off guard and to "force" him to open in a manner that
will set forth some of his proof.

Will he succeed? Let us make a mental note to return to this courtroom later to find out just what the risk is in making this kind of
opening.

In the meantime, we visit another courtroom, where counsel is obviously going to rely on photographic exhibits and is preparing the jury for them. This is how he does so:

> I am a great believer in the adage that a photograph is worth a thousand words. In this case, the plaintiff hopes to establish that the defendant was driving up a one-way street in the wrong direction when the accident occurred, and the photographs will tell much.
>
> During the trial I shall show you photographs which, in my opinion, will be extremely helpful to you in arriving at the truth. Please try not to prejudge the case. Please wait until all the testimony is in and the Court has charged you on the law. A case is like a mosaic. It is put together a little piece at a time—a little piece here, a little piece there—and when the pieces are all in place, you must examine it to understand the whole picture. And that is the way a lawsuit is. The testimony, like the pieces of mosaic, must all fit right. The facts in this case are . . .

But not every attorney is as skillful in phrasing his opening as the ones we have heard so far. At one of the trials we hear plaintiff's counsel saying to the jury, "I *promise* to prove the following things in this case . . ." and then listing everything he hopes to demonstrate. Here the jury has the right to hold him to strict accountability to his promise, and we can be sure that his adversary will see to it that they do so.

More cautious is the introductory statement heard in another courtroom:

> I shall give you an outline of the plaintiff's case. The plaintiff's witnesses will supply the details. What I am going to give you is a picture of this case as it will develop from the lips of the plaintiff and his witnesses. Here is what they told me . . .

The last trial we have time to visit before the lunch break is one in which the plaintiff has apparently suffered unusually severe injuries. His counsel has reached the point where he is saying, "My function now, in the opening statement, is to review the facts that led to the injuries sustained by the plaintiff." But we find that, in reality, he spends comparatively little time on these matters. Instead, he dwells upon the severity of the injuries and enters into details concerning the period of hospitalization. Elaborating upon the gravity of his client's disability, he stresses the loss of earnings suffered by the plaintiff and concludes by emphasizing the permanency of the bodily damage sustained. Without using any technical terms, he assures the jury that the medical testimony will corroborate the extent, nature, and seriousness of the injuries. In other words, he so pitches his opening statement that the jurors' attention is fixed, throughout, more on his client's injuries than on the issue of liability.

Upon returning to the courthouse after lunch to resume our observation of lawyers at work, we find that it is now the turn of defense counsel to open to the jury.

Let us begin, then, in the last of the courtrooms we visited to see what can be done by the defendant's attorney in an accident case to tip the scales in his client's favor after his adversary has dwelt at length upon the severity of the injuries received by the plaintiff.

We arrive just in time to hear counsel saying:

> You have just heard my adversary describe the injuries that the plaintiff, his client, is alleged to have suffered as a result of the accident. I hope you will not allow yourself to be carried away by such expressions as "excruciating pain" and "unbelievable disfigurement" which counsel for the plaintiff has used to prejudice you against my client. Please bear in mind that the injuries are of no moment until you decide who is liable. That is the crucial issue in this case. Before you can award damages, as I am sure the learned Court will instruct you later, you must decide whether the defendant was negligent and whether the plaintiff was free from contributory negligence. Please pay strict attention to what the witnesses will testify to on this point when they take the stand. And make up your minds only when the case is completed and the learned Court has instructed you on the law. Please keep an open mind throughout the trial.

In another court where an accident case is being tried, defense counsel is likewise seeking to counteract the effect of his opponent's stress on the extent of the injuries which the plaintiff suffered:

> Please listen to the testimony. No doubt the plaintiff was hurt, but not through the defendant's fault. The defendant did everything he was supposed to do. Please keep your minds open, and listen carefully to the defendant and his witnesses as they tell you how the accident occurred.
>
> What I tell you now is not evidence. What my adversary just said is not evidence. What counts as evidence is only what you hear from the lips of the witnesses in that witness chair [pointing to it]. My client denies that he was in any way at fault for what happened.

Following the same procedure we adopted earlier, we do not stay to hear the rest, but move on to a different trial, where the defense is confronted with a similar problem. There counsel deals with it thus:

> I join my adversary in his statement that we are not trying to persuade you at this time. Now, no one questions that an accident happened.

But did it happen substantially as the plaintiff says, or as the defendant says? That is for you to determine, after you have heard all the evidence, and the Court will instruct you on the law.

Evidently, then, there are a number of different ways in which the defendant's attorney can cope effectively with the same type of situation.

As counsel proceeds to give his client's version of the occurrence of the accident, we leave the court in order to look in on a trial in which the defense concedes liability. Here, obviously, a different approach is called for and adopted:

Let me be perfectly frank with you. I represent the defendant, and he admits being at fault in the accident. He does not deny that he was careless. What he does dispute, however, is that the plaintiff sustained the injuries he complains of. Whatever injuries he suffered were slight. Please, therefore, focus your attention on whether the plaintiff was as seriously hurt as he, through his lawyer, says he was. That, members of the jury, will be the sole issue for you to decide.

Elsewhere, we find counsel's prefatory remarks even briefer:

This is a simple case. The facts are not too much in dispute. Practically the only question at issue is the extent of the injuries. On this point, please keep an open mind until you have listened to the medical testimony.

Without waiting to hear him set forth his position on the nature, extent, and seriousness of the injuries, we return to the courtroom where, earlier in the day, we heard plaintiff's counsel try to make his adversary feel obliged to go beyond vague generalities and disclose the nature of his defense. Let us see what response this tactic evokes. Defense counsel begins as follows:

I thank my distinguished adversary, who is a shrewd and seasoned trial lawyer, for suggesting that I tell in detail what my defense will be. However, under the law, as he so well knows, I need not prove anything. As the judge will tell you in his charge at the end of the trial, the burden of proof rests with the plaintiff. Throughout this entire trial I need offer no proof at all. I can remain mute and not even talk at this time, and the burden of proving his case continues to be with the plaintiff. It never shifts, and therefore any gratuitous suggestion made by my adversary is entirely out of order, and he knows it. So I will say nothing about my proof now until I hear the plaintiff's case. This is my legal right, and I am confident you will fully understand my position.

Not only has defense counsel avoided the trap laid for him, but he has succeeded in scoring a point against his opponent.

Proceeding to still another courtroom, we hear the shortest defense we have encountered so far:

> I have but one request as I rise to make an opening statement on behalf of my client, the defendant. Please pay attention to the evidence. I am confident you will find the truth. As the case progresses, you will see where the truth lies.

An opening like this should be used with extreme caution. It is possible, of course, that counsel has in his possession some contradictory statements by the plaintiff or his witnesses which are to be held in reserve until they can be most appropriately introduced. In that case, the defendant's attorney is on safe ground in relying on this kind of opening statement, which avoids giving his adversary any inkling of the nature of the forthcoming defense. But if opposing counsel already knows what the defense will be, it is wiser to go into a little more detail.

Further perambulation brings us to a court where counsel for the defendant is faced with a quite different problem. His opponent evidently tried to explain a point of law to the jury. Here is how that situation is handled:

> What I say to you now in my opening remarks is not evidence. It is only what I have learned of this case from my client and his witnesses. The same is true of the plaintiff's lawyer. What he has told you just now is only what his client and his witnesses told him. That is not evidence. Please pay no attention to the law as he just set it forth for you. The learned judge, who knows the law applicable to this case, will take care to instruct you in it at the proper time. The judge knows the law better; so wait until the case is completed, and then apply the law to the facts in the case as the judge gives it to you in his charge.
> That is all I ask of you.

Earlier in the day we found one of the attorneys for the plaintiff emphasizing that what he said to the jury was not evidence. Back in the same courtroom his adversary now picks up that remark:

> My adversary has just told you that what he has related as his client's case is not to be construed or accepted by you as evidence. He is right. It is not what he says or what I might say now on behalf of the defendant that you are to consider as evidence. I would prefer to have the defendant and his witnesses tell their story.
> As I know it, it is briefly this . . .

Finally, we have time for just one more visit. We come upon the scene as counsel is saying:

The point or objective of an opening is to outline what a lawyer intends to prove. You have just heard the plaintiff's lawyer tell you what he intends to show. It is now my duty to tell you what I intend to prove on behalf of my client, the defendant.

As he outlines his defense, we reflect on the simplicity of his manner and language. To the seeker after thrills and excitement, the absence of flourishes and fireworks, the plain talk and unpretentious directness of his approach may seem rather disappointing. Where is all the explosive tension, the drama, the conflict, that one usually associates with a trial? It should be remembered, however, that these are but preliminary skirmishes. The real battle has yet to be joined. The combatants are still cautiously sparring. They are gauging each other's strength and agility before letting go with everything they have.

Naturally, a quite different tack would have to be taken by a lawyer defending a client charged with a crime. In fact, even before he himself addresses the jury, he has to chart a course that, under favorable conditions, might take the wind out of his opponent's sails.

In the first place, the rule with respect to the taking down of an opening statement in a criminal case is different from that in a civil case. Whereas in the latter a record of counsel's opening is made, as we have seen, only on request, in criminal prosecutions the court reporter *must* record it.

In criminal cases, it is the prosecutor who opens first, and it is he who has, throughout, the burden of proving each count in the indictment and every element of the crime charged. Usually, he can be expected to state the issues and outline the evidence with considerably more definiteness and in much greater detail than would counsel for the plaintiff in a civil suit.

Yet there are bounds which the prosecutor may not overstep without invalidating the entire proceedings. If, for example, he reads the entire indictment to the jurors, as he may do, he is not permitted to create prejudice in their minds by suggesting that it carries proof of guilt. Nor may he at any point voice his own opinions or conclusions, refer in derogatory terms to the character of the accused, or so much as mention the defendant's past crimes or arrests, if any.

Defense counsel must therefore listen very carefully to every word of his adversary's opening in order to make sure that the right of the accused to a fair trial is in no way impaired. If the prosecutor becomes argumentative or abusive, assails the character of the accused, or says anything that even borders on the prejudicial, it is the duty of the attorney for the defendant to enter an immediate objection and move for withdrawal of a juror and a mistrial.

On the other hand, if the prosecutor refers to matters which defense counsel knows cannot be proved, because the requisite testimony is either unavailable or legally inadmissible, there is no need to object at this point, unless there is risk of substantial damage to the rights of the accused. By objecting during the prosecutor's opening, counsel merely alerts him to the fact that there is a weakness in his case which he must do something to overcome or minimize before the trial ends. It is therefore wiser for the defense, in such circumstances, to remain mute and simply take notes while the prosecutor addresses the jury. Later, in the summation, the time will be opportune to expose any discrepancies there may be between what the prosecutor promised to prove and the subsequent testimony.

An alternative course followed by some trial counsel is to object immediately, on the theory that if the judge sustains the objection, his ruling would have a favorable impact on the jurors by implying to them that the prosecutor is using unfair, if not illegal, tactics. In addition, the reference to such inadmissible evidence may form the basis for the granting of a motion for a mistrial.

To be sure, it is not mandatory, in criminal trials, that the defense open to the jury. In fact, there may be some cases in which the attorney for the accused will be inclined to waive his right to do so, particularly when he wishes to delay revealing the defense strategy or when he intends to interpose no defense whatsoever. He may choose the latter tactic if he expects that the prosecutor will fail to prove the accusation or that a defense can be established through the prosecutor's own witnesses.

However, even then it is generally dangerous to dispense altogether with an opening statement. For counsel's failure to open is often regarded by the jury as an indication of the hopelessness of his defense. At least something should be said that might include the following:

> You have heard the prosecuting attorney state his case. Now I ask you to watch carefully to see whether, in fact, he succeeds in establishing it beyond a reasonable doubt. The defendant, by his plea of not guilty, has denied having committed the crime. He still denies his guilt.

Of course, if the attorney for the defendant, from his preparation of the case, knows definitely that the accused will not take the stand, this

information should certainly be conveyed to the jurors either in selecting them or in the opening statement. But in that event it is necessary
to emphasize that the defendant is not required to take the stand or
offer any proof in his defense, that the obligation to prove his guilt beyond a reasonable doubt rests with the prosecutor, and that the defendant is presumed to be innocent throughout the trial. On the
other hand, in the more likely event that counsel is uncertain until the
last moment whether the defendant will in fact take the stand, no
reference whatever should be made to the possibility of his testifying.

For the rest, the opening in a criminal case should conform to the
same basic principles that ought to be observed in a civil suit. In other
words, the presentation should be clear, brief, and natural.

By way of illustration, I may cite what has been characterized as the
finest opening by counsel for the defense in a murder case. It is the
short but compelling statement made on July 8, 1857, by John Inglis
to the jury in the trial of Madeline Smith before the High Court of
Justiciary at Edinburgh:

> Gentlemen of the jury, the charge against the prisoner is murder, and
> the punishment of murder is death; and that simple statement is suffi-
> cient to suggest to us the awful solemnity of the occasion which brings
> you and me face to face.

"Well begun is half done." The lawyer who starts off right should,
by the end of the first round, already have won some points in his
favor, whether for landing a telling blow himself or skillfully side-
stepping a potentially damaging one from his adversary. At any rate,
he should have maintained his balance throughout, kept his guard up
at all times, probed for weak spots, and nicely gauged the precise effect
of each of his jabs, swings, and hooks. For all this will stand him in
good stead later. If he has handled himself well at the outset and
emerged so far unscathed, he should be able to face the rest of the
trial with confidence. Whatever fortune awaits him, he will at least
have stepped forth to meet it manfully.

IV

DIRECT EXAMINATION

11

"Call Your Witness, Counsellor"

Once both sides have completed their opening statements to the jury, the time comes for what is called "direct examination," sometimes also referred to as the "examination-in-chief." In this part of the trial, counsel for each of the parties has his chance to offer in evidence the testimony of his witnesses and any supporting proof he may have in the form of documents, photographs, and other exhibits. The purpose of direct examination is to build up the case affirmatively. If cross-examination gives color to the trial, then direct examination may well be said to give substance to the case.

And so a stir of anticipation rustles through the courtroom as the spectators lean forward to see what is going to happen next. If a civil suit is being tried, the judge nods from the bench toward counsel for the plaintiff and says, "Proceed, counsellor; call your first witness." In a criminal case, of course, the prosecutor would be the first to call his witnesses.

Before taking the stand, each witness solemnly swears or affirms that he will "tell the truth, the whole truth, and nothing but the truth." It then becomes counsel's duty to elicit from his own witnesses as clear and concise a presentation of his case as he sketched in his opening remarks to the jury.

But this is more easily said than done. It is one thing for him to have stated his case, in his own words, in a lucid, organized, and forthright manner. It is quite a different and far more difficult task for him to attain the same clarity, order, and brevity in presenting the testimony of a variety of witnesses—including, possibly, the diffident, the garrulous, the inarticulate, and the forgetful. Indeed, to impose any kind of coherence on the testimony of a heterogeneous collection of individuals of diverse education, experience, and intellectual competence is one of the most challenging problems facing the trial lawyer.

For, no matter how well prepared he may be, unanticipated developments are bound to occur. Sooner or later his resourcefulness will be

put to a severe test. All he will then have to rely on will be his ability
to think quickly on his feet, conceal any surprise or disappointment,
and gloss over embarrassing moments. These happen to even the best
of lawyers and can sometimes put counsel in a ridiculous light, as the
following incident shows:

A talented and dedicated attorney of my acquaintance was once trying a case involving a claim for a back injury. In preparation for the
trial, he had elicited from the plaintiff's wife a description of all that
she had done to administer to her husband the medication prescribed
by the doctor. Among other things, she had told counsel that she had
prepared a hot-water bottle and applied it to her husband's back.

But, alas, when she took the stand, she forget to mention this
particular item in the catalogue of her helpmeetly ministrations. Mind-
ful of the injunction against asking the witness a leading question, like
"Didn't you also prepare a hot-water bottle and apply it to your husband's back?" counsel kept pressing her to recall everything that she
had done to ease the plaintiff's pain. But to no avail. No matter how
counsel phrased his question, the desired information was simply not
forthcoming.

Finally, in desperation, he asked her, "Now, Mrs. G., please tell the
judge and jury everything that you did for your husband after he got
into bed."

There was such a loud roar from the jury box that the judge had to
declare a ten-minute recess.

To be sure, there is no way of guaranteeing that awkward and embarrassing slips of this kind will never occur during the course of direct
examination. Nevertheless, there are many precautions that a prudent
lawyer can take to minimize the likelihood of unexpected setbacks or
disappointments.

In the first place, he should come to court with a thoroughly mapped-
out strategy for marshaling his troop of witnesses so that their testimony, as it develops, is arranged in an easily intelligible order,
preferably—though not necessarily—chronological. This point is amusingly illustrated in Sir Alfred Denning's book *The Road to Justice*:

> Perhaps I may remind you of the famous rebuke which Mr. Justice
> Maule once made to counsel who was blundering along in haphazard
> fashion:
> "Mr. Smith, do you not think that by introducing a little order into
> your narrative, you might possibly render yourself a trifle more intel-

ligible? It may be my fault that I cannot follow you—I know that my brain is getting old and dilapidated, but I should like to stipulate for some sort of order. There are plenty of them. There is the chronological, the botanical, the metaphysical, the geographical; even the alphabetical order would be better than no order at all."

Certainly, before a lawyer ventures to ask his witnesses any questions when they take the stand, he would do well first to put a few silent questions to himself and be sure he knows the answers to them:

Which witnesses shall I call? (The most credible, of course, and the ones who have something pertinent to say—no others. If counsel has few or no witnesses, and his opponent has many, it is only prudent to move that all witnesses but the one giving testimony be excluded from the courtroom. This will prevent the other side from allowing its witnesses to sit in the courtroom listening to one another testify and being "educated" accordingly to conform their own testimony to the prevailing pattern.)

In what order shall I call my witnesses? (Any order, chronological or climactic, that is coherent and readily understandable. However, the first witness should be the one best able to withstand cross-examination, since he generally has to bear the brunt of an extended interrogation by opposing counsel. Similarly, wherever possible, a strong witness should be selected to close the case and thereby leave the jury with a good impression of it.)

How much information shall I seek to elicit from each witness? (No more than he has given in the interview before the trial, and in no case anything not already known to counsel.)

It is amazing how far a lawyer can go toward losing an otherwise good case simply by failing to adhere to these three elementary principles of relevance, logic, and brevity. Let us consider each in turn.

Indispensable in achieving relevance in direct examination is the elimination of all evidence, no matter how interesting, that has no bearing on the issues. Unless counsel separates the wheat from the chaff in advance of trial, he runs the risk, after objection from his adversary, of having this done for him by the Court as he examines his witnesses. For, under the rules of evidence, testimony is legally admissible only if it has probative value. If it does not, it will be ruled out. Obviously it is better for counsel to prune the evidence himself, before the trial, than to find a good part of his direct examination excluded by the judge as "incompetent and immaterial."

But even if this should not happen, it is desirable, for other reasons, that direct examination be confined to the issues in dispute and the main points of the case. For one thing, unnecessarily enlarging the trial minutes may prove burdensome and costly in the event of an appeal. Then, too, the jury is likely to be confused if the testimony is allowed to wander far from the point at issue. It is, of course, desirable that the witness be allowed to tell his story in his own words without interruption. Yet if he strays from the narrow path and meanders into byways, it is counsel's job to lead him tactfully back on the right track. Indeed, a lawyer, during direct examination, has to be constantly on the alert to check such errant tendencies on a witness' part before opposing counsel raises an objection or the trial judge becomes impatient. This is particularly true in cases where the witness does not have a good command of English or where he must be questioned through an interpreter.

For all these reasons, counsel should have prepared his questions, in writing, in his office and arranged them in proper sequence for each witness. These then become his script. Unlike the actor on the stage, who has to memorize his part, counsel can refer to it during his direct examination and so keep his questioning under control at all times.

Since the courtroom is the "stage" on which he will appear, it is desirable, too, that he familiarize himself with it somewhat in advance of playing his role in the trial. Just as an actor on tour may find himself playing in theaters of all sizes and shapes, so a lawyer tries his cases in many different courtrooms that are by no means uniform in their structure and layout. In some there may be only one jury box; in others, two. In one the bench may be only ten feet from the counsel table; elsewhere it may be as far as twenty or thirty feet away. There are courtrooms in which there is only one counsel table to be shared by the attorneys for both sides; in others there may be separate tables for each side. It is therefore important for a lawyer, in advance of trial, to visit the courtroom and become as well acquainted with its exits, arrangement, and appointments as he is with those in his own apartment. Instead of rushing into court at the last moment, breathless and full of apologies, he would do well to cultivate the habit of arriving ahead of time. He will thereby be able to walk around the room, acquaint himself with the position of the counsel table, set his papers on it for easy access, gauge the distance from jury box to witness stand, and envision himself in action. Incidentally, he will, at the same time, feel more comfortable and "at home" in his surroundings and may be able to convey his ease and assurance to his client and witnesses as he calls them to the stand.

In fact, proper "stage technique" and placement is just as important for the trial lawyer as it is for the actor. In conducting his direct examination, counsel will have to be concerned with the same two problems that confront any performer on the stage, namely, audibility and visibility. Consequently, he should stand back from the witness box so as to avoid placing himself between the jury and the witness. He should look directly at the witness when questioning him, turn to the judge when addressing him, and glance from time to time at the members of the jury to let them know that he is aware of their presence, too. Out of courtesy as well as necessity, he should make sure that everyone can see and hear all of the proceedings. He should ask all his questions clearly, distinctly, and slowly. And, of course, he should instruct his witnesses in advance and remind them during the trial, if necessary, to speak up so that their replies to his questions can be heard by all.

In any action in which the emotions and feelings of the witnesses are just as important as the words they speak, it is essential that counsel so position himself that the witnesses necessarily face the jury in answering his questions. To this end, he may even find it necessary to stand behind the jury box or, because of the design of the courtroom, at the head of the jury box facing both witness and jurors.

The best way of ensuring that witnesses under direct examination will give short, responsive answers, instead of embarking on extended, rambling monologues, is for counsel to put to them questions that are themselves brief, uncomplicated, and readily comprehensible. Consequently, he must know the capacity of his witnesses to understand the words that are likely to be needed in questioning them, and he should be prepared to adjust his vocabulary accordingly.

A trial lawyer once said to his client, "Please continue your narrative."

Whereupon the witness replied, "I only went to the seventh grade in public school. Please bring it down to my level, those words you use."

How easy it would have been for counsel to have said to this witness, "Please go ahead with your story."

I have heard lawyers ask witnesses of limited education the following questions and receive these answers:

Q. Did you have any destination in mind?
A. I don't understand the word.
Q. Prior to the event, did Mr. Jones say anything?
A. What means "prior"?
Q. Did you observe what happened?
A. What does "observe" mean? Are you trying to put me in trouble?
Q. Was the area illuminated?
A. What do you mean?
Q. Was it lighted?
A. Why didn't you say so in the first place?
Q. Pursuant to this agreement, what did you do?
A. Counsellor, don't mix me up with fancy words.
Q. Now tell us what transpired.
A. Mr. Lawyer, I no understand.
Q. Were these complaints registered in the presence of the lawyer?
A. Please explain your question.
Q. Did this incident precipitate anything between you and your husband?
A. What? What?
Q. Can you fix the date with some precision?
A. (No answer.)
Q. Can you tell the date when it happened?
A. Oh, yes.
Q. As the car went across the shoulder, did you feel it jouncing?
A. I don't know what you're talking about. Whose shoulder? My arm was hurt!

In testifying in a recent case in which he was called as a witness, Rocky Graziano, former middleweight boxing champion, took umbrage when he had trouble understanding all of the District Attorney's questions. When the judge cautioned him to keep his testimony to the point, he complained that the prosecutor was jabbing him unmercifully with big words and getting him confused. Here is an excerpt from the trial record:

THE WITNESS: But I got to say something, because the way I talk, I don't understand big words like this guy brings out.
THE COURT: Well, try to—
THE WITNESS: I just can't. That's the way I am. I went to fourth grade in school. That's me. I'm sorry.
THE COURT: All right, you listen.
THE WITNESS: That's the only guys get me mixed up with those big words, and I don't understand them. I'm sorry, Judge, believe me.

In a matrimonial action in which the infidelity of the wife was a crucial issue, a key witness for the plaintiff, when asked on direct exam-

ination by the husband's attorney whether the defendant had a reputation of being chaste, unhesitatingly replied, "Yes." Counsel was
amazed and momentarily taken aback. Then he thought of asking the
witness:

Q. How do you spell "chaste?"
A. C-H-A-S-E-D.

A classic of its kind is the question I once heard used in court:

Q. Were you knocked unconscious by this automobile?
A. That's right.
Q. How long were you unconscious?

Of course, the proper question is: "What is the next thing you remember?"

If counsel is not careful how he frames his questions, his adversary
may rise and say, "I object. Learned counsel is trying to confuse the
witness by using words of more than one syllable."

Special problems are raised if a witness has to testify through an
interpreter in a language with which counsel is not familiar. In such
circumstances, it is best to have someone on hand who understands it
well. For it is not advisable to depend exclusively on even a court interpreter's translation. Although the caliber of court interpreters has
improved in recent years, there are still areas where they may err or
honestly differ in their rendering of the testimony.

In the first place, an interpreter needs to have such a thorough
knowledge of the language or dialect used by the speaker that every
implication, every overtone, every shade of meaning can be accurately
translated. He must, besides, be able to interpret the significance of
words and phrases in the light of their accompanying facial expressions
and gestures, as these are commonly understood in the speaker's lin-
guistic community. "In other words," as Professor Willem L. Graff of
McGill University concludes in his *Language and Languages* (New
York: D. Appleton and Co., 1932), "the interpreter has to combine
the knowledge of a linguist, the clairvoyance of a psychologist, and the
shrewdness of a detective."

It will therefore be readily appreciated that, well-trained and knowledgeable though a court interpreter may be, honest mistranslation is
a possibility to be reckoned with. An amusing example occurred in the
course of a trial some years ago. The plaintiff, who was suing a bus
company for damages for personal injuries, was a man eighty-two years

of age, with a long, flowing beard. Bent, tottering, and unable to see more than a few feet ahead of him, he had to be assisted to the witness chair. Since he could speak no English, it was necessary for an interpreter to translate his testimony.

In response to the question (in Yiddish): "What is your occupation?" he replied, "*Ich bin a shochet.*"

(A *shochet*, in the Jewish ritual, is a slaughterer of chickens and cattle.)

"What did he say his business was?" the judge inquired.

"He says he is a chauffeur," answered the interpreter.

A titter went through the courtroom.

The judge rapped his gavel and asked incredulously, "*What* did he say his business was?"

Again the interpreter responded, "He says he is a chauffeur."

The judge was shocked and indignant. "This," he said sternly, "will require an investigation. I'd like to know how this man got his chauffeur's license—or, for that matter, even a driver's license. He is a menace and a danger behind the wheel. I am going to order an investigation at once!"

When informed of the interpreter's little error, the judge joined in the laughter that rang through the courtroom.

Other examples of the same kind could be cited. I remember a separation action in which a husband charged his wife with cruelty. In response to a question concerning an incident that involved some soup he had complained about, he said, in Yiddish, that he could not digest the soup his wife had served him because it had too much "*negalach.*"

This the interpreter translated as "nails" or "tacks." The reaction in the courtroom can well be imagined. But the wife's lawyer corrected the interpreter, explaining that *negalach* referred to a condiment, such as cloves, added to the soup to give it flavor.

Yet in spite of the precautions that must be taken to guard against misunderstandings like these, there are times when an interpreter is indispensable. If there are dangers in relying exclusively on his translation, it is equally risky to try to do without him when he is needed.

Should a lawyer have any doubt whatsoever about the ability of one of his witnesses to understand and speak English, it is best to discuss the problem frankly with him in advance of trial. To be on the safe side, his attorney would do well to test him beforehand by asking him all the questions to be put to him in court. Nothing should be taken for granted, especially in the case of a witness who has—or thinks he has—some amount of familiarity with the English language. "A little learning is a dangerous thing." The trouble is likely to come in precisely those areas in which the witness' acquaintance with English is most spotty. If it proves too limited to be safely trusted, it is generally advisable for counsel to disclose this fact to the judge before the witness takes the stand and to request the services of an interpreter.

Once this decision has been made, it is a good idea to stick to it. No doubt the process of translating every question and every answer is tedious and time-consuming. And there is always the risk of distracting or boring the jurors by the whole procedure. For the sake of expediting the direct examination, counsel may therefore be strongly tempted to request that the interpreter's services be dispensed with if, after a few minutes, his witness seems to indicate that, after all, he can get along quite well without one.

But just how perilous a procedure this is can be seen from the following incident, which occurred during a trial involving a claim for injuries caused to a pedestrian struck by an automobile. The plaintiff had been walking on the shoulder of the road along which the vehicle had been moving.

After counsel for the plaintiff had made use of an interpreter for about twenty minutes, he began to become impatient. Accordingly, he suggested that perhaps, in order to save time, the interpreter could be bypassed entirely, since his client might have sufficient knowledge of English to answer the questions directly. But, to make sure, counsel decided to test the witness himself. After cautioning his client not to answer any questions unless he completely understood them, the attorney for the plaintiff inquired whether he had understood the questions that had been put to him in English up to that point.

"Yes," replied the witness, without any hesitation whatever.

"Good. But just so that we can all know that you understand my questions, let me ask you this: You say that you were walking along the shoulder of the road?"

"Yes," the witness answered.

"And so that I can be quite certain you understand: Do you know what the shoulder of the road is?"

"Oh, yes," the plaintiff promptly replied. "That is the part of the road where you're not supposed to walk."

Before putting any witness on the stand, a lawyer should have a clear idea of just what information he expects to elicit and how far he can depend on the witness to supply it. This is one of the reasons why the well-prepared attorney takes the precaution of coming to court with a complete set of written questions, drawn up on the basis of interviews, for every witness he expects to call upon to testify in his client's behalf.

When he has asked the last question on his list, he should end his examination of the witness, and not try to squeeze anything more out of him. For extending the interrogation beyond this limit usually means that counsel is venturing onto hitherto unexplored territory and asking questions to which he himself does not already know the answers. To proceed along any road where one cannot see ahead is always risky, and nowhere more so than in direct examination.

By way of illustration, I may cite a trial of a negligence case in which the testimony indicated that immediately following the accident the plaintiff refused to go to the hospital for treatment. It was only several weeks afterward, according to the plaintiff's testimony, that he first entered a hospital for a thorough physical examination. The results, by his own admission, were negative.

But his lawyer was not satisfied to leave this point and pass on to something else. He asked the plaintiff, "Do you recall whether they gave you a blood test at the hospital?"

"Yes," the witness replied, "they did give me a blood test, but I don't remember what it showed."

Still unwilling to desist, counsel pressed on, prodding the witness with question after question about the hospital's blood test, presumably in an effort to impress upon the jury the seriousness of the injury that his client had suffered. Finally, in his zeal, the plaintiff's attorney threw caution to the winds and improvidently ventured on a question to which he could not foretell the answer: "Do you mean to tell me that you don't know what the hospital's blood test showed?"

Visibly embarrassed, the plaintiff innocently and truthfully replied, "Oh, yes, they said I had contracted a slight case of venereal disease."

On hearing this response, the plaintiff's lawyer began to shuffle his papers as though he were looking for a misplaced one-way ticket to Cambodia.

Indeed, not knowing when to stop can prove disastrous in conducting a direct examination. I recall a divorce proceeding in which an experienced and supposedly able lawyer was representing the husband, who alleged that his wife had committed adultery. Counsel had succeeded in eliciting from two of his star male witnesses testimony to the effect that while his client was away on a weekend, they and the defendant had spent the entire time together, nude, in the couple's home, disporting themselves continuously.

However, the plaintiff's attorney was not content with this testimony, even though it established a prima facie case by demonstrating both opportunity and inclination for adultery. Evidently feeling that he had to go beyond mere inference, and desiring to clinch his case with an outright admission, he proceeded to ask one of the witnesses, "And did you have intercourse with the defendant?"

Realizing that he might be liable to prosecution if he said that he had, the witness naturally denied doing any such thing.

Whereupon the judge leaned over the bench and said, "Counsel, you asked just one question too many!"

It is, in fact, this effort to "paint the lily" that tempts some lawyers to extend their direct examination beyond the point of no return. The tendency to overreach oneself in this phase of the trial is particularly apparent in cases where the qualifications of an expert, such as an engineer, an architect, or a medical specialist, need to be established. If they are unusually impressive, counsel will quite understandably want to have them enumerated for the benefit of the jury, so that as much as possible may be known of the expert's background, education, and experience. For example, if a physician is to testify, he will normally be asked to state the year in which he was admitted to practice, his hospital connections, the field in which he has specialized, and the titles of any books or articles he may have written.

But often opposing counsel will, after hearing some of this testimony, interrupt the interrogation of the witness and say, "I concede the doctor's qualifications."

If counsel feels that his expert is unusually well qualified, instead of abruptly rejecting his adversary's offer, he may courteously respond to it by saying, "I would rather that the jury heard Dr. _____'s qualifications and that the record contained them." But if these have been sufficiently established on direct examination, a lawyer would be well advised to think twice before stubbornly and arbitrarily rejecting such a concession. For counsel to go on questioning the doctor at length and in great detail, in an effort to wring out every last bit of information bearing on his background, may prove, in the end, to be self-defeating.

I remember a case in which the direct examination of a doctor concerning his qualifications as an expert continued for almost an hour.

Counsel insisted on extracting every piece of evidence touching on the doctor's many achievements in his long and distinguished career and twice ignored a proffer by his adversary to concede the witness' competence.

"I don't want any concessions," he said, and rashly proceeded, for another twenty minutes, in pressing the doctor to detail all his varied professional activities, publications, and affiliations.

But the moment of reckoning finally came when one of the jurors raised his hand and asked permission of the Court to put a question to the witness.

"Doctor," asked the juror, "so when do you sleep?"

In another case, tried before me by an attorney of at least thirty years' experience, the plaintiff, a trumpet player in a nine-piece band, alleged that while he was in the act of taking his seat, after he had stood up to play a solo, his chair slid backward off the stage, causing him to sustain severe injuries. He further testified that he was rushed to a hospital by some of his fellow musicians, including his brother, who was also a member of the band at the time of the accident.

However, none of the musicians who played with him and his brother that night was called as a witness to corroborate his story. The reason was that not a single member of the band was available at the time of the trial, because it was on tour far beyond the jurisdiction of the Court. Unfortunately, counsel failed to call this fact to the jury's attention.

When, just about the time for the lunch recess, the plaintiff's attorney rested his case, it was quite obvious to everyone in the courtroom that the absence of at least one corroborating witness could be fatal to his case, especially when so many had been present at the time of the accident.

After lunch, a man of good appearance and demeanor walked over to the counsel table where the plaintiff and his lawyer were seated and, in plain view of the jury, embraced the plaintiff, whom he obviously resembled, and gave him a hearty kiss. Following a brief huddle between the lawyer and his client, counsel moved to reopen his case for further proof. I granted the motion. The plaintiff's attorney then called this new witness, who testified that he had seen the accident, as he had been sitting right next to the plaintiff on the stage when it happened.

Thereupon counsel asked the witness, who by that time had identified himself as the plaintiff's brother, "Did you then accompany your brother to the hospital?"

Never shall I forget the pained expression on counsel's face and the audible groans from the spectators as the answer came from the lips of the witness: "Oh, no, I waited around to see the boss to collect my day's pay."

When the trial was over, I invited the lawyer for the plaintiff into my chambers and asked him why he had called his client's brother as a witness.

Utterly dismayed, the lawyer replied, "I didn't call him. The plaintiff called him during the lunch hour and asked him to come down to testify."

"But didn't you talk to him before you put him on the stand?" I asked.

"No, I did not," he replied.

"Why didn't you?" I persisted.

"Because I figured he knew the facts," answered the lawyer.

"Then, before interrogating him, you didn't know that he would testify as he did?" I inquired incredulously.

"Of course not!" he exclaimed.

Only after the witness had left the stand did counsel learn that his client had not seen his brother for about three years. During this entire period, and up to a few days before the trial, the witness had been confined to a mental institution. The plaintiff told his lawyer that the kiss which his brother had planted on his lips was simply his brother's way of announcing to him how happy he was to be out in the world again.

The pitfalls facing a lawyer who puts a witness on the stand without having previously interviewed him are further illustrated by a case recently brought to my attention. It involved a claim for damages allegedly imputable to defective work done on real property owned by the plaintiff.

The trial was marked by conflicting testimony. On the one hand, the plaintiff testified that the premises had never before been in need of repair, and that independent contractors had had to be retained to repair the damage caused by the defendants' work. They, on the other hand, sought to cast doubt on the veracity of the plaintiff, contending that much of the damage complained of had pre-existed the repairs they had made. Moreover, they argued, their work did not require any repairs, and, contrary to the plaintiff's testimony, these had been made by his own employees.

The plaintiff presented several independent witnesses, tenants in the building, who gave versions favorable to his case. Indeed, at this point in the trial, counsel for one of the co-defendants had the feeling that the jury had been swayed slightly in favor of the plaintiff.

Then, upon the conclusion of the plaintiff's and the defendants' case, counsel for the plaintiff produced a new witness in rebuttal, without having first discussed his testimony with him. In fact, the witness was brought directly from his home to the witness stand.

Essentially, the direct examination of the witness by the plaintiff's attorney took the following form:

Q. Were you present during a conversation between the plaintiff and defendants' workmen?
A. Yes.
Q. What was said by the plaintiff, and what was said by the defendant?
A. The plaintiff said that he had some cracks in the wall. The defendants' employees said they would check them.
Q. What happened after that?
A. Nothing. We were all laughing and thought the whole thing was a joke. I told them to pay Mr. So-and-So $100,000.00 and let's go home. Everybody thought it was a big joke.

Cross-examination proceeded as follows:

Q. Did you personally know the employees of the plaintiff?
A. Yes, I knew all of them.
Q. Did you ever see them repairing the premises?
A. Yes, they were always patching up various cracks in the front wall.
Q. When?
A. Ever since I was a tenant.

(The witness testified that he had been a tenant for some time before the alleged occurrence.)

According to this witness, the plaintiff's employees "always did the work around the premises." A few further questions were asked, and the answers generally helped the defendants' case. Thereupon, the witness was discharged without any further redirect examination by counsel for the plaintiff.

To be sure, the jury did find in favor of the plaintiff, but the verdict was very nominal—in fact, far less than the amount offered in settlement. Apparently, the last witness had tipped the scales in favor of the defendants, since much of his testimony had discredited that of the plaintiff and his witnesses. The plaintiff's attorney later expressed regret that he had ever produced the witness. He stated that he had never interviewed the witness but had thought his additional testimony would be "the icing on the cake."

Many another case could be cited to show how dangerous it is for a lawyer to call any witness without knowing in advance exactly what testimony he is going to give. Nevertheless, there are times and situations when the risk may be taken. Knowing full well all the hazards involved in putting on the stand a witness who has not been previously interviewed, counsel may still feel justified in taking a chance on doing so, especially if he is convinced that his case is otherwise quite hopeless. For there is always the possibility that the testimony he hopes to elicit may turn defeat into victory.

That this risk is sometimes worth taking is illustrated by a case I once tried. My client was a former lawyer who, before being disbarred ten years earlier, had had an extensive criminal practice and was well known in the profession. What had led to his disbarment was his conviction for second-degree larceny for having allegedly misappropriated funds belonging to one of his clients.

He told me that at his trial the prosecution introduced into evidence a check made payable to an estate and endorsed over by the complainant in her capacity as administratrix. She testified that Mr. R., my client, was supposed to have deposited the check to the credit of the estate. However, he stated that at the trial he produced a written authorization, signed by the administratrix, for him to cash the check and retain the proceeds for his own account in reimbursement of sums that he had advanced. The complainant, for her part, denied that she had signed the authorization.

As the issue turned on the authenticity of the signature, the defense attorney called a handwriting expert, who testified that it was indeed that of the complainant. No handwriting expert was called by the State in rebuttal.

In questioning my client, I ascertained that a man he did not know had appeared in court briefly as a handwriting expert for the People, but he did not testify. I thereupon went to see the handwriting expert who had testified on Mr. R.'s behalf, and I learned that on the morning of the trial he too had seen the expert witness for the prosecution in court for a few minutes.

Once I knew who this mysterious witness was, I paid him a visit and tried to have him recall the circumstances of the case. However, he said he could remember nothing about it, and I was unable to elicit any information from him.

Finally, in desperation, and still having no idea what his testimony would be, I had him served with what is called a *subpoena duces tecum*, ordering him to bring with him his diary for the year during which my client had been convicted.

The following excerpts from the trial record—with a few alterations in the names of some of the participants and some slight editing for the sake of brevity—illustrate how I fared with the risk I took:

Q. Are you a handwriting expert?
A. Yes.
Q. In 1936 and for some time before that, were you called by the then District Attorney of Kings County into consultation in connection with matters pending in that office?
A. Yes, I have a diary entry of having been in the District Attorney's office.
Q. Look in your diary for June 23rd, and let me know whether you have an entry of any kind for that day.
A. Yes, I am looking, and I see an entry.
Q. Was that entry made in the regular course of your business?
A. Yes.
Q. And is it in your handwriting?
A. Yes.
Q. Will you please read it.
A. "In Brooklyn for Assistant District Attorney X.–R. case."
Q. When you came to Brooklyn on June 23, 1936, do you have any recollection as to whether you saw the Assistant District Attorney handling the R. case?
A. None whatever. I cannot remember a thing about the case.
Q. Does that date suggest anything to you regarding any conversation you had with anyone on that day regarding the R. case?
A. Just so far as the entry is concerned, I have no independent recollection, but that entry would not have been made had I not seen the Assistant District Attorney on that day about the case.

Now I had at least an admission that he had seen the Assistant District Attorney. But I suspected that the witness was not prepared to tell the whole story. Was it because he could not remember an event which had taken place ten years earlier, or was he just "not talking"?

At this point, I requested and received permission for an adjournment of the trial. I felt that I needed additional time to consider my next move.

I decided that I had nothing to lose in assuming that the witness was not motivated by bad faith. Accordingly, I sent to his office "blow-ups" of the signature appearing on the authorization in question and of the signature of the complainant appearing on documents she had signed in connection with another case in which she was involved. My purpose was as much to refresh the expert's recollection as to give him an opportunity to make the necessary comparisons.

Recalled at a later date, he testified as follows:

Q. Mr. W., you recall testifying in this case some time ago?
A. Yes.
Q. And at that time you had with you your diary, you recall?
A. Yes.
Q. And that diary was offered in evidence, is that correct?
A. Yes.
Q. You recall that the diary contained a notation that you were to meet or that you came to the County Court on the day of Mr. R.'s trial and met the Assistant District Attorney in charge of the prosecution of the case, you recall that?
A. Yes.
Q. Since the time you testified here last, you made an independent investigation, is that correct, of the facts in this case?
A. Yes.
Q. Will you tell His Honor what you found?
A. At the time that I testified before, I could not remember a thing about what I had done in this case. My diary was the sole record. I have since that time examined the file in a certain estate, and the papers in that case have recalled to my mind what was done. Shall I recite what was done?

The witness continued:

I was called to the court by the Assistant District Attorney, and I can recall examining the standards, that is, the papers that were written by the complainant by request, and that after I had examined them, I talked to the Assistant District Attorney about my reaction to these papers, and told him that the disputed signature was a genuine signature.

Q. Now, let us go back to the occasion when you were in the County Court. The time is so long ago that you may not recall definitely everything that happened.

(In saying this, I was letting him know that I had forgiven him for his past failure to recall the circumstances of the case.)

But you have testified that you had a talk with the Assistant District Attorney, is that correct?
A. Yes.

At this point, I still had no idea what further information might be forthcoming from the witness, but I continued to probe further:

Q. And you told him, if I recollect correctly, that in your opinion, having looked at the specimen of the handwriting of the complaining witness, you considered it a genuine signature and the handwriting of the complaining witness, is that correct?

A. Yes.

Q. What did the Assistant District Attorney say to that when you made known your opinion?

A. My best recollection is that he then told me to leave without being noticed by anyone in the court, and I can recall that I did not go through the courtroom when I left.

Thus the calculated risk proved to be worth taking after all. There was, it seemed, another door in the courtroom, leading to a small corridor, thence to the judge's chambers, and thereby to the elevators used by the general public. The questioning continued:

Q. Did you tell him that you were ready, willing, and able to testify in the trial of the People of the State of New York against R. in effect, or in substance, that the signature was, in your opinion, that of the complaining witness?

A. I am sure I did. I know I did.

Q. Did he indicate that perhaps it might hurt his case or be unfavorable to the People's case were you to testify?

A. I am sure of that, because he did not want me to be seen in the courtroom.

Q. Did the Assistant District Attorney in effect, or in substance, or by innuendo, indicate to you that he did not want that testimony because it might help the defendant?

A. Yes.

Q. What did he say to you when he discharged you, when he said you were not required as a witness? Tell me in substance, if you can, what he said.

A. In substance, it was that he did not want me to be seen in the courtroom or that I let it be known that I had examined these papers, and he wanted me to get out surreptitiously.

Q. Did you say to him, "Please, now, you had me come here. I have given my opinion. Don't you want me to testify in this case?" Did you say anything like that?

A. I cannot remember about that. I can remember that I did report to him that it was a genuine signature, absolutely, according to my opinion.

To sew up the case, I put the final question to him:

Q. Tell me, if you can, the exact language that the Assistant District Attorney employed when he said in effect, "I don't want anyone to

know that you have identified the signature, and I don't want you
to be seen in or near the courtroom."

A. My best recollection is that when I made my official report to him
after having seen this petition to open the safe deposit box, he did
not want me to be seen in the courtroom, and that he would like
me to go out a different way.

Of course, the behavior of the prosecutor in this case was altogether
reprehensible and was strongly condemned by the Court. But I must
add, in all fairness, that this was one of the rare instances of such misconduct that I have encountered in my professional career. I certainly
should not want to give the impression that it is the usual practice for
prosecutors to act in this way. On the contrary, I have generally found
them extremely cooperative and anxious to help a defendant wherever
there is the slightest doubt of his guilt.

In this connection, I recall a case tried before me in which the Assistant District Attorney, knowing full well that the answer to a certain
question would lead to the defendant's acquittal, suggested to defense
counsel during the trial that he put the question to his client on direct
examination. But, apparently distrustful of the prosecutor, and believing he was being led into a trap, the defendant's lawyer failed to take
the proffered advice. Thereupon, the prosecutor himself asked the
question of the defendant and, on obtaining the reply he had expected,
promptly moved for his acquittal.

No less exemplary was the action taken by District Attorney Aaron
Koota of Kings County, New York, in a recent case in which two young
men were charged with robbery, grand larceny, and assault. The victim,
a sixty-seven-year-old night watchman for a trucking company, had been
set upon by two individuals who knocked him to the ground, kicked
him, and took his wallet. Six days later he thought he recognized his
assailants in two youths who stopped at the company garage where
he worked and asked him about an automobile part. After taking down
the license number of their car, he called the police. Upon his positive
identification, the pair were arrested, booked, and later indicted. If convicted, they could have been sent to prison for ten to thirty years.

With the jury already chosen, and the victim ready to take the stand
to repeat his identification under oath, Mr. Koota's office received last-
minute information indicating that one of the defendants had had a
breakdown of his automobile in a town in Long Island at the very time
that the robbery was alleged to have occurred in Brooklyn. An affidavit
from an official of the Long Island State Parkway Commission stated

that a sergeant and a patrolman in a patrol car had come upon this defendant stranded in his car.

Upon the motion of the prosecution, a recess was declared while detectives were sent to check the police records and to bring the defendant in question to confrontation with the garage man who had serviced the disabled car. He signed an affidavit identifying the defendant as the man who had been in the vehicle.

Meanwhile, friends of the other defendant came forward to corroborate his story that on the night of the robbery he had been in a town in upstate New York.

Accordingly the prosecution's motion to dismiss the indictment was granted.

12

Eliciting Direct Testimony

When the direct examination of witnesses is depicted in radio, television, or movie representations of courtroom dramas, the questioning is almost invariably shown as brisk, pointed, and climactic. No irrelevancies or superfluities are allowed to weaken the vividness of its impact. It proceeds straight to its goal with admirable clarity, and then stops.

Unfortunately this is not what actually happens in most trials. Many lawyers seem never to have mastered the art of keeping the direct examination of their witnesses brief and to the point. In this respect, they might learn something from our dramatists and scriptwriters for the mass media. Too often, the process of eliciting the facts of the case is unnecessarily drawn out, meandering, and feebly ineffectual. The essential information is lost in a welter of tedious and picayune details, until the jury's sensibilities are numbed and its patience exhausted.

Yet such fumbling ineptitude is certainly not difficult to avoid. Frequently all that is required to make the difference between a weak and a strong performance on counsel's part is a little more forethought about the pattern of the questioning and strict adherence to a few basic principles.

Why, for example, do so many lawyers think it necessary to repeat verbatim every single answer given by the witness? Do they not realize that this practice, besides needlessly lengthening the trial record, bores and annoys the members of the jury? If the answer given by the witness is audible, counsel should pass on to the next question. If, on the other hand, he has any doubt about whether the jury heard the answer, he should instruct the witness to speak up and repeat it. Only very rarely—perhaps to emphasize some especially significant point —does an attorney have to repeat for the benefit of the jury the witness' answer to his question.

Equally time-consuming and ultimately self-defeating is the practice of calling a flock of witnesses to testify to the same effect. No doubt there are situations in which the testimony of a number of independent witnesses may be required to corroborate a doubtful or disputed version of the facts. But ordinarily, if a fact has been established by credible testimony on the part of one or two witnesses, it is as good as if counsel called on ten or twenty. Adding numbers does not necessarily increase the weight of the evidence. After all, what counts is not the quantity of witnesses, but the quality, completeness, and pertinence of their testimony. Calling many witnesses who merely parrot one another's answers, without adding anything significant to what has already been testified to, tends to increase the risk of weakening the case. The fewer the witnesses, the less danger there is that their testimony may backfire.

Once, when sitting in the Criminal Court, I heard a young Assistant District Attorney suggest to an experienced lawyer who had specialized in criminal cases that he "take a plea" for his client, that is, offer a plea of guilty to a lesser charge, since the prosecution's evidence was so overwhelming. When defense counsel turned down the suggestion, the prosecutor added, "I've got ten witnesses who will testify against your client."

"Good," the defendant's lawyer replied. "If there were only one, I'd be worried. But ten is just fine. I'll have no trouble in creating, during cross-examination, all kinds of confusion and in finding contradictions galore in their testimony. It will be easy for me to establish a reasonable doubt of my client's guilt."

And that is exactly what he did.

The fact is that juries are not generally impressed by testimony that is repetitive, and sometimes they may find the whole process of eliciting it very irksome indeed. While listening to it, some jurors may begin to wonder why it was necessary to summon five or six people to swear to exactly the same story. Others may come to feel that the testimony no longer rings true and may suspect that the case is being deliberately built up with a parade of witnesses. And jurors whose business experience has accustomed them to expect and demand economy in the use of time may strongly resent the waste of their own time, not to say the affront to their intelligence, in being compelled to hear the identical story over and over again.

If, then, an attorney finds himself in the fortunate position of having an abundance of witnesses, all ready to testify to the same facts, the best procedure for him to follow is to select from among them the one or two who seem most likely to score a point for him. Normally they should be the ones whose testimony is most credible and who are best able to stand up under cross-examination. The rest can be safely allowed to stay home.

There are other ways, too, in which lawyers—even those with good cases—manage, in examining their witnesses, to alienate the jurors. Sometimes the very manner in which the examination is conducted is enough to set one's teeth on edge. Certainly an attorney should be friendly and courteous in his demeanor toward each witness, but there is no need to be unctuous or obsequious. I remember presiding over a trial in which counsel, after each answer the witness gave, would say, "Thank you," in a tone so saccharine that it became positively nauseating. On at least three occasions, I told him, "Counsellor, you need not thank the witness every time he makes a reply." But, no doubt a victim of habit, he persisted in pursuing this course of conduct, until finally I felt compelled to admonish him: "Counsellor, if you want the trial record to be unencumbered, will you please refrain from thanking the witness every time he answers a question!"

Perhaps the most common fault is the tendency to ask leading questions, that is, to frame the questions so as virtually to put the answers into the mouth of the witness and to leave him little else to say than yes or no. The temptation to conduct a direct examination in this way is understandably strong, especially if the witness is forgetful, inarticulate, or prone to indulge in elaborate irrelevancies. But such questions give rise to objections by opposing counsel and incur the displeasure of the Court.

For example, testimony obtained in the following way is of little value, since it is the lawyer who is, in effect, testifying, and not the witness:

Q. Is your name Alice Brown?
A. Yes, it is.
Q. Have you been living in a four-room apartment on the second floor of 16 Smith Street, Brooklyn, New York, since June 4, 1953?
A. Yes, I have.
Q. Were you married on June 30 last year to Homer Brown in Maryland when your maiden name was Smith?
A. Yes, I was.

In point of fact, no lawyer would long be allowed to go on in this fashion without being challenged. The appropriate method of eliciting the desired testimony from the witness in such a case would be to propound the questions in the following manner:

Q. What is your name?
Q. Where were you living on June 4, 1953?
Q. What kind of apartment did you occupy at that address?
Q. What is your husband's name?
Q. When were you married?
Q. What was your maiden name?

Obviously, it is better for counsel to frame the questions properly in the first place than to have to be admonished by the Court to correct his procedure in the midst of his direct examination.

Of course, a lawyer is supposed to know in general what kind of questions he may legitimately ask a witness. For the rules of evidence, which determine what testimony is admissible, are not the expression of each judge's individual caprice. Although a certain area of discretion in interpreting them is allowed to the trial judge, they constitute, on the whole, a body of knowledge in which the legal experience of the ages has been crystallized. They serve to exclude testimony that is immaterial or prejudicial. Every attorney is expected to be familiar with them and to abide by them.

Actually, putting improper questions to a witness is bad trial tactics. Any lawyer who asks questions that he knows are objectionable is, in effect, gambling with his client's case. He may think that he has escaped unscathed if his adversary fails to object, and if the trial judge says nothing against his questions. However, counsel should not congratulate himself too soon, for he is still not out of danger. He may yet have to reckon with a reversal on appeal. This means a new trial, an inordinate waste of time, additional expenses, and, very probably, a dissatisfied client.

Indeed, even if the trial judge sustains an objection to improper questions, the error made in asking them may not thereby be remedied, as counsel may learn when a higher tribunal is called upon to deal with it. This is precisely what happened in a recent case. Plaintiff's counsel, in questioning a doctor, sought to instill in the minds of the jurors the suggestion that the plaintiff's pain could be compensated "on a unit-of-time basis," that is, by the payment of a definite sum of money per hour of suffering. On appeal, objection was raised in particular to the following questions:

Q. So that we now have some measure of the value of pain, $45.00 to save her a half hour of pain, is that right, Doctor?
Q. You doctors, aside from what is charged for the period of anesthesia, have no other dollar value in measuring pain, do you?

The higher court held that even though the defendant's objection to these questions had been sustained by the trial judge, they were no less prejudicial. Plaintiff's counsel should have known in the first place that they could not be properly asked.

All this, of course, serves only to substantiate what has been said about the importance of adequate preparation for this phase of the trial. Yet, as we have seen, no matter how carefully prepared a lawyer may be, he can hardly anticipate every answer that his witness will give. There are bound to be some unpleasant surprises sooner or later. No attorney can hope to escape them altogether. By the time the witness is called to the stand, he may have forgotten much that he said in his interview in counsel's office, or he may no longer be as sympathetic as he once was. There is, besides, always the possibility that a witness may innocently add some new and damaging testimony not even hinted at in advance of trial. In any event, an attorney has to be ready to shift gears quickly during his direct examination in order to adjust to un-expected jolts, turns, and roadblocks along the way.

One of the most upsetting of these shocks comes when a witness whom counsel has interviewed before the trial flatly denies under oath that any such discussion ever took place. Ordinarily, under these cir-cumstances, the proper procedure is to try to rehabilitate the witness by asking him questions that may help to bring him round to the right path. However, I know of at least one instance in which a veteran trial lawyer found it more advantageous to adopt a far bolder tactic.

In this particular case, through some sixth sense that comes only from experience and constant application, he got the feeling that this wit-ness would deny on cross-examination that he had ever talked with counsel before the trial. Therefore, the first question put to the wit-ness in direct examination was, "Did you ever talk about this case with me before today?"

When the witness said no, counsel immediately asked him to step down from the stand.

This prompt action in withdrawing the witness and excusing him from any further testimony made a most favorable impression on the jury. Had he been permitted to testify and to be cross-examined, it might well have appeared to the jury that counsel had put an untruth-ful witness on the stand. As it was, when the case was concluded, some of the jurors volunteered the statement that they felt the witness had not given a truthful answer to the only question asked of him, and that counsel had done the right thing by them in refusing to subject them to testimony from such a witness.

Like a general, then, a lawyer has to be resourceful enough to alter his grand strategy on the spur of the moment in terms of the concrete tactical situation that confronts him in the heat of battle. Suppose, for example, that he elicits from one of his witnesses, to his surprise, testimony harmful to the case. He has to be able, on the instant, to decide on its seriousness and to adjust his procedure accordingly. If he judges the testimony to be of relatively minor significance, the best thing for him to do may be simply to ignore it and to move directly on to something else. In other circumstances, however, it may be desirable for counsel to ask additional questions that might take the sting out of the adverse response or place it in its proper context. But whatever he does, he must conceal his surprise and proceed unhesitatingly, in order to avoid emphasizing something that might otherwise pass unnoticed.

Indeed, this is a situation that calls for the utmost delicacy on counsel's part. After all, he can hardly afford to question the veracity of his own witness, much less cross-examine or assail him. Like an actor on the stage who suddenly finds himself under the necessity of ad-libbing to conceal his own or someone else's lapse of memory, counsel has to find some way of bridging over the ugly moment and rendering it as inconspicuous as possible.

Sometimes the only thing to do is to call another witness to explain away the discrepancy. If none is available, and it is impossible to rehabilitate the recalcitrant witness because objections to his testimony are being sustained by the Court, the only alternative left is for counsel to meet the problem during his summation. But before making such a decision, he would be wise to bend every effort toward bringing the errant witness back on the right track. Otherwise, no amount of forensic oratory later in the trial may be equal to the task of undoing the damage done by counsel's own witness under direct examination.

The problem involved is so difficult and arises so frequently that an illustration may perhaps make clear how an expert trial lawyer might go about solving it.

Let us, then, envision him as counsel for the plaintiff in a negligence action. His client has been hit on the left side by the defendant's automobile, sustaining injuries to his left arm, knee, and leg. The defendant has not contested liability or contended that there was any contributory negligence on the plaintiff's part. Consequently, plaintiff's counsel has concentrated, in the preparation of his case, on the injuries suffered by his client. In opening to the jury, he has stressed their extent and severity, specifically enumerating each, and mentioning in particular the left arm, the left knee, and the left leg.

But, alas, when the plaintiff takes the stand, counsel immediately receives a heavy blow to his case from a most unexpected quarter:

Q. What side of your body was hit by the defendant's automobile?
A. My right side.
Q. Which side? [In restrained surprise.]
A. My right side.
Q. Which leg was hit?

(Here counsel is trying to get the witness on the right track.)

A. My right leg.
Q. Which knee?
A. My right knee.
Q. And which arm?
A. My right arm.

What to do? His client's testimony now stands in direct conflict with the facts, with the allegations in the pleadings and the bill of particulars, and with the opening statement to the jury! To add to counsel's difficulties, he has no other witness available to explain away the discrepancy. He is, besides, haunted by the vision of a sharp cross-examiner eagerly awaiting his opportunity to pounce on the plaintiff, pummel him, and add to his confusion. If counsel hopes to explain the discrepancy in his summation, he may find himself talking to a jury that is unable to blot out the memory of the damaging testimony that came from the lips of the plaintiff.

Clearly, such an impasse calls for all the tact, poise, and skill that a lawyer can muster. Attempting to repeat the questions previously put to the plaintiff will only bring objections from opposing counsel that will surely be sustained by the Court. By the same token, leading questions asked in desperation, like "Are you sure it was your right side?" "But didn't you tell me before coming to court that it was your left side that was hurt?" will not only be just as objectionable but, even if they are allowed, may confuse the witness even more.

Here is where delaying and diversionary tactics may well be in order. A good way to straighten out the witness is to try to take his mind off his injuries entirely—at least for the time being. So counsel has him revert to the circumstances of the accident and to all the events that led up to it, reconstructing in detail the whole scene as the witness remembers it, until he gradually returns to his recollection of the moment of impact. Now counsel makes another attempt to develop a description of the injuries. But this time he begins by showing the witness photographs of the defendant's car, has him point out the part of the automobile that struck him, and finally asks him to point to the side of his body where he was hit. With a combination of diplomacy and psychology, counsel so absorbs his client in recounting the manner in which the accident occurred that the required testimony is readily obtained. Once the witness correctly identifies the part of the body where he was injured, it is relatively easy for counsel to receive from him an explanation for the mistaken testimony that he previously gave. After that, there should be smooth sailing.

Above all, counsel should beware of succumbing to panic, keep his head, and take command of the situation until he extricates himself.

On the other hand, there are times when it pays to be quite frank in eliciting adverse testimony from one's own witness. If there is anything in his background that may tend to discredit him or his testimony, bringing it out into the open on direct examination is preferable to having it dragged out to public view by opposing counsel in his cross-examination.

Here, for instance, is the way in which an attorney conducted the direct examination of a defendant who was charged with being the father of three children born to the complainant out of wedlock:

Q. Are you the father of child #1?
A. Yes, sir, I admit it.
Q. How about child #2?
A. There's a fifty-fifty chance. My cousin from South Carolina stayed in my apartment for almost a year before #2 was born.
Q. Are you the father of child #3?
A. No, sir, I deny it. The year the third child was born, Marie [the complainant] went to live with my cousin for a few months, until he left her to go back to his wife in South Carolina.

By his straightforward admission, the witness completely eliminated the third count of the information and cast doubt on the second count. Certainly it was far better for him to have made the disclosure under direct examination by his own lawyer than to have the facts paraded before the jury during cross-examination by the complainant's attorney.

The manner in which this direct examination was conducted illustrates an important principle frequently overlooked by many lawyers. They labor under the delusion that their obligation to protect the credibility of their witnesses begins only when opposing counsel starts his cross-examination. Often, however, it is too late by that time for a lawyer to do anything effective on their behalf simply by raising objections to the searching questions his opponent puts to them. The proper time for an attorney to begin setting up his defenses against the cross-examination of his witnesses is while they are giving their direct testimony.

The wisdom of adopting this strategy becomes particularly evident in criminal cases in which counsel decides to put on the stand a defendant with a record of previous convictions. Under the circumstances, a lawyer owes it to his client to bring this fact into the open at the earliest opportunity—preferably during the *voir dire* and again in the introductory statement to the jury. Then, when the defendant is called upon to testify, his criminal record should be made a subject of frank inquiry on direct examination. He will thus be left in a strong position to withstand cross-examination on this point. For his counsel to wait until the District Attorney forces the defendant to divulge his previous convictions is to invite possible disaster.

Direct examination, in such a case, should proceed substantially as follows:

Q. Are you the defendant in this case?
A. Yes.
Q. In June, 1950, in this county, were you convicted of grand larceny?
A. Yes.
Q. In November, 1953, in New York County, were you convicted of robbery?
A. Yes.
Q. And altogether for these two convictions, how many years have you served in State Prison?
A. Nine years altogether.
Q. Now, since the commission of these crimes, have you been convicted of any others?
A. No.

By eliciting these answers from the witness on direct examination, counsel steals the prosecutor's thunder and forestalls his scoring what might otherwise appear to the jury as a telling, if not a devastating, blow.

But besides derogatory information, there are other facts about a witness which, while not actually discreditable to him, can be made to appear in a most unfavorable light if they are left to the cross-examiner to discover. Often the psychological effect of a revelation on the jury depends not so much on the fact disclosed as on who reveals it. For example, if a witness is someone related to counsel, or in his employ, it is generally better to make this fact known at once—perhaps even before the witness is sworn and gives his name—than for it to be brought to light later, either by the attorney for the opposing party or inadvertently by the witness himself. All counsel has to do in such a situation is to say, "Your Honor, I now call my secretary (or associate or brother-in-law)."

Holding back information of this kind can sometimes lead to awkward complications. I remember in particular the embarrassment suffered by the lawyer for the defendant in a case over which I once presided. Counsel came to court appareled as if he were going to the opera or to a wedding at which he was to appear as "best man." Approaching the counsel table, he carefully placed upon it his black Homburg, slowly removed his elegant gloves, laid them neatly on top of his hat, and then proceeded, with the same studied deliberation, to take off his velvet-collared overcoat, fold it, and drape it smoothly over a chair. All eyes turned to him as he stood there before me, impeccably dressed—if not, in fact, overdressed—in a black suit of the most fashionable cut, with a fresh flower in his lapel, spats, and a resplendent, multicolored vest. Indeed, he looked out of place in a courtroom crowded with people in ordinary, workaday clothes somewhat the worse for wear.

But the contrast with his client was even more striking. The defendant, dressed in an old sweatshirt, unpressed trousers streaked with grease stains, and unpolished shoes rather worn at the heels, looked positively unkempt.

Counsel gave him a cursory glance and then, before putting him on the stand, turned to me and said apologetically, "Your Honor, I hope you will excuse my client's attire. You see, he is a truck driver, and he returned only half an hour ago from an eleven-hundred-mile trip."

I nodded understandingly, and the witness was sworn. When he took the stand, the first question counsel put to him was, "What is your name?"

A look of pained incredulity came over the witness' face, and he asked to have the question repeated. When it was, he exclaimed indignantly, "What's the matter with you? Don't you know my name? I'm your brother-in-law!"

13

"Received in Evidence"

Very often, an important part of the direct examination of witnesses consists in having them identify or interpret exhibits, such as photographs, charts, maps, and records. Once these have been "received in evidence," as the expression goes, they form part of the trial record and may be examined and taken into account by the jury in its deliberations. However, it is the trial judge who decides what documentary proof or exhibits are admissible in evidence.

The procedure followed in having such evidence accepted during the conduct of an examination is very simple. Let us assume that an eye-witness to an automobile accident is on the stand. Counsel has a photograph of the intersection where the accident occurred. Showing it to the witness, he says, "I show you this photograph. Please look at it and tell me whether it fairly represents the intersection where the accident happened at the time of its occurrence." If the witness says that it does, the photograph may then be offered in evidence. But before the trial judge receives it in evidence, it will be shown to opposing counsel. If there is no objection from him, the Court will direct that the photograph be marked, for example, "Plaintiff's Exhibit 1."

If any objection to the introduction of the photograph is raised, the Court will rule on the objection, and if it is sustained, the exhibit will not be marked in evidence. This means that the jury will not be allowed to see it. It may, however, be marked for identification only. The reason for doing so is that if an appeal is taken, the appellate court may view the exhibit to determine whether the trial judge's ruling on the objection was correct. If, on the other hand, the objection is overruled, the exhibit will be received in evidence and given an exhibit number. It will then carry the same weight as any testimony or other admissible evidence.

Similarly, counsel may have occasion to offer in evidence a photograph showing that his client's car was damaged. While the plaintiff is on the stand, he should be shown the photograph and asked whether it fairly represents the condition of the automobile immediately after the accident. If he says that it does, the photograph may then be offered in evidence. At this point the witness should be asked whether any of the damage indicated on Plaintiff's Exhibit 1, in evidence, was on the car before the accident.

It is generally advisable, in such cases, for counsel to ask the Court, after each exhibit is introduced, to permit the jurors to see it. In this way, they can obtain a better visual understanding of the issues. In a negligence case, for example, viewing photographs may enable them to become oriented to directions and distances. Sometimes, if a series of exhibits is to be introduced, the judge may suggest that counsel withhold them from the jury until all of them are received in evidence. But in my opinion it would better serve counsel's cause for the jury to see each exhibit as it is introduced. He should therefore have no hesitation in saying to the Court, "May it please Your Honor, I respectfully request that the jury be permitted to see each exhibit as I introduce it, since I believe that it will be helpful to them in following the testimony." Certainly if the exhibit contains any writing, unless it is inordinately long and complicated, it should be read to the jury at once. This is particularly true of letters, which can easily be lost during the trial or misplaced by counsel or the clerk.

In matrimonial actions, the sole means of identifying the defendant may be a photograph which was furnished to the process server by the plaintiff or his attorney. In that event, the process server, at the trial, should be called upon to testify to the facts of service and to swear that the person he served with the summons and complaint was the one depicted in the photograph. This should now be marked for identification. Thereafter, a person who knows the defendant—preferably the plaintiff—should be called upon to identify the photograph. It can then be offered in evidence. This procedure may be used by the attorney for the plaintiff to identify the defendant in an action for annulment or separation, and such means of identification have been held to be permissible in a divorce action as well.

Another powerful buttress in support of one's case may consist of documentary evidence, in the form of records, charts, and notes. During the trial of a negligence case, for example, it may be very important to offer in evidence a hospital record containing entries of treatment received by the plaintiff, as well as the diagnosis and the prognosis of his physical condition.

It goes without saying that counsel should familiarize himself with every word in the hospital records before having them produced in court. The pertinent medical facts are extremely helpful in establishing the amount of damages to be awarded in a negligence case. Yet I have seen many such cases tried before me in which it was obvious that counsel for the plaintiff had concentrated almost exclusively on preparing his client and witnesses to establish the defendant's negligence and liability, but had failed woefully to give adequate attention to the medical evidence. Often I have heard lawyers, when reading a hospital record to the jury, say, every few minutes, "This word I can't make out." The procedure I myself followed, when I prepared cases of this kind for trial, was to have extracted and typed every part of the hospital record that I wanted to read to the jury. In this way, having examined it in advance, I could read it with ease and understanding.

If it is dangerous for an attorney to place on the stand a witness whom he has not previously interviewed, it is equally risky to offer in evidence records that have not been thoroughly scrutinized well in advance of trial. Counsel may find that they contain damaging admissions made by his client or statements by attending physicians that are at variance with what his client told him. For this reason, the records should be studied before counsel drafts the complaint and bill of particulars.

On the other hand, hospital records may contain statements that could be very helpful in establishing the nature and extent of the injuries sustained by the plaintiff. By familiarizing himself thoroughly with the records, counsel will be able to prepare his client before he testifies, and be ready to object to such parts of the record as are not admissible, and to request the deletion of any hearsay statements, that is, those attributed to someone who is not available for cross-examination.

How are medical records offered and received in evidence? Generally any memorandum recording an act, transaction, or occurrence is admissible in evidence, provided it was made at the time, or within a reasonable time thereafter, in the regular course of business, and that it was the regular course of the business to make the record. In most cases, counsel for the respective parties have no difficulty in arriving at an agreement between them with regard to documents that will be offered in evidence. However, in the absence of such agreement, or in the face of objections from opposing counsel, an attorney who wishes to introduce hospital records into evidence may issue a subpoena to be served on a representative of the hospital who is in charge of records. In addition, he should be served with a *subpoena duces tecum*, as it is called, ordering him to produce the records in question.

When he does so, he may be questioned as follows:

Q. Are you employed by the XY Hospital?

Q. In what capacity are you employed by the hospital?

Q. What are your duties?

Q. Have you produced, as ordered by the *subpoena duces tecum* served on you, the hospital records showing the treatment received by the plaintiff, John Smith, while he was a patient in the XY Hospital between January 1 and February 10, 1963?

Q. Does this folder which you have just handed me contain the hospital record of John Smith?

At this point, addressing the Court, counsel says, "I offer this file and its contents for identification." If, thereafter, a doctor is called upon to testify from these records, he should be handed the folder when he is sworn. Then, after saying, "I now offer the hospital records in evidence," counsel may proceed to question the doctor concerning them. If, on the other hand, no doctor is called upon to testify, counsel may offer the hospital records in evidence immediately after the hospital representative has produced and identified them. Thereupon, counsel may read from them such excerpts as he wants the jury to hear.

In like manner, the attorney for either of the parties in a negligence case may wish to offer in evidence a police blotter or record relating to the circumstances of the accident. But he will not always be able to have such documents accepted. If the policeman who made the report was not a witness to the accident, or if he relied on the statements of a third party in preparing the report, the Court will consider it hearsay and will refuse to receive it in evidence. Nor is the police blotter admissible if the information contained in it was received by the police officer from the party on whose behalf he is testifying. His report will also be excluded if it contains mere inferences, rather than descriptions of what the police officer himself directly observed.

On the other hand, there are occasions in which the police blotter is admissible in evidence, even though the police officer who made the report was not himself a witness to the accident. For example, at the time the report was being prepared, one of the parties directly involved in the case may have made an admission damaging to his own interest. If such an admission is contained in the report of the police officer, it may be introduced into evidence.

Here, for instance, is a case in which counsel represented the plaintiff, a pedestrian run down by the defendant's car at an intersection. Policeman Brown arrived at the scene after the accident took place and included in his report a statement made by the defendant: "Operator of the car said he did not see the STOP sign near the intersection and went into the intersection without stopping at the corner."

In order for counsel to have the police blotter containing this damaging admission received in evidence, he subpoenaed the police officer and asked him on direct examination the following questions:

Q. What is your badge number and rank in the Police Department of this city?
Q. Were you on official duty on August 17, 1963, at 2:00 P.M.?
Q. Did you respond to a call to the scene of an automobile accident at the intersection of X Street and Avenue A?
Q. Did you witness the occurrence of the accident?

If the police officer had been a witness to the accident, his report could have been received in evidence at this point. However, as this was not the case here, counsel proceeded as follows:

Q. In the course of your official duties, did you prepare a report known as "Police Accident Report"?
Q. I show you this certified copy of your police report and ask you if this is a true copy of the report you made.
Q. I offer this report as Plaintiff's Exhibit 3 for identification. Now, before you prepared this report, Plaintiff's Exhibit 3 for identification, and before you entered the statements it contains, did you have a conversation with the defendant?
A. Yes.
Q. What was the conversation?
A. I asked the defendant what happened, and he said, "I didn't see the STOP sign until after I drove part of the way across the intersection."

Since this is an admission made by the defendant against his own interest, counsel now addressed the Court as follows: "I offer in evidence the police blotter dated August 17, 1963, as Plaintiff's Exhibit 3."

Then, after the police blotter was received in evidence, counsel asked for permission from the Court to read the damaging statement to the jury and to have the police blotter examined by each of the jurors.

In a recent case, a deputy sheriff who was not a witness to the accident made a report which included an admission by the defendant indicating that she was at fault: "Driver of Car 2 said she did not know where her car stopped." Defense counsel objected to the introduction of the report on the ground that it constituted hearsay and was therefore inadmissible. However, the trial Court received the report in evidence over this objection. On appeal, the judgment in favor of the plaintiff was affirmed. It was held that the document had been properly received as a "business record."

Whatever may be said concerning accident or police reports, medical records are not generally self-explanatory. Their interpretation usually requires the expert knowledge of a physician. If they are introduced in evidence, they must be supplemented by competent professional testimony. Since such testimony often plays a crucial role in negligence cases, no lawyer can afford to be anything but thorough in familiarizing himself, in advance of trial, with all the relevant medical details.

To this end, it is essential that, in addition to his own independent study of the records, counsel go over with the doctor, before putting him on the stand, every piece of paper he has relating to the plaintiff's physical condition. The doctor should be asked to review and interpret all written medical reports on the case and to explain technical terms in simple language.

At the same time, definite financial arrangements should be made, well in advance of trial, to compensate the doctor promptly and adequately for his appearance in court and for the time spent in examining records, X-rays, and medical data. His testimony is too important for counsel to risk losing it by leaving such matters to chance. A casual telephone call to the doctor the day before the trial is hardly the way to ensure his attendance. A busy member of the medical profession may simply fail to appear just when he is wanted the most. If counsel then rushes a subpoena to him, the process server may bring the disappointing news that the doctor is nowhere to be found. On the other hand, if the doctor is brought to court under the compulsion of a subpoena, but without having received prior assurances of appropriate compensation for his services as a witness, he may prove uncooperative, and his testimony may turn out to be of little value.

Indeed, both counsel and the doctor need to come to court thoroughly prepared. Counsel should bring with him a complete medical file of data, including the doctor's name and address, his telephone number, age, physical appearance, academic background, hospital affiliations, medical specialty, years of experience in the practice of medicine, and publications, if any. Prior interviews with the doctor should also have given counsel a good idea of the kind of person he is going to have to examine. For this purpose, he should ask himself a number of questions about the doctor:

Is he given to long-winded answers, or is he the type that confines himself to a categorical yes or no?

Is he a patient, understanding, sympathetic person, or is he likely to prove crotchety, finicky, cranky, and uncooperative?

Does he talk slowly, softly, deliberately, and in a pleasant tone of voice, or does he shout, bellow, roar, and race through his testimony?

Does he keep accurate records of the dates of his visits, the nature of his treatments, the amount of his dosages, and the appliances and medications he prescribed?

Are his answers given in language that a layman can understand, or does he talk like a walking medical dictionary?

Clearly, the way in which the doctor is to be handled on direct examination will depend, to a considerable extent, on the answers to these questions. It is certainly better for counsel to know his man beforehand than to acquire this knowledge, possibly at some cost to his case, only after the doctor takes the stand.

For it should never be forgotten that the primary criterion of a doctor's usefulness as a witness is not how much he knows, but how well he can present the medical evidence on behalf of the client. Of course, if the doctor has testified in court before, the task of examining him when he takes the stand will be relatively simple. But sometimes even a recognized authority in his field may have had no prior experience as a witness in a court of law. He may be "at home" in his office, the X-ray room, or the hospital, but in the courtroom he may be nervous, ill at ease, forgetful, or unable to speak in a voice that can be heard by judge and jury. No matter how knowledgeable he may be, he may appear to them to be confused, and he may even give an impression of the plaintiff's injuries prejudicial to the case.

This type of doctor needs, first of all, to have his confidence bolstered. I would try to make him realize that he would be testifying in his professional capacity as a recognized expert in his field, that the jury would respect him because of his medical background, and that the judge would extend to him every courtesy to which a member of the medical profession is entitled. In addition, before the trial, I used to give the doctor some orientation concerning courtroom procedure. Accordingly, I would ask him to meet with me, a reasonable time before the case was expected to come to trial, for the purpose of going over all the questions I intended to ask him on direct examination and those I anticipated would be put to him on cross-examination. I found that it was usually the fear of being cross-examined that caused the greatest reluctance to testify. This apprehension can be considerably allayed by adequate, comprehensive preparation.

When the doctor was called to the stand, I made it my first task to acquaint the jury with his medical background in order to establish his qualifications as an expert. Direct examination for this purpose would proceed somewhat as follows:

Q. Dr. Jones, are you duly licensed to practice medicine in this State?
Q. What college or colleges did you attend?
Q. When were you graduated?
Q. With what hospitals are you affiliated, and in what capacity?
Q. Do you specialize in any particular branch of medicine?
Q. How long have you specialized in this branch of medicine?
Q. Are you the author of any medical treatises?
Q. In what medical schools in this country is your book used as a text for medical students?
Q. Are you associated with any medical school?
Q. In what medical schools have you taught?

(Of course, questions concerning the doctor's publications and educational affiliations would not be asked unless he was indeed the author of some book or article and it was in fact used by medical students or cited in the literature on the subject and he himself had some experience in teaching medicine.)

Q. Did you have occasion to treat the plaintiff, Mary Smith, at your office on September 4, 1961?

If the doctor was the physician who had treated my client for injuries sustained in an accident, I would then have him relate the history of the case, as told to him, as well as his diagnosis, prognosis, and treatments. Such testimony would involve, first of all, a description, in minute detail, of each injury suffered by the plaintiff. In this connection, I would have the doctor report his objective findings regarding all scars, lesions, fractures, defects, and functional disturbances and disabilities. I would then ask him to express his medical judgment concerning the permanency of the injuries. Next, to fill out the picture, I would also have the doctor testify concerning the number of visits the plaintiff had made to his office, the number of house calls he had made in treating the plaintiff, and the nature of the medications and appliances he had prescribed.

In support of all this testimony, I would, wherever possible, refer the doctor to medical notes, X-rays, or other visual aids, which I would then have shown to the members of the jury to assist them in grasping the meaning of what the doctor said. Indeed, I made every effort to get into evidence as many written statements or memoranda as possible bearing on the medical testimony. In this way I made sure that when the jurors retired to deliberate, they would have before them in the jury room exhibits that had been received in evidence as tangible "props" for my case. The jurors could then point to these and discuss them without quibbling over what one juror thought the doctor had said or another juror denied having heard him say.

I found X-rays particularly helpful where a fracture was involved. In such cases, I would generally have opposing counsel consent to allow the X-rays to be marked in evidence. But even then, they are of little value unless the doctor who treated the injured party can discuss them intelligently. Whenever I had any doubts on this score, I preferred to call a competent roentgenologist to interpret the X-rays. If, on the other hand, the attending physician referred the patient to an associate who specialized in taking X-rays, I would have the specialist come to court with his records, prepared to read them and explain their meaning to the jury.

In cases of this kind I found the following line of questioning useful:

Q. Dr. Jones, are you a graduate of the X Medical School?
Q. Do you specialize in any branch of medicine?
Q. What are your qualifications as an expert in this field?
Q. Did you take X-rays of the plaintiff, Mary Brown, on October 5, 1962?
Q. Here are four X-ray films. Can you identify them?

After the doctor had identified the X-rays as those of the plaintiff taken on a certain date, I would show the film to opposing counsel and then state, "I offer these films in evidence." Of course, I would never offer a batch of X-ray films in evidence as a single exhibit, since it would later be difficult to follow interpretations of particular ones in the collection. Each would be offered separately. The Court would receive it in evidence and direct the reporter to mark it. When the entire set had been so marked, I would continue:

Q. Do these X-rays in their present condition correctly show the part of the plaintiff's body you X-rayed?

Further questioning would elicit from the doctor what the X-rays showed, whether they indicated any fractures, what kinds of fractures they were, how permanent the condition was likely to be, and what the effect of such an injury would be on the plaintiff's ability to stand, bend, turn, run, or make any other movements. At all times I was careful to have the doctor explain his medical terms in language that the jury would understand. Finally I would ask the doctor to state the amount of his charges for treating the patient, and I would inquire whether these charges were fair and reasonable.

My method of dealing with all these matters can best be illustrated by the following typical line of questioning:

Q. Doctor, look at Plaintiff's Exhibit 3, the X-rays you took of her left leg on October 5, 1962, and tell us what they show.

A. This film shows a comminuted fracture of the patella.

Q. Doctor, please tell the Court and the jury what that means.

A. The patella is the kneecap, in this case the left kneecap. A comminuted fracture is a pulverized break in the bone, a crushed bone.

Q. What effect does such a fracture have on the patient?

A. It causes severe pain whenever the patient attempts to move or bend the knee.

Q. What treatment did you prescribe for the plaintiff?

A. I applied a cast from above the left knee to her ankle. She wore it for some time.

Q. Doctor, did you bring your records in this case with you?

A. Yes.

Q. Are those records in your own handwriting?

A. Yes.

Q. When were they made?

A. At the time I treated the patient.

Q. Do they refresh your recollection?

A. Yes, they do.

Q. Tell us from your records how long the cast remained on the plaintiff's leg.

A. From October 5, 1962, for about six weeks. I removed the cast on November 16th.

Q. Doctor, have you formed any opinion as to the permanence of the plaintiff's injury?

A. Yes, it's a permanent condition.

Q. In your opinion, in what way will the plaintiff be affected by this injury?

A. Since she is an operator of a power press on housecoats and lingerie and is required to use her left leg and foot in her employment, she will no longer be able to do that kind of work. She will not be able to drive an automobile without feeling pain in the left knee joint. She will experience pain on standing or walking.

Q. In your opinion, can anything be done medically to help the plaintiff?

A. Yes, she can continue to receive treatments to relieve the pain, or she can undergo surgery to correct the damaged knee.

Q. Doctor, what is the total charge for the services you rendered?

A. My records show four visits, a series of X-rays, and treatment, for which I charged and was paid $125.00.

Q. Is that a fair and reasonable charge for a roentgenologist of your standing in the profession to make for all the services you rendered to the plaintiff?

A. Yes, sir, it is.

Of course, the same principles apply to the direct examination of any other type of expert witness called upon to interpret the significance of an exhibit, whether in the form of blueprints, technical documents, charts, tables, or handwriting. Whatever may be his specialty, his qualifications first have to be established, and then he must be led, step by step, through a detailed but at all times clearly understandable exposition of his professional findings and conclusions. Only if counsel is fully confident that such testimony will support his case should he put the expert on the stand, and only after thorough and precise questioning of the kind exemplified here may counsel safely turn his witness over to his adversary for cross-examination.

14

Getting Down to Cases

The particular questions a lawyer asks on direct examination will depend not only on the kind of witnesses he calls but also on the type of case he is trying. To be sure, the concrete circumstances of each case are unique and have to be individually mastered in preparing for it. Nevertheless, it is still possible to learn much, in a general way, about the art of direct examination, and to appreciate its fine points, by watching an expert trial lawyer at work questioning his witnesses.

Why do we not, then, return to the courthouse we visited earlier and see whether we can find anything going on there that is worth noting in this connection? Rather than immerse ourselves in all the details of each case, as counsel for each side has to do, let us follow our previous practice of moving from one courtroom to another, remaining only long enough to observe the crucial or significant parts of the direct examination and to comment on whatever may prove instructive. This procedure will also give us an opportunity to see how lawyers adapt the conduct of their direct examination to the nature of the case and to the type of witness on the stand.

We time our arrival in the courtroom to coincide with the beginning of the direct examination of a witness called by defense counsel in a criminal case for the purpose of establishing the good character of the accused. The problem here is a common one in this type of trial, but it is rarely handled well. Indeed, during the time I was an Associate Justice of the Court of Special Sessions, I was shocked to find how few attorneys knew how to go about performing this task for their clients.

Since our main concern is with the questioning, let us, in this case, disregard the witness' answers and concentrate exclusively on counsel's general approach.

The witness on the stand is a clergyman. Questioning begins as follows:

Q. What is your name?
Q. Where do you live?
Q. What is your occupation?

At this point, counsel could well have enlarged somewhat on the witness' background with questions about his years in the parish, his experience elsewhere, his work in the community, the size and composition of his congregation, the scope of his responsibilities, etc. Naturally, the same can be done for any professional person called for a similar purpose, such as a doctor, a lawyer, a judge, an engineer, or a businessman of some consequence and reputation.

Counsel now continues:

Q. Do you know the defendant?
Q. How long have you known the defendant?

Here, too, counsel might have had the witness expatiate on the nature and extent of his relationship with the defendant. Questions on this point would be especially appropriate if the witness has ever visited the accused at his home, spent time with him socially, or known him professionally as an active member of his congregation. In general, it is a good idea, when eliciting testimony regarding the good character of the accused, for counsel, wherever possible, to try to have the witness fill in the details of his experience with the defendant.

But let us turn our attention once again to the questioning, which proceeds as follows:

Q. Do you know people who know the defendant?
Q. Did you ever have occasion, before the date of the alleged crime, to discuss with people the defendant's reputation for truthfulness?

(This question is needed in most cases, and especially in those in which the accused is to testify in his own defense.)

Q. Did you ever have occasion, before the date of the alleged crime, to discuss with people the defendant's reputation for peaceableness?

Here the crime charged is evidently assault. Had it been larceny, a question concerning the defendant's reputation for honesty would have been appropriate. In general, any witness called for the purpose of establishing the good character of the accused in a criminal case should be asked to state what his reputation is in regard to any traits of character that might be relevant to the charges against him.

Finally, counsel asks:

Q. Will you tell the Court and the jury what the people of the community say about the defendant's truthfulness and peaceableness?

An alternative method of establishing the defendant's good character is by negative testimony, in response to the question: "Have you ever heard anyone say anything against the defendant?"

Quite another matter, however, is the trial of an action for separation on the ground of cruelty, which we find taking place when we return to court in the afternoon. In such a case, the handling of direct examination puts a lawyer—especially one accustomed to trying personal injury suits—to a severe test.

Following the usual procedure in negligence cases, counsel simply asks the plaintiff, after she takes the stand and has been identified, "Now tell the Court and jury just what happened on January 2, 1960, in your apartment."

Now there is no denying that a question like this is most appropriate in an action for personal injury resulting from alleged negligence on the part of the defendant. The plaintiff in such a lawsuit testifies, for example, that on a certain day, at a particular time and place, while he was standing at the street corner, he looked to the left and the right to see whether there was any traffic. There being none, he stepped into the roadway and was immediately knocked down by a speeding automobile that seemed to have come from nowhere. In other words, the event complained of happened "out of the blue."

But how utterly different the whole situation is when counsel is seeking, on behalf of his client, a separation on the ground of cruelty! We can best appreciate what a mistake it is for a lawyer to ignore this difference if we consider the answer given by the plaintiff to counsel's question in the present case:

"Well, I was standing at the kitchen sink, washing the dishes, when my husband came in and hit me."

Just like that!

The trouble with this kind of answer, of course, is that, unlike accidents, such things simply do not happen without a background of developing events that give them meaning. It is for this reason that a trial for separation on the ground of cruelty has no counterpart in civil jurisprudence. It is, in fact, something of a unique phenomenon. Counsel has to frame his questions in such a way as to bring out the whole chain of events that led up to each overt act of cruelty.

Fortunately, we have an opportunity to appreciate the superiority of a seasoned lawyer's method of presenting the evidence in a similar case in progress elsewhere in the courthouse. As we arrive, the plaintiff has just finished describing the physical arrangement of the premises at the time the incident complained of took place. Here is the testimony of the wife in her own words:

Q. Where were you?

A. I had just come downstairs to the kitchen after making the beds. I was standing at the stove, four or five feet away from the door leading to the foyer.

Q. Where was your husband at this time?

A. He was putting on his hat and coat. He was getting ready to go out.

Q. And where were your children?

A. They were still upstairs in bed. But then the telephone rang, and my daughter started to come downstairs to answer it.

Q. Did she answer it?

A. No. As she made for the phone, my husband ordered the child away and said he would take the call himself.

Q. Did your husband say anything else?

A. Yes, he made a very nasty remark about me. He called me a foul name and said I was getting telephone calls from strangers, and he was going to get to the bottom of it.

Q. What did your husband do at the telephone?

A. He picked up the receiver and answered the call, then hung up, walked into the kitchen, and in a loud tone of voice said I was soliciting calls from strange men who hung up when they heard his voice.

Q. What did you say to that?

A. I protested that I did not know what he was talking about. I told him I deeply resented his statement.

Q. What response did your husband make to that?

A. He told me that he would not tolerate such tactics any more, and he threatened to beat me if I did not stop.

Q. How did you react to this threat?

A. I became frightened and started to leave the kitchen, but he grabbed me by the arm and told me I would have to stay and listen to him until he was through.

Q. Did you offer any resistance?

A. Well, I tried to shake my arm loose, but he pushed me back.

Q. What did you do then?

A. I began to cry.

Q. Where were the children at this time?

A. When I started to cry, they were both standing right beside us.

Q. Did they see you crying?

A. Yes.

Q. What did they do when they saw you crying?

A. They began to cry too.

Q. What did your husband do when he saw the children crying?

A. He began to yell that I was inciting his own children against him.

Q. Did you try to leave?

A. Yes, but when I tried to push my way out of the kitchen, he raised his arm and with full force struck me on the side of my face, knocking me to the floor.

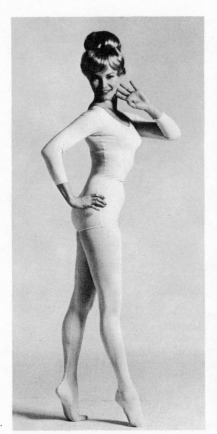

EXHIBIT 1: "If your client has been publicly photographed as shown at left . . . do not let her appear in court as shown at right. The jury will see through the pretense and exaggeration." (See Chapter 2.)

BROOKLYN, N. Y.

No.

BROOKLYN, N. Y. 11201
360 ADAMS STREET
ROOM 156
DIVISION OF JURORS   FIRST CLASS MAIL

. . . .

TELEPHONE
643-8023
643-5257
643-5256

THIS IS A LEGAL NOTICE

DO NOT DESTROY IT.   **BRING IT WITH YOU.**

The Penalty for Failure to Attend is Contempt of Court Punishable by a Fine Not Exceeding TWO HUNDRED AND FIFTY DOLLARS OR 30 DAYS IN JAIL

You are hereby summoned to appear personally at the office of the County Clerk, Division of Jurors, for the County of Kings, Room 156, 360 Adams Street, in the

Borough of Brooklyn, The City of New York, on

between the hours of **9 A. M.** and **3 P. M.,** for examination as to your competency and qualification to serve as a Trial Juror, as provided by Law.

Robert J. Crews

County Clerk   Kings County

Upon the willingness of those selected for jury service depends the proper administration of justice. Those who serve as jurors have the distinction of rendering a worthwhile civic service. To them must come the satisfaction of knowing that they are helping to protect our democratic form of government, which cannot "long endure" without the sustaining interest of the people who make up the community.

SEE INSIDE   66-1001-50M-701209(66) ⊂═══⊃ 114

EXHIBIT 2: Sample of Examination Summons mailed to potential jurors. (See Chapter 5.)

...LIFICATIONS TO SERVE AS JUROR
...BE FILLED OUT IN OWN HANDWRITING

DATE	RESULT	BY WHOM EXAMINED

DO NOT WRITE IN THIS BOX

...A PERSON WHO KNOWINGLY MAKES A FALSE STATEMENT OF A MATERIAL FACT IN
...ESTIONNAIRE IS GUILTY OF A MISDEMEANOR, PUNISHABLE BY FINE OR IMPRISONMENT

{ EXPLANATIONS OR REMARKS CONCERNING ANSWERS }
{ MAY BE MADE IN RULED BOX ON REVERSE SIDE }

...dersigned certifies to the following answers
...nt name
...ull

Married............ Single............ Widower............
Ever............ Ever............ No. of............
Divorced............ Separated............ Children............

FIRST NAME	MIDDLE NAME	LAST NAME

...te of
...h

Color............ hair
Color............ eyes
Wear............ glasses
Weight............
Height............

MO.	DAY	YEAR

...nt residence

P.O. Zone............
Apt. No............
Tel. No............

...ner or
...ant

If not, with............ whom do you live

How long living............ at present address
How long in............ N. Y. State
In Kings............ County

...nt former residences
...past six years

...e any other name you
...ve used or been known by............

If None State "None"

Did you register............ at last election
Where did you............ live then

...ce of
...th

If not American born,............ how became citizen

When............ naturalized
Where............

CITY	STATE

...ucation: Primary, High School,
...llege, degrees, special studies, etc............

...nt
...cupation

Employed............ at present
Business............ address
Tel. No............

...nt firm name
...employer

How long in............ present employment

...at other employment
...ring past six years............

...fe's
.... Her occupation
Her............ firm
Her busi-............ ness address

...you or your wife own property (such as bank account, furniture,
...urance, trust funds, stocks, bonds, mortgages, land, etc.) worth $250............

Describe............ property

...er before filled out
...s or similar form

Are you............ on relief
Ever served............ as a juror
In what court and............ when did you last serve

...er been denied listing as a qualified juror
...been stricken from any list of jurors............

Where............ and why

...e you physically
...abled or incapacitated............

Is your hearing or eyesight so impaired that............ you could not intelligently follow a case in court

Ever confined to a State............ or Private Institution

...your answer to any question on
...e 16 is "Yes," give all particulars............

...er arrested or
...dicted on a
...minal charge

Ever............ convicted

Ever summoned or notified to............ answer charges before any admin-............ istrative Bureau or Public officer

Any judgment ever entered against............ you in a civil court on allegations............ of fraud or misconduct

If "Yes" Explain On Back	If "Yes" Explain On Back	If "Yes" Explain On Back

...y judgments
...tstanding
...ainst you............

Nature of............ action in............ which obtained

Are you knowingly a member of any party or organization which advocates, advises
or teaches the duty, necessity, desirability, or propriety of overthrowing or destroying
the government of the United States, the government of any state, territory, district
or possession thereof, or of any political subdivision therein, by force or violence?............

...ave you ever been in
...nkruptcy or made a general
...signment for the benefit of creditors............

Have you such views concerning the death penalty
as would prevent you from finding a defendant
guilty if the crime charged be punishable by death............

If "Yes" Explain On Back

...ave you any opinion as to circum-
...antial evidence which would prevent your
...ding a verdict of guilty upon such evidence............

Do you doubt your ability to lay aside an opinion or impression formed
from newspaper reading or otherwise, or to render an impartial verdict
upon the evidence, uninfluenced by any such opinion or impression............

...re you aware of any prejudice against any
...ate law which would prevent a finding
...guilt for violating such law............

Have you such a prejudice against any particular
defense to a criminal charge as would prevent your
finding a fair and impartial verdict upon its merits............

If "Yes" Explain On Back	If "Yes" Explain On Back

...y law the failure of a defendant in a criminal case to
...stify is not considered as any evidence of his guilt.
...ould you give a defendant the benefit of this law............

What months of the year between
September 1 and June 30 would you
prefer to serve (Name at least two months)............

...there anything which would influence you as a juror, as affecting any person,
...class of persons because of nationality, sex, color, race, religion, wealth,
...cupation, political affiliation, social or economic belief or any other reason............

If "Yes" Explain On Back

...KING OF A FALSE STATEMENT OF A MATERIAL
...IN THIS QUESTIONNAIRE IS A MISDEMEANOR,
...JNISHABLE BY FINE AND IMPRISONMENT

THE FOREGOING ANSWERS ARE TRUE IN ALL RESPECTS

...NT
...O.

107-15M-701965 (65) ◆◆◆ (101)

SIGN HERE............

...XHIBIT 3: Questionnaire filled out by prospective juror at office of Division of Jurors.
...ront of form is shown above; back of form on reverse side. (See Chapter 5.)

I, ...do hereby certify;
I do not dwell or lodge nor do I have or maintain a dwelling or lodging in the
County of Kings for the greater part of the time between the first day of
October and the thirtieth day of June next thereafter, and I am not a resident

of said County; but I reside permanently at...

City of.........................., County of.........................., State of.........................., and have

resided there since...

                                    Signature

Dated :..196..........

I, ...do hereby certify;
I am entitled to and claim exemption } from doing jury service for the
I am disqualified

following reason ....

....

....

                                    Signature

Dated :..196..........

Explanation of any answers on oppos.
this form, or remarks, may be mad

DO NOT WRITE IN SPACE BELOW THIS LINE

| NAME | ADDRESS | BIRTH DATE | INDEX N |

RECORD OF JURY SERVICE

| DATE PLACED IN WHEEL | TERM DRAWN | COURT | DAYS | | IF EXCUSED REASON | DATE PLACED IN WHEEL | TERM DRAWN | COURT | DAYS | | IF E R |
			IN ATTEND-ANCE	ACTUAL-LY SERVED					IN ATTEND-ANCE	ACTUAL-LY SERVED	

CHANGES OF ADDRESS

BUSINESS ADDRESS

RESIDENCE

CERTIFICATE OF EXEMPTION OR NON-RESIDENCE

I, ...

do hereby certify that I reside at

....

and have resided there since ....

I claim that I am exempt from or not liable for jury service in Kings County, by reason of the following:

....

....

Date of birth ....

Occupation ....

Firm Name ....

Firm Address ....

SIGNATURE ....

THE MAKING OF A FALSE STATEMENT IN THIS CERTIFICATE IS A CRIME PUNISHABLE BY FINE AND IMPRISONMENT (PENAL LAW, SEC. 1232-a).

. . . .

EXEMPTIONS FROM JURY DUTY: The following, although qualified, are the only persons entitled to claim exemption:

1. A clergyman or minister of religion officiating as such and not following any other calling.

2. A practicing physician, surgeon, podiatrist, or dentist having patients requiring his daily professional attention, a licensed pharmacist, or embalmer actually engaged in his profession as a means of livelihood, and an optometrist actually engaged in the practice of optometry.

3. An attorney or counsellor at law regularly engaged in the practice of law as a means of livelihood.

4. A person belonging to the armed forces of the United States, and the active national guard and naval militia of the state.

5. An active city fireman or policeman: an exempt volunteer fireman, as defined in section two hundred of the general municipal law.

6. A captain, engineer, or other officer, actually employed upon a vessel making regular trips; or a licensed harbor or river pilot actually following that calling:

7. A woman.

8. An editor, editorial writer, a sub-editor, reporter or copy reader, actively and regularly employed in the handling or gathering of news for a daily, semiweekly or weekly newspaper.

The claimant for exemption, or another person in his behalf, must fill out the adjoining certificate, stating the facts in detail, which must be filed with the County Clerk.

RESIDENCE: (Sec. 596 Judiciary Law) A person dwelling or lodging or having or maintaining a dwelling or lodging in the County of Kings for the greater part of the time between October 1 and June 30 next thereafter, is a resident of Kings County, within the meaning of this section. If, under the foregoing provisions, you claim non-liability for jury service, please fill out in detail the adjoining certificate and return to the County Clerk.

EXHIBIT 4: Certificate of Exemption attached to Examination Summons. (See Chapter 5.)

BIRTH

NAME

RES

OCC

66-2001-6750-701541(59)   371

EXHIBIT 5: "Ballot" card prepared for each juror. (See Chapter 5.)

SUPREME COURT OF THE STATE OF NEW YORK

COUNTY OF KINGS

SUPREME COURT BUILDING, CIVIC CENTER AT MONTAGUE ST., BROOKLYN, N. Y.

You are hereby SUMMONED to attend a TRIAL TERM of the SUPREME COURT of the STATE OF NEW YORK, in the CENTRAL JURY PART, Room 261, SUPREME COURT BUILDING, Civic Center at Montague St., in the Borough of Brooklyn, as a TRIAL JUROR, for the 12 jury days of said term or as otherwise ordered by the Court, commencing

at 9:30 o'clock in the forenoon.

BRING THIS NOTICE WITH YOU

Robert J. Brown

County Clerk, Kings County

A FAILURE TO ATTEND WILL MAKE YOU LIABLE TO A FINE, NOT TO EXCEED $250, OR IMPRISONMENT NOT TO EXCEED 30 DAYS, OR BOTH, FOR CONTEMPT OF COURT.

AN APPLICATION TO BE EXCUSED FROM JURY SERVICE, IN ACCORDANCE WITH THE PROVISIONS OF LAW (SEC. 604) AS SET FORTH ON THE BACK OF THIS SUMMONS, MAY BE MADE AT THE CENTRAL JURY PART BETWEEN THE HOURS OF 9:30 A.M. AND 3:30 P.M., FROM TUESDAY THROUGH FRIDAY PRIOR TO THE RETURN DAY, BUT IF SUCH PRIOR APPLICATION CAN NOT BE MADE, THE JUROR MAY MAKE SUCH APPLICATION ON THE DATE AND AT THE TIME HE IS REQUIRED BY THIS SUMMONS TO ATTEND. NO APPLICATION WITH REGARD TO THIS SUMMONS MAY BE MADE TO THE COUNTY CLERK.

66-2019-5M-701204(66)   114

EXHIBIT 6:   Jury Subpoena mailed to prospective juror. Front of form is shown above; back of form on reverse side. (See Chapter 5.)

SEC. 603. The county clerk must notify each juror drawn for jury service by serving upon him a notice to that effect and specifying the place where and the time when he is required to attend. The notice may be served by mail, personally, or by leaving it at the juror's residence or place of business with a person of suitable age and discretion.

SEC. 604. The judge of the trial court may, in his discretion, on the application of a trial juror, excuse him from a part or the whole of the time of service required of him as a juror or may postpone the time of service of a juror to a later day during the same or any subsequent term of the court.

A person who has been notified to attend and who applies to be excused as prescribed in this section must present the notice to the judge in open court. If he can not personally attend he must send it by a person capable of making the necessary proof in relation to his claim to be excused.

SEC. 749-c. All jurors including those in a criminal action or special proceeding in a court or before an officer duly summoned and who served as provided for by the laws of this state and are entitled to payment therefor, must present their claims to the proper official designated by law for the payment of jurors' fees, on or before the thirty-first day of December of the year succeeding or following the year in which such services were rendered and performed, and failure to comply with this provision shall be a forefeiture of the payment for such claims or services thereafter.

REPORT PURSUANT CH. 202, SEC. 604 LAWS 1940 TO BE FILLED IN BY CLERK OF COURT.

Date to which
Service Postponed ....

IF EXCUSED—
REASON ....

....

....

PUNISHMENT IMPOSED—
SEC. 751, Judiciary Law ....

Judicial Signature
or Initials ....

JUROR must fill in **(use ink)** before appearance in court and deliver to Clerk of Court, whether or not applying to be excused.

Signature of Juror..

Tel.
Residence.. *No*..................
Brooklyn, N. Y.

Business
Firm Name..

Business
Address..

Tel.
Occupation.. *No*..................

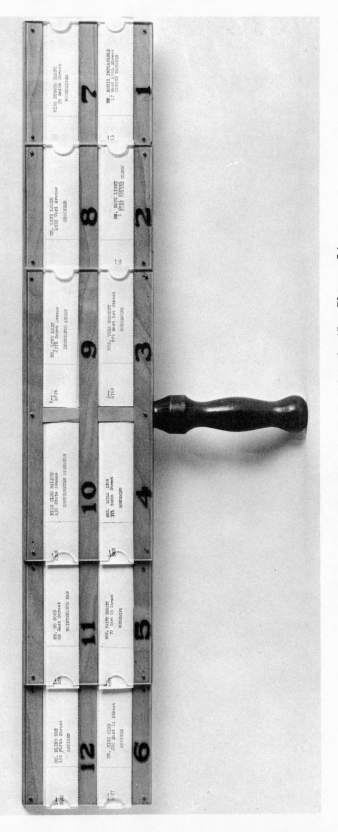

Exhibit 7: Panel Board with jurors' cards. (See Chapter 5.)

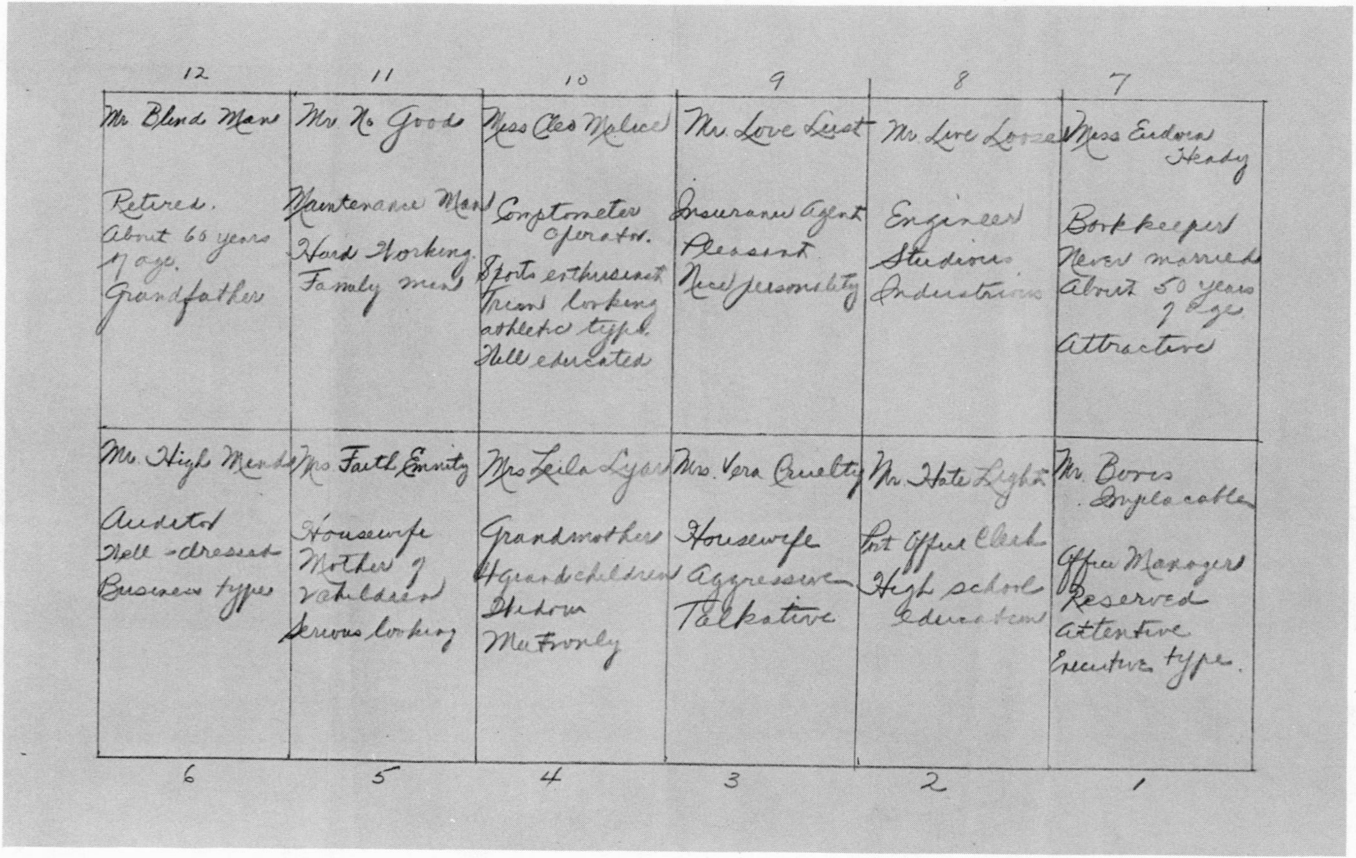

EXHIBIT 8: Diagram of jury box with useful notes. (See Chapter 6.)

12 — Mr. Blank Man
Retired. About 65 years of age. Grandfather

11 — Mrs. R. Goode
Maintenance Man. Hard Working. Family man

10 — Mrs. Geo. Wallace
Construction Operator. Sports enthusiast. Keeps working. athletic type. full education

9 — Mrs. Love Scott
Insurance Agent. Pleasant. Responsible

8 — Mr. Love Lorn
Engineer. Studious. Intensive

7 — Mrs. Edms. Henry
Book-keeper. Never married. About 50 years. ? Eye. Attractive

6 — Mr. High Mind
Arrested. Well-dressed. Business type

5 — Mrs. Fat'l County
Housewife. Mother? schooled. serious to hear

4 — Mrs. Zila Lynch
Grandmother. Grandchildren aggressive. Modern. McFinley

3 — Mrs. Vera Quality
Housewife. Talkative

2 — Mr. Ash Right
Post Office Clerk. Slight active. Education

1 — Mr. Butis
Bright active. Office Manager. Reserved. attentive. executive type.

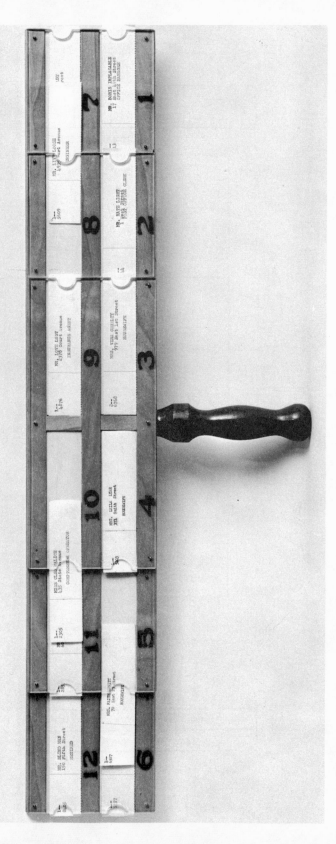

EXHIBIT 9: Panel Board showing cards 5, 8, and 10 moved to one side as reminders that jurors 5, 8, and 10 are to be excused from serving. (See Chapter 6.)

IN GOD WE TRUST

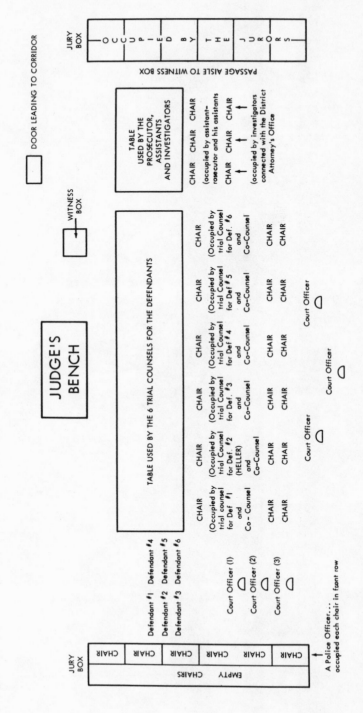

EXHIBIT 10: Diagram of courtroom in which author defended one of six youthful defendants accused of murder. (See Chapter 17.)

We are certainly proceeding very slowly. At this rate, it seems, the trial is going to drag on for a long, long time. Will not the judge become impatient with such a long-drawn-out recital of what he said and she said? Possibly. But a contested separation action, involving a number of different acts of alleged cruelty, may require several days of testimony like this. There is absolutely no short cut that a lawyer can safely take in this type of case. He must prove it with facts. Otherwise he is not giving his client proper representation. If the judge becomes impatient, that is a hazard that counsel must be prepared to face. It is his duty to try to convince the judge that every reasonable effort is being made to expedite the trial, and not to prolong the proceedings unduly. But the proof must be set against its background and in the context of all the relevant circumstances.

We have time to observe just one more trial before the day is over. Shunning any more matrimonial actions, we take our place in a packed courtroom where a man is on trial for manslaughter. The accused, charged specifically with vehicular homicide on the New York Thruway, is on the stand and has just finished identifying himself, stating his address, his occupation, and the place where he was on the night of the alleged crime. His attorney proceeds with the direct examination as follows:

Q. After you left your home on the morning of December 8, 1962, do you remember whether anything happened while you were driving out of New York City?
A. Yes, an attractive woman standing at the side of the road put her hand up to thumb a ride with me.

Here counsel took care to avoid asking a leading question, like "Did you see an attractive woman trying to thumb a ride?" Instead, he phrased his question in general terms that permitted the witness to supply the details.

The questioning continues:

Q. What did you do?
A. I stopped my car.
Q. What happened then?
A. The woman asked for a lift.
Q. What did she say?
A. She said, "Mister, are you going upstate?"
Q. What did you reply?
A. I told her I was going to Newburgh.
Q. What, if anything, did she say?
A. "That's just where I am going!"

These are all excellent questions, precise and pointed. Each contains only five or six words, and each calls for a brief response.

But now counsel is coming to a crucial part of his direct examination. There is, apparently, a contradiction between the statement made by his client when he was questioned by the State Police and the allegations made in the defense. Here is how the problem is approached:

> Q. What did you tell the State Police after your arrest when they asked you whether anyone else was in the car with you?
> A. I told them that no one was in the car with me.
> Q. Was that true?
> A. No.
> Q. Do you have any explanation?
> A. I was lying when I said no one was in the car with me. Frankly, I didn't want my wife to know I took a day off from work and that I was driving upstate and had a woman in my car.
> Q. Do you realize your predicament now?
> A. Yes.
> Q. Have you anything further to say?
> A. I am sorry I lied, and that is all I can say.

Thus, by adroit questioning, defense counsel has succeeded, on direct examination, in explaining the conduct of the defendant immediately after the alleged manslaughter. At the same time, the accused is no longer seen in the unfavorable light in which he placed himself by making untrue statements to the police.

In the cases we have just observed, our attention was concentrated so much on the questions being asked that we probably failed to notice a very significant fact. During the direct examination, the judge, in virtually every instance, was constantly poring over his notebook, or writing feverishly in it, as the witnesses testified. In fact, I myself take more notes on the testimony given during direct examination than during cross-examination, and I believe my practice in this respect is typical of that of most judges. Sometimes a judge will even stop a witness and ask the reporter to read back an answer, or he may have the witness himself repeat it, just to keep the notebook record in order.

Nor will the judge relax until the cross-examination begins. Indeed, I would say that for every ten pages of material written in his notebook during a trial, only about one page is set down during cross-examination. Moreover, when the time comes for the judge to charge the jury, the chances are that in summarizing the respective contentions of the parties, he will rely, to a considerable extent, on the notes he has taken and the data he has culled from the testimony given during the direct examination.

We see, then, how important it is for a lawyer to make sure that the answers given to his questions by his client and witnesses constitute a clear and complete statement of his case. To this end, he may sometimes find it necessary, after one of his witnesses has been cross-examined, to repair or qualify his testimony by redirect examination. Occasionally a witness who has given a good account of himself in his direct testimony can be made to look confused or unreliable by a clever cross-examiner. A perfectly innocent fact, for example, may be put in such a light as to appear quite sinister simply because something in the context is left unexplained. Under such circumstances, the temptation is strong for counsel to re-examine his witness in order to clear up the uncertainty, fill in the missing details, and set the record straight once again.

However, there are grave dangers in this procedure. Unless a lawyer is absolutely certain that harmful or damaging statements made by his witness under cross-examination can be corrected, it would be better to forego any effort to rehabilitate him by questioning him further. Otherwise, counsel may well be running the risk of emphasizing a weak point in his case. Besides, the witness may not know how to exculpate himself. Consequently, redirect examination should be used sparingly. Apparent contradictions and confusions in the testimony of a witness can often be cleared up better in counsel's summation.

Under no circumstances should a lawyer employ redirect examination in an attempt to bolster solid testimony already given by his witness. It is best to leave well enough alone, as the following incident shows.

The case involved a collision between two ships, one of which was lying at anchor in a harbor at the time of the accident. The owner of this vessel engaged an experienced maritime lawyer on its behalf. On direct examination of a qualified expert, a master mariner, counsel succeeded in eliciting testimony to the effect that the ship could not possibly have backed down sufficiently to avoid being hit. Direct examination included the following testimony on this point:

Q. Now, suppose a man had been present on the bow of the anchored ship, and, at the first sign of danger, about a minute before the collision, he had been ordered to pull up the anchor, could the vessel have been maneuvered out of the way of the other ship by putting the engines promptly at full speed astern?

A. Quite impossible. The ship could not possibly have been backed down enough.

When direct examination had been completed, the cross-examination began. This was followed by redirect examination and a second cross-examination of the same witness. Throughout, he remained unshaken in the conviction, which he repeatedly made perfectly clear, that the anchored vessel could not, by any action on her part, have avoided the collision.

Nevertheless, perhaps feeling that he must have the last word, counsel for the owner of the anchored ship could not resist a further question on an additional redirect examination:

Q. Just one more question I forgot to ask you. If you were a chief officer on the lower bridge of a ship like the one involved and saw a vessel bearing down on you off your port bow in the fashion that I have asked you to assume before, what is the first thing that you would do?

A. If I were the chief officer on that ship, and there were indications of a collision, or a ship was bearing down on me, I couldn't decide in an instant whether that ship was going to hit my ship or not, just because he let his anchors go, and it would probably take me five seconds or more to decide whether there was going to be a collision, and then I would try to shout to the man on deck to stand by the windlass and feed chain, and at the same time rush to the telegraph and ring standby, and immediately after that full speed astern. That is what I would have done.

Not one of these measures had been taken aboard the anchored vessel!

Many lawyers, I find, are like counsel in this case. They think that when their adversary has completed his cross-examination, they must, as a matter of course, rise again to conduct a re-examination, if only to give added emphasis to the points they have already established. They seem to be afraid that otherwise the jury may forget their witness' direct testimony and remember only something he may have said during cross-examination. Generally, however, if the direct examination has been properly prepared and conducted in the first place, there should be no need for counsel to return to his witness after he has been cross-examined. At any rate, if a lawyer has any doubt whatever that he can accomplish anything to overcome the effect of a destructive cross-examination, the best policy for him to follow is to permit the witness to leave the stand without further questioning.

At last the moment comes when counsel finds that he has called all his witnesses and has completed his direct examination of them. This is an appropriate time for him to take a backward glance at the proceedings thus far in order to assure himself that all is in order, before he "rests" his case and allows his adversary to present his. Certainly there is no reason for any lawyer to be hasty in making a decision to terminate this phase of the trial, and there are many good reasons for giving the matter some careful thought.

No doubt counsel may take some comfort from the fact that, on the whole, those whom he has called upon to testify have done well, thanks to his efforts to prepare them. Most of them have, besides, withstood satisfactorily a searching cross-examination. In the few instances where they did not, one or two pointed questions on redirect examination sufficed to straighten everything out.

But is this all that counsel has to be concerned about now? By no means.

For one thing, as he reviews in his mind the direct testimony he has elicited, he may recall that some of it was not strictly in accord with the allegations made in the pleadings. In that case, fortunately, the remedy is quite simple. All counsel needs to do is to move "to conform the pleadings to the proof."

But there are other considerations, much more weighty, that should give him pause at this time, especially if he is representing the plaintiff. For once he utters the fateful words, "Plaintiff rests," he must be prepared to have his entire case, as presented so far, put to its first important test. If it fails that test, the trial is over, and counsel has lost his case, no matter how well he thought his witnesses testified.

There is no avoiding the test, either. The moment counsel rests his case, he can expect that his adversary will rise, as a matter of course, to make a "pro forma" motion for a judgment on the defendant's behalf.

On what grounds? Anything that opposing counsel can find. And he can surely be counted on to find something. Generally it will be something lacking from the testimony or the evidence, but not always. If, for example, an accident case is being tried, he may seek to show that the plaintiff was guilty of contributory negligence. Did not the plaintiff admit operating his automobile about thirty-five miles an hour in a zone where the speed limit was twenty-five miles an hour? Did not his testimony show that he failed to yield the right of way when he reached the "Yield" sign at the intersection where the accident occurred, and that he misjudged the distance between his car and the defendant's? Opposing counsel may even quote from the trial record to substantiate his argument.

But, more often, he will try to find some insufficiency in the testimony or evidence offered on the plaintiff's behalf. The decision in either case is a matter of law and rests with the judge, not the jury. What the judge has to decide is not a question of fact, but whether sufficient legal evidence, direct or circumstantial, has been presented by the witnesses for the plaintiff to warrant submitting the case to the jury. If the judge thinks not, he will grant the defense motion, and the case will be ended then and there. If, on the other hand, the Court denies the motion, the defense presents its case. Sometimes, however, the Court may choose to reserve decision on the motion to dismiss the complaint. In that case, too, the trial will continue. But then, at the end of the case, before the issues are given to the jury to decide, the defendant's attorney can still move for judgment on his client's behalf, as a matter of law, on the ground that the plaintiff failed to prove his case "by a fair preponderance of the credible evidence."

Such a motion, at this point in the trial, is tantamount to a motion for a directed verdict for the defendant. If the Court grants the motion, the judge, in effect, takes the position that there is nothing for the jury to decide after all, and therefore the judgment will be given in the defendant's favor. In that event the Court will tell the members of the jury that there are no questions of fact to deliberate on. If, however, the motion is denied, the questions of fact raised during the trial will be given to the jury to resolve.

To be sure, in deciding on a motion to dismiss the complaint at the end of the plaintiff's case, a judge is required to consider the evidence adduced at the trial in the aspect most favorable to the plaintiff. In other words, the plaintiff is to be given every favorable inference which can reasonably be drawn from the evidence and testimony.

Nevertheless, it is not a good idea for the plaintiff's counsel to rely on the benefit of the doubt if he can possibly avoid doing so. Before he rests his case, he had better be reasonably certain that the evidence he has offered is sufficient to withstand the legal attack that he knows will immediately be made upon it. Only after he has satisfied himself on this point may he safely and confidently bring his affirmative presentation of his client's case to a formal conclusion.

V

TAKING EXCEPTION

15

"I Object!"

The popular image of a trial is certainly very far from reflecting the rather colorless and sedate proceedings I have described so far. Are not the courtroom scenes depicted on stage and screen—to say nothing of those to be viewed on television—full of tension, conflict, and excitement? Where is the clash of personalities between opposing counsel? May we not expect to see each jump up at every moment to register a heated objection to the questions and tactics of the other? Where do we find the eyeball-to-eyeball encounter of unbudgeable antagonists, resorting to every conceivable stratagem, licit or illicit, to score a point in their favor? And where are the shouting matches between contending lawyers, or the barbed insults and stinging taunts they hurl at each other in the heat of their fury?

Do these outbursts really occur, or are they not rather the frothy fabrications of sensation-mongering scenario writers intent on whipping up a synthetic drama for their audience?

Ideally, of course, a trial is supposed to be conducted with dignity and decorum, on the very sound theory that the search for truth is best carried on in an atmosphere of dispassionate inquiry. It is normally the responsibility of the presiding judge to ensure that the conditions prevailing during the trial are conducive to a calm, judicial assessment of the pertinent facts in the case. Temperamental flare-ups on the part of counsel are as out of place as demonstrations of emotion or partisanship on the part of the spectators, and both will usually meet with a prompt rebuke from the Court. Indeed, judges are empowered to take, if necessary, stern measures to uphold and preserve the majesty of the law and to enforce the respect due to its authority.

Nevertheless, we have to reckon with the all-too-human tendency of lawyers to become emotionally involved in the cases they are trying. After all, their prestige is at stake, as well as monetary considerations, and they feel also an understandable obligation to do all in their power to protect the rights of their clients. It is hardly surprising, therefore, that a good trial lawyer keeps a sharp watch over every word spoken by opposing counsel as he examines witnesses. If anything objectionable is said or done, this is the signal for the alert advocate to rise in defense of his client's rights and to ask that it be stricken from the record as immaterial, incompetent, irrelevant, or prejudicial, as the case may be.

For, as we have seen, the rules of evidence forbid the introduction of such testimony on the ground that it is not, properly speaking, evidence at all. Evidence, in the strict sense, includes all the means by which an alleged matter of fact in dispute in a case is either established or disproved. Before a trial judge can admit oral testimony or documentary proof as evidence, it must meet certain requirements. It is relevant if it has the legal capacity to prove or to disprove a principal fact in dispute. It is material if it has a direct, effective bearing or influence on one or more pertinent facts at issue in the case on trial. And it is competent if it is given in the form of testimony by a properly qualified person, or if it was produced by such a person.

Although the rules of evidence are interpreted and applied by the judge, he may very often depend on counsel for guidance in the particular instances when they are invoked. In order to keep up his guard, a lawyer must therefore pay close attention not only to every question asked by his adversary, but also to every answer given by the witnesses for the other side. As soon as counsel is convinced that an objection is in order, he should not hesitate to make it, whether it is sustained or not. Any laxity or delayed reaction on his part in this respect only permits objectionable testimony to keep piling up while his adversary covers a great deal of ground that cannot later be recaptured.

The importance of being "on one's toes" to make timely objections is well illustrated by the following excerpt from the record of a case in which the daughter of the injured plaintiff testified as to what she had done for her mother:

Q. Where was she hurt, did she tell you?
A. She said she fell, and she hurt her knee, and she had terrific pain.
Q. Which knee?
A. Left knee. And she was in terrific pain. And I phoned the doctor immediately. When I phoned the doctor, I said, "Mother fell, and she is in terrible pain. What shall we do?" He suggested I go around the corner to Dr. Carlson and have an X-ray taken.
Q. Was that done?
A. Yes, immediately, and Selma helped me, Mrs. Hall helped me, and we helped Mother over to Dr. Carlson, and then Dr. Carlson

took Mother, and she still was in pain, and Dr. Stone is right across the street, and we went right from Dr. Carlson. We didn't wait for the X-ray. We went right over to Dr. Stone, and Dr. Stone looked at Mother, and she said she had terrible pains, and he gave her some pills that he had there, and from there we came home, and I tried to ease her, but it seemed anyway we raised the leg—.

DEFENDANT'S COUNSEL: I haven't objected to—.

THE COURT: That is your business. If you don't object, I don't rule.

DEFENDANT'S COUNSEL: I move that the testimony of the witness with regard to what transpired or what she did be stricken out as immaterial.

THE COURT: Motion denied.

Q. After you took her home from Dr. Stone's office, did you do anything for your mother?

A. Yes, I tried. I gave her a pillow underneath the knee. She said nothing helped. So I phoned the doctor again.

DEFENDANT'S COUNSEL: I move that it be stricken out.

THE COURT: That what be stricken out?

DEFENDANT'S COUNSEL: That nothing helped.

THE COURT: Granted.

Here, the result of counsel's tardy reaction was that much objectionable testimony based on inference and hearsay was left in the record, all of it prejudicial to his client's case.

More often, however, the mistake made by counsel is in the other direction. Far from failing to capitalize on opportunities to make valid objections, many lawyers tend to "protest too much." These "overconscientious objectors," as I like to call them, keep popping up at the slightest pretext, almost from the moment opposing counsel has begun his direct examination, and sometimes even before they have heard the entire question or the witness has had a chance to answer it. Immediately they launch into a vociferous cry of indignation at the outrageous tactics of their adversary. The courtroom resounds with their clamorous protests against virtually every move made by opposing counsel. If only the strength of a case could be measured in decibels!

Unfortunately, too often those who cry the loudest have the weakest cases, and it is only too obvious that they are hoping to substitute vocal vehemence for legal validity. But even more lamentable is the situation of the attorney who has a good case, but who merely succeeds in arousing the suspicion of the jury by his niggling, pettifogging obstructionism. For a lawyer can generally expect to get very little mileage by raising continual objections, even if most of them are sustained.

Indeed, he may do his case more harm than good if he insists on the exclusion of relatively innocuous and inconsequential matter that does not substantially affect the issues in the case. The only effect he is likely to have on the members of the jury is to give them the impression that he is trying to becloud the issues and to keep from them matters they should know.

This impression is likely to be reinforced if counsel's objections are frequently overruled by the Court. To be sure, the unfavorable effect on the jury may be somewhat mitigated by a technique in favor with a certain Assistant District Attorney much admired by one of my colleagues on the bench. Whenever his objections are overruled, he invariably says, "Thank you, Judge." The jury, unacquainted with the technical aspects of the objection, is presumably left with the feeling that he is always being sustained.

But even this is not enough. It is quite possible for a lawyer to win any number of verbal skirmishes over the exclusion of evidence that is technically inadmissible, and yet lose the war as far as the jury is concerned. Sustained objections to the admission of evidence do not necessarily count as milestones along the way toward a favorable verdict. A lawyer may score point after point over his opponent in these respects and still be as far as ever from achieving his goal. In the last analysis, what counts is the headway he makes with the jurors. If he cannot win *them*, all the legal acumen in the world is of no avail.

Such considerations may at first be somewhat disconcerting to a conscientious advocate, eager to do his duty by his client, especially if counsel is convinced that this requires him to take advantage of every right that the law allows. The rules of evidence are necessarily framed in such general terms that harmless technical deviations from them are almost bound to occur quite naturally in the course of any recital of events by the average witness unfamiliar with the law. Is it really counsel's obligation to object to *everything* said by a witness that might be inadmissible on the strictest and most literal interpretation of the rules?

The best way to answer this question—which is really a question of trial tactics—is to consider a few cases in which it might arise. Several are mentioned by Justice Samuel J. Silverman in an article in the *New York Law Journal* of March 24, 1966, on some absurd technicalities in the rules of evidence.

Suppose, to cite an example mentioned by the Justice, a witness is asked to state the source of a spark that caused an explosion. Being cautious and well informed about matters of this kind, he may begin by saying, "Well, there are a number of possibilities." Before he can go any further, opposing counsel raises an objection. The witness may not, strictly speaking, indulge in speculation about mere possibilities. Yet it is questionable whether, in fact, counsel has gained anything by insisting on the exclusion of such a statement once the members of the jury have heard it. Can they really ignore it or put it out of their minds, even if they are promptly instructed by the Court to do so? Will they not be likely to conclude that something significant is being deliberately withheld from them?

Or suppose a witness is asked to mention something he remembers about a person he met that might help to identify the individual. On reflection he answers (to cite another of Justice Silverman's illustrations), "Well, I did notice that she spoke English rather poorly." Technically this is an inference or a conclusion. The witness is supposed to avoid such statements and to confine his testimony to what he knows directly. But what sense would it make for a lawyer to raise an objection to such an answer? Even if it were to be expunged from the record, it could not very well be replaced by any other testimony on this point, nor could it be erased from the minds of the jurors. A lawyer would be well advised to let it pass without objection.

The same is true, of course, of answers like "I think so" or "I believe so" in response to questions inquiring whether a particular event took place. It is simply absurd for opposing counsel to insist on excluding such answers on the legalistic ground that they are "conclusions." Yet there are lawyers who can be counted on to leap up with an objection as soon as they hear anything like this said by a witness for the other side.

Then, too, some lawyers like to make a big to-do about what are called "unresponsive" answers that are not directly relevant to the question. Yet very few people not especially trained in the law can testify for very long without wandering somewhat from the point, interjecting an irrelevancy, or gratuitously adding something not asked for. This, in fact, is the pattern of normal discourse, and it is not likely to be altered substantially when a person takes the stand. If, for example, a witness is asked whether he had a conversation with a given party on a particular date, it is common for him to begin his answer by saying something like, "Well, now, let's see. That was twelve years ago."

Up jumps Mr. Objector: "I move to strike out the answer as unresponsive."

In effect, what he is asking the judge to do is to tell the jury to disregard the fact, known to all of them, that twelve years have elapsed since the conversation in question! The impression made on a jury by this kind of quibbling may well be imagined.

Still another rule of evidence excludes testimony referring to "operations of the mind." And so, there is always some stickler for legalism to insist on his last ounce of flesh if a hapless witness says something like "I was so scared when I saw the car coming at me that I was paralyzed with fright," or "I was so ashamed when he called me nasty names in front of our children," or "He became infuriated with rage," or "Both of them came to see what was going on." It is hard for me to understand how any lawyer can really believe he has taken a step forward toward a favorable verdict for his client when he raises an objection to such testimony. It seems to me that this kind of advocate has become so accustomed to a purely mechanical application of a set of misunderstood legal formulas that he has completely lost sight of his ultimate goal. Once again, he has failed to reckon with the impact of his conduct on the jury.

Perhaps the area in which there is the greatest abuse of the demand to exclude testimony is that of hearsay. Statements made out of court by persons not called as witnesses are, with certain notable exceptions, inadmissible as evidence of the truth of the facts they allege. The reason for excluding hearsay is the absence of the necessary safeguards to ensure or check the reliability of the testimony, such as the oath administered to the witness, cross-examination, and the opportunity to observe his behavior on the stand.

But not everything that seems like hearsay is really that. It is understandable that a layman might have some difficulty in distinguishing actual from merely apparent hearsay, because the legal definition of hearsay is a technical one. But there is little excuse for a trial lawyer, who should know better, to jump up and cry, "Hearsay!" every time a witness begins to relate what somebody else said. Often no hearsay is involved at all.

The difference between the substance of hearsay and its shadow can best be seen in a landmark case in which the defendant was on trial for the first-degree murder of his wife. Here, the prosecution had to prove that the accused had killed his victim with both premeditation and deliberation. The husband's defense was that he had committed only manslaughter, because he had killed his wife in the heat of passion. As proof of this contention, he alleged that immediately before he killed her, his wife had incited his fury by telling him that she had become pregnant by another man.

When the defendant sought to testify that his wife had made this statement to him, the Court admitted the testimony as not in violation of the rule excluding hearsay. Although the wife's statement had been made out of court and could not, in the very nature of the case, be independently verified by calling her to the stand, what she said to her husband the moment before the slaying was not being offered in evidence as proof of its truth, but only to show the effect it had produced on the defendant's state of mind at the time. Whether or not his wife was telling him the truth was not at issue in this case. What made his statement admissible was that it was relevant to the contention of the accused that he had become so enraged by what his wife said to him that he killed her then and there, in the heat of passion, without premeditation or deliberation.

We see, then, that a lawyer has to use good judgment in deciding what to object to. He may sometimes better discharge his duty to his client by refraining from an objection, even when it may be technically valid, than by pressing for the strictest adherence to the letter of the law in every instance. It takes experience and a certain emotional maturity to know just when to object and when not to insist on one's right to do so. Indeed, the ability to exercise this kind of precise discrimination is one of the distinctive marks of the expert trial lawyer. Between neglecting to protect his client's lawful rights, on the one hand, and a self-defeating excess of zeal, on the other, an attorney has to find the middle way of prudence, moderation, and good sense.

In order to steer a safe course through these treacherous seas, counsel would do well, in advance of trial, to chart for himself, so far as possible, not only the landmarks needed to get his bearings but also some of the rocks on which he could founder. After all, he should have a rather good idea, before going to court, of the testimony his adversary expects to elicit from the witnesses for the other side. It is not, then, difficult to draw up at least a tentative plan for dealing with anticipated possibilities in the area of inadmissible evidence. Certainly counsel will do this anyway in preparing to counter expected objections to the evidence he himself proposes to adduce, and he should extend his preparation to include the essentials of his own strategy for meeting inadmissible evidence likely to be offered by his adversary. The basic question counsel should ask himself in each instance is the extent, if any, to which the objectionable testimony is likely to damage or prejudice his client's case. Unless the evidence is deemed to be positively harmful or prejudicial, counsel should consider carefully whether it is worth protesting against at all, whatever may be the technical merits of his objection.

Unless an attorney learns to curtail excessive and unnecessary objections, he may one day find himself a bit groggy and may say, as one weary advocate once did at the end of a long, hard day in court, "I object to the testimony on the grounds that it is incompetent, immaterial, and irrelevant—and on any other grounds that may be applicable that I can't think of at this time."

Perhaps because of the publicity they have received in our mass media of entertainment, those members of the legal profession who are engaged in trial work seem to have attracted to their ranks more than their share of frustrated actors. For these "hams," the courtroom is primarily a theater in which they can satisfy their suppressed yearning for playing to the galleries. What they thrive on most is the laughter and applause of the multitude. They look upon the trial chiefly as a showpiece for themselves and an excuse for displaying their histrionic talents. Nothing pleases them so much as to be the center of attention, and they like best of all those parts of the trial—the opening to the jury and the summation—in which they have the whole stage to themselves, as both prologue and epilogue. They revel, too, in the scenes of dialogue—direct examination or cross-examination—in which they take an active role. But what they cannot tolerate is having to yield place to opposing counsel for even a limited time and to stand waiting in the wings while he examines his own witnesses.

And so these scene-stealers seek every opportunity to stay in the limelight as long as possible. They will not allow the jury to forget them for an instant. Any pretext will do for an interruption, whether in the form of an objection, a "wisecrack," or a gratuitous sneer, so long as it gives them a chance to be the star performer. They will just as soon play the clown as strike a tragic pose, if only they can get the spotlight to shine upon them for a blazing moment. Never mind what happens to their client's case in the meanwhile!

I am not, of course, referring here to the carefully calculated theatrical effect—the dramatic pause, the surprise witness, the spectacular exhibit, the climactic sequence of questions, the contrived suspense, or the sharp change of tone. These are certainly legitimate when sparingly employed for a definitely intended effect by a lawyer gifted with a flair for showmanship. Later, in discussing the art of cross-examination, I shall have occasion to describe some of these techniques at greater length. There is undoubtedly a proper place for a certain amount of theatricality in the work of a trial lawyer, as long as it effectively subserves his ultimate end, which is that of winning his case. It is only when he has lost sight of this end in a narcissistic preoccupation with his own image that his courtroom theatrics become self-defeating.

This is exactly what happened in a case recently tried before me. The plaintiff, who had sustained serious injuries in an accident, was on the stand undergoing direct examination by his lawyer:

Q. What was the next thing you remember, after the accident?
A. I was lying in bed in a hospital, with a nun holding my hand—I thought I was in heaven.

Counsel for the defendant knew exactly what the witness meant, namely, that he was hit so hard he thought he was dead. But, trying to be funny at the plaintiff's expense, he arose and, looking straight at the jury, asked in "deadpan" fashion, "With whom were you lying in bed?"

As I observed the expressions on the faces of the jury, I got their reaction: a telepathic message of six words, saying: "Judge, now *that lawyer* is dead."

"Smart aleck" tactics of this kind usually backfire badly, and the attorney who resorts to them generally gets what he deserves.

No less obnoxious and inept are those who cannot seem to resist butting in with gratuitous comments during direct examination by opposing counsel. Almost invariably they suffer some setback as the price of their compulsive imprudence. Not content to remain quiet while they are ahead, they brashly rush in where they have no business venturing and soon become involved in a mess from which they cannot possibly extricate themselves.

A case in point is a negligence action tried before me some years ago, in which the plaintiff was suing two defendants—let us call them Clark and Jones. Only Clark's lawyer had had a doctor make a physical examination of the plaintiff. As the plaintiff's attorney was concluding his direct examination of his client, he turned to Clark's counsel and, addressing him only, asked him to concede for the record that he had had his physician examine the plaintiff. Clark's lawyer promptly rose, made the concession, and even supplied the doctor's name, the date, and the place where the examination had been conducted.

At this point, Jones's lawyer raised an objection, shouting, "But let the record show that *our* doctor did not make such an examination!"

Whereupon counsel for the plaintiff quietly said, "You know very well that if you had wanted a physical examination, all you had to do was request it or make a motion ordering us to grant you the examination, and no judge would have denied you the relief, even if I had opposed it, which I would not be so foolish as to do. Am I correct, Mr. Adversary?"

To this, Jones's lawyer had no rejoinder. Unfortunately for him, his failure to say anything was, at this point, a little belated. It would have served him better had he been quiet in the first place. For the jury well understood the significance of his sudden silence, and somewhere in their verdict it was amply reflected.

Another mistake I have seen some lawyers make is to attempt to berate a witness while he is being questioned on direct examination by his own lawyer. This tactic too can sometimes boomerang dangerously. I recall a case in which, after the witness had been on the stand a minute or two, he asked for a glass of water. As he drank it, he stealthily slipped a pill into his mouth. Instantly opposing counsel was on his feet, protesting vehemently that "the witness is courting sympathy and should not be permitted to make a spectacle of himself."

"Well, then," his attorney calmly continued, "now that my adversary has broached the subject, tell us just what your trouble is. Why did you ask for water?"

"To swallow a pill," the witness replied. "I have chronic leukemia."

"Is that cancer of the blood?" asked his attorney.

"It's a rough way of putting it," said the witness, "but I guess that's it."

It would have been a hardhearted jury indeed that did not feel, at this point, some sympathy for the unfortunate witness. Thus the lawyer who tried to abuse him succeeded only in defeating his own purpose.

That, in fact, is what usually happens to an attorney who attempts to browbeat a witness or to bluff or bluster his way through this phase of the trial. Even the slightest suggestion of an overbearing manner or of high-handed tactics does not sit well with the average juror. It is wiser for counsel to exercise self-restraint in the course of his adversary's direct examination. Rather than pop up continually with a host of petty or querulous objections, he can best occupy his time during this period by paying close attention to the testimony. He should listen carefully for any material that can later be turned to good account in cross-examination, and take note of significant gaps or inconsistencies in the evidence presented. Certainly, counsel should be sure he has heard every word of an answer before he objects to it. Then, if an objection is in order, it should be stated firmly but calmly, without undue vehemence or lengthy speeches.

Indeed, the tone in which an objection is made is often quite as important as its substance, at least as far as the jury is concerned. A heated protest may sometimes magnify a minor situation that might otherwise have passed unnoticed. Besides, strong emotion tends to cloud the judgment and frequently leads to regrettable excesses. In the excitement of the moment, the witness may be misquoted, or his lawyer may be falsely accused of putting into his mouth words actually spoken by the witness in response to a perfectly proper question.

The following incident aptly illustrates the dangers of too great haste and warmth in objecting to testimony. The plaintiff in the case was suing to recover for an alleged fall on the ice in the defendant's parking lot. Counsel for the plaintiff had called as a witness one of the defendant's former employees and was in the midst of his direct examination when a lengthy conference at the bench took place.

After this interruption, counsel resumed his questioning of the witness by asking, "What did you do after you had observed the icy, hard-packed snow?"

Immediately defense counsel jumped up and protested vigorously against this question: "I object! There was no reference to icy, hard-packed snow by this witness. Plaintiff's attorney is putting words into the witness' mouth! I ask for a mistrial."

This outburst by the attorney for the defendant caused the jury, which had fallen into a rather relaxed posture, to sit bolt upright.

When counsel for the plaintiff indignantly denied the accusation, his adversary reiterated it even more heatedly. Finally the judge decided to settle the issue by directing the court reporter to read back the witness' answer to the last question asked before the interruption. By this time a good deal of suspense had been aroused in the outcome of the tussle between the lawyers on each side, and every juror leaned forward to hear the record read. The only sound in the courtroom was the rustling of pages as the reporter leafed through his notes. Finally he found the place and read, in a lifeless monotone, the witness' last answer:

A. I had gone out into the parking lot and looked at the icy, hard-packed snow.

THE COURT: Objection overruled. Proceed with your interrogation.

In the absence of defense counsel's violent objection, the witness' rather offhand and incidental reference to the "icy, hard-packed snow" might well have escaped notice. Instead, the tone and manner in which the attorney for the defendant called attention to it impressed it indelibly on each juror's mind. Shortly thereafter the case was settled for a substantial sum.

In this situation defense counsel should have used an altogether different tactic. Instead of rudely breaking into the questioning with an indignant outburst, he should politely have requested—after apologizing for the interruption—that the previous answer be read in order to refresh his recollection. If it then became apparent that the attorney for the plaintiff was indeed putting words into the witness' mouth, the jury would see this, and an objection would be sustained. But if, as was the case here, the question asked by the plaintiff's attorney proved to have been based on the witness' previous answer, all that defense counsel would need to do would be to thank everyone concerned for accommodating him and permit the questioning to proceed.

A particularly offensive form of rude behavior on the part of some lawyers is their practice of muttering under their breath insulting remarks audible only to opposing counsel, but not to judge or jury. These are foul blows—below the belt, so to speak—and an attorney who resorts to them must expect, sooner or later, to be on the receiving end himself.

In a bitterly contested case, recently tried before a judge who shall remain nameless, defense counsel kept relentlessly interrupting his adversary with constant objections. Finally, after one lengthy and especially acrimonious argument between them, in which each gave his opponent as vicious a verbal pummeling as he received, the plaintiff's attorney muttered something under his breath which he thought was heard only by his adversary, to whom it was addressed. The judge, however, overheard the remark and, turning to the plaintiff's attorney, ordered him to repeat what he had said. For a moment the attorney stood mute. Then the judge again ordered him to repeat the remark.

"Your Honor," he said, "I called the attorney for the defendant a dirty son of a bitch."

The judge smiled at the attorney and said, "I thought I heard that, but I wanted the record to show it."

It certainly takes an enormous amount of self-discipline for a lawyer to maintain his composure in the face of a constant stream of verbal abuse directed at him by his adversary. Persistent needling will eventually exhaust the patience of the most even-tempered of men and provoke an angry retort that he may later regret. A good trial lawyer has to learn to control his natural impulse to reply in kind and must cultivate the art of preserving an unruffled exterior under the most trying conditions. He must never allow his adversary to goad him into saying or doing anything out of keeping with the dignity of his position. No matter how severe the provocation, he must strive always to remain outwardly calm under fire and present an image of imperturbability. In this way, he will earn the respect of both Court and jury.

Accordingly, I do not agree at all with the often quoted dictum of Leo Durocher that "nice guys finish last." This may be the way to separate the winners from the losers under the fiercely competitive conditions of the baseball diamond, but certainly not in the courtroom. There, at least, it has been my observation that it is no disadvantage whatever for a lawyer to appear in the eyes of judge and jury as a gentleman. This is the type of advocate who, while representing his client with ardor and devotion, remains pleasant, decent, and cooperative at all times and never finds it necessary to resort to vitriol or overt combativeness. Indeed, one of the hallmarks of the good trial lawyer is that he is precisely what is known as a "nice guy": he treats not only the judge but his adversary with unfailing courtesy and courtliness.

There is no doubt in my mind that counsel has everything to gain and nothing to lose by doing so. Jurors do not like the lawyer who is rude, offensive, or antagonistic. An attorney who baits the judge, interrupts his opponent, or indulges in snide remarks for the benefit of the jurors generally ends by alienating them.

There are some lawyers who, through obstinacy, foolishness, or an unconscious tendency to think of themselves as one of the parties to the litigation, refuse any request made by the other side in the course of a trial. Such conduct could do their clients a great deal of harm. Unless a request is clearly unjustified, it is better for counsel to give his adversary what he asks for. It is most unwise to put him to the trouble of proving matters that are obvious or easy to establish. In such circumstances it is far preferable to concede the point graciously and to enter into what members of the legal profession call a "stipulation" with opposing counsel as often as is practicable rather than to raise needless objections.

In a negligence case once tried before me, the plaintiff, in testifying about his injuries, gave the name of his attending physician. When asked by his attorney whether the doctor would take the stand, he replied, "No, he's dead."

Instantly the attorney for the defendant jumped to his feet and objected, "That's no way to prove he's dead."

Thereupon, plaintiff's counsel made a statement substantiating the assertion. But defense counsel would not accept this either. "My opponent," he screamed, "knows full well he needs legal proof of the doctor's death. I'll accept nothing short of that—legal proof!" He made the rafters ring with his cry of protest.

As it was near the lunch hour, I suggested to plaintiff's counsel that he try to obtain the proof during that time, and, as he was a heavy-set fellow, I jestingly added, "You can afford to miss a meal and take off a little weight." I then adjourned for lunch.

When we resumed, plaintiff's attorney rose and said, "Your Honor, I went to the Board of Health on Pearl Street, but I could not obtain a death certificate. Apparently he did not die in Brooklyn. However, I found out that a son of the deceased is practicing medicine in Westbury, Long Island. I called him, and he told me that his father, upon retiring, went to live with him in Suffolk County and died there. This young doctor is a very kind man and, realizing my predicament, he has consented to be here to give the 'legal proof' of his father's death. He promised to be here by 4:00 P.M. May I continue?"

At this point the defendant's attorney rose and wanted to concede the doctor's death, but counsel for the plaintiff very courteously said, "There's no way to stop him from coming now, since he promised to take the 1:15 train. Thank you."

When the young doctor arrived and testified, the embarrassment of defense counsel can well be imagined. The jury rendered a verdict far in excess of the amount that the case could have been settled for.

It is never wise to underrate one's adversary or to behave toward him in any manner that even suggests an attitude of condescension. He should at all times be accorded the respect which his professional position deserves. For one thing, the opponent whom a lawyer treats with indifference or discourtesy today may not prove generous or forgiving if he is encountered in later years, as sometimes happens, as a judge or in some other official capacity. But even when such an eventuality is most unlikely, it is neither gracious nor prudent for a lawyer to put on high and mighty airs or to adopt a haughty tone with opposing counsel. "Pride goeth before a fall," and the comedown can often be quite sharp and painful.

Occasionally a lawyer advanced in years and ripe in courtroom experience, in opposing a younger member of the bar, will try to throw his weight around. He will become personal in his remarks, ridicule his adversary, lecture him, or take him to task when objecting to statements that the young lawyer makes to the Court and the jury. I suspect that the members of the jury resent such conduct. They cannot show their displeasure by breaking out in revolt, but my guess is that they will remember it in the jury room.

Once a young lawyer of ability was trying a case against a gray-haired opponent of many years' experience at the bar. During the course of the trial it became increasingly evident to everybody that the junior advocate was getting the better of his adversary. The young man had just finished citing a point of law favorable to his case when the veteran lawyer, bristling with the pride of seniority, arose and objected, "In all my forty years of practice I never heard of any such proposition of law."

To which the young lawyer promptly retorted, "My grandfather has been playing pinochle for forty-five years, and he still doesn't know the game."

Objections, then, are to be made with discretion. Like everything else in a well-conducted trial, they have their proper place, but the right to raise them must not be abused. They are not in themselves a substitute for adequate preparation, but rather ought to be based upon it to a considerable extent. Moreover, the manner in which they are presented, as well as their frequency and validity, has a subtle influence on the jury that must at all times be carefully taken into account. To this end, a lawyer has to be always in full control of himself, and he has to weigh every word he utters not only to judge and jury but also to his adversary.

In short, an attorney must be, as we have seen, more than a legal specialist; he has to be something of a psychologist as well. For everything he does in court contributes in one way or another to the total picture that the jury forms of him and, indirectly, of his case. The image so presented has to be all of a piece. His bearing throughout the trial must be consistently dignified and professional.

Keeping this in mind, let us now consider what counsel still needs to do in order to defend properly the interests of his client and at the same time remain worthy of the respect of the Court and the jury as he proceeds to the next phase of the trial: the cross-examination of the witnesses on the other side.

VI

CROSS-EXAMINATION

16

"Your Witness!"

There is generally a momentary feeling of suspense in the courtroom when, at the conclusion of direct examination, counsel turns to his adversary and says, "Your witness!" Immediately a noticeable increase seems to take place in the tension felt by everybody—the witness on the stand, counsel for both sides, the parties to the dispute, and the spectators. Each, of course, has his own reasons for responding to these words with a flush of excitement.

Almost invariably a change can be seen to come over even the most phlegmatic witness. Up to now, under direct examination, he has been treated rather gently. Questioned in a friendly and sympathetic fashion by a lawyer disposed to accept uncritically his version of the facts, the witness has so far had things more or less his own way. But now he braces himself for a very different type of encounter—something more in the nature of a duel, in which he may have to cross swords with a wily and seasoned antagonist. The most apparently innocuous question may appear to the witness as a dangerous trap for the unwary, to be approached only with the utmost caution. No wonder that the average witness becomes a little tense as he hears himself being handed over, as it were, to the enemy!

Will he have to eat his words? Will he be caught in some contradiction? Does that paper which opposing counsel holds in his hand contain some damning piece of evidence that will show how mistaken the witness' memory is? Will his confidence be shaken in the end? Will he leave the stand with his credibility impaired?

These fears and doubts, felt to some extent by every witness, may also be quite disturbing to the lawyer who called him to the stand in the first place. For counsel knows that the purpose of cross-examination is to dilute, lessen, neutralize, or completely destroy the effect of the witness' direct testimony. And the cross-examiner can be counted on to do everything he can to achieve this end. No matter how confident a lawyer may be in his witnesses, he can never be altogether sure of their reaction to a searching cross-examination.

Nor is the witness the only participant in the forthcoming psychological and verbal tussle who feels somewhat apprehensive about it. The lawyer, whether experienced or not, who is about to conduct a cross-examination is also very likely to be assailed by a certain disquietude as he rises to confront the witness. Up to this point in the trial, he has examined witnesses who have testified on his client's behalf, and, for the most part, he knew what to expect of them. But now he is faced with a quite different situation. The road ahead is no longer so clearly marked, and the steps he is about to take are fraught with much risk. Success is by no means assured, even for an attorney with years of practice behind him. The pitfalls are many, and there are no set rules to guide him in framing his questions.

As for the spectators, as well as the litigants themselves, they probably have read and heard so much about the way witnesses are completely annihilated during this phase of the trial that they have a grossly exaggerated idea of the devastation that is going to be wrought before their eyes by the withering fire of cross-examination. The fact is that it is extremely rare for a witness to be completely discredited or his testimony demolished, except on the stage, in the movies, and on television. There is only one Perry Mason!

Under ordinary circumstances a lawyer cannot expect always to be successful even in diluting, much less in destroying, a witness' testimony during cross-examination, nor is he obliged to do so in every instance. After all, his adversary's witnesses, like his own, are generally prepared to state the facts as they know them. Cross-examination is therefore not always likely to yield something worth while. In that case, it is better for counsel to forego it altogether.

The first question, then, that a lawyer has to ask himself at this point in the trial is: Shall I take up the challenge and cross-examine this witness, or shall I decline the opportunity? Time and again I have observed how lawyers are trapped into cross-examining as soon as they hear the words, "Your witness!" when actually a cross-examination serves no useful purpose whatever except to strengthen their adversary's case. They seem to be afraid to say, "I have no questions." Some advocates, particularly inexperienced ones, evidently fear that their client will criticize them if they refrain from cross-examining every witness for the other side.

What such attorneys forget is that, in the courtroom, the lawyer is the doctor, and the client is the patient. A patient does not tell a doctor what instruments to use while operating, nor should fear of criticism by his client deter a lawyer from using whatever strategy will best serve his cause. If he is successful, he will escape criticism; if he is not, he will be criticized no matter what he does. Or, as Abraham Lincoln said, "If the end brings me out all right, what is said against me won't amount to anything. If the end brings me out wrong, ten angels swearing I was right would make no difference."

There are many occasions in which counsel would do well to refrain from cross-examination altogether. If an adverse witness has said nothing on direct examination that is of value to the other side, cross-examining him may merely provide him with a second chance to say something that could really hurt counsel's case. For the same reason, it is worse than pointless—it is positively dangerous—to cross-examine a witness on some matter that has no bearing on the issues in dispute. And it is equally unwise to conduct a cross-examination in regard to matters on which the witness' answers could well have the effect of neutralizing, weakening, or destroying the very position that counsel is seeking to maintain.

In this connection, I recall a negligence case tried before me in which the defendant's counsel, in his opening statement to the jury, denied that there had been any accident such as the plaintiff alleged. He further stated that his client had no notice or knowledge of any accident involving the plaintiff. Without even disputing the nature, seriousness, or extent of the plaintiff's injuries, defense counsel contended that they must have been received in some way other than as the plaintiff's lawyer had alleged.

Yet, after the plaintiff's doctor had testified briefly about the injuries, the attorney for the defendant, instead of keeping him on the stand for a reasonable length of time or even declining to cross-examine him at all, proceeded to question him about the injuries for a day and a half. Repetitious and unnecessarily protracted, the cross-examination of the doctor entered into the most minute details concerning the nature, extent, and seriousness of each injury sustained by the plaintiff. Before long it was apparent to me that the jury was becoming impatient. By continually hammering away at the doctor's testimony, which counsel had previously said was of no concern to the defense, he did more than incur the jurors' disfavor; he undoubtedly caused them to forget the position on which his whole defense was based, namely, that there had been no such accident involving the defendant as the plaintiff had alleged. In the end, the jury returned a substantial verdict for the plaintiff.

If a witness' testimony is essentially neutral, if he has said nothing to damage counsel's case and he has contributed nothing to the case of the other side, it serves no useful purpose to pepper him with a fusillade of questions just for the sake of asking them. There is nothing to be gained by cross-examining him, and much to be risked. The consequences could be disastrous.

In another case tried before me, the plaintiff called to the stand a doctor who, throughout his direct examination, gave every indication of wanting to get back as soon as possible to his job at the Compensation Bureau. His testimony, delivered in an utterly bored, listless, and indifferent manner, in no way enhanced the plaintiff's case. Nevertheless, defense counsel felt obliged to bombard him with a volley of questions, none of which elicited anything significant. The doctor's testimony continued to be entirely neutral.

Thereupon, the cross-examiner, instead of desisting, simply redoubled his efforts. Relentlessly he kept up an unabated flow of questions, until he succeeded in casting the doctor in the role of a very important witness.

Finally, the doctor, his patience sorely tried, turned to me and said something, but his words were inaudible. I motioned to the witness to resume his former position on the stand. As he did so, he placed a card on the bench on which were written the words, "Don't Aggravate Me," as well as an article entitled "Relax!"

Instantly his cross-examiner demanded to know what the witness had said to me.

"Nothing," I replied, because I had not given the doctor a chance to talk to me.

The lawyer then insisted on seeing what it was that the witness had laid on the bench. I took a quick look, smiled, and assured him it had nothing to do with the case. Instead of accepting my statement, counsel persisted in demanding to know "everything that was said."

"I want to see what he gave Your Honor," he proclaimed.

Whereupon I handed him the card and the article. As he was examining them, the doctor said—and the effect of his words was not lost on the jury—"Counsellor, the card, as you can see, simply reads, 'Don't Aggravate Me,' and my article, which you are looking at, is entitled 'Relax!' This is a valuable piece of advice—particularly for fellows like you. Take the article home tonight and study it. You really should learn how to relax."

So perhaps the first principle of cross-examination is that it should be skipped entirely if it promises to yield nothing of value. For weeks during the prosecution of the Eichmann trial, Dr. Robert Servatius, the defense counsel, listened attentively as scores of witnesses recounted anguished stories of persecution, terror, and slaughter. The testimony was repetitive and cumulative. But he seldom cross-examined. Instead, he would rise slowly from his chair at the end of a witness' direct testimony and announce to the Court, "I have no questions." Apparently he felt that cross-examining such witnesses might do more harm than good. It could only add emphasis to the damaging testimony and give the witnesses an opportunity to elaborate upon it.

Ultimately a lawyer's obligation is to his cause. Dr. Servatius had to take a good deal of abuse from his client, but he nevertheless proceeded to try his case as he thought it should be tried, and he won the respect of lawyers all over the world for the exemplary manner in which he conducted Eichmann's defense.

On the other hand, there are times when a lawyer can use cross-examination not only to destroy the effect of the witness' direct testimony but to bolster his own client's case. This is precisely what was done by counsel for the plaintiff in a case tried before me. He made his cross-examination serve as a means of vividly portraying the extent of the pain suffered by his own client, the mother of a girl who was killed in an accident involving several cars at a street intersection.

Here is an extract from his cross-examination of one of the other plaintiffs in the case (the name of the deceased child has been changed):

Q. Where did you see Mary Jones?
A. Lying in the road.
Q. What did you observe about Mary?
A. Her left leg was split open this way [indicating]. And it was lying to her side this way [indicating]—from the knee to the ankle along the shinbone.
Q. What else did you observe about Mary?
A. She had a big cut here, this way [indicating], diagonally across the chest from the left shoulder down to the right side. She had another cut here [indicating], directly under the chin. And this [indicating]—the chin was all broken. And while she was talking, she was spilling out teeth.

Q. What did she say?

A. She was screaming for her mother.

It need hardly be said that the result of this line of questioning was highly dramatic and most effective in eliciting testimony that might not otherwise have been presented to the jury.

Similarly, cross-examination can sometimes be used effectively to bolster the status of a witness on the cross-examiner's side of the case. If, for example, counsel has on his side a general practitioner, while the other side has an expert, he is not taking much of a risk in asking the expert, on cross-examination, whether he will not admit that Dr. X, the general practitioner, is a competent and honorable medical doctor. It is hardly likely that a doctor would say anything detrimental about another doctor. Thus, almost invariably, the reply will be, "Oh, yes, of course," and the expert will have been used to build up counsel's own witness.

But knowing when to cross-examine and when to refrain from cross-examination is just the beginning of wisdom in this phase of the trial. Such a decision must itself form part of a larger plan of action that needs to be carefully thought out in advance. If the decision is to cross-examine, then the problem is to know *how*. Even from the few cases I have already cited, it must be evident that successful cross-examination is rarely the result of sheer luck or momentary inspiration. It is an art whose mastery requires much practice and experience, founded, of course, upon a thorough knowledge of its underlying principles. Like the conduct of warfare, cross-examination has its strategy and its tactics. Let us, then, follow step by step the process by which an effective cross-examiner maps out each move and brings his attack to a victorious conclusion.

To the spectator in the courtroom, it may seem as if the questions asked in cross-examination have been improvised on the spur of the moment or, at best, hastily prepared in court solely on the basis of what the cross-examiner heard the witness say in giving direct testimony. Indeed, to the uninitiated, it may appear incredible or, at least, remarkable that counsel, knowing in advance substantially what each witness would testify to, could have prepared before the trial a rather full outline of the questions to be asked on cross-examination. How could he have anticipated what the witness was going to say on the stand?

In fact, however, the successful cross-examiner, as a general rule, comes to court thoroughly prepared in these respects and then proceeds according to a well-conceived plan. Long before the trial he puts himself in the place of his adversary and tries to anticipate the types of witnesses who may be called for the other side and the testimony they will give.

If a negligence case is being tried, these witnesses are likely to include the other party to the dispute, an eyewitness, a police officer, a doctor, and perhaps an expert. In a criminal action, the prosecution may reasonably be expected to call the complaining witness and perhaps other witnesses in order to establish a prima facie case. The line of questioning to be pursued will then depend on the nature of the crime charged. If, for example, the defendant is accused of burglary, that is, breaking and entering a building with the intent to commit a felony, defense counsel must be ready to dispute the contention that his client broke into the building, if that is his defense. Moreover, the cross-examination of the police officer must be planned to offset any statement that the accused may have made to him and to throw light on any acts of the defendant bearing on the issue of intent. And, of course, if counsel's investigation discloses that other witnesses will be called, such as a fingerprint expert or one who will identify burglars' tools, a series of questions will have to be prepared with the object of casting doubt on their testimony. To this end, the attorney for the defendant must have done his homework in advance so that he may learn something about fingerprints, burglars' tools, etc.

In order to avoid an aimless, hit-or-miss cross-examination, counsel should, as part of his plan, prepare to pursue a line of questioning directed toward a clearly defined goal. Instead of attempting to interrogate each witness on every single point brought out in direct examination, a good lawyer prepares to direct his fire upon what he can reasonably expect to be the crucial and possibly vulnerable parts of the testimony. By concentrating his attack upon a few major issues and hitting one or two weak points relentlessly, he may expose important inconsistencies or omissions in the testimony and thereby succeed in impeaching the witness' credibility. A cross-examination conducted along such lines may make it possible for counsel later, in his summation, to cast a pall of doubt over the entire testimony of the witness.

The procedure involved here is a common one in military strategy. Whereas a frontal attack on an easily defensible position may prove worse than futile, it may often be overthrown quite readily by an outflanking maneuver. Even though there may be no specific reason for doubting the witness' credibility in regard to certain matters, any line of questioning that succeeds in shaking the jury's faith in his veracity or reliability with respect to other points in his testimony may be enough to undermine it completely. For it suffices to dislodge only a few keystones for the whole structure, no matter how well built, to come tumbling down.

On the other hand, asking too many questions on cross-examination, in an effort to touch on every point made by the witness in his direct testimony, merely dulls the effectiveness of any solid blows that may have been struck at the weak spots. An excess of questions may even elicit responses that are unfavorable to the cross-examiner's cause. Prying into everything said by a witness on the stand just provides him with a chance to buttress his statements and give them added weight and credibility. It also permits the witness to explain away or enlarge upon points not brought out effectively during direct examination. Indeed, there is even the danger that the witness may seize the opportunity to testify to matters that on direct examination would not be admissible as evidence.

A case in point, in which overzealous cross-examination merely opened the door to the introduction of adverse testimony otherwise inadmissible, involved a suit instituted by a salesman for commissions allegedly due him. During the course of the trial, a written contract between the parties was produced, which, on its face, included the terms and conditions of the salesman's employment. However, it made no mention of how much he was to be paid.

When the plaintiff took the stand, he attempted to show that he had entered into a supplemental contract with the other party to the dispute, in which the amount and terms of payment were explicitly set forth. His direct examination on this point proceeded substantially as follows:

Q. Where is this supplemental contract?
A. The defendant has it.
Q. How did he get it?
A. A few days after I signed it, the defendant told me he had lost his copy of it and asked me to lend him mine so that he could have it copied for his records.
Q. Did you comply with this request?
A. I did.
Q. Did the defendant ever return to you the copy of the supplemental contract that he had borrowed from you?
A. No. He never did.

Immediately, defense counsel quite properly objected to the introduction of testimony setting forth the alleged sum to be paid and the mode of payment provided for in the supplemental contract. Under what is called the "parol evidence" rule, the proffer of such proof was inadmissible because it was oral. The trial judge sustained the objection, and all references to the supplemental contract were excluded.

This brought the direct testimony of the plaintiff to an end. Thereupon, the Court asked defense counsel whether he had any questions.

"I certainly do," he said. He then proceeded as follows:

Q. You say you had a supplemental contract in which the sum to be paid and the mode of payment were set forth?
A. Yes, sir.
Q. And it was in writing?
A. It was.
Q. You read it, did you?
A. I sure did.
Q. What do you claim it said?

Bewildered, in view of the Court's previous ruling barring such testimony, the witness turned to the judge and asked, "May I answer?"

"Certainly," the Court replied; "now you can, since counsel has opened the door to permit you to give an answer."

The witness then proceeded to explain the terms of the supplemental contract, and, as the judge later put it, "There went the ball game."

Of course, it is impossible for counsel to anticipate, before the trial, all the adverse testimony to be presented by the other side. No matter how well prepared a lawyer may be when he comes to court, he still has to reckon on unexpected possibilities and opportunities. He may find himself confronted with a surprise witness, or he may be struck with a revealing observation gratuitously interjected by a voluble witness on direct examination. And sometimes counsel may take his cue from some significant peculiarity in the witness' demeanor on the stand.

It is therefore a lawyer's duty, from the moment an adverse witness enters the courtroom, to scrutinize him carefully and to follow his direct testimony with the utmost attention. The purpose of this vigilance is not so much to find something to object to as to discover a possible basis for a searching cross-examination, to assess the witness' state of mind, and to estimate the extent to which he might be vulnerable to attack. Close observation of opposing witnesses while they are giving their direct testimony can sometimes bring rich rewards to a lawyer perceptive enough to take note of significant clues to their character or personality. Indeed, even the physical appearance of a witness may provide counsel with telltale grounds for questioning his credibility or may help to stir suspicions about the reliability of his testimony.

This is exactly what happened at the trial of Frank "the Dasher" Abbandando and Harry "Happy" Malone, two members of the notorious "Murder, Incorporated" gang. One of the defense witnesses, who gave his occupation as that of a laborer, testified to a version of the facts which, if truthful, could have wrecked the prosecution's whole case.

However, the prosecutor, my valued friend, Burton Turkus, who is credited with having broken up "Murder, Incorporated," had trained himself to be observant. Nothing escaped his sharp eye. Accordingly, he began his cross-examination substantially as follows:

Q. Did I understand you to say you are a laborer?
A. That's right.
Q. Where do you work?
A. In a garage.
Q. What kind of work do you do there?
A. I'm a mechanic. I repair automobile engines and work on auto parts.

At this point the prosecutor asked for the Court's permission to have the witness show his hands to the jurors. Instead of horny calluses and grimy fingers, what they beheld was a pair of smooth, lily-white palms and a set of exquisitely manicured fingernails. This was enough to raise so serious a doubt about the witness' credibility as actually to destroy the defendants' case. They were convicted and died in the electric chair, as did many of the remaining officers and directors of their organization as a result of a series of such prosecutions by the same District Attorney.

A civil case recently brought to my attention likewise illustrates the importance of observing the physical appearance of the witnesses for the other side. Suit was brought on behalf of a child who had sustained a fracture of the jawbone in an accident. As a result, it was alleged, the plaintiff was left with a receding chin, which would require cosmetic surgery to correct.

When the child's father took the stand to give his direct testimony, defense counsel noticed that he too had a receding chin. After pointing this out to the Court and the jury, the attorney for the defendant called to the stand, on his client's behalf, a doctor who testified that a receding chin is usually hereditary. This testimony served to mitigate the claim that the defect was attributable to the accident. Here defense counsel's alertness made it possible for him to discredit the father's testimony without even having to cross-examine him!

But it is not only the physical characteristics of a witness that may be helpful in guiding a vigilant attorney toward a successful cross-examination. No less significant in this respect are the intellectual and psychological traits exhibited by the witness while he is on the stand. A lawyer must learn to assess these too as he listens to the testimony and observes the reactions of the witness to the questions put to him by opposing counsel. Indeed, being able to judge the mental celerity, emotional balance, and general personality of a witness as he gives his testimony requires very much the same kind of experience and knowledge of human nature that enables a shrewd advocate to "size up" prospective jurors during the *voir dire*. This is a skill not taught in the law schools and impossible to acquire from reading law books, but still indispensable to a trial lawyer's eventual success in his profession. It is generally the product of wide contact with people of every type in all walks of life.

Yet even a lawyer lacking in experience can train himself to form a fairly accurate judgment of the strengths and weaknesses of adverse witnesses, provided he knows what to look for. As he observes each witness on the stand and listens to his testimony, counsel should be asking himself such questions as the following:

Is the witness cocksure, or is he diffident?

Is he voluble or closemouthed?

Is he prone to digress into irrelevancies, or does he stick to the point?

Is he quick to sense the direction of counsel's line of interrogation, or is he slow in seeing the point of a question?

Is he inclined to be precise or vague about dates, places, persons, or other crucial points?

Does his story sound too pat, as if it was memorized, or does it seem natural and plausible?

Is he tense and "on guard," or relaxed and at ease?

Is his language highly colored and exaggerated, or is his account sober and straightforward?

The answers to these questions can often be very revealing. Even if they provide counsel with only a hint of a possibly promising line of inquiry, this is sometimes all that he needs to set him on the right track.

An example of the way in which alertness to such significant details can help to give shape to a lawyer's cross-examination is the experience of an acquaintance of mine who served as defense counsel in a lawsuit brought by a former employee of his client. The plaintiff complained that he had been fired from his job as a dress designer in violation of the terms of a written contract of employment. The defense contended that the employee had been justifiably discharged for incompetence and that he had failed to mitigate the damages by seeking other employment.

From the direct examination of the plaintiff, defense counsel concluded that the witness was prone to exaggerate and would respond affirmatively to negative suggestions. Accordingly, the attorney for the defendant began his cross-examination by asking the plaintiff whether he considered himself to be a competent designer, and whether he had a good reputation for ability in that line of work in the ladies' garment industry. Just as counsel had expected, the witness gave himself an excellent rating. The cross-examination then proceeded somewhat as follows:

Q. After you were discharged, you did not look for work, did you?
A. Oh, yes. I certainly did.
Q. But you didn't look for work every day, did you?
A. I most certainly did—every day.
Q. But you didn't see more than one or two people a day, did you?
A. Oh, many more than that.
Q. Well, how many more?
A. I'd say as many as eight to ten people every day.
Q. You didn't ask them all for employment, did you?
A. I did. I asked each one for a job.
Q. But you didn't go looking for a job every day, did you?
A. I told you before. I went out every day hunting for a job.
Q. Please multiply eight by five and tell me what you get.
A. Forty.
Q. Good. Now be good enough to multiply forty by fifty and tell me what you get.
A. That comes to two thousand.
Q. Now take half of two thousand, and what's left?
A. Why, one thousand, of course.
Q. And if you add two thousand to that, what will the final sum come to?
A. Three thousand.

The contract had a year and a half to run from the date when the plaintiff was fired. During all that time he had secured no employment.

The inference for the jury to draw was clear: either the plaintiff was really incompetent if he was turned down by three thousand prospective employers, or he was not telling the truth about the number of people he had seen in his attempt to secure employment. Naturally counsel bore down hard on this point in his summation, and there can be little doubt that this masterly cross-examination was a decisive factor in his obtaining a verdict in favor of the defendant.

But the witness is not the only one who provides opposing counsel with the material to cross-examine him with. Occasionally, while a lawyer is pondering the questions he should ask on cross-examination, he will receive a real—though, of course, unintended—assist from his adversary. The only trouble is that the average lawyer often does not know how to identify such opportunities even when they are offered to him or does not know what to do with them in order to turn them to his own advantage. Like a good football player, an attorney has, as it were, to learn how to intercept the opposing team's pass or to pick up the ball when it is fumbled by the other side, and carry it forward for his own team as far as he can.

A perfect illustration of the way in which a watchful lawyer immediately seized upon the material inadvertently supplied to him by his adversary and used it to excellent effect is a case in which a single remark by defense counsel sufficed to spark a devastating cross-examination by the plaintiff's attorney. The plaintiff had lost his right arm as a result of his having been run over by a truck. Defense counsel—an able and experienced advocate—called to the stand a witness in his late forties, who was prepared to testify that the plaintiff had dashed from between two parked cars directly into the path of the oncoming vehicle. After the witness had given his name and address, defense counsel said to him, "Sit back, sir. I understand that you are a shell-shocked war veteran."

Plaintiff's counsel—likewise a top-notch trial lawyer—refrained from objecting to this statement. He hoped, in his summation, to remind the jury that millions of Americans had done their patriotic duty and that some of them, including members of his own family, had lost their lives in the war.

The first question he put to the witness was a carefully calculated trap:

Q. Please tell this jury in what battle you were shell-shocked, to

what hospital in Europe you were confined, and for how long a
period you were hospitalized.

Naturally counsel was well aware of the fact that this was a triple-
barreled question and was, therefore, objectionable. But he was afraid
that if he asked simply, "Where were you treated?" the answer might
very well be nothing more than "in France, but I don't remember the
name of the hospital." The question was purposely cast in this form
to let the witness know that if he decided to lie, he would be leaving
himself open to searching examination in regard to many details of his
alleged shell shock. If, on the other hand, it turned out that the
witness had indeed been shell-shocked, counsel was prepared to conclude this phase of his cross-examination by asking, "Certainly you don't
expect any greater consideration than any other witness who takes the
stand, do you?"

However, the witness answered, "I am not exactly shell-shocked. I'm
just a little nervous."

Here, then, he was caught in an obvious lie. The question was what
to do with it. The rest of the cross-examination is a masterly example
of the way in which damaging admissions by an adverse witness may
be made to yield rich dividends by a skillful attorney:

Q. Nervous, are you?
A. Yes, sir.
Q. When Mr. _____ [defense counsel] made the statement, "Sit back.
    I understand you are a shell-shocked war veteran," you must have
    told someone that you were, right?
A. I did.
Q. Did you tell it to Mr. _____'s assistant?
A. Yes, sir.
Q. Certainly Mr. _____'s assistant didn't tell you to lie and say that
    you are a shell-shocked war veteran, did he?
A. He did not.
Q. Did you expect more money for your court appearance if you were a
    shell-shocked war veteran?
A. I did not.
Q. No one suggested or told you to say that you were a shell-shocked
    war veteran?
A. No, sir.
Q. Since no one suggested you say it, and no one told you to say it, and
    you didn't expect any more money for your court appearance, it is
    true, is it not, that for no good reason at all, you lied when you
    stated that you were a shell-shocked war veteran?
A. Yes, sir.

There was no need for plaintiff's counsel to proceed any further. The witness was thoroughly discredited in the eyes of the jury by a cross-examination wholly based on a single remark by opposing counsel!

In a recent murder case in which Percy Foreman was defense counsel, the prosecution put on the stand a convict from the State penitentiary. In order to buttress the witness' credibility, the District Attorney sought to establish that his character had undergone a remarkable transformation while he was in jail. Asked about his spiritual life, the witness averred that he had discovered God, and he was a changed man after that. In fact, he added, he intended to become a minister of the Gospel and was taking a correspondence course in the Holy Scriptures while serving his sentence.

This was all that Foreman, an ordained Baptist minister, needed for his cross-examination. Disregarding the damaging testimony the witness had given, Foreman directed his attack on the convict's credibility with the following line of questioning:

Q. Did I understand you to say that you are now a student of Holy Writ?
A. Yes, sir.
Q. You mean you are a student of the Bible?
A. That's right.
Q. Have you studied about a character in the Bible by the name of Ananias?
A. I certainly have.
Q. Do you or do you not propose to model your ministry after this individual?
A. No, sir, I do not.
Q. Who was Ananias?
A. Sir, I will preach you a sermon if you would like to hear one.
THE COURT: We do not want a sermon. Just answer the question.
Q. Tell the jury who Ananias was.
A. At this time, sir, I couldn't tell you.

At this point Foreman drew himself up to his full height, an imposing six feet, four inches, and turning halfway around, so that he faced both the jury and the witness, he thundered: "He is the biggest liar in all antiquity. Does that help you?"

Of course, it takes good judgment and a certain amount of experience for a lawyer to know at just what point to concentrate his fire during cross-examination. It is not always easy to ascertain whether a witness is lying or exaggerating or what parts of his testimony are most vulnerable to attack on these counts, and some risk is involved in probing inexpertly to find out. Often questions designed to test the witness' credibility serve only to bring out his honesty all the more. Unless there is good reason to suppose that the witness is not telling the truth, it is generally most unwise for counsel to gamble with questions designed to catch him in a lie.

An example of the way in which such questioning can badly backfire is a case in which the defendant was charged with malicious mischief for having allegedly smashed the plate-glass window of a store and wrecked its interior by throwing all kinds of objects about the place. The complainant testified that while the defendant was making a shambles of his store, he cowered under a desk at the back until the police, whom he had called, arrived.

On cross-examination, the defendant's lawyer decided to make capital of the complainant's statement that he had summoned the police:

Q. Is there a telephone in your store?
A. Yes.
Q. Did you use it to call the police?
A. No.
Q. Did you say you were hiding under the desk all the time the defendant was destroying your store?
A. Yes, sir.
Q. Then explain to His Honor how you called the police.

Whereupon the witness took a police whistle out of his pocket and blew a long, ear-splitting blast on it while he was on the stand. Immediately, policemen, with their guns drawn, poured into the courtroom from every direction. Needless to say, counsel succeeded in convicting his client.

The danger of questioning a witness' credibility in the absence of positive proof that he is lying is that counsel never knows what reply he may get to his questions. In the trial of a murder case in which a very able lawyer of my acquaintance represented the defendant, he called a witness to establish that the accused had acted in self-defense. The witness, who spoke broken English, testified, with the aid of an interpreter, that the man whom the defendant killed had first pulled a revolver out of his pocket and fired a shot at the defendant, and the bullet went whistling past the witness' head. On cross-examination, the Assistant District Attorney said, "I understood you to testify that the victim of this killing first shot at the defendant, and the bullet went whistling past your head. What did you do when the bullet went whistling past your head?"

The witness, without the aid of the interpreter, said, "I shita my pants."

"I take it, Mr. District Attorney," the Court interposed, "you have no doubt that the witness told the truth on that score, have you?"

Still, there are times when it may pay a lawyer to take a chance on testing a witness' credibility. If the case looks hopeless, and the one witness who made it so is on the stand, and the odds against winning are overwhelming, there is so little to lose that counsel may safely risk an attack in this direction.

In a recent negligence case, such a desperate stab in the dark succeeded in striking home. The plaintiff contended that as she was crossing the street at the crosswalk, she was struck by a bus coming around the corner. The bus company argued, on the contrary, that she was crossing the street diagonally more than thirty feet from the crosswalk, so that, for the most part, her back was to the oncoming vehicle. Hence, the defense maintained that the plaintiff was contributorily negligent.

The only witness was a man called by the plaintiff. He testified that he was a passenger on the bus, and that he had observed the plaintiff standing at the crosswalk. According to this witness, before starting to cross, the plaintiff looked to her left—the direction from which the bus came. Then, when she was almost across the street, the bus, which was going fast, made an uncommonly wide turn and struck her.

On cross-examination, the witness said that he was eighty-two years of age. He had been born in the South and had come to New York in his early twenties.

Where had he come from the evening of the accident? Why, from work.

What did he work at? As a plumber's helper.

Seated in the bus, would he not have been facing front, so that he could not see the plaintiff as she came from his right? Why, no. It was very warm, the window of the bus was open, and he had stuck his head out of it to get a breath of fresh air. In that position, he averred, he could not fail to see the plaintiff.

The witness' manner was sweet and kindly. He had obviously made a good impression, and the cross-examination seemed only to be strengthening it. What to do in the face of such testimony? In desperation, counsel decided to cast his net in another direction to see whether he could catch in it anything worth while.

How long had the witness worked as a plumber's helper? About three years.

What did he do before that?

At this point the witness' manner changed, and he appealed to the Court: "Judge, must I answer that?"

THE COURT: Yes, you must.
A. I did not do anything.
Q. Were you ever convicted of a crime?
A. It's none of your business.
DEFENSE COUNSEL: Your Honor, I demand he answer.
THE COURT: You must answer.
A. Yes.
Q. What crime did you commit?
A. Perjury.
DEFENSE COUNSEL: No further questions.

This last question was, of course, a shot in the dark. However, up to that point, the case for the defendant was as good as lost. Under the circumstances, what alternative did counsel have?

On the other hand, it should not be supposed that the revelation of unsavory details in a witness' past will automatically or necessarily suffice to impeach his credibility. No matter how shameful a witness' background may be, the exposure of it in cross-examination may have little effect in undermining the jury's faith in his veracity. There is very little that a lawyer can do about such a situation. He must be content to bring the matter to the jury's attention during his summation, but indirectly and with a certain amount of finesse in order to avoid any suggestion of harshness or uncharitableness.

Illustrative of these observations is a case in which an acquaintance of mine was defending a man charged with robbery. The chief witness for the People was a madame. Asked under cross-examination what her occupation was, she demurely replied, "I'm a housewife." When defense counsel insisted that she tell the Court and the jury her true vocation, she turned to the judge and asked whether she had to answer the question.

Before the judge could reply, counsel asked the witness, "Isn't it a fact that you are a madame?"

"Yes," she replied, "but not a high-class one."

The jury—all male, of course—believed her testimony in spite of this admission.

In another case, the plaintiff, a foreign-born unmarried woman, had sold a house and received a check in payment for it. The defendant, a builder, on learning of this fact, contrived to meet her as she was emerging from the building where the check had been given to her. Engaging her in conversation, he suggested that he could arrange to have the check cashed for her, enticed her into his automobile, and drove her around until the banks had closed. Determined not to let her go until he had the check in his possession, he then induced her to accompany him to his home. There he finally obtained possession of the check and endorsed it by forging her name. However, it was deposited in the account of the wife of a plumbing contractor and eventually cleared with the endorsement of the Federal Reserve Bank.

An action was brought to recover the proceeds of the check from the builder, the bank, and the plumber's wife. During the course of the trial the question of the relationship between the builder and the plumber's wife became a matter of great importance in shedding light on the reason why the check had been deposited in her account. The plumber was called to testify on behalf of the defendants. Under cross-examination, he stated that he had been doing business with the builder for about a million dollars a year. Although he knew that the builder had been having an affair with his wife for a long period of time, the plumber had done nothing about it.

Thereupon, the cross-examiner, Robert H. Elder, one of the great trial lawyers of his era, exploded the following question:

Q. Then you were a pimp, sir. Is that correct?

Over the objection of defendants' counsel, the plumber was compelled to answer the question. It bore, of course, directly and savagely on the issue of the witness' credibility. This is the only case I know of in which a husband was actually accused on the stand of being a pimp for his wife and admitted it without resorting to the Fifth Amendment.

17

Cross-Examination Strategy

If there is one fact on which counsel can depend, it is that most witnesses, however well they may bear themselves in giving direct testimony, are unlikely to be self-possessed under cross-examination. It is at this point in the trial that they begin to feel unsure of themselves and are easily bewildered. In short, they may look like fair game for a wily cross-examiner—helpless and at his mercy.

But there is such a thing as being *too* effective in annihilating the testimony of a confused or intimidated witness, as Allan Nevins shows in his *Herbert H. Lehman and His Era*. In his youth Lehman was called as a witness in a trial involving a textile firm in which he was an officer. He did well enough on direct examination, but he collapsed completely under the vigorous and relentless cross-examination of Max Steuer. In the end, all he could say was, "I'm sorry. My memory on that point is a complete blank"; "Yes, I suppose you are right about that"; "I guess I was mistaken about that"; "I'm afraid I have forgotten that." When he left the stand, he felt deeply abashed and apologized abjectly to his firm's lawyer for the execrable showing he had made.

"Yes," the lawyer agreed, "you were simply awful."

Yet the jury lost no time in bringing in a verdict for the firm. As the foreman explained later, "It was Herbert Lehman's testimony that convinced us. He made such an exhibition of himself there on the stand under cross-examination that we could see he was being completely honest in everything he said."

So before counsel is tempted to take advantage of his apparently dominant position, he should remember that the average jury tends, at least initially, to be sympathetic toward a witness undergoing the ordeal of cross-examination. As John Alan Appleman, an attorney of Urbana, Illinois, says, in an article entitled "Cross-Examining for the Jury" which appeared in the *Legal Aid Brief Case* in December, 1965:

> Jurors identify not with the lawyer, but with the witness. They visualize themselves in the witness chair. A lawyer who . . . attacks too vigorously will invariably alienate the jury.

Besides, the witness is not quite as defenseless or friendless as he may look. He has the lawyer who called him to the stand, as well as the Court, to protect him against being bullied, browbeaten, or imposed upon by his cross-examiner.

Under the circumstances, therefore, it is only sensible for counsel to exercise sufficient self-restraint to avoid the all-too-common practice of asking the witness unfair questions, insidiously phrased in such fashion as to assume that something has been stated or established when in fact it has not. In a matrimonial action, for example, there may have been testimony to the effect that the defendant was in arrears in his alimony payments. It would, however, be grossly unfair for counsel, on that account, to ask him, on cross-examination, "When did you decide to violate the order of this Court by failing and neglecting to pay the alimony?" since it is for the Court to determine, on the basis of the evidence in the case, whether or not its order has been violated.

A question as obviously improper as this is almost certain to arouse opposing counsel to a vigorous objection that the Court will sustain. Besides, there is always the risk of a rebuke from the Bench. The judge may interrupt and say, "Don't you think, counsellor, that whether the defendant violated the order of the Court is for the Court to determine?"

In any event, if an unfair question is asked, the colloquy between the cross-examiner and the judge, whose duty it is to keep the cross-examination within proper bounds, may give the jury the impression that the offending attorney has been taking undue advantage of the witness. Hence, counsel has to be careful to say or do nothing in his cross-examination that could put the witness in the position of the underdog and cast himself in the role of a bully or a trickster.

However, a question does not have to be unfair in the technical sense—that is, legally impermissible—to affect the jury unfavorably. The impression that the witness is being browbeaten is often unwittingly conveyed as much by the tone or manner in which a question is asked as by its form. Even the position and posture of the cross-examiner as he questions a witness can suggest an affront to his dignity. I have noticed, for example, that some lawyers, while conducting a cross-examination, will stand facing the jury, with their backs to the witness. Others will walk toward or away from him in a continual pilgrimage around the courtroom or will menacingly approach within inches of the witness, shout, and shake a finger under his nose. When such conduct does not actually distract the jury, it suggests that counsel has a weak case and is trying to badger, rattle, or intimidate the hapless witness. Often a judge will reprove this kind of behavior by saying, "Counsel, won't you please stand at the rail or at a respectable distance from the jury box as you are examining the witness," or "Counsel, there's no need to harass the witness. Please stand back a few feet and don't breathe into his face or down his neck." Opposing counsel, if he is at all alert, will likewise protest against such tactics. In short, they win favor with nobody—least of all with the members of the jury.

Indeed, any action or statement on a cross-examiner's part that suggests arrogance is likely to boomerang badly, especially if contempt is shown for a witness who is uneducated, speaks with an accent, or has difficulty in making himself understood. After all, if a lawyer is not deterred from demeaning himself in this fashion by a decent regard for the ordinary courtesies expected of a member of the legal profession, he should at least consider that some of the jurors or their close relatives may also be poorly educated. Besides, few people esteem a man who takes advantage of his superior knowledge to belittle or downgrade another.

I once heard a lawyer cross-examine a woman close to seventy years of age who spoke with a heavy Yiddish accent. She had given damaging testimony against his client. Counsel was unable to shake her. Although her lack of education was apparent, it in no way affected the substance or logic of her testimony.

Finally, in a desperate attempt to impeach her credibility on the ground that she was illiterate, counsel asked her, "Do you know how to read or write English?"

"Counsellor," she replied, "I am a true witness. No, I can't read or write English. But I just came from my lawyer's office, where I signed my name to a will, and I gave away ten thousand dollars to wonderful Jewish and Christian hospitals. I got the will in my pocket. Would you like to see it? You can read it, I'm sure."

The fact is that it is extremely risky for a lawyer to assume that the witness he is cross-examining is his intellectual inferior. Appearances can be very deceiving in this respect. That a person is engaged in a humble occupation is no reason for concluding that he is ignorant or dull-witted.

A colleague of mine told me of a negligence case in which a bus driver was called to testify on behalf of the defendant, the company that employed him. On direct examination he stated that there was an impact between the bus he was driving and the plaintiff, but the accident had been caused by the plaintiff's walking along the roadway into the right side of the moving vehicle.

On cross-examination, the plaintiff's attorney tried to drive home the point that the bus driver was looking straight ahead while operating the vehicle at the time of the accident, and so he could not have seen the plaintiff walking some distance to its right. Counsel put the crucial question thus:

Q. How come you were able to see the plaintiff to the right of your bus while you were looking straight ahead?

Instead of being floored by the question, the witness calmly answered:

A. Counsellor, haven't you ever heard of peripheral vision?

When counsel appeared stunned and perplexed at hearing such learned language issuing from the lips of a bus driver, the witness added:

A. It means the formation of the sight image at some part of the retina which forms indirect vision.

At this point the attorney for the plaintiff should have brought his cross-examination to an end or at least terminated this phase of it and passed on to something else. He ought to have realized that he had encountered an extremely intelligent and knowledgeable witness, and he should have beaten a gracious but hasty retreat. Instead, evidently still trying to downgrade the witness, counsel pressed on with a further question:

Q. How do you know what "peripheral vision" means?
A. Well, I've been attending college at night for the past four years in order to prepare myself to become an ophthalmologist.

Thus, counsel succeeded unwittingly in enhancing the testimony of the witness.

In another case, the plaintiff complained that the defendant had characterized him as being "consciously arrogant." During the cross-examination of the plaintiff, defense counsel, underestimating the witness' intelligence, made the mistake of asking him how he would define "conscious arrogance."

"I would say," the plaintiff replied, "that conscious arrogance is the outward manifestation of overweening self-esteem."

High-pressure tactics generally prove just as ineffectual, if not actually self-defeating, in the conduct of a cross-examination. A display of impatience or ill-temper by a cross-examiner in questioning an unresponsive or uncooperative witness is very likely to be interpreted by the jury as nothing but an implied confession of counsel's failure. Berating a witness is an almost sure way of unwittingly admitting defeat and putting him on top.

I recall a case in which the plaintiff was on the witness stand being cross-examined by the defendant's lawyer. The witness was obviously being cautious in formulating his answers. Apparently sensing a trap in every question, he took plenty of time to reflect on each one before committing himself. At one point, after counsel had addressed a question to him, there ensued a silence of about a minute or two while the plaintiff sat in the witness chair placidly contemplating the ceiling.

Finally, defense counsel lost patience and shouted at the witness, "Why don't you answer? Why don't you answer my question?"

Still getting no reply, he turned to the judge and asked that the plaintiff be directed to answer the question. But before the judge could say anything, the witness also turned to him and said, "Look at him, Your Honor. He had three years to think up the question, and he won't give me three minutes to think up an answer."

Instead of being impatient or angry with a witness who takes an inordinately long time to answer a question, counsel would do better to make a note of any unusually lengthy interval between question and answer. In the end, he will generally find that he will get more mileage out of such evidences of hesitation if he points them out to the jury during his summation than if he tries to make an issue of them during cross-examination.

Similarly, a cross-examiner deludes himself if he thinks he is making any headway when he seizes upon trifling discrepancies in a witness' testimony regarding such matters as distances, colors, heights, weights, etc. It is just as bad to underestimate the intelligence of the jury as to underrate that of the witness. Jurors are not fools. They know well enough that exactitude on points of this kind is not to be expected of anyone, and that witnesses are bound to differ somewhat in their estimates and impressions in these respects. The jurors are also well aware of the fact that a witness' memory is not unfailingly accurate as to dates, measurements, conversations, and the like. To keep badgering him about inconsequential matters like these only lessens a cross-examiner's chance of gaining the jury's support. Unduly prolonged inquiry into such details is worse than tedious; it may actually weaken counsel's case.

In this regard I may cite what happened in the course of the trial of a negligence action. Suit was brought against a railway company for the recovery of damages sustained in an accident that resulted in the amputation of one of the plaintiff's legs. The plaintiff contended that he was thrown under the wheels of a trolley car that suddenly began to move just as he was getting off. To corroborate the plaintiff's testimony, his counsel produced a witness who had been standing on the corner at the time of the accident.

The able attorney for the railway company began his cross-examination of the witness by asking him how far he was from the trolley when the accident occurred. Counsel sought to place the witness at least fifty feet from the corner, but the witness insisted that he had been standing only thirty feet from the scene. The tug-of-war over this point between defense counsel and the witness went on for about fifteen minutes, with the cross-examiner trying all the while to pull him ever farther away from the corner.

Finally, one of the jurors raised his hand to ask a question. When the Court granted permission, the juror inquired, "What difference does it make how many feet the witness was from the scene? The leg came off, didn't it?"

The presiding judge promptly declared a mistrial. But if the juror in this case had not raised this question in open court, he could hardly have been the only member of the panel to whom it must have occurred. Moreover, it surely would have been raised in the jury room.

By the same token, the average jury is not likely to form a favorable impression of a lawyer who turns the cross-examination into an occasion for making sneering or sarcastic remarks at the witness' expense in an obvious effort to "needle" him into an intemperate outburst. Some attorneys, for example, comment on each answer that the witness makes with a derisive "So that is what you say, huh?" "That is what you saw, huh?" "You remember it that way, huh?" Besides being personally demeaning, such conduct is unworthy of a member of the legal profession, and it is virtually certain to arouse resentment on the part of the jurors. A lawyer's function during cross-examination is to ask questions, not to indulge in snide remarks, make little speeches for the benefit of the jury, or vent his venom on the hapless witness on the stand.

Counsel must keep in mind that in the duel in which he is engaged, a poisoned foil can all too easily be turned against its user. There is always the possibility that he will meet his match, and that the witness may wrench the tainted weapon from his attacker's hand, return the thrust, and come out on top. Consider, for example, the following bit of dialogue between witness and cross-examiner:

WITNESS: Well, I spent a good bit of money in taking a year's course of study at Johns Hopkins, after I obtained my M.D., and thereafter I spent two years studying at Vienna, Austria.

CROSS-EXAMINER: (*Sarcastically*) Well, doctor, I believe by now you know everything.

WITNESS: No, sir, I am not fortunate enough to be a lawyer.

That even so experienced and talented a lawyer as Percy Foreman can sometimes come off second best in such encounters with a witness may be seen from the following excerpts from the record of a recent murder case in which he figured prominently:

Q. Do you know Christine M_____?
A. I don't recall her name.
Q. You say you don't know her, and yet might not you have once lived with her?
A. I knows the ladies I live with, Mr. Percy.

When another witness said that at his first meeting with one of the defendants he had a feeling she wanted to talk about something bad, Mr. Foreman asked:

Q. Oh, you just perceived that out of thin air?
A. What would a woman like that want with the likes of me?
Q. How did you know what she was going to talk about?
A. I didn't assume we were going to play tiddlywinks.

One of the other defense attorneys in the same trial fared little better with some of the witnesses he cross-examined:

Q. Why were you passing worthless checks when you had the money you extorted from the defendant?
A. You've got money, Mr. Woody . . . and you're still down here tryin' this case.

Asked to describe the size of the man who allegedly accompanied the defendant at their first meeting, the same witness shot back:

A. I didn't measure the man, Mr. Woody . . . I didn't happen to have a tape measure on me at the time.

Making jokes at the witness' expense can also prove a risky venture, unless counsel is reasonably sure he can "top" anything the witness says. As a general rule, an attempt at humor, even if it is successful, is out of place and even in bad taste during this phase of the trial. Cross-examination is a very serious matter. It is a search for truth, and it should be undertaken with the earnestness befitting its gravity. However, there are occasions when a touch of drollery or an apt witticism may be in order. Any question that reveals the absurdity of the witness' testimony or the ridiculousness of his position may get the jury to laugh at it and so score a point against him.

To illustrate: A lady in her late seventies was on the stand. She proved a shrewd witness. Suddenly, in the midst of her cross-examination when counsel raised a question touching on her credibility, she turned to her interrogator and asked, "Son, are you suggesting that I am not trying to tell the truth?"

Bowing from the waist, counsel retorted, "Not at all, Mother, but will you please try a little harder?"

Then, too, there was the Irish gentleman who, during a rather lengthy direct examination, stated, "Before this accident, I was so strong I could wrestle a bull."

His cross-examination, by contrast, was very brief:

Q. Mr. Reilly, you stated that before the accident, you were so strong you could wrestle a bull?
A. Indeed, I could.
Q. Isn't that precisely what you have been doing for the last hour and a half?

The tough, hard-hitting cross-examiner, who batters away relentlessly at the witness until he crumbles, is chiefly a figure of fiction. Such tactics bear very little resemblance to the actual realities of courtroom procedure. There are, to be sure, occasions when it may be necessary for counsel to take a firm and even an aggressive tone in conducting his cross-examination, but it requires some experience to recognize them. More often than not, high pressure and a hard line on the part of a cross-examiner succeed only in stiffening the witness' resistance.

Generally, the most effective practitioners of the art of cross-examination adopt a quite different approach. Instead of attempting to storm the witness' position with a direct assault, they prefer to lay siege to it and slowly and insidiously to undermine it before the witness is aware of what is happening to him. The crowning triumph of this type of interrogation comes when the witness leaves the stand without even realizing that the props have been knocked out, one by one, from under his testimony.

A somewhat similar technique consists in disarming the witness with feigned friendliness. The aim here is to put him completely at ease, lull his suspicions, and lead him along gently and almost imperceptibly from one admission to another, by a rather roundabout route, until he allows his guard to drop for a moment. Then, when his defenses are down, he is wide open for a sudden knockout blow—perhaps a single devastating question that ends everything.

In short, whatever method is used, more is to be gained by calmness, courtesy, and indirection than by bluster or bluff. The scalpel and the probe, rather than the sledgehammer or the bludgeon, are the preferred instruments of the masters of this art, and the operation is best performed when the witness has fallen under the anesthetic influence of an ingratiating tone and a friendly, patient manner on counsel's part.

This also has a salutary effect upon the jury. By showing no outward sign of hostility to the witness, counsel will appear in their eyes as a fair advocate whose only concern is to arrive at the truth. If, for example, the Court suggests that he rephrase his question, he will do so without anger or resentment, prefacing his new question by saying to the judge, "I'm obliged to Your Honor for the suggestion."

To the same end, I would often begin my cross-examination by saying to the witness, "If you do not understand a question I put to you, please do not answer it. Just ask me to repeat or rephrase it, and, with His Honor's permission, I will be glad to do so."

This promise should, of course, be scrupulously kept. If the witness says he does not understand a question that is a little confusing—for example, one that really consists of two or three questions—counsel loses nothing in readily agreeing with him by saying, "I don't blame you. I now see that it certainly needs clarification." This kind of frankness will help to dispose a jury favorably toward a lawyer.

As an illustration of the advantage to be gained from the subtle and courteous approach in disarming a witness suspected of untruthfulness, I may cite an experience I had when I represented one of six youthful defendants charged with murder. Ranging in age from seventeen to nineteen, they strikingly resembled one another: each weighed between 125 and 135 pounds; each was between 5'8" and 5'10" in height; each had a crew haircut; and each wore a black "zoot suit" with tight pants. Jointly indicted for a fatal stabbing, they were accused of inflicting about forty knife wounds upon a young lad whom they had allegedly strung up on a pole.

The case took approximately six weeks to try, with frequent recesses during each day of the trial to accommodate the Court, the jury, eighteen defense lawyers (each trial counsel had two assistants), and three or four Assistant District Attorneys with their investigators. During the course of the first three or four days of the trial, I noticed that after every such recess, the defendants would be returned to the courtroom by the court officers and seated in the very same chairs they had occupied from the beginning of the trial. These chairs were arranged in two rows of three. Invariably, Defendant No. 1 sat with Defendant No. 4 at his side; Defendant No. 2 sat beside Defendant No. 5; and Defendant No. 3 was paired with Defendant No. 6.

There were two jury boxes in this courtroom. One was occupied by the jury; the other, by six burly policemen, who were seated side by side in the first row. The rear row of this second box was unoccupied.

Since there were, besides, at least six court officers in attendance at the trial, it seemed to me that the presence of the policemen, so conspicuously placed where the jury could have a good view of them throughout the proceedings, was little more than a kind of "side show," calculated to create a little atmosphere for the benefit of the jury. My argument at the bench—of course, out of hearing of the jury—was directed toward dispensing with the presence of the policemen on the ground that it was prejudicial to the defendants. However, the Court denied my request.

As can be seen in the sketch (Exhibit 10), the courtroom in which the case was tried was jammed with court officers, policemen, defendants, and lawyers. My client, Defendant No. 2, was seated in front of the jury box occupied by the policemen. Sitting between my client and me were Defendant No. 5, the three lawyers who represented Defendant No. 1, a number of court officers, and others.

After each of the numerous daily recesses, as the defendants, in the custody of the court officers, were led back through the door near the witness stand to the area in the courtroom where they were requested to sit, I remember I would turn to one of my associate counsel, Mr. Benjamin Spector, an extremely able lawyer, and ask, "Which one is our client?" They all looked so much alike that my associate too, although he had interviewed Defendant No. 2 on several occasions in the city prison, had difficulty in picking him out as he walked with the remaining defendants to his chair.

About the tenth day of the trial, the prosecution called a witness whom I shall never forget. Led gently through his direct examination by the able prosecutor, he testified that on the evening of the slaying he had been looking out of the window of his apartment on the first floor of his house. Suddenly, he alleged, he saw six boys dragging a youth of between seventeen and eighteen along the street from the direction of a certain juke-box parlor frequented by teenagers. The witness further testified that he saw the defendants strap their victim to a pole, and that thereupon each defendant inflicted upon him at least half a dozen knife wounds. He had no doubt that when they had finished, the young man they had stabbed was dead.

Now, for the first time, the pattern followed in returning the defendants to the same seats after each recess began to appear significant to me. The witness' testimony was letter-perfect. He identified each defendant. Apparently his eyes were like a Polaroid camera that could focus on a distant object, snap a series of pictures in quick succession, and develop them instantly. In addition, he must have had a filing cabinet stored somewhere in the recesses of his brain. In reciting the distinctive identifying features of each of the alleged assailants, he talked glibly of a "thin mustache," "a scar on the left cheek," "a round face," "protruding ears," "thick lips," "a long nose," "bulging eyes," "bushy eyebrows," "a receding chin," etc.; and he was likewise able to state in every instance the young man's approximate height and weight.

In itself, this was certainly a remarkable feat of observation and memory. But the witness did even better than that. In response to questions from the prosecutor, he succeeded in correlating each set of features with the individual defendant to whom they belonged. Typical of this part of his direct examination is the following extract from the trial record:

Q. The young man who had a "thin mustache," can you point him out?

The witness pointed to Defendant No. 1.

Q. And how tall would you say he is?

The witness estimated his height within an inch.

Q. And how about the young man with a scar on his cheek, can you point him out?

The witness did, pointing to Defendant No. 2.

Q. And about how tall is he?

The witness had no trouble in correctly estimating his height too. Similar questions were asked in regard to the rest of the defendants, and the witness gave similar answers. He identified all of them as having participated in the crime.

The cloud of uncertainty as to why the defendants were always led back to the same seats was by this time completely dispelled. I could hardly wait for my turn to cross-examine this witness. His story was just too pat, and I strongly suspected his reliability and truthfulness.

While counsel for Defendant No. 1 was cross-examining the witness, I left my seat at the counsel table and mingled in the crowd of lawyers that thronged the courtroom. Meanwhile, I arranged for Defendant No. 2 to change seats with Defendant No. 5. When I rose to conduct my cross-examination, I stationed myself directly behind the chair occupied by the prosecutor. During the cross-examination, whenever I noticed the prosecutor move his head toward his left, in the defendants' direction, I would maneuver my body to the prosecutor's left to insure that at all times I obstructed his view of them. I then asked the witness to look directly at me while he testified.

The tone I took with this witness was deferential and friendly.

"I want to compliment you," I began, "on your excellent memory. You certainly gave a very clear description of each defendant. I have only a few questions."

The witness was obviously flattered. I could see that he felt relieved that he would be spared a hammering cross-examination. He relaxed visibly.

Then I continued along these lines:

Q. You haven't been in the courtroom during the last ten days of the trial, have you?
A. No.
Q. Were you somewhere in this building?
A. Yes.
Q. In a room on this floor, is that right?

(I knew that the District Attorney had a witness room on the same floor.)

A. Yes.
Q. Can you tell us where that room is located?

(Just an insignificant question to give the witness a chance to show his honesty.)

A. Down the hall, to the left of the elevator.
Q. You mean the District Attorney's room, don't you?
A. Yes.

Q. And have you been in that room on each of the last ten days?
A. Yes.
Q. From about ten o'clock each morning?
A. Yes.
Q. While you were there, did you talk to anyone about this case?
A. Yes.
Q. With whom did you talk?
A. With a detective.
Q. Besides talking with him, were you shown photographs of these defendants?
A. Yes.
Q. Under each of those photographs, was there a name and a description?
A. Yes.
Q. Were these photographs laid out on a desk or table before you in the same order as the defendants are now sitting in this courtroom?
A. Yes.
Q. By the way, were the photographs numbered 1, 2, and 3 laid out on your right side, and 4, 5, and 6 on your left side?
A. Yes.
Q. So that while you were in the District Attorney's office during the past ten days, were you able to memorize a description of each defendant?
A. Yes.
Q. And that's why you know them so perfectly?
A. Yes.

At this point, as an "aside," I commented, "I certainly want to compliment you on your marvelous memory." (A lawyer can sometimes indulge in a side remark, provided it is serious and not just horseplay.)

With this statement I sought to give the impression that I had no further questions and was about to take my seat. Thinking that I was finished with him, the witness again relaxed. Instead, I said, apologetically, "I have just a few more questions, not many." My cross-examination then proceeded as follows:

Q. Please look at the defendant in Seat No. 1.
A. Yes.
Q. Did you take a good look?
A. Yes.
Q. Now, looking at me, what is his name?

The witness correctly stated the name of Defendant No. 1.

Q. Please continue to look at me and describe him.

The witness described him exactly as he had on direct examination.

Q. Now look at the defendant in Seat No. 2.
A. Yes.
Q. Did you take a good look?
A. Yes.
Q. Now, looking at me, what is his name?

The witness gave the name of Defendant No. 2.

Q. Will you please describe him.

The witness described Defendant No. 2 as he had previously.

I proceeded in the same quiet tone, asking similar questions about the rest of the defendants. Of course, when the witness reached Seat No. 5, in which Defendant No. 2 was now sitting, he described Defendant No. 5.

Defendants No. 2 and 5 were acquitted.

Yet this witness, who had just torpedoed the prosecutor's case, left the stand convinced that he had performed a Herculean feat of memory. As he stepped down from the stand, he raised his hand to his brow as if to salute me. It was a gesture of triumph on his part. I had no compunction about returning a full salute to him, as if in recognition of his extraordinary achievement, and then, turning to the members of the jury, I shaped my lips to convey to them, as one would in speaking to the deaf, the unspoken but clearly understandable words, "What a lying scoundrel this witness is!" I later made this the theme of my summation.

Thus, there is no need for a cross-examiner to adopt either the stance or the weapons of a dragon-slayer if he has doubts about a witness' credibility. What is called for in such cases is not a sustained, vicious, and violent attack with a battle-ax, but a more subtle strategy aimed at impaling the witness on the sharp point of a rapier. The cross-examiner's task, in such a situation, is to bring to the attention of judge and jury relevant matters at issue that would otherwise pass unnoticed.

By way of illustration, I may cite the manner in which this technique was employed to discredit a witness whose story counsel suspected had been memorized.

The case was a suit for malpractice brought against a physician. It was alleged that in removing some callous from the plaintiff's foot, the doctor had used an unsterilized razor blade taken from the medicine cabinet in the patient's home. As a result, the plaintiff had to have his leg amputated. An expert witness, called on behalf of the plaintiff, testified that if the doctor had indeed performed the operation as alleged in the complaint, the loss of the leg could be attributed to the resulting infection.

In support of the allegation concerning the doctor's use of the razor blade in such a grossly unprofessional manner, the plaintiff called one of his sons as a witness. However, defense counsel noticed, on raising some objections during the course of this witness' direct testimony, that he seemed to lose track of his version of the facts and had to start all over again from the beginning. Accordingly, in the cross-examination, the doctor's attorney pursued the following line of questioning:

Q. When you were a student at school, were you given assignments to memorize poetry and then recite it in class?
A. Yes, we had lessons like that. We had to memorize passages from Shakespeare.
Q. And did you find that, after committing a passage to memory, if you were interrupted in reciting it, you had to go back and start all over again?
A. Yes, that always happened.
Q. Is it not a fact that you memorized your testimony, and that was why, when interrupted, you had to start at the very beginning?
A. Yes, that's true.

Later, in speaking with two or three of the jurors, defense counsel was told that they were convinced the witness had presented a memorized version of the facts; otherwise, he would have been able to pick up his story where he had left off before the interruption. The defendant prevailed.

In general, a cross-examiner would do well to avoid asking questions that call for lengthy explanations or that give the witness an opportunity to exculpate himself. Hence, whenever practicable, questions should be so phrased as to call for a brief, definite answer, preferably a yes or a no. To ask for anything more is to take a great risk.

The most dangerous question to put to a witness on cross-examination is "Why?"—"Why did you do that?" "What was your reason for saying that?" "What purpose did you have in mind?" "What did you hope to accomplish?" "What was your motive?" "Why didn't you?" No matter in what form it is put, the "why" question is always fraught with peril, because it allows the witness to talk at length and to "get off the hook" if he is on one. It is an avenue of escape conveniently opened up for him in case he has trapped himself. It gives him a chance to extricate himself from difficulties his testimony may have got him into. It makes it possible for him to bolster his testimony and appear to be honest. Counsel can never know what answer such a question will evoke or where it may lead.

I once heard opposing counsel ask one of my witnesses in an action for breach of contract, "Why did you come here to testify?"

I raised no objection to the question.

Without batting an eyelash, the witness replied, "Because from my experience with your client, I know he is unreliable and a crook, and he pulled the same thing on me as he did on the plaintiff. So I came to see justice done."

In another case, the defendant was charged with petty larceny. The complainant testified that one afternoon, while she was seated, watching a movie, in a practically deserted section of the theater, the defendant entered and sat next to her. After a while, he dropped his hat and, in picking it up, touched her ankle. Later, he placed his hand on her knee, and still later slid his hand along her thigh and under her skirt. There, under the top of her stocking, he felt a bill concealed. He snatched the twenty-dollar bill and ran for the exit. The complainant screamed, and the defendant was apprehended by the manager of the theater.

On cross-examination, defense counsel asked the complainant:

Q. When the defendant put his hand on your ankle, and later on your knee, why didn't you scream?
A. I didn't think it was my money he was after.

Still another illustration of the dangers involved in a cross-examiner's probing into a witness' motives is provided by a case in which a wife sought to have her husband declared incompetent in a proceeding brought under the Mental Hygiene Law. The strongest evidence presented to establish his mental incapacity was the fact that he was conducting bicycle races in the garage which he operated in Coney Island. A former champion bicyclist, he had had show cards printed to be distributed in the area, inviting people to his garage on a Saturday evening to watch the races in the bicycle track he had built there. Using this as evidence that he must have been mentally ill, since he had squandered his money on such a harebrained project, his wife provided her attorney with a copy of the show card to prove her point.

When her husband was called to the stand, he admitted building the bicycle track and planning to hold races in his garage. He testified that he had done so because bicycling was his chief hobby. Moreover, he said it was his belief that if he attracted people to his garage, he would substantially increase his sale of gasoline.

On cross-examination, his wife's attorney confronted him with what counsel thought would be a very damaging question:

Q. Is it not a fact that, although you had the show cards printed, you never actually distributed or used them?
A. Yes, it's true. I never did use them.
Q. Even though you had them printed at great expense?
A. Yes, they cost me a lot of money.

With a complacent smile, the wife's attorney looked at the jury as if to say, "You can see for yourselves that the man is crazy. I have proved it beyond a doubt."

However, counsel apparently would not let well enough alone. He felt he had to ask one final question:

Q. Why didn't you distribute the show cards?
A. Because they contained a mistake in spelling. Look here: You see "Saturday" is spelled "Satuday."

The card had been passed from the attorney to the judge and among all the jurors. No one had noticed the error. The witness' answer apparently proved conclusive in regard to the basic issue of his mental competence, for within five minutes after the members of the jury retired to deliberate, they returned with a verdict in his favor, and the wife's proceeding was dismissed.

The risk that a cross-examiner runs in asking a witness a "why" question is just as great in a criminal action as it is in a civil suit. In the prosecution of a husband for the murder of his wife, the District Attorney put on the stand the couple's nine-year-old son solely to show that his mother and father quarreled. After he had so testified, counsel for the accused, on cross-examination, asked the following questions:

Q. You don't like your father, do you?
A. No, I don't.
Q. As a matter of fact, you hate your father, don't you?
A. Yes, I do.
Q. Why do you hate the father who has supported and raised you?
A. Because he killed my mother.

Similarly, in the trial of a murder case, an old Polish lady testified that a skeleton found by the authorities was that of the murdered man.

Defense counsel foolishly asked her how she knew that this was the skeleton of the deceased.

"Because," she replied, "the defendant told me he had killed him and buried him just where the skeleton was found."

The "why" question, of course, can be phrased in many ways: "How come?" "How do you explain . . . ?" "How do you account for . . . ?" etc. These "how" questions are, as can easily be seen, simply variants of the "why" question, in the same category, and subject to the same criticism. For example, in a recent negligence case, the plaintiff complained that he had suffered "brain damage." The defendant called a medical expert, who disputed this contention. No amount of questioning by the plaintiff's attorney, an experienced practitioner, could shake the expert's testimony. Finally, after lengthy cross-examination without apparent favorable result, counsel asked, "Doctor, how do you account for the fact that the plaintiff has serious headaches and spells of dizziness?"

The doctor replied, "I can easily inform you. He has a wife, five children, and no job."

In addition to the "why" question, there are certain stock questions which seem to form an essential part of the standard repertoire of some trial lawyers whenever they cross-examine a witness. One of the questions that apparently enchants many cross-examiners is that old stand-by, "To whom have you talked about this case?" Sometimes they will make the question more specific: "Did you speak to your lawyer? Other witnesses? Your wife?"

I do not think that this type of question should be asked indiscriminately. To be sure, a negative answer, if obviously untruthful, will tend to undermine or even completely discredit a witness' testimony. Nevertheless, such questions are so dangerous that counsel would be well advised to avoid them altogether unless he knows in advance that the witness will answer in the negative. If, when I was trying a case, I concluded that a witness had told the truth in giving his direct testimony, and that he had no financial or other interest in the outcome of the case, I would never ask him whether or with whom he had discussed it.

The risk involved in putting such a question to a witness is well illustrated by a criminal case in which an elderly couple, who spoke with a decided Yiddish accent, were witnesses for the prosecution. They operated a luncheonette in an area where holdups had become frequent and were robbed at knife point of several hundred dollars. At the trial, the wife testified first, while her husband waited outside the courtroom for his turn to take the stand. She positively identified the defendant as the man who had held them up. Next her husband was called to the stand. After he had completed his direct testimony, which corroborated that of his wife, defense counsel put a few preliminary questions to him and then asked, "By the way, did you discuss the facts of this case with your wife?"

The old man, who was somewhat deaf, cupped his hand to his ear and asked, "Hah?"

The attorney for the defendant repeated the question. For a moment the witness just stared at his cross-examiner with an expression of incredulity. Then he asked, "Vat's de matter? You t'ink I'm mad at mine wibe?"

The presiding judge stated that this wholly unexpected response was the best possible answer to such a question that he had ever heard.

Incidentally, when the wife was testifying on cross-examination, she too proved more than a match for defense counsel. Seeking to undermine her credibility, he asked her, "How many people were in your luncheonette that evening?"

"Vy esk soch foolish kvestions?" she retorted. "Comes by night, ve count de money, not de customers."

Equally shattering, in a case tried before me, was the response given by a youngster of twelve, who was asked on cross-examination whether he had talked to the lawyer about the case. To the obviously complete satisfaction of the jury, the child promptly replied, "Nope! But I talked to my mother about it a lot of times, and she talked to the lawyer when she went to his office, and the lawyer always told me to tell the truth."

I may best sum up the essential principles of cross-examination strategy by quoting the excellent advice of Sir Sidney Littlewood on this subject:

Cross-examination needs much thought.

First, assess the witness you have to cross-examine, and on that assessment decide how you will deal with him. Some witnesses will respond best to kindly treatment; some to firm treatment. By the time the witness has given his evidence in chief, you should have made up your mind which course you will adopt.

An advocate should always know exactly what he wants when he starts to cross-examine. Many ask questions for the sake of asking questions, and ask questions on points that do not affect their own case at all. This tends to irritate the Court and helps no one. If you know exactly what you want, you will cease cross-examining as soon as you have got it. In my view, it is a mistake to ask any question in cross-examination unless it is directed to something that you have already decided you want to elicit. It is true that there are times when you have to approach your point in a roundabout way, but, even so, every question that you ask while proceeding in that roundabout way should lead up to the point that you seek to establish or destroy.

There are instances, and they are not infrequent, where there is no point in cross-examination. In such cases do not cross-examine.

Let us see how these principles might be applied to the cross-examination of the various types of witnesses that a trial lawyer is likely to encounter.

18

Trials and Errors of a Cross-Examiner

The approach that a trial lawyer takes in conducting a cross-examination will depend not only on the nature of the case and the issues in dispute but also, to a considerable extent, on the type of witness he is dealing with. In other words, an attorney has to tailor his questions to fit the person he is cross-examining. To this end, he should know something about the witness' experience, educational background, relation to any of the litigants, possible financial or other interest in the outcome of the trial, and general character. Indeed, ideally a lawyer would like to have as much prior information about a witness to be cross-examined as about a prospective juror.

Ordinarily, as we have seen, it is not difficult for an enterprising and alert attorney to gather data of this kind about a witness for the other side before he takes the stand. But sometimes counsel may be taken unawares. Testimony damaging to his case may be given by a "surprise" witness called by the opposing party without prior notice. In the absence of adequate information about the unexpected witness, a lawyer is handicapped in cross-examining him.

In such cases, counsel should waste no time. As soon as the witness takes the stand to give his direct testimony, an effort should be made to get as much information about him as possible. Is the witness a stranger, or is he a friend of the party for whom he is testifying? How well known are they to each other? Do they belong to the same social club or political organization or business firm? Is the witness interested financially in the outcome of the litigation? Was he subpoenaed, or did he appear voluntarily? Is he being paid a fee for testifying?

Possibly the answers to some of these questions may be given in the witness' direct testimony or may be inferable from it. Often the best person to ask is one's own client, if the facts are not forthcoming from other sources. They may not be questions to put to the witness himself—at least not directly. But with a certain amount of tact and finesse, such information may be gathered from him indirectly.

Indeed, tact and finesse are qualities that counsel will have particular need of in cross-examining certain kinds of witnesses. For example, he must be especially careful not to offend clergymen or members of religious orders. Unless there is compelling evidence to contradict their testimony, it is most injudicious to grapple with such witnesses. The best thing to do is to bow graciously and say, "I have no questions."

I recall a case tried before me in which a rabbi who was an eye-witness to an accident was subpoenaed by the defendant. The witness' testimony was direct, precise, and to the point. He told what he remembered of the event. If he did not recall some of the details he was asked about on his direct examination, he said so quite frankly.

The plaintiff's attorney cross-examined him as follows:

Q. When for the first time did anyone get in touch with you about this accident?
A. Oh, several years ago, in West New York—I lived there.
Q. I mean recently.
A. Someone called at my office—a gentleman by the name of Maloney.
Q. When was that?
A. A few days ago.
Q. Just one more question: Did they arrange to pay you to testify? Yes or no?

The rabbi looked as if he had received a left hook to the heart. He was completely overcome at being asked that "one more question." From where I was sitting, I could easily see, and I remember to this day, his glazed look, the squint of his eyes as he looked down his nose, the downward curve of his lips, and his pained expression. When he had regained his composure, the rabbi turned toward the members of the jury. Their eyes were riveted upon him. Then, he slowly bowed his head, so that his black "yarmulka," or skullcap, was in their full view, and, speaking with deep and obviously sincere emotion, in the manner of a chant, as if addressing his congregation, replied, "God forbid! No! No!"

Needless to say, the verdict was for the defendant.

No less inept was the cross-examination of a clergyman which concluded with the utterly incredible question, "Have you ever been convicted of a crime?" What did counsel hope to gain with a question like that? The witness, of course, answered no. His cross-examiner neither produced nor had any evidence of a conviction. Naturally, opposing counsel, in his summation, stressed the outrageous unfairness of the question. The jurors later admitted that the asking of that question had influenced them in reaching a verdict "against the lawyer who propounded it." In this case, as in so many others, the sins of the lawyer were visited upon his client.

In another case, a seventy-five-year-old pedestrian sued to recover damages for serious personal injuries he sustained when he allegedly was hit by a truck. The defendant called as a witness the ambulance physician, a nun attached to the hospital staff.

On the date of the alleged accident, the nun was assigned, in a medical capacity, to ambulance duty at the hospital. She testified that she responded to the call for an ambulance. When she arrived at the scene, she found the plaintiff lying on his back. She asked him what had happened. He replied that he had "fainted." The nun then specifically asked him whether he had been hit by a truck or an automobile, and he said no. She thereupon examined the plaintiff and found that, except for a scalp abrasion over the occipital area, his torso and extremities showed no sign of any traumatic injury. The plaintiff was then removed by ambulance to the hospital, where he was X-rayed. By this means, a skull fracture and other serious injuries were discovered. The nun concluded her direct testimony by expressing the opinion that the plaintiff had fainted and fallen to the ground, hitting his head and sustaining his injuries.

The plaintiff's counsel, a well-known trial lawyer, subjected the nun, who was dressed in her habit and carried a Bible in her hand as she approached the witness stand, to a grueling cross-examination. He attempted to attack the credibility of her testimony by insinuating that she was not a bona fide physician at all, but an investigator of accidents. Counsel even went so far as to intimate that the questions she had asked the plaintiff in the course of her professional examination of him were altogether unnecessary and beyond the scope of her medical responsibilities.

Because of the seriousness of the injuries the plaintiff had sustained, the damages he incurred were very substantial. His lowest settlement demand was $35,000, and the Court had recommended a settlement of $25,000.

After approximately ten hours of deliberation, the jury returned a verdict in favor of the plaintiff in the sum of $15,000. Later, conversations between counsel and some of the jurors disclosed that the low verdict had been influenced to a considerable extent by the jury's resentment of the tactics of the plaintiff's attorney in cross-examining the nun.

For similar reasons, a lawyer must be very careful about the way he cross-examines a child. Here, for example, is what happened when defense counsel in a negligence action examined the plaintiff, a youngster of ten, who was seriously injured when he was struck by a car while he was crossing the street:

Q. Now tell me, sonny, what class are you in?
A. 3B.
Q. What hours do you attend school?
A. From eight to three.
Q. Was the day of the accident a regular school day?
A. Yes.
Q. Did you go to school that day?
A. No.
Q. Were you ill?
A. No.

This would have been a good point for counsel to have ended his cross-examination. Instead, he asked "one more question":

Q. Now, sonny, did you play hookey that day?
A. Oh, no. I am an orphan. I have no mother or father and was staying with my aunt, who was very sick, and I had to go to the drugstore to get her medicine, when I was hit by the car.

Defense counsel strenuously objected to this answer and moved that it be stricken out. But to no avail.

"You asked for it!" the judge said, in overruling his motion.

A generous verdict was, of course, rendered in favor of the child.

Another type of witness who poses a special problem for a cross-examiner is the person called to testify to the character of the accused in a criminal case. Here again, a quick assessment of the witness' education and background must be made, often in the course of the cross-examination itself. If it appears that there is a chance of impeaching the witness' credibility, the prosecutor should certainly make the attempt. Thus, if the witness has stated on direct examination that the defendant's reputation for veracity is good, it may be advisable to ask him the meaning of the word "veracity." If he does not know its meaning, there is no need to berate or abuse him. All the prosecutor has to do in that case is to end his cross-examination right then and there. Later, the witness' ignorance of the word may be mentioned in the summation—but charitably, without vindictiveness or gloating. Much discretion is required in discrediting a character witness because the jury well understands that he may have consented to testify only to accommodate a friend. It is therefore more prudent for the prosecution to dismiss such testimony as essentially of little or no account than to launch an attack on the motives or the character of the witness himself.

As an excellent example of the right way to handle a character witness, I may cite the cross-examination of a retired judge called to testify on behalf of a defendant charged with fraudulent stock transactions. On direct examination, the witness testified that the defendant's reputation for veracity was "the very highest." Here is how the Assistant United States Attorney pressed the witness during cross-examination:

Q. Have you heard that the defendant considers himself a friend of Tony Stiletto [an alleged member of Murder, Inc.]?
A. No, never heard of Stiletto.
Q. Have you heard that the defendant considers himself a friend of Jake Jacobs [a gambler]?
A. No.
Q. Do you know that he socialized with and recommended the employment of a man who pleaded guilty to a stock fraud case?
A. Never heard of any such thing, and I don't believe it.
Q If you had heard it, would this have changed your opinion?
A. Of course it would.

When the witness uttered these words, in my opinion his testimony exploded with megaton impact.

In another case, a Catholic priest was called as a character witness on behalf of the defendant, who was charged with impairing the morals of a minor. Under direct examination, the priest testified that he knew the defendant, that he knew others who knew the defendant, that he had had occasion to discuss with them the defendant's reputation for honesty, veracity, and morality, and that his reputation was excellent.

On cross-examination, the prosecutor asked the witness, "What was the occasion for your conversation with others concerning the defendant's morality?"

The priest promptly replied, "Well, he sought admission into the Holy Name Society. Before the application could be approved, I did everything I could to verify my own impression of the defendant's character and reputation."

The prosecutor readily agreed with the unanimous verdict of "Not guilty" which the three-judge Bench rendered.

Often counsel is faced with the problem of the witness who keeps on repeating, in response to virtually every question, "I don't remember." One of the most amusing cross-examinations I have ever heard was made of one of my own witnesses who professed to be unable to recall practically everything he was asked about. Conducted by Leon Morgan, one of the most able and skillful lawyers I have ever encountered in a trial, the questioning went something like this:

Q. When you say you don't remember, Mr. Jones, do you mean by that that you remembered it and forgot it, or that you never remembered it at all?

A. I remembered it and forgot it.

Q. Your accident happened on January 10, 1948, and today is March 14, 1953. I know that you cannot give me the exact date that you forgot it, but you certainly can give me the year, can you not?

A. It was in 1952.

Q. Thank you for your assistance. Now that you remember that you forgot it in 1952, I know that you cannot remember the precise month you forgot it, but can you tell us what time of the year it was.

A. Some time in the middle of the year.

Q. Would it be a fair statement that it was some time between June and August? Is that what you mean by the middle of the year?

A. Yes, sir.

Q. I know you don't remember the precise time of the day that you forgot it. I am sure, however, that you can tell us whether it was early morning, afternoon, or evening.

A. It was some time in the afternoon.

Q. From your answer, I take it that you forgot it in the year 1952, some time between June and August, and during the afternoon. Is that right?

A. Yes, sir.

Unlike the witness who has trouble with his memory, the flippant witness is a cross-examiner's delight. The best thing to do with him is to encourage him to talk to his heart's content. The more he babbles, the more likely it will be that sooner or later he will blurt out something brash or bumptious that will be enough to provide counsel with ammunition for a devastating summation.

By way of illustration I may mention a case in which I represented one of the defendants. Leo Durocher, the fiery and popular erstwhile manager of the Brooklyn Dodgers—or "Bums," as they were affectionately called by their devoted fans—and a special police officer at Ebbets Field, where the team played, were charged with assaulting a spectator.

The complainant alleged that the defendants first enticed him to leave his seat in the grandstand; then, when he reached the vicinity of the dugout, they beat him with a blackjack, breaking his jaw, so that for some months he was unable to eat solid food.

When I cross-examined the complainant, I asked him how often he came to see the Dodgers play. It turned out that he was in practically daily attendance at the ball park when the "Bums" played at home. He admitted that it was his habit to hurl unflattering and unprintable epithets at Durocher whenever Durocher called for a play that failed.

My cross-examination then proceeded along substantially the following lines:

Q. How is it that you have the time to attend almost every game the team plays?
A. Well, it's part of my job, you could say.
Q. What kind of job is that?
A. I make book. You get me?
Q. You mean you take bets on the outcome of the game?
A. That's it. You got it exactly.
Q. Then you're what's called a "bookie" or a "bookmaker," is that it?
A. Yep. I make out all right.
Q. So you're not really a Dodger fan at all, are you?
A. Nah. I don't go for that stuff.
Q. You don't really care about seeing the Dodgers win, then, do you?
A. Not a bit.
Q. You mean you don't feel sorry when the home team loses or glad when it wins?
A. Not at all. That's not what I go to the game for.
Q. So what makes you come to see the game?
A. Look, I'm a bettor. All I'm interested in is "cabbage," see? That's all.

Imagine a Brooklynite making such an admission! In "Dodgertown" this was tantamount to confessing a kinship to Hitler or Mussolini. Later, when the two defendants were indicted for felonious assault, I appeared for the police officer, and Hyman Barshay, now my distinguished colleague, appeared for Durocher. In our summations (I think we each consumed two and a half hours) we made much capital out of the complainant who dared to attend our hallowed ball park, not as a loyal "rooter," but as a gambler, intent only on the sordid business of picking up a little "cabbage." Again and again we referred, with the utmost contempt and disdain, to his flippant remark about "cabbage," until, by the time we had concluded our respective summations, the jurors were enraged at him.

I shall never forget the tumultuous scene when the jury reported its verdict. Hundreds of spectators filled the courtroom, corridors, and sidewalk outside. I sometimes wonder what would have happened to the complainant if the police had not rushed him out under their protection.

The question is sometimes asked: How should a lawyer cross-examine a woman? The implication is, of course, that women pose a special problem for the cross-examiner. But do they? On this point there appears to be some disagreement. Some lawyers would say that there is nothing unusual about a female witness that makes her any harder or easier to cross-examine than a man. Yet there is a considerable body of opinion—chiefly masculine, of course—to the contrary. Many lawyers would agree with Kipling that "the female of the species is more deadly than the male"—at least when she takes the stand.

This, at any rate, appears to be the view of the Honorable Daniel J. Gillen, Associate Justice of the Municipal Court of Boston, and a jurist of experience and distinction. In an article entitled "More Deadly Than the Male—in the Courtroom," which appeared in the March 1965 issue of the *Massachusetts Law Quarterly*, he risks the wrath of his female readers by asserting quite flatly that a woman on the stand is "dangerous every second she is unfolding her story."

Why?

For one thing, the Justice warns the cross-examiner that a woman is generally determined not to allow the spectators to get the impression that she is being bested by his questioning or that he is making her look bad. Hence, she is likely to be unresponsive and to insist on having the last word.

On the other hand, Justice Gillen does admit that women tend to take a greater personal interest in the proceedings and outcome of a trial than men, and that they are both positive and firm in their sympathies as well as in their antipathies. I too have often observed that a woman will hold to her view of a case more tenaciously than a man. As Judge Gillen puts it:

> When a clever trial lawyer, by a series of questions gently propounded, leads her into a position where it looks as if her original story was incorrect in many details, she fights back . . . She bandies back and forth with the lawyer. She means to tell the truth, but her . . . loyalty will not permit her to admit she is mistaken.

And, of course, as a last resort, she can always cry if the cross-examiner is too rough with her, and thus she can make him appear like a brutish bully in the eyes of the jury.

In the end, Judge Gillen tends toward the opinion of Rufus Choate, one of America's greatest trial lawyers of yesteryear, that an attorney should never, except in a desperate situation, cross-examine a woman.

I would not, myself, go that far. But I do agree with him that "the successful way to examine a woman is to know how few questions to ask her." Yet I would also add that this excellent advice is equally applicable to the cross-examination of a man. The real problem here, as I see it, is presented not so much by the sex of the witness in itself as by its subtle impact on the members of the jury. If an attractive female witness is testifying before a predominantly male jury, any cross-examiner who questions her story starts with quite as much of a handicap, it seems to me, as he would if he tried to undermine the testimony of a suave, handsome male witness under the fond and tender gaze of a panel of gushy matrons. I need not labor the point that the effect of each witness on a jury of his or her own sex would probably be quite different. In either case, then, counsel must select his questions with the utmost care.

A particularly difficult type of witness to cross-examine effectively is the expert. His specialized knowledge, his years of experience, his reputation in his field, and the authority of his pronouncements all combine to give him prestige in the eyes of the jury and an enormous advantage over any lawyer who may presume to question his professional judgment in the area of his competence. Indeed, unless counsel has prepared himself well enough to pick the expert's testimony apart and, as it were, to challenge him on his own home ground, the best course to follow is simply not to tangle with him at all.

In this connection, my friend, the Honorable Thomas F. Murphy, Judge of the United States District Court for the Southern District of New York, told me the following story of an experience he had when, as Chief of the Criminal Division of the United States Attorney's Office in Manhattan, he was preparing for trial the prosecution of Alger Hiss. Knowing that the defense was going to call as a witness a renowned psychiatrist, he had "boned up" on the more abstruse technicalities of that esoteric profession in anticipation of cross-examining the expert. However, he still felt that he needed some practical advice and therefore consulted one of the most experienced trial lawyers he knew.

His friend advised him never to examine an expert in regard to his specialty.

"Ask him questions," the lawyer suggested, "about baseball, mechanics, education—anything but psychiatry. I remember once cross-examining a brain surgeon. He got me inside the human brain, and it took me two days to get out!"

To be sure, in many cases, the direct testimony of an expert witness is given in response only to a hypothetical question. In that event, a simple question may suffice for cross-examination: "Did you ever see or examine the party (or thing) that you testified about?"

If the answer is no, all counsel has to do is to turn from the witness and say to the Court, "I have no further questions." He then has an effective argument for his summation: "How does the expert know? He was just guessing! He was a paid expert testifying about a condition not known to him from personal observation or examination."

Unless a lawyer feels confident that he has as much knowledge as the expert on the subject under inquiry, the best policy is to refrain entirely from cross-examining him. If, however, it is deemed advisable to tackle an expert witness, counsel must be sure to be thoroughly prepared, so that he understands the matter at issue in all its ramifications. All that is required to become knowledgeable is application and homework. Often this is sufficient to place a lawyer on a par with the expert in regard to the particular area of technical knowledge relevant to the point in dispute. For it is amazing how many experts prove to be poorly grounded in the literature on the subject they are being examined on. Doctors, for example, often do not know or have forgotten the medical literature in their field. Many cannot name the meninges, are unable to tell the differences among the arachnoid, the dura, and the pia mater, do not know that there are holes in the sacrum called foramina, or have no idea how many of them there are.

By way of example, I recall the manner in which a neurologist failed a test administered to him in a masterly cross-examination by one of my former frequent adversaries, Isidore Halpern, a brilliant and skillful trial lawyer and lecturer, who, in my opinion, probably knows more about the technicalities of forensic medicine than some of the best medical experts.

The doctor in the case, testifying for the defendant, took the position that the plaintiff had suffered no brain injury. The cross-examination proceeded substantially as follows:

Q. Doctor, medicine has equipped the doctor with some tests that he can make to determine whether or not an injured person has a brain injury; is that correct?

A. It has.

Q. I take it, sir, that you will agree with me that the neurological tests are of great diagnostic value?

A. They are.

Q. You will agree with me, will you not, that the frontal lobes of the human brain do not yield up their secrets to the neurological tests?

A. As a general statement, that is true.

Q. In other words, there can be brain damage in the frontal lobes, and all of the neurological signs may be negative?

A. That is correct.

Q. Likewise, X-rays and the electroencephalogram can be negative, and yet there may be damage to the frontal lobes?

A. That is true.

(This was all by way of preliminary.)

Q. Doctor, you stated that you subjected this patient to all the neurological tests, and that they are within normal limits. Is that correct?

A. Yes.

Q. Did you test the patient for hyperalgesia?

A. I did, and it showed nothing.

Q. Anesthesia?

A. I did, and it showed that nothing was wrong.

Q. Hyperesthesia?

A. I did, and it likewise showed nothing.

Q. Hemianopsia?

A. It showed nothing.

Q. Polynesia?

A. That was likewise negative.

Q. You know, doctor, do you not, that the test for polynesia takes at least fifteen minutes?

A. It takes longer; it occupies a half hour.

Q. You told this jury you went to the trouble of subjecting this patient to that test. Is that right?

A. I most certainly did.

Q. When you made the test for polynesia, in what position did you examine the patient? Was he standing or lying down?

A. He was lying down.

Q. Doctor, where did you look to determine whether or not the polynesia test was negative or positive?

Evidently feeling that this had something to do with polyps, the doctor gave the following reply:

A. In his nose.

Q. You say that when you looked into his nose, you did not find it.

A. No.

Q. If he had an injury, could you have discovered it by way of the polynesia test?

A. Yes.

Q. Doctor, don't you know that Polynesia is a group of islands in the South Pacific?

A. I am not so good on my geography.

Q. How are you on your neurology?

Obviously, even to venture on this kind of cross-examination, a lawyer must be well "up" on his medicine. He has to have sufficient technical knowledge of the witness' field to evaluate the accuracy, relevance, and adequacy of the expert's testimony. But in cases like this, even a thorough grounding in the pertinent scientific literature is not enough. Mere book learning, such as could be acquired by some hours of diligent study in a library, would not have sufficed, in itself, to reveal the fatal flaw in the expert's character that led him, in the case just cited, to pretend to knowledge that he did not have. It also takes native shrewdness, experience, and a knowledge of human nature for counsel to be able to judge the personality of the expert while he is under direct examination. A lawyer's decision to examine an expert witness has to be made not only on the basis of a solid body of well-digested factual information of a highly specialized kind, but also in the light of the witness' demeanor on the stand as he is giving his direct testimony.

Indeed, there are times when all that is needed to arouse the suspicions of an alert cross-examiner and put him on the right course is a slight tremor in the witness' voice, a momentary faltering in his response to a critical question, a shadow of incertitude flitting across his face, a hardly noticeable moistening of the lips or constriction of the throat, or a hint of defensiveness and rigidity in his tone or posture. Especially in a criminal prosecution, where the life of the accused—or at least many years of his life—may depend upon the weight to be attached to expert testimony, defense counsel cannot afford to ignore these telltale signs.

A case recently brought to my attention provides a striking example of the way in which nothing more than a "hunch," founded on just such apparently insignificant clues, can ultimately lead to the discrediting of a witness accepted as an expert by both the prosecution and the Court. John P. Walsh, one of our most distinguished criminal lawyers, was representing a defendant accused of murdering a woman in a Philadelphia hotel. At the preliminary hearing, held before a magistrate without a jury in order to ascertain whether the State had established a prima facie case against the accused, it was brought out that the body, fully clothed, had been found on a bed in the room occupied by the deceased, one floor above that on which the defendant was living. Death was attributed to strangulation. On the night of the murder the accused had been seen in the company of the victim, first at a nearby bar, then at a restaurant, and finally going up with her in the hotel elevator.

A "medical technician" detailed to the Police Chemical Laboratory testified for the State at some length on the results of her microscopic, micrometric, and spectrophotometric examination of bits of hair and clothing taken from the body of the dead woman and of hair, clothing fibers, and fingernail scrapings taken by the police from the defendant the day after the crime. Using such technical terms as "follicles" and "epithelium," the laboratory technician gave it as her judgment that the physical characteristics of specimens of hair from the body of the deceased were similar to those of the accused, and that fibers from the clothing found on the body were of the same color, size, and weave as those taken from the defendant's clothing.

In support of the laboratory technician's qualifications to testify as an expert on these matters, the prosecution brought out, on direct examination, that she had "graduated from Temple University" and was also taking medical courses there, "in connection with this work," in forensic laboratory techniques, biology, botany, and zoology. She further alleged that she had spent a year at the Philadelphia College of Textiles and Science studying fibers and fabrics, and that for the past eight years she had been doing "this type of work" for the Police Department. She estimated that in the course of her work as a police laboratory technician within the previous year alone she had made reports on twenty-five hundred hairs and had "probably in reaching that figure," examined five thousand or more.

At this point the prosecutor, turning to defense counsel, asked, "Any question as to her qualifications?"

Mr. Walsh's client, if convicted, faced the possibility of a death sentence. It was obvious that the State was going to rely heavily on the testimony of the police laboratory technician to send the accused to the electric chair. It would hardly have been prudent to be precipitate in admitting her qualifications.

"I think you made out enough to pursue questioning," Mr. Walsh cautiously replied. "I have some questions."

He began his cross-examination by carefully going over the ground previously covered by the witness in outlining her education and experience. In response to his questions she filled in the details. Twenty years before working for the Police Department, she testified, she had been employed for six years as a "medical technician" in the city laboratory of the Board of Health, where she had worked as a bacteriologist making microscopic examinations of various organs. Her cross-examination continued as follows:

BY MR. WALSH:

Q. What were your qualifications as a bacteriologist at that time?
A. At the time I had been working as a . . . [Here the witness' voice trailed off into inaudibility.] I had graduated from Temple University.
Q. What year?

There was a moment's hesitation before the witness responded.

A. Well—I guess it was about 1934.
Q. What?
A. I graduated from Temple University about 1934—I guess.

It was at this point that Mr. Walsh's suspicions were first aroused. After all, when one receives a diploma from an institution of higher learning, one is normally referred to and always considered thereafter as a member of a "class" designated by the year of graduation; and one is not likely to be unsure, even twenty or more years later, about whether one is or is not an alumnus of the "class of '34," especially as one is customarily reminded by periodic class reunions or solicitations for contributions.

"Playing a hunch," Mr. Walsh decided to probe more deeply. He resumed his cross-examination as follows:

Q. What degree?
A. Actually, I have a certificate as a medical technician.
Q. You said you graduated from Temple University, didn't you?
A. I said as a medical technician I graduated from the course as a medical technician. At the time it was a two-year course.
Q. Why did you tell me you graduated from Temple University? You gave me the impression that you were the recipient of some degree.
A. I had no degree.
Q. Isn't it a matter of fact that you never graduated from Temple?
A. No, I graduated from the course as a medical technician.

When, at this point, the prosecutor intervened and said, "I thought you had agreed to her qualifications," Mr. Walsh, realizing that he had struck "pay dirt," by no means agreed and continued to follow up his suspicions by plying the witness with further questions about her educational background, courses, and schools attended. Had she graduated from Germantown High School? Yes. What year? 1928. Had she gone immediately to Temple University? No, she had been employed for seven years by a drug company, as a laboratory technician, interrupting her work there for two years to take a course at Temple University. The witness testified that she had received a medical certificate between 1934 and 1936 in medical technology to give her the necessary background for her work with the drug company.

Q. Did the studies that you pursued at Germantown High School and in the two-year period at Temple University qualify you to render an opinion on, or have anything to do with, the similarities between hairs taken from the bodies of different people?

A. No, they did not.

Q. Was there anything in the nature of your work for the drug company that qualified you to express an opinion as to similarities in the size or color of hairs taken from different persons?

A. No, there was not.

In response to further questioning by Mr. Walsh, the witness testified that she had attended evening classes at Temple University in 1938 three times a week, two hours a night, taking a year's course in botany and receiving a certificate.

Q. Has botany anything to do with what we're talking about here?

A. That is about plant material.

Q. That has nothing to do with what we're talking about here, does it?

A. That is correct.

Under further cross-examination she testified that in 1939 she took a course in zoology for six months by attending Temple University one night a week. But she had to admit that zoology had nothing to do with the subject matter of her direct testimony.

Two years later, she alleged, she took a course in biology.

Q. What is biology?

A. Why, biology is the study of human life.

Q. Biology is the study of human life?

A. Yes, sir.

Q. Anything else?

A. It is the study of animal and plant structure and function of the
animal and plant and life structure.

She testified that she had taken this course one night a week, for
three hours a night, for a year. Between 1939 and 1945, she stated, she
had not pursued any formal studies.

Q. You had never, up to 1945, conducted an examination such as
this?
A. No, I did not.
Q. Based upon your educational attainments at the time, or any experiences you felt you had, you were not qualified to express an
opinion such as you gave here, were you?
A. No.

When, then, did she first become qualified to express such opinions?
Only after she came to work in the police laboratory, when she took a
one-semester course, two hours a week, in forensic laboratory techniques
at Temple University.

Q. When did you take this course?
A. Let's see. About four years ago.

(She had testified that she had been working for the Police Department as a laboratory technician for eight years.)

Q. And you made an application for this position in which you stated
your qualifications?
A. That's right.
Q. Did you say in your application that you were a graduate of Temple
University?
A. My application has on it all my educational background.
Q. Did you say you were a graduate of Temple University?
A. No.

She had, she said, also taken, three years earlier, a sixteen-week course
in chemistry for three hours a week, and two years later—that is, in
1963 and 1964, a year or so before the hearing—she had attended the
Philadelphia College of Textiles and Science for two sixteen-week
courses in the identification of textiles, two nights a week, three hours a
night, receiving a certificate stating that she had completed the course
with a passing mark.

Q. You have stated here all your educational attainments?
A. Yes, sir.
Q. And you have stated where you have worked?
A. Yes, sir.

Q. Now, I would like to know what qualifies you to express an opinion on hair.

The witness contended that it was her eight years' experience as a police laboratory technician that had made her an expert on bacteriology, human hair, blood, and fibers. "There is no course," she said, "that I could take which would actually fit me for this job."

After Mr. Walsh had questioned her at some length on the equipment and the methods she used for identifying, measuring, and comparing hairs, the Court intervened:

THE COURT:
Q. I have something to ask the witness. Have you made similar examinations prior to this examination?
A. Yes, sir. I have, Your Honor.
Q. How many?
A. Thousands.
Q. As a result of those examinations, have you ever testified in court?
A. Yes, sir. I have.
Q. Have you ever been qualified in court before?
A. Yes, I have.
Q. On how many occasions?
A. Innumerable occasions. I have been qualified by Philadelphia, Delaware County, and Bucks County.
THE COURT: For the sake of this hearing, I think she is qualified.

But Mr. Walsh did not agree. As he had proceeded with his cross-examination of her, he had a feeling that she was lying about her educational background. Accordingly, between the time of the preliminary hearing and the date of the trial, he made a thorough investigation of all the information she had provided in her testimony in this regard. Keeping in mind that she had said, "My application has on it all my educational background," he personally checked that document, as well as the records of Temple University, Germantown High School, the Board of Education of Philadelphia, and the Philadelphia College of Textiles and Science. He continued his research by delving into the files of the local Civil Service Commission to verify the witness' testimony concerning her experience as an employee of the Board of Health. He also examined class yearbooks and rosters, interviewed the registrars of the various educational institutions which the witness alleged she had attended, and studied the transcripts of several previous trials in which she had been certified as an expert.

Mr. Walsh told no one what he was doing, nor did he reveal his findings to anyone. When the case came to trial, the prosecution called the Police Laboratory technician to the stand as an expert and key witness. During the eight years she had been the Police Department's chief technical witness, she had testified in more than thirty murder trials, most of which had ended in convictions; one defendant against whom she had given testimony was executed in the electric chair.

In her recital of her educational background, on direct examination, she said she had taken courses at Temple University in medical technology, forensic techniques, laboratory techniques, chemistry, criminal law, and police science. She also cited her course on textiles and her years of experience on the job. She stated that the "American Society of Forensic Pathologists" had given her a satisfactory rating on her work.

On cross-examination, Mr. Walsh, thoroughly prepared, threw his bombshell. He began by asking her to trace her entire educational background from elementary school. When she said that she had graduated from Germantown High School, he asked her, "When?" She expressed uncertainty about the year because, she said, "a record as to my course at Temple and records of courses that I took during my employment after I graduated were lost." Did she have a diploma? No, she did not have one in her possession. Was her picture in the yearbook for 1931 (the year she said she thought she had been graduated)? No. Nor could she recall the name of the principal at the Germantown High School or, indeed, of any of the teachers who had taught her there.

Her application for employment filed with the personnel department of Philadelphia and her application for the Civil Service position of criminalistic technician, after being marked for identification, were next shown to her. She had to admit that she was not sure whether the dates she had put down on these documents in regard to her school attendance were correct. "In making out the application," she said, "I just probably put down the dates because I didn't want to get involved in trying to remember the dates when I went to the other school."

Q. Didn't you go to the Fitler School between 1920 and 1928?
A. I don't remember what year it was.
Q. Did you say you graduated?
A. No.
Q. Did you graduate? What did you write in your own handwriting?
A. I am sorry. I did write in my own handwriting that I graduated, yes.
Q. Did you graduate from the Fitler School?
A. No, I did not graduate from the Fitler School.

She said that she had attended Gratz High School and also German-town High School.

Q. Now, in answer to that question about Gratz, in answer to the question, "Did you graduate?" what did you say in your application?

A. Yes.

Q. Is that true?

A. No. I couldn't graduate from both.

Q. I direct your attention to Question 27 and ask you what you filled in there with respect to your high-school education.

A. Germantown High School, 1929 to 1934.

Q. Did you get to the column where it says, "Did you graduate?"

A. I said yes.

Q. Did you graduate from Germantown High School?

A. Yes, I did.

Q. Now, what years did you say you attended Germantown High School?

A. 1929 to 1934.

Q. Then you would have graduated in 1934?

A. Yes.

Q. If you were born, as it says here, in 1913 . . . that is the date of your birth, isn't it?

A. Yes, it is.

Q. You would have been twenty-one years old when you graduated from Germantown High School, wouldn't you?

A. I think I was seventeen.

Q. Now I show you Exhibit 9 [the application for employment with the City] and ask you what you stated about Germantown High School in this application?

A. 1928 to 1932.

Q. What does the column say: "Did you graduate?"

A. Yes.

Q. In here you said you graduated in 1934, but now you say you think it must have been 1931; is that right?

A. Probably 1931 or 1932, I am not sure.

Q. What year did you graduate? We all remember when we graduated from high school.

A. I am sure it was 1931.

Q. Do you recall my asking, when you testified at the preliminary hearing, when you graduated, and under oath you said you graduated in 1928, and in Exhibit 8, which you filed with the Civil Service Commission, you said you attended Germantown High School from 1929 to 1934 and you graduated; and in Exhibit 9 you said you attended Germantown High School from 1928 to 1932 and that you graduated; is that right?

A. Yes.

Asked whether she had the certificate that she said, in her application, she had received from Temple University for her course in medical technology, the witness said she did not have it and had not seen it for fifteen years.

Q. Now will you explain this: On Exhibit 8 you stated that you went to Temple University from 1934 to 1936 during the day. And on Exhibit 9 you say you went to Temple University from 1933 to 1935 at night. And you also say that you were working at the National Drug Company between the hours of 9:00 and 5:00 from 1933 to 1936. I would like you to explain how you could, in those years, have gone to school day and night and worked for the National Drug Company too; could you explain that?

A. No, I cannot.

Q. May I suggest to you that you never attended Temple University, and you were never certified in medical technology, as you stated in these applications. Now, let's have the truth. You never attended Temple University, and you never received a certificate in medical technology. Now, isn't that the truth under your oath?

A. Yes, that's the truth.

Q. Now, you admit, then, that when you put that in your application for a Civil Service examination, it was untrue?

A. That is true.

Q. And, you admit, then, that when you put that in your application for a position in 1958, it was untrue?

A. That is also true.

Q. When you said that you went to Temple in 1934 and 1936 and that you received a certificate in medical technology, you were lying, were you not?

A. That is true.

Q. And when you said that you went to Temple University from 1933 to 1935 at night and you received a certificate in zoology, botany, and biology, you were lying?

A. Yes.

However, the witness still insisted that she had graduated from Germantown High School, although she had been confused about the date.

Mr. Walsh then had her read, from the application she had filed, the declaration above her signature certifying to the truth of the statements she had made in that document and concluding with the words: "I realize that any misstatement on my part will be cause for my rejection or dismissal."

The admissions thus far wrung from the witness came as a complete surprise to both the Court and the prosecution. Under the circumstances, the District Attorney, at this point, felt constrained to with-draw the claim that the witness was qualified to testify as an expert. However, he moved that she be permitted to testify as a nonexpert in regard to the chain of causation connecting certain fibers and hairs, mounted on slides and produced as evidence for the State, with the defendant and with the body of the slain woman. The prosecution then proposed to have the witness' superior in the Police Laboratory testify as an expert regarding the interpretation of this evidence.

Over Mr. Walsh's objection, the Court granted this motion. Conse-quently, he was free to continue with his cross-examination. Up to this point, he had used only a small part of the ammunition with which he had come prepared.

By the time the witness was recalled to the stand a few days later to resume cross-examination, she had had the opportunity to consult with counsel of her own and to read the record of her testimony at the preliminary hearing.

Mr. Walsh concentrated on demolishing her credibility. He began as follows:

> Q. Last Wednesday, before you left the stand, I asked you whether
> or not you graduated from Germantown High School. In one docu-
> ment filed with the Civil Service Commission you said you gradu-
> ated in 1934. In another document filed with the City you said you
> graduated in 1932. Under oath at the preliminary hearing you
> stated that you graduated in 1928. And you said here under oath
> before this Court and jury that you graduated in 1931.
>
> Do you still maintain that you graduated from Germantown
> High School?
> A. No, I do not.
> Q. Then, what you told the jury here last week was an absolute lie
> when you testified that you had graduated in 1931; is that cor-
> rect?
> A. That is correct.
> Q. At the preliminary hearing in this case, did you tell the truth in
> every respect, or did you lie?
> A. No—I did not tell the truth.
> Q. And you were under oath?
> A. I was under oath.
> Q. You knew you were testifying against a man charged with murder,
> didn't you?
> A. That is correct.
> Q. And you knew the enormity of that offense and the importance
> of the case; is that correct?
> A. Yes.

Q. Did you in answer to the question, "What type of training had you had for this occupation?" testify at the preliminary hearing, "I graduated from Temple University"? Do you recall saying that before you were cross-examined by me?

A. I do recall saying that I graduated from Temple University, and I recanted that at the hearing.

Q. Do you recall, when you were cross-examined by me about your qualifications as to a bacteriologist, answering, "I had graduated from Temple University"?

A. I don't recall saying that, no.

Q. Would you deny that you said it if it is right here in the transcript on Page 74?

A. No, I would not deny it, Mr. Walsh.

Q. That was not true, was it?

A. No, it was not true.

Q. And when I asked you what degree, you said, "Actually I have a certificate as a medical technician." Do you recall saying that?

A. Yes, I do.

Q. That wasn't true either, was it?

A. No, it was not true.

Q. You said you graduated from Temple University. Was that true?

A. No, it was not true.

Mr. Walsh next read from the record of the preliminary hearing her statement that she had graduated from the course as a medical technician.

Q. Was that true?

A. No, it was not true.

Q. Did you testify under oath at the preliminary hearing (Pages 77, 78, 80, 82, 84, and 87) that between 1938, 1941, and with specific reference to 1938, you received a certificate from Temple University in the subject of botany?

A. Yes, I did.

Q. And that was untrue?

A. That was untrue.

Q. And did you not also testify under oath at the preliminary hearing that in 1939 you studied zoology for one year at Temple University?

A. That was also untrue.

Q. You testified under oath in the preliminary hearing (Pages 86 and 87) that you went to Temple and studied biology for ninety-six hours, didn't you?

A. Yes, I did.

Q. And that was all untrue?

A. All untrue.

Q. And it was all given under oath?

A. All given under oath.

Q. In a case where you recognized and knew that the defendant was charged with murder; you knew that, didn't you?

A. Yes, I did.

Mr. Walsh was by no means through with this witness. He had plenty of additional material. If she was going to be allowed to testify even as a nonexpert, he wanted the jury to see the whole picture. He now turned to a case in which she had testified for the prosecution. After citing it and having her recall that she had taken the stand against the defendant, he proceeded as follows:

Q. Do you recall testifying that you instructed in laboratory techniques at Temple University?

A. No, I do not.

Mr. Walsh read the relevant excerpts from the trial record, in which, among other things, she had testified that she had "instructed in laboratory techniques in Temple University." Had she so testified? Yes, she had. She had assisted her superior in the instruction of the students.

Q. Were you a member of the teaching staff of Temple University?

A. I assisted the instructor of the course.

Q. Were you a member of the teaching staff of Temple University?

A. No, I was not.

Q. Were you a member of the faculty of Temple University?

A. No, I was not.

Q. Now, you stated that your work has been evaluated by the American Society of Forensic Pathologists; did you so testify?

A. That is the American Academy of Forensic Pathologists.

Q. Are you a member of it?

A. No, I am not.

Q. Are you a pathologist?

A. No, I am not.

Q. Who evaluated your work?

A. I have no idea. I understand it is a board which evaluates all the criminalistic laboratories in the country.

Q. Did they tell you this by word of mouth, or did they write a letter?

A. They write a letter to the laboratory.

Q. Do you have the letter?

A. No, I do not.

Q. Do you know the name of anybody who is an officer or director of the American College of Forensic Pathologists?

A. No, I do not.

Q. Do you recall testifying that you are considered a hematologist (Page 548)?

A. I am considered a hematologist, yes.

Q. Who considers you a hematologist?
A. My employers considered me.
Q. Did you tell all these doctors that you graduated from Temple University?
A. Yes, I did.

But then the witness corrected herself. "I didn't tell them I graduated from Temple University, never. I told them that I had a course in medical technology at Temple University, but I never—"

Q. Which was not true?
A. What was not true.
Q. Under oath, when you were asked at Page 548 whether you had formal education and training in hematology, did you not testify that you did and that you had a certificate as a medical technician from Temple University?
A. Yes, I did.
Q. Was that true?
A. That is not true.

The witness was thoroughly discredited, and the jury acquitted the defendant. Moreover, the disqualification of the Police Laboratory technician in this case has led to a review of a number of murder cases in which she testified.

One cannot help wondering whether these cases would have turned out as they did if defense counsel in any one of them had gone to the lengths which Mr. Walsh went to in checking on the qualifications of the prosecution's expert witness. Of course, it takes a lawyer of Mr. Walsh's consummate skill and acumen to sense the possibilities implied by the slenderest of clues and to follow their lead to the stunning victory achieved in this case. But it does illustrate the transcendent importance, especially in a criminal case, of alertness to every nuance in the demeanor and testimony of the witness under cross-examination, of courage in refusing to be overawed even by an "expert" with apparently well-attested credentials, and of dogged perseverance and thoroughness in conscientiously checking every fact in preparation for the trial.

Sometimes, in fact, counsel does not even need to rely on a ponderous mass of painstakingly studied standard treatises and texts to confute the testimony of an expert. Here is how one lawyer attained the same end with a simple survey.

The case grew out of an accident which occurred on board a vessel that had blundered into a mine field. The ensuing explosion blew the plaintiff into the air, without, however, rendering him unconscious

more than momentarily, if at all. Nevertheless, he sued the ship company, contending that his epilepsy was of traumatic origin attributable
to the shock of the blast.

A very prominent neurosurgeon was called as the medical expert
for the defendant. According to him, just about every authority on the
subject of epilepsy was either his student or his colleague. He opined,
with the utmost confidence, that the explosion could not have caused
the plaintiff's epilepsy because the blow he had received was not of
sufficient force. The positiveness with which the expert testified to this
effect and his repeated assurances of the absolute impossibility of traumatic epilepsy in the circumstances of this particular accident appeared
to have made an enormous impression on the jury.

All that counsel for the plaintiff produced, in cross-examining the
witness, was a somewhat lonely report of a survey, made by three neurosurgeons, of some four hundred war veterans, all of whom unquestion-
ably suffered from traumatic epilepsy.

Q. Have you heard about this survey, sir?
A. Not only do I know about it, but of these three neurosurgeons,
   one was a student of mine, and the other two are my colleagues.

This was just the kind of answer counsel was hoping he would get.
He then steered the cross-examination toward the issue of the plaintiff's
unconsciousness during the moment of the explosion. But with an obvious display of much patience and tolerance, the expert said, "I want
to remind you again, young man, as I have repeated many, many times
before, that your client was not unconscious."

Thereupon counsel whipped out the survey, which showed that of
the veterans examined, a small percentage were suffering from traumatic
epilepsy, even though they had not been rendered unconscious by the
shock they had sustained. With this, the arrogance of the neurosurgeon
vanished. The effect was startling, and the verdict for the plaintiff was
substantial.

In another negligence case, a doctor long in practice but short on
knowledge of new developments, after having testified for the plaintiff,
was cross-examined in detail by the attorney for the defendant as to the
nature of the injuries and his prognosis. The doctor was asked whether
he had refreshed his recollection by reference to any medical textbook.
He replied in the affirmative. Asked whether *Modern Clinical Psychiatry*
by Noyes is a recognized authority, he not only said that it is but that
he had consulted this particular work to refresh his recollection. At

this point defense counsel produced the book and asked the doctor to point out the particular page which referred to the illness described in his testimony concerning the prognosis. Unfortunately for the doctor, no such page could be found.

The average attorney, however, is not likely to emerge unscathed from an encounter with an expert who is honest. There is just no way of matching the witness' technical knowledge, and the best thing for counsel to do ordinarily is to concede his own inferiority in this respect and decline the opportunity to grapple with so formidable an opponent.

But if a lawyer does try to place himself on a par with an expert, he should come to court ready to confront the witness with the very latest works published on the subject. For it should never be forgotten that all sciences, including medicine, undergo change. What was considered a scientific fact ten, five, three, or even two years before the date of the trial may in the meantime have been superseded by more recent findings that render earlier publications on the subject altogether obsolete.

Unless counsel keeps this in mind, he may, in cross-examining an expert witness, suffer a fate similar to that of an acquaintance of mine. A lawyer of unusual talent, he was representing one of several defendants accused of having asphyxiated a man while he slept by holding up to his mouth and nose a pipe filled with illuminating gas. The charge was first-degree murder.

The chief issue in the case was the cause of death. On this point the State called as a witness a toxicologist, who testified that he had performed an autopsy about six months after the victim's death, the body having been exhumed for that purpose. In the expert's opinion, based on this autopsy, death was due to asphyxiation by carbon monoxide.

Defense counsel had prepared himself for his encounter with the toxicologist by consulting what he thought was a standard treatise on poisons. Armed with his new-found knowledge, he confronted the expert with a quotation from this work:

Q. Doctor, do you know a book by Wharton and Stilles called *Medical Jurisprudence?*
A. Yes, sir.
Q. Have you read it?
A. Years ago.
Q. Supposing I were to read this statement to you, will you tell me whether you agree or differ with it? . . . I want to call your attention, please, to page 120 of this book, under the general head-

ing of "Carbon Monoxide," Sec. 60, Vol. 2, on Poisons, and I am going to ask you . . .

"The presence of this gas may be found in the blood of a person poisoned by its inhalation if acute and provided the examination be made almost immediately after death."

A. Oh, I disagree with that absolutely. . . . This book is thirty years old. At that time they did not even have a method for the quantitative determination of carbon monoxide.

The doctor then pointed out that since the publication of the book the whole new science of blood chemistry had come into existence. Indeed, the witness himself had contributed to its development. Moreover, he testified that he had performed many autopsies upon persons asphyxiated by the inhalation of illuminating gas, and that the signs of its presence were unmistakable. The doctor had, in fact, published several papers explaining how it was now possible to conclude, with complete certainty, that death was due to this cause, even though the autopsy was performed months or years later. He explained further that these new and effective means of discovering the presence of carbon monoxide included the Van Slaight method and five tests—dilution, alkali, tannic acid, spectroscopic, and lead acetate—all of which he had performed in this case. Finally, the witness referred counsel to a more modern treatise (Webster's) which fully supported his contention.

In short, when the cross-examination was over, any lingering doubt that the jury may have had on the point was resolved in favor of the prosecution. All the defendants were found guilty as charged and sentenced to death in the electric chair.

As we can readily see, the cross-examination of a doctor is not to be undertaken lightly. To make any progress at all in this difficult task, a lawyer needs all the knowledge and assistance he can get from his own researches and from recognized medical experts.

To be sure, if counsel has proof that the doctor made prior statements inconsistent with his present testimony, or that he took a contrary position in other cases in which he appeared as a witness, there is some chance of discrediting him. But in the absence of such proof, an attorney has to be able to adduce some authoritative source, such as a medical textbook, that contradicts the doctor's testimony in a crucial respect. In any event, counsel must take the time to inform himself thoroughly concerning the medical aspects of the case. For example, if the plaintiff suffered an injury to the brain, counsel had better know all he can learn about this subject from a study of the relevant literature. I used to spend a great deal of time poring over the standard works in the field before going to trial. Then, after I had gained a working knowledge of the problem involved, I would consult my friends in the medical profession for guidance and advice. They would often provide me with useful hints or suggestions. In this way, I was able to cross-examine a doctor with confidence.

I recall a case I tried against the Prudential Insurance Company on a claim for double indemnity. I had so thoroughly researched the literature on the heart, septicemia poisoning, etc., that a few minutes after I had begun my cross-examination of the defendant's physician, he proceeded to preface his answers by calling me "Doctor." Naturally this gratuitous addition of a medical title to my law degree did not hurt me in the eyes of the jury. At the same time, the witness realized that he was being questioned by a knowledgeable cross-examiner, and that he could not take refuge in presumably incomprehensible technical jargon. For I made sure, also, to familiarize myself with the medical terms likely to be employed in referring to the type of injury involved in the litigation.

Over the years I have had occasion to observe the ineptness of many trial lawyers in cross-examining doctors. In this connection, I am reminded of one of the witticisms of a distinguished attorney of my acquaintance: "To the average lawyer, the word 'Babinski' means that a Communist doctor is practicing in an American hospital, and a complaint should be made to the Un-American Activities Committee." (The word, in fact, is a medical term referring to a reflex movement when the sole is tickled. If the great toe turns upward instead of downward, it indicates an organic lesion in the brain or spinal cord. This test was originated by the French neurologist Babinski.)

There is, alas, a certain measure of truth in my friend's jocular remark. Too often, indeed, I have seen a cross-examiner ask not a single question of a doctor, either because counsel was unprepared or because he felt that he could gain no advantage from interrogating the witness. No doubt, under certain circumstances, as we have seen, to refrain from cross-examination may really be the prudent thing to do. But, in my opinion, it is not generally wise for a cross-examiner to allow a doctor to leave the stand without asking him any questions at all. For the jury may interpret counsel's failure to cross-examine as an admission that the witness' testimony was true and reliable. Such an implied concession may very well prove fatal to counsel's case. He should therefore make the cross-examination of his adversary's physician the rule rather than the exception. But he had better know his subject!

Since doctors, unless they are general practitioners, specialize only in certain branches of medicine, the cross-examination should begin with an inquiry into the nature of the witness' practice, somewhat along the following lines:

Q. Doctor, are you a general practitioner?

If the answer is no:

Q. Do you have any specialty?
Q. What is it?

If he says he is a neurologist, and the injuries involved concern orthopedics, counsel has already established a beachhead from which, as we shall shortly see, he may make further inroads on the doctor's testimony. If, on the other hand, the witness says he is a general practitioner, this statement too can be used later, in summation, to persuade the jury that the doctor is not qualified to testify concerning the injury because of his lack of specialized knowledge of the subject.

If hospital records exist, the witness should be asked whether he examined them, and, if he did, where and when he saw them. Often counsel will discover that the doctor did not see the records at all, or, if he did see them, they were shown to him in court a few minutes before he was called to the stand. This line of cross-examination will elicit testimony that counsel may profitably capitalize on later in his summation.

Let us first see how the attorney for the plaintiff might proceed from here with his cross-examination of the defendant's doctor. If, as often happens, the witness examined the plaintiff some time after the accident, the odds are 100 to 1 that the doctor will testify that he could not see or find any evidence of pain or injury. The witness may even go so far as to say that, as all the plaintiff complained of was having headaches, his trouble was entirely subjective. In that case, plaintiff's counsel might continue his questioning of the doctor somewhat as follows:

Q. Doctor, have there been experiences in your own practice where you have been pessimistic in making a diagnosis?
A. Yes, sir.
Q. Later on, you were happy to learn that despite your original pessimism, your patient had recovered?

A. Yes, sir.

Q. Doctor, haven't there been cases in your practice as well where you have been optimistic, and subsequently found that events did not bear out that optimism on your part?

A. Yes.

Q. Now, doctor, the plaintiff says she has headaches. Do you deny it, and say it is not so?

(Rarely will a doctor deny it.)

Q. The plaintiff says that she cannot sleep nights. Do you deny that?

(The same type of question can be put to the doctor concerning all the other symptoms of which the patient complains: dizziness, nervousness, etc.)

Q. Did you examine the hospital records?

If the doctor says no, the best thing to do is to be satisfied with the answer, since it will supply ammunition for the summation that counsel is preparing. To prod the doctor any further on this point is to make the mistake of giving him a chance to explain why he did not examine the hospital records.

However, there is an alternative approach that can be quite effective in this situation, as the following questions may suggest:

Q. Doctor, Mt. Sinai Hospital, in which the plaintiff was a patient, is a fine, recognized hospital, is it not?

A. Yes, sir.

Q. Do you know Dr. Burke of that hospital?

If the answer is no, counsel should read the hospital record at this point to indicate that Dr. Burke treated the plaintiff. Then he should proceed with his cross-examination:

Q. You have told us that you did not read the hospital records, is that right?

A. That is right.

Q. Doctor, will you please try to answer yes or no to the following question: Were you not concerned and interested to find out what this fine hospital and Dr. Burke had to say concerning the plaintiff's condition?

If the witness answers in the negative, this is an ideal place to end the interrogation, or at least this particular line of questioning, for the doctor has strengthened the basis of counsel's argument during summation. If, on the other hand, the witness answers in the affirmative, questioning can proceed as follows:

Q. When did you examine the records and where?

Q. Did you make a notation in your report to that effect?

The chances are he made no such notation—another evidence of carelessness, haste, or lack of concern that could carry much weight with the members of the jury if their attention is later called to it. Here too, then, is a good place for counsel to stop, if he has made his point.

If the doctor says that he examined the records in court, the following question becomes pertinent:

Q. How long did it take you to examine them?

No matter what the doctor's answer is, he should next be asked:

Q. Doctor, would it not have been helpful to you if you had examined the report at the time you made the physical examination of the plaintiff?

Once again, whatever the witness' answer, plaintiff's counsel is building up another potential argument for his summation, as we shall see later.

So far, the cross-examiner has made his points without having any need of entering into medical technicalities. Now, since the doctor has already testified that he found nothing wrong with the plaintiff, and that the plaintiff's complaints were subjective, it is appropriate to ask the witness the following question:

Q. Doctor, cannot a person have pain without objective evidence of it?

If the doctor says yes, counsel should stop right here, for he has elicited a significant admission. But if the witness says no, questioning should continue as follows:

Q. Doctor, what are remissions and exacerbations?

A remission is a period in which a patient may feel better and show no symptoms. Stedman's *Practical Medical Dictionary* defines it as "a lessening in severity, a temporary abatement of a disease." An exacerbation, on the contrary, is a worsening of the patient's condition and a flare-up of painful symptoms, or, as the same source defines it, "an increase in the severity of a disease or any of its signs or symptoms." I know of no instance in which a doctor was unable to give a satisfactory definition of these terms. But, of course, there is always a first time for everything, and if a cross-examiner does come across a physician who flounders or falters in attempting to answer this question, counsel will know that he has hit "pay dirt."

If the doctor defines the terms correctly, the questioning should proceed as follows:

Q. When you examined the plaintiff on February 10, which was seven months after the accident, is it not possible he was in a period of remission?

It would be very difficult indeed for a doctor to answer no to this question. But if he does, he should next be asked:

Q. Doctor, would you say the plaintiff is a malingerer?

If the doctor says yes, the cross-examiner should at once ask to see his report. Of course, as counsel already has a copy of it and has studied it in advance of trial, he will know whether it contained any such statement. Nevertheless, after the doctor hands the document to his cross-examiner, the latter should go through the motions of scrutinizing it, as if he were reading it for the first time, then return it to the witness, and ask:

Q. Doctor, did you say so in your report?

Since his answer must be no, there is no need for counsel to pursue this line any further. Instead of belaboring the point, he should turn to something else, for he has added another argument to his summation.

Next, inquiry should be directed toward the doctor's physical examination of the plaintiff:

Q. Where did the examination take place?

The usual answer is: At the office of the plaintiff's attorney.

Q. Who were present?

The answer will probably be: The plaintiff and his attorney or representative.

Q. How long did the examination last?

The answer may range from ten minutes to half an hour.

Q. How much were you paid for the examination?
Q. How much are you being paid for your time to testify here?

The witness may say anything from twenty-five to a hundred dollars or more for the examination and from seventy-five to two hundred fifty dollars or more to testify.

Q. By the way, Doctor, what percentage of your income is derived from testifying in court?

He may admit that 20, 30, or 40 per cent is thus derived. Whatever figure he sets should be accepted. But if he says, "I don't know," or "I never figured it out," or "I've never thought about it," or something similar, then he should be pressed, substantially as follows:

Q. Doctor, I don't expect you to know exactly what portion it represents, but maybe I can help you if you will be good enough to answer these questions:
Q. How many similar examinations do you make each day?
Q. And approximately, each week?
Q. And approximately, each month?
Q. Is it therefore safe and conservative to say you make twenty, thirty, forty examinations per year?

The number set should be reasonable and fair. It is better to understate than to exaggerate. Once the approximate number has been fixed, the doctor should be asked:

Q. And what is the average charge for an examination?

When the figure is stated, it should be multiplied by the number of examinations. The next questions should then be:

Q. Would it be fair to say you have an income of two thousand dollars, three thousand dollars, or four thousand dollars from these examinations?
Q. And roughly, what portion does this sum bear to your entire yearly income as a physician?

If the witness does not wish to commit himself to a definite answer, he should be pressed no further. Counsel has found here a good enough place to end this particular line of questioning, since the doctor's evasiveness can be dwelt upon later in the summation.

Next, he should be asked:

Q. By the way, Doctor, how much time did you spend at my office examining my client?

If the doctor testifies that he spent no more than ten or twenty minutes, counsel may proceed to the next point, because in his summation he will have an opportunity to ask the jurors whether, in their opinion, such a brief time was adequate for a really thorough examination. But if the witness exaggerates and says he took half an hour to examine the plaintiff, he should be asked the following questions:

Q. How many other examinations did you make on that day?
Q. How many examinations did you make before you examined my
client?
Q. How many after?
Q. What time did you examine someone after you left my office?

If the doctor says that he does not remember, he should be requested
to refresh his recollection by consulting his appointment book. In case
he says the book is not with him, counsel should ask, in a surprised
tone of voice:

Q. Well, don't you have a memo with you which will indicate your
appointments for that day?

If his answer is no, he should next be asked:

Q. You knew you were going to testify today, didn't you, Doctor?

This is a good place to stop. These questions, none of which required
the cross-examiner to enter into the technicalities of the doctor's substantive testimony, have raised enough doubts, have created enough
suspicions, to supply plaintiff's counsel with material for a summation
bristling with insinuations, innuendoes, and inferences tending to discredit the witness.

Let us now return to the doctor who, called to testify about a neurological ailment, fails to mention, in setting forth his qualifications, that
he is a diplomate. His cross-examination should proceed as follows:

Q. Doctor, what is a diplomate?

His answer will be to the effect that a diplomate is a doctor who has
taken and passed certain examinations in a particular branch of medicine.

Q. What is your branch of medicine?

If he says he is a neurologist, counsel should accept the answer without argument. But if he says he is an orthopedist or some other kind of
specialist, he should be questioned further along these lines:

Q. Doctor, when one is approved and certified as a diplomate, is he
considered a specialist in that particular field?
A. Yes.
Q. Doctor, are you a diplomate in the field of neurology?

His answer will have to be no, as it will be to the following questions:

Q. You do not possess such certification?

Q. Then you are not an expert in this field?

Q. So that you are not a diplomate in neurology?

Next the witness should be asked:

Q. Are you a diplomate in your own field—orthopedics?

If the answer is yes, the final question should then be:

Q. You realize, of course, that the plaintiff's injury has no relationship to orthopedics?

His answer will have to be yes. Counsel has thus made his point and
should stop here. If the doctor answers no, then, of course, this is all
the more reason to end the cross-examination at this point and leave
the rest to the summation. We shall see later what capital a lawyer can
make of such answers when he sums up his case before the jury at the
end of the trial.

More or less the same procedure would be followed by counsel for
the defendant in cross-examining a physician called to testify on behalf
of the plaintiff. However, under these circumstances, there is one additional factor that must be taken into account. The doctor's office records
should be subjected to close scrutiny. Quite often they fail to record
objective signs or symptoms and merely indicate his conclusions. In
other words, the record may read, "cerebral concussion," without listing
a single positive neurological finding. In that case, the cross-examination might well follow these lines:

Q. Doctor, medicine has discovered a way of looking into the human
brain, hasn't it?

A. Yes.

Q. Doctor, you keep a record and naturally note thereon all findings of
importance, don't you?

Counsel can then proceed to show that the doctor's record is utterly
devoid of neurological findings.

The same could be done in a case involving a claim for alleged "back
injuries." Although there are several different tests for them, such as
Lasègue's and Patrick's, the average doctor's record card rarely contains
any notation referring to such tests. But, of course, the cross-examiner
must himself know what he is looking for, and for this he needs to acquire the relevant technical knowledge.

We see, then, that to practice successfully the difficult art of cross-
examination, a lawyer must draw upon a broad range of resources. He

must have a good understanding of human nature as it is exemplified in the various types of witnesses he will confront. He has, besides, to have a thorough knowledge of the law applicable to the case and of the subject matter in dispute. And he needs to know how to plan a strategy that will allow him the maximum tactical flexibility. This means that he must be able to anticipate the possible divergent paths his questioning will take in following up the answers of each witness. Moreover, at every crossroads along the way, he must be ready to decide, on the instant, which fork to take and how far to proceed along it before stopping and returning to the main road.

This is, in fact, one of the most difficult problems facing the cross-examiner. How can he know where to stop following a particular line of inquiry and when to bring his whole examination to an end? How does he know when he has reached his destination? And what are the dangers of not stopping in time, of pushing on too far in a given direction, of overshooting the mark?

These are such important questions that their discussion deserves extended consideration. Now that we have seen how a cross-examination is set in motion, let us turn our attention to the proper way to steer it and to bring it safely to a full stop when it has reached its predetermined goal.

19

"Just One More Question!"

Being a witness on the stand under cross-examination is in some respects even worse than being a member of a "captive audience." For the witness may not close his ears to the stream of questions coming at him, nor may he turn his attention to something else. Twist and writhe as he may, he is, as it were, backed into a corner from which there is no escaping until he is released by his cross-examiner. Meanwhile, he is bound not only to listen but to respond to every question put to him as long as it is not excluded by the judge. His tormentor, on the other hand, can go on indefinitely, it seems, asking all the questions he can think of until everybody is utterly exhausted—witness, judge, jury, and counsel.

And this is precisely what many cross-examiners do. Once they get up a head of steam, they keep on going just as far as they can. These marathon interrogators leave nothing unexplored in their interminable inquiries into when, where, who, what, why, and how. One question seems to feed on another, and they go on for days on end, reluctant to let the luckless witness out of their grasp until they have squeezed out of him every last ounce of information—or misinformation—he has.

Boring and alienating the jury are the least of the penalties that this type of cross-examiner risks by his seemingly endless interrogation. He also is in danger of blunting the effect of whatever telling blows he may have struck during the course of his cross-examination. Even worse, as we have already had occasion to observe, he never knows when that "one more question" may get him into real trouble.

So whenever I hear those often-used words, "Just one more question, Your Honor," I can't help wondering whether it is going to be worth the risk. Why cannot counsel learn to stop when he's ahead? Why must he insist on pushing his luck? Is the impulse to ask one more question like that of a gambler whose appetite for placing wagers is whetted by a winning streak or a single lucky throw of the dice? I sometimes think so. But at least counsel should consider that it is not only his own fortune he may be risking, but his client's as well.

I myself learned about the wholly unpredictable consequences of overreaching oneself by asking "just one more question" shortly after I became a lawyer, but, fortunately for me, not in the courtroom. Nor was it I who asked the additional question that unwittingly lifted the lid of Pandora's box, although I was the one who felt most imminently threatened by the host of troubles and vexations that I thought the answer to that question would inevitably release.

I had recently been admitted to the Bar, and I was keenly aware of the provisions of the Code of Ethics prohibiting the direct or indirect solicitation of cases. Naturally I made up my mind to be very circumspect during my career as a lawyer, and I resolved not to permit anyone to "chase" after cases on my behalf. But how can you prevent a mother from being a "chaser"?

Of the first hundred cards I had printed, my mother dealt out five to me and kept ninety-five for herself. She was a remarkable woman, and she was confident of her ability to get clients to "go to my office," as she put it. She spoke very little English, but that was no impediment to her. Although most of her busy day was spent in shopping, cleaning, mending, washing, baking, and working in the kitchen preparing meals for my father, my two brothers, my sisters, and me, she managed to find time to get out into the streets to interest people in her son's career. Her typical sales talk as she accosted strangers on the street went something like this: "Mister, you look like a man who would never get into trouble—a good man, *balibotish* [meaning, in Yiddish, a respectable person of upright character]—but you never know when you might have an accident—God forbid!—or some friend could be locked up, or somebody may ask you for a lawyer; so take my son's card just in case you ever need it—God forbid!—and if you or one of your friends should ever need a lawyer, you will know where to get in touch with my son. Believe me, you will always thank me for this."

DeKalb Avenue, between Throop and Tompkins Avenues, in Brooklyn, was only about four blocks from our home. The street overflowed with pushcarts and was filled with a variety of small retail shops selling meat, dairy products, vegetables, clothing, etc. It was a replica of old Orchard Street on the lower east side of New York City. People not only from our neighborhood but from all parts of Brooklyn came there "to shop for bargains." My mother was no exception.

Almost forty years ago, just after my admission to the Bar, my mother was walking along DeKalb Avenue, going from one store to another, doing her daily chores, when she noticed that one of Food Fair's grocery stores, which was then just a small shop selling dairy products, was open for business, while five or six stores on either side of it were being torn down. Upon inquiry, she learned that Food Fair had purchased all the stores adjoining it. The common talk was that the company was building a supermarket.

The supermarket was built, and one day my mother found herself in it. As she walked through the store, she was overcome with bewilderment. She was amazed to see that she could do all her shopping there— butter, eggs, meat, vegetables, every type of food imaginable. As she was browsing around amid this unaccustomed plenitude of inviting edibles, a saleslady standing at one of the counters called her over and asked her whether she would like to taste a piece of gefüllte fish. Now my mother regarded herself as just about the best maker of gefüllte fish in the world, and she was. She couldn't imagine that gefüllte fish could be sold in a market. Nevertheless, she tried the proffered sample. As she did so, she noticed a number of very small jars of gefüllte fish displayed on the counter. Finally, the saleslady asked her, "How do you like the fish?"

"It was delicious," my mother promptly replied, eying with ravenous longing the little jars on the counter, which she surmised were being distributed as samples for advertising purposes. As my mother later explained, her thinking was confirmed, for the lady thereupon gave her a small jar and said, "Take it home and let your family taste it, and please come back next week on Friday at 11:30 A.M. and let me know what they think of it too. If they like it, I will give you this large jar of gefüllte fish," which she took from underneath the counter. My mother looked at the large jar, and she was hooked. The next week couldn't pass fast enough for her. Imagine getting such a big jar of fish for nothing!

I can't say Mother had sleepless nights during the week, because that might be an exaggeration, but I do remember that each day she would inquire, "What's today?" She was looking forward to that Friday appointment at 11:30 A.M. Finally, the longed-for day arrived! She went back to the store and immediately walked over to the counter where she had received the sample. The saleslady greeted her by name and asked, "Mrs. Heller, did your husband eat the gefüllte fish?"

"Of course he did," my mother said (in Yiddish).

"And how did he like it?"

"He loved it," my mother answered. "*Er hat opgelekt die fingers* [he licked his fingers]."

"Did he say how it compared with your fish?"

Keeping her mind on the big jar, my mother promptly answered, "He said it's better than my fish."

The saleslady concluded that she had the right prey. She then asked my mother, "Have you heard of the Jewish Hour?"

This was a radio program broadcast at noon each day. Practically every Jewish family listened to it, for between commercial advertising of clothing, food, and home products, it featured nostalgic Yiddish songs.

"Of course I am familiar with the Jewish Hour," my mother replied. "I listen to the program every day."

Whereupon the saleslady told her, "In a few minutes I am going to put you on the air and ask you the same questions I just put to you. I want you to give me the same answers."

My mother agreed. At noon she was standing before the microphone with the saleslady. The same questions were asked, and my mother gave the same answers. But then the saleslady decided to ask her "just one more question":

"And tell me, Mrs. Heller, did any of your children remark about how good the fish was?"

This was all the opportunity my mother needed. She quickly replied, "Yes, my son, the lawyer, Louis B. Heller, 16 Court Street, Brooklyn, New York (get off at Borough Hall), thirty-second floor, TRiangle 5-2729, said it was the most delicious gefüllte fish he ever had."

I happened to be in the barbershop at the time I heard this over the radio, and I really panicked. I expected that within a matter of hours I would be hearing from the Bar Association that I had been charged with indirect solicitation of cases. I could hardly wait for my mother to come home from the supermarket. As soon as I could, I telephoned her and started to remonstrate with her. Her calm reply was, "Don't be nervous! If Food Fair could use me to advertise their gefüllte fish, which isn't half as good as mine, I can use them to advertise my son, the lawyer. Now, son, hurry back to your office, because there must be a crowd of people waiting for you, and tonight you will eat *my* gefüllte fish."

But let us return to the courtroom.

The important thing for a cross-examiner to bear in mind is that when he has made a telling point or succeeded in getting a witness to admit a material fact favorable to counsel's case or adverse to the other side, the best procedure is to drop the subject at once. To pursue it is only to give the witness an opportunity to bail himself out. He should not be given a chance to explain previous testimony that is damaging. For this material can be used later in summation, as we shall see.

Somewhere I read or heard—and perhaps the story is apocryphal— of a renowned trial lawyer who delivered a lecture at one of the law schools on "How to Try a Case." He neglected to touch upon the subject of cross-examination. As he was about to conclude his address, a student rose and said, "I had hoped to hear you discuss how to conduct a cross-examination. That is the phase of the trial that worries me the most, and I think I express the sentiments of the rest of the students in this room."

Thereupon, the lecturer, taking out his watch, looked at it for a moment and then replied, "I see that I have about twenty-five minutes to catch a train back to New York, but I think I can cover that phase of my subject in less than one minute. Young man, do you drive a car?"

"Yes," answered the student.

"What was the first thing you were taught when you learned to operate it?" continued the lecturer.

"How to stop," the young man promptly replied.

"Good! If you and your classmates can remember how to stop when you are cross-examining a witness, you will master the problem that disturbs you."

This is a lesson that had evidently not yet been learned by the plaintiff's attorney, an experienced trial lawyer, in a case tried before me, when he conducted the following cross-examination of one of the witnesses in regard to a crucial point in dispute:

Q. And did the sidewalk have ridges of ice on it?
A. I don't know whether it had ridges on it or not, sir.
Q. You don't know? All right. Now let us go back to page 12 of your testimony [referring to an examination before trial]. Let me go to Questions #106 and #107. Do you remember these questions being asked and giving these answers:
"Q. #106: Tell us what you observed on the public sidewalk adjacent to this entranceway.
"A. There were slight, thin ridges or a coat of ice.
"Q. #107: Tell us, did they extend across the entire entranceway, along the public sidewalk?
"A. Yes, sir."

Q. Do you remember these questions being asked and giving those answers?
A. If it is there, sir, yes.
Q. Were they true when you gave them?
A. No, sir.

Here the witness admitted that he had not told the truth. What an excellent place for counsel to have stopped! Instead, he continued:

Q. It was not true?
A. No.

Counsel was lucky. The witness here gave him another chance to stop. But again he went on:

Q. In other words, what you are telling this Court and jury now is that your memory is better today, a longer distance in time away from the accident, than it was on May 28, 1960, which was much closer to the time of the accident. Is that what you are telling the Court and jury?
A. Yes, sir.

And so counsel gratuitously gave the witness a chance to get "off the hook" on which he had been impaled!

As a comment on this performance it would be hard to find anything more appropriate than what C. P. Harvey, Q.C., said in his book *The Advocate's Devil*, in reference to a different cross-examiner who made the same kind of blunder, also, strangely enough, after he had asked five questions:

Why in the world did he not stop when he had got the answer to the fifth question? The explanation, of course, is that he fell into the same trap . . . the thing seemed to be going so well that he yielded to the temptation to make it go just a little better.

Another illustration of the same fatal propensity to overreach oneself, to press on beyond the point of no return, is provided by the record of an action tried before me in which a wife sued her husband for a separation. The attorney for the husband, in cross-examining the wife as to her financial condition, proceeded as follows:

Q. Do you mean to say you have no property of your own?
A. That's right. I have none.
Q. Now think again. Don't you own stock?
A. Oh, yes, I forgot.
Q. I thought so. Now take your time and tell us how much you paid for your stock.

(Counsel evidently thought he had hit "pay dirt" and decided to proceed quite blindly.)

A. About fifty dollars.

Instead of immediately dropping this line of inquiry, counsel went on:

Q. Where did you get the money to buy it?
A. I borrowed it from my mother-in-law four years ago, and now she has a judgment against me for this loan.

Of course, it was a mistake for counsel to have asked the last question. After the third question it was apparent that he was engaged in a "fishing expedition"—a pointless, rambling, hit-or-miss cross-examination. If he did not have undisputed proof that the plaintiff owned stock of substantial value which she had purchased with her own funds, it was foolish to examine her along these lines. Later, when I asked counsel, "Why did you ask these questions?" he blamed his client, who, he said, had suggested them to him. Had counsel taken the trouble, in advance of trial, to make a careful investigation of the wife's stock transactions, he could have avoided leaving himself open for a staggering blow. Then, instead of rolling with the punch, he made the further mistake of coming back for more of the same with his fourth question.

In general, unless a lawyer has convincing and reliable proof to counteract testimony damaging to his client's case, he should avoid harping on it in cross-examination, for he may succeed only in impressing it more deeply on the minds of the jurors.

This is precisely what happened in a criminal case in which the accused was charged with passing counterfeit money. Several witnesses for the Government testified that on the day in question, about eight months before the trial, the defendant, driving a green Buick, had stopped at various stores in the same neighborhood and made small purchases, for which he paid in each case with a counterfeit ten-dollar bill, receiving the change in good money. In order to corroborate the testimony of these witnesses and show that the defendant was in the neighborhood on the day of the crime, the Government put on the stand the owner of a gasoline station in the area, who testified that the defendant, driving a green Buick, had stopped at his station that day for gas.

The cross-examination of this witness by defense counsel, an experienced trial lawyer, proceeded as follows:

Q. How many cars stop at your gas station each day?
A. A couple of hundred.
Q. Do you remember any other car that was there on this particular day eight months ago?
A. No, not offhand.
Q. And yet you remember this one?
A. Yes.
Q. How is it that you remember this particular car and that the defendant was the driver?
A. Because he paid me with a phony ten-dollar bill.

The very fact that the defendant had purchased gas at the witness' station should have been enough to put counsel on his guard before engaging in this standard type of cross-examination. Certainly he should have checked with his client as to whether the gas was paid for with a counterfeit bill. Had counsel done so, he would have stopped before asking the last question. The effect would then have been to leave the impression in the minds of the jurors that the testimony of the gas-station owner was, to say the least, implausible.

Once a cross-examiner has cornered a witness on some important point and maneuvered him into a position from which he cannot extricate himself unaided, it is folly to play around with him further, like a cat with a mouse, in the hope of drawing more blood. Just how foolish this is can be seen from the unhappy experience of defense counsel, an eminent attorney, in a negligence action brought by a person who had fallen into a hole and fractured his leg. At the examination of the plaintiff before trial, the defendant's attorney noticed that the plaintiff was not wearing glasses. However, when he took the stand at the trial, he was wearing a pair with thick lenses.

Defense counsel, after giving the plaintiff a very thorough cross-examination, finally asked him:

Q. At the time of the accident, were you wearing your glasses?
A. No, I was not.

This would have been an excellent place to stop. But the cross-examiner thought he had hit on something good and decided to make the most of it. He asked the plaintiff to show him the glasses. Then, holding them up before his eyes, counsel made a great show of moving them vertically and horizontally, just as an optician would do, and he offered them in evidence. Next, the glasses were handed around among the jurors for inspection, and each went through the ritual of holding the thick lenses in front of his eyes and moving the glasses back and forth and up and down. All in all, it looked like an impressive piece of evidence that spoke for itself only too eloquently.

Then a luncheon recess was taken.

Why the witness should have been called back after lunch for further cross-examination, after the impression left by the morning session, or what more counsel hoped to gain by additional questioning, is beyond me. At any rate, when the witness returned to the stand, he was no longer wearing his glasses. Defense counsel could not restrain himself from making a comment about this and calling it to the attention of the jury.

On the back wall of the courtroom, about forty feet away from the witness, was a clock about eighteen inches in diameter. The time was 2:17. The first question the defendant's attorney asked the witness, after noting the absence of his glasses, was:

Q. What time is it by that clock?

Without the slightest hesitation, the witness replied:

A. 2:17.

The judge and jury burst into laughter. That was the end of the cross-examination. The case was settled immediately thereafter.

I may also cite the experience of a colorful and deadly cross-examiner, defense counsel in a bankruptcy fraud case. He was grilling a witness, obviously Jewish, who, although involved in the fraud himself, had testified for the prosecution:

Q. Mr. W., you were involved in the Chelsea case, and you cheated your creditors there, didn't you?
A. Yes, sir.
Q. And you were involved in the Bates case, and you cheated your creditors there, didn't you?
A. Yes, sir.
Q. And you were involved in the Onyx case, and you cheated your creditors there?
A. Yes, sir.

At this point, defense counsel, drawing himself up to his full height to deliver the *coup de grâce*, turned to the jury and shouted:

Q. Now, Mr. W., do you want this Court and jury to believe that you are reformed?
A. No, Counsellor, I'm Orthodox.

The witness' answer drew a hearty laugh from a jury that had up to that moment been following the cross-examination with apparently tense absorption. Unwittingly the witness seemed to have put his character in a different light. What effect his last answer would have had on Orthodox Jewish jurors, had there been any on the panel, is, of course, purely conjectural. But from the point of view of cross-examination strategy, we may well ask whether the last question was really necessary. What purpose was it designed to serve? Was the cross-examiner trying to rub salt into a mortal wound he had inflicted? Was he afraid the jury wouldn't get the point?

It seems impossible for some lawyers to leave well enough alone. In a case tried before me, a doctor, testifying for the plaintiff, stated that he was suffering from a permanent injury. On cross-examination, defense counsel brought out the fact that the doctor had last examined the plaintiff over a year before the trial. Instead of being satisfied with this admission and trying to make whatever capital of it he could on summation, counsel pursued the point further by asking:

Q. Can you state whether the injuries are permanent at the present time?
A. They were permanent as of a year ago when I examined him. That is all I can say.
Q. But I'm asking you about his condition now.
A. I can tell you only that on the basis of the examination I made a year ago, I found his injuries to be permanent.

Counsel then went after the witness savagely in a futile attempt to shake him. Finally he thrust the following question at him:

Q. Doctor, would you examine him now and give us your findings?
A. I'd be glad to.

While the jury waited, the doctor left the witness stand and, in my chambers, made a physical examination of the plaintiff. When he returned to the stand, the doctor stated:

A. Now I can testify that the permanency of the plaintiff's injuries has continued up to the present time.

It goes without saying what the effect of defense counsel's ineptitude was on the verdict of the jury. Had he been content to let well enough alone and not challenged the doctor to examine the patient again, counsel would have had a powerful argument for his summation. For example, he could have said something like this:

If the plaintiff now claims that his injuries are permanent, why didn't his own doctor examine him today, yesterday, last week, or a month ago, and tell you today that they are permanent? In view of his own doctor's guarded testimony that they were permanent over a year ago, the only possible inference is that they are not permanent today.

What an opportunity to fling to the winds!

It would not be difficult to match these with other instances, equally horrendous, of what I call the "foot-in-mouth" disease of many cross-examiners. As C. P. Harvey says, in the book already cited, quoting Mr. Justice Hilbery on this subject:

> The temptation to ask just one more question in cross-examination seems to be irresistible. Moreover, it occurs in examinations-in-chief as well. At any rate, if you go round the courts, you will be able to see this very mistake made, not merely by beginners, but by practiced hands, almost every day.

On occasion, the presiding judge will ask the cross-examiner who has either made his point or is engaged in an exercise in futility, "Are you through with the witness? Have you any more questions?" Much too often I have heard counsel, both experienced and inexperienced, answer, "No, Your Honor, I'm not through yet. I have just one or two more questions." (Generally this means a dozen or more questions, very frequently including one or two that do irreparable damage to counsel's case.) If I think additional questions are unnecessary, I ask counsel, "Can you count up to two?" This is my way of hinting that he quit before it is too late and not yield to the temptation to try for a little more when he already has enough. Unfortunately, few attorneys take the hint. They seem rather to get their second wind, and as the cross-examination proceeds, they end by snatching doubt from the jaws of certainty.

In this connection I am reminded of the story told about Rigby Swift, a judge who sat on the English Bench some time ago. A rather naïve young attorney appeared before him and was laboring a point at unnecessary length. A more experienced lawyer sitting behind him handed the young man a note, which read, "Sit down! The old reprobate is in your favor."

Seeing the note being passed, the judge said, "I see you have a note."

"Yes, Your Honor," the young advocate responded.

"Hand it up to me!"

"It is a private note, Your Honor," counsel protested.

"Hand it up to me!"

With much embarrassment counsel tremblingly handed up the note,

and Rigby Swift read it. Then the judge turned to the red-faced young
man and asked, "Have you read it?"

"Yes, Your Honor, I have," he replied.

"Then read it again," said the judge.

We see, then, that the kind of self-discipline called for in successful
cross-examination involves a deliberate—though rapid—assessment of
the situation after each answer given by the witness before counsel proceeds to the next question. If he is not to flounder aimlessly, a cross-
examiner must know at all times where he is on the course that he has
charted for himself, and this means that he must take his bearings quite
frequently. Effective cross-examination is thus a series of starts and
stops, of twists and turns, of sudden rerouting and backtracking, of subjects picked up and dropped, with fresh beginnings along hitherto
untried channels, always under the control and guidance of counsel.
Any sign of evasiveness, any admission of error, carelessness, incompetence, or unethical conduct on the part of the witness, is just so
much gained along the way, to be quietly gathered up by the cross-
examiner as he proceeds and set aside for later use. In other words,
cross-examination should be looked upon primarily as a source of material for counsel's summation.

The effect of this kind of cross-examination upon the witness can be
most disconcerting. More or less dimly aware that some of his answers
do not put him in a very favorable light, he would like nothing better
than to explain, clarify, elaborate, and correct the poor impression he
is making, but counsel never gives him a chance. Forced to shift from
one subject to another in a pattern not of his own making and by no
means clear to him, the witness finds it hard to anticipate what is coming next. He is not always able to appreciate the thrust of a question
before it is too late to take back or to qualify what he has said, nor
does he know just how much his cross-examiner is holding back in reserve. If he is not thrown off balance completely, he at least has the
sense of not being in full control. The cross-examiner is in the saddle,
and the witness, like a docile horse equipped with blinders, is being
gently but firmly goaded, checked, reined in, and driven toward his
master's chosen destination.

The fact that the jury may not appreciate, during the cross-
examination, the full significance of some of the witness' admissions is
of no immediate importance. As we have seen, counsel only courts
disaster if he tries to use the cross-examination to underline or em-

phasize a point already elicited, solely for the sake of impressing it upon the jurors. To do so is also seriously to misconceive the function of this phase of the trial. The cross-examiner's task is chiefly to collect the ammunition he will need later when he addresses the jury. There will be time enough then to set everything in its place, to expatiate on each important point, and to use all the resources of logic and rhetoric to put the witness' testimony in the poorest possible light.

How, exactly, is this done? Summation is an art in itself whose theory and practice require discussion in greater detail.

VII

CLOSING TO THE JURY

20

The Art of Summation

If the opening to the jury is the prologue to the trial, then the summation may well be called its epilogue. This rounds out the presentation of counsel's case and brings it to a conclusion. The summation is his last opportunity to address the members of the jury. It is in his closing remarks that he seeks to persuade them of the justice of his client's cause and of his interpretation of the facts as they have been brought out in the testimony. To this end, he tries to marshal all the arguments he can muster in his client's favor and to present them as convincingly as possible.

Obviously, what he says will depend, to a considerable extent, on whether he or his adversary speaks first. The order of precedence in this matter is determined by law. In both civil and criminal actions, the attorney for the defendant is the first to sum up. However, in criminal cases the reverse is true in certain jurisdictions. For example, in Florida, if the attorney for the defendant in a criminal prosecution calls no witnesses, he is permitted to sum up last.

Lawyers, I believe, have often felt—and I fully concur—that the one who speaks last enjoys an inestimable advantage. I think that in all criminal cases this opportunity should be afforded to the accused as a matter of right. After all, a man's life, or at least many months or years of his life, may be at stake. Surely the outcome ought not to depend on a procedural technicality that could adversely affect the interests of the defendant, especially in a country such as ours, which so studiously seeks to safeguard every man's constitutional right to a fair trial and due process of law.

In commenting on this anomaly in our judicial system, an able lawyer of my acquaintance has recommended that we follow the example of the State of Israel, which allows the defendant's attorney to sum up last in a criminal action. He continued:

The right of the defendant in a criminal case to close last to the jury is not a new reform. Sir Walter Raleigh argued for it in his own trial. From *The Advocate's Devil* by C. P. Harvey, I quote:

> Coke: Have you done? The King must have the last word.
> Raleigh: Nay, Mr. Attorney, he which speaketh for his life must speak last.

> Raleigh was profoundly right. Every defendant, without exception, should have the right to close last to the jury. In England, if the defendant testifies and calls no other witness, he has that right. The defendant's life, liberty, and reputation are in the balance. In that solemn moment, his should be the final words.

I agree wholeheartedly with this reasoning.

At any rate, as conditions are now, defense counsel in a criminal case, since he speaks first, has to be extremely careful in his summation not to say anything that the prosecutor can later seize upon and use against the defendant. A single mistake may be enough to undermine the whole defense. On the other hand, it is sometimes possible for the attorney for the defendant to anticipate and forestall the tactics of the prosecution in summation. A clue to them may often be found by paying close attention to the prosecutor's opening statement. From it and other indications an alert attorney may be able to infer the content of his adversary's summation and frame his own accordingly.

For example, in a criminal case I tried, I noted that the District Attorney, in his opening remarks to the jury, asked them more than once to "show no mercy" toward the defendant. Here, substantially, is how I couched my summation:

> Members of the jury, the District Attorney, in his opening statement, on several occasions asked you, in weighing the evidence in this case, to "show no mercy" toward my client. Before you permit yourself to give heed to such a plea, I beseech you to ask yourself: Who of us is perfect? Is there anyone in this world who always does everything he ought to do and never does anything he ought not to do? Is it not true that we all stumble now and then? Some stumble many times; some, only a few. Which one of us is without fault? Should not justice, particularly in this type of case, be seasoned with mercy? Does not God forgive our sins? An understanding of God's infinite mercy should make it possible for us to imitate Him in our dealings with our fellow men and should enable us to show mercy to others, even as God does to us.
>
> In judging my client, I would rather have you follow the precepts of religion as found in the Bible. There we are adjured "to love mercy." I would remind you, too, of the divine beatitude: "Blessed are the merciful, for they shall obtain mercy." It is this noble thought, also, that animates those immortal lines of Shakespeare which we all know so well:

And earthly power doth then show likest God's
When mercy seasons justice.

And please consider, as well, that your showing mercy is not to be
understood as a sign of weakness. On the contrary, it is a sign of nobility
and greatness of spirit.

The great disadvantage of having to speak first, of course, is that
counsel not only has to avoid providing grist for his adversary's mill but
also has no opportunity to rebut or correct anything opposing counsel
may say.

Here, for example, is the way in which the right of the plaintiff's
attorney to have the last say was used by a resourceful advocate to good
effect against the defendant, who was left powerless to reply. In an action to recover for a salesman's commissions, the defense was that the
plaintiff had not made the sales in question and so was not entitled to
the commissions he claimed. Before the trial, the plaintiff's attorney
served on the defendant corporation a notice to produce its books. The
defendant, however, did not produce the books at the trial when
called upon to do so by the plaintiff's counsel. In his summation he
accordingly argued as follows:

The defendant was required to produce its books but did not do so.
It is plain that the reason the books were not produced is that the
plaintiff made the sales in question and is entitled to the commissions
on them.

The verdict was for the plaintiff. Upon appeal, a new trial was ordered because of an error made by the Court in admitting certain evidence. On the retrial, the defendant came to court with voluminous
books and piled them up in the courtroom where the jury could see
them plainly. The trial proceeded and concluded, but this time the
plaintiff's attorney did not call for the production of the books, and
they were not used. Now he resorted to a different argument in his
summation:

You saw the defendant come here with a truckload of its books. But
did the defendant open up so much as a single book? No! And why not?
Because the defendant knew that if those books were opened to the
jury, they would show that the plaintiff made these sales and is entitled to the commissions he is suing for.

Again the plaintiff obtained a favorable verdict, and this time it was
affirmed on appeal.

There is no rule of thumb for beginning a summation, nor is there any set form or pattern to follow. Each summation must be determined both as to form and content according to the individual circumstances of the case. If I venture to generalize at all on the practical aspects of this art, on the basis of almost forty years' experience on both sides of the trial bench, I do so with an acute awareness of the possible exceptions to virtually every "principle" of summation that I might suggest. I well realize that what may be recommended as an advisable course of conduct for counsel to follow may prove on occasion to be the very opposite. Whoever gives advice on matters of this kind risks the possibility of having his own artillery some day turned against him and being hit with his own ammunition.

That even the most learned and experienced dispenser of legal wisdom may sometimes have to swallow a bitter dose of his own medicine was strikingly brought to my attention by my revered friend, the Honorable John C. McCrate, a former Justice of the Supreme Court of the State of New York, and later Justice of the Appellate Division, Second Judicial Department. He amusingly illustrated this point by recounting to me what happened in an action in which he presided. It seems that Francis Wellman, a leading cross-examiner of his day, was being opposed by a young unknown adversary. At about the time of the trial, Mr. Wellman had gained considerable acclaim for his excellent book *The Art of Cross-Examination*. It has, indeed, since become a classic in its field. In it, he touched, as I have, on the importance of not asking the witness any questions unless the situation warranted a cross-examination.

Mr. Wellman's opponent, counsel for the plaintiff, had called the only eyewitness to testify on behalf of his client. At the conclusion of the witness' direct examination, the young lawyer turned to Mr. Wellman and, with great trepidation, said, "You may cross-examine."

Mr. Wellman rose from his seat at the counsel table, looked for a suspenseful moment at the witness, and, for reasons best known to himself—and he certainly must have had good ones—said to the judge, "Your Honor, no cross-examination." He was a great exponent of these magic words, but they did not serve him well on that day.

His adversary, talented and adept, kept this dramatic incident in mind. When it was his turn to present his summation, the young man drove home a winning blow with an argument substantially as follows:

You heard Mr. Jones, a witness for my client, the plaintiff in this case, testify at length about what he saw. You will also recall that when the witness had concluded his direct testimony, and my learned adversary, the distinguished Mr. Wellman, was afforded the opportunity to cross-examine him, not one single question did Mr. Wellman put to the witness. Mr. Wellman waived his opportunity to test the witness' story when he uttered those fateful words, "No cross-examination." Now, Mr. Wellman is the well-known author of a book that I use, as do many other members of the bar. It is called *The Art of Cross-Examination*. In it he advises lawyers not to cross-examine a witness who is obviously telling the truth. Now we can understand why Mr. Wellman declined the opportunity to cross-examine Mr. Jones. It was because Mr. Wellman knew that the witness was telling the truth from the moment he took the stand until the time he left it. From his long and varied experience as a great and accomplished cross-examiner, Mr. Wellman knew that you cannot shake a witness who tells the truth. This circumstance, in and of itself, should convince you that my client, on whose behalf this witness testified, should prevail.

He did.

Again and again, the underlying factor which comes to the fore at a trial, especially in summation, is the personality of the advocate. It is impossible to find a universal rule of conduct in summation that will apply equally to all members of the bar. Each has his own quirks, idiosyncrasies, winning ways, or annoying mannerisms that go to make up a combination of strengths and weaknesses. Just as, out of the same clay, one sculptor models a man, another a dog, and a third a tree, so different lawyers will produce different effects with the same material. "Style," said Buffon, "is the man himself."

Consequently, it is not surprising that there are as many different styles of summation as there are trial lawyers. There is the quaintly jocular, the intimately "folksy," the eloquently orotund, the quietly conversational, the learnedly allusive, the coldly logical, and the strikingly histrionic—to name but a few of the better-known types. There is the clown who plays it for laughs, and there is the subtle master of innuendo and insinuation. There is the silver-tongued spellbinder, and there is the table-thumping shouter. There is the slobbering sentimentalist, and there is the virtuoso of invective. There is the advocate who deftly ticks his points off, one by one, on his fingers, and there is the colorful showman, with his dramatic pauses, sweeping gestures, and rolling eyes. And, of course, trailing in the rear is the army of mediocrities, droning monotonously on from irrelevancy to irrelevancy, rambling, repetitious, colorless, and tedious.

There is a school of thought which holds that, ideally, a lawyer, like an actor, should be able to assume any of these roles (except, of course, the last-named), as circumstances may demand. He will, in short, suit his style not only to the nature of the subject but to the jury he is addressing. There will, accordingly, be times when a quiet, earnest tone will prove more persuasive than the most dazzling display of oratorical prowess. On other occasions, a little "hamming" may not be out of order, and even a somewhat "corny" approach—safe platitudes and homely sentiments—may be called for.

Indeed, counsel for the plaintiff in a civil action, since he speaks last, may take his cue from the style of his adversary and decide on a sharp contrast in tone. Thus, after a fiery, high-pitched, emotional summation for the defense, a speech that is calm, sober, and reasonable in tone may help to bring the members of the jury down to earth. Contrariwise, an impassioned appeal to the jury's feelings, according to some lawyers, may be just what is needed after a boring enumeration of factual details concerning dates, medical terms, hospital records, and statistics. By the same token, a witty summation, if it is kept within the bounds of good taste, may reduce the position of the other side to absurdity.

I should be the last to deny that a lawyer needs a certain amount of versatility in these respects. The more resources, natural or acquired, that he can call upon, the better. Certainly there is a place for the advocate who has a flair for the dramatic, and he should not hesitate to exploit whatever natural talents he may have when the time comes for summation.

In fact, some lawyers go so far as to play the "ham" to divert the jury from what their adversary is saying. This is precisely what Clarence Darrow is alleged to have done during a criminal prosecution in which he was representing, as usual, the accused. The District Attorney, who had an ironclad case against the defendant, was summing up. Darrow was seated near the jury box and in full view of the jury. In those days lawyers could smoke during the proceedings. As the prosecutor began his speech, Darrow struck a match and lit a cigar into which he had secretly inserted a wire. Holding it high enough for each juror to see, he took a puff on it from time to time, but he never flicked the ashes off the end of it. Slowly but surely a gradually lengthening cylinder of remarkably cohesive cigar ash held the fascinated gaze of the jurors. They kept watching and waiting to see when the ashes would fall off or be flicked off. And so the jurors concentrated on Darrow's cigar, which he smoked very slowly, while the prosecutor talked on. Needless to say, the ashes never came off, and the jury's attention was effectively distracted from the prosecutor's speech.

Yet Darrow would probably have been the first to agree that most cases are not won by trickery or showmanship, but by solid factual evidence and logical reasoning, presented, of course, in the clearest light and in the most convincing manner. If there is an art to summation— and there certainly is—it is not the magician's art of illusion, but the art of setting off the jewel of truth so that it may be seen to best advantage in all its luminous purity and splendor. No legerdemain is needed to do that. Nor can counsel expect to get along by memorizing some particular set of formulas to be used in summation at all times and under all circumstances. He must be prepared to cope with each situation as it arises, drawing upon his experience, training, and stock of knowledge to produce the summation best suited to the particular case he is trying.

This does not mean, however, that a lawyer should not have stored in his memory a set of apt phrases or striking quotations generally appropriate for the occasion or commonly applicable to various types of cases. I knew one prominent trial lawyer who successfully opened summation after summation by quoting the words inscribed over the entrance to the courthouse of the Supreme Court in New York County. If the case was being tried there, he would say, in substance:

> As I walked up the steps of this courthouse, I observed, as undoubtedly you did too, those profoundly impressive and significant words inscribed over the portal. They read, "The true administration of justice is the firmest pillar of good government."

If he spoke elsewhere, he varied his remarks somewhat:

> I wonder whether you have ever seen the words inscribed over the entrance of the Supreme Court Building in New York.

Then, after quoting them, he would proceed to remind the jurors that, as sworn judges of the facts, they constituted the bulwark of the administration of justice, and so they had an obligation to arrive at their verdict without passion or prejudice and to be concerned only with the weight of the credible evidence, in the light of the law as expounded by the judge in his charge.

I must confess that I too have used these words in my closing remarks. But in order not to sound like a phonograph recording playing back the same speech at every trial, I invented a few variations. If, for example, I was speaking last, I would borrow whole passages from my adversary's summation, particularly those in his concluding sentences—still, presumably, ringing in the jurors' ears—and I would tell them, "I intend to use his words as my text." Then I would point out to the jury those statements of my adversary which were distortions, exaggerations, inaccuracies, logical fallacies, misrepresentations, or prejudicial appeals to false sentiment. Of course, I would support my characterization of my adversary's arguments, in each instance, with appropriate references to the testimony, reading some of it verbatim.

Another technique I acquired rather early in my career as a trial lawyer was to use in my summation one or more of the aphorisms that I found inscribed on the wall behind the judge's bench in almost every courtroom. I made a collection of these and did not hesitate to draw upon this rich treasury of the wisdom of all ages and nations whenever I had need of an appropriate quotation. I was thus able to lend the weight of ancient and honorable authority to my summations by citing, for example, Aristotle's dicta that "justice is to give each man his due" and that "good law must necessarily mean good order," or by going even further back in time to the days of Amen-En-Apt, the Egyptian sage of the tenth century B.C., who described justice as "a great gift of God." Among the other wise men of antiquity whose words on this theme I sometimes called to mind was Agesilaus II, king of Sparta in the fourth century B.C., who characterized justice as "the first of the virtues."

On the same subject I could also cite modern authorities: Joseph Joubert, the eighteenth-century French moralist and theologian, who called justice "truth in action"; Joseph Addison, the famous British essayist of the age of Queen Anne, who said, "To be perfectly just is an attribute of the Divine nature"; and James Anthony Froude, the nineteenth-century British historian, who wrote, "Justice without wisdom is impossible." Nor should one forget Sir William Watson's twentieth-century English translation of an ancient Latin maxim: "Let Justice be done though the heavens fall." I likewise often found apposite Thomas Jefferson's famous declaration in favor of "equal and exact justice to all men" and the noble sentiment embodied in the United Nations Charter: "All persons are equal before the law."

In another context, it might suit my purpose to remind the jurors of the observation of Edmund Burke, the great eighteenth-century English statesman and political writer, that "law and arbitrary power are in eternal enmity," and the statement of William Pitt, Burke's contemporary and peer: "Where law ends, there tyranny begins."

And to buttress the demand for the exercise of reason and logic in the jurors' deliberations, rather than blind prejudice and emotion, I could fortify my argument by calling to witness, as it were, a host of great writers and jurists. First among them would be Thomas Fuller, the seventeenth-century British preacher, who said, "Reason is the life of the law" and "Law governs man; reason, the law." Next would come Sir John Powell, his contemporary and compatriot, who, in the course of his distinguished career on the bench, said very much the same thing: "Nothing is law that is not reason." And backing them both up to the same effect would be the words of Sir Edward Coke, the greatest of all the masters of English law: "The common law itself is nothing else but reason."

Each quotation, of course, would be attributed to its source. Sometimes I would figuratively don the toga of Cicero, the greatest lawyer and orator of ancient Rome, whose rhetoric became the model for schools throughout the world, and I would tell the jury that "the good of the people is the chief law." At other times I might speak with the voice of Sir Edward Coke and say the same thing in different words: "The welfare of the people is the supreme law." On still other occasions I would borrow the words of Sir William Blackstone, the eighteenth-century judge and commentator on jurisprudence: "Law is the embodiment of the moral sentiment of the people." Or I might fall back on the wisdom of Sir Edward Hyde Clarendon, the seventeenth-century British statesman and historian, who said, "The law is the standard and guardian of our liberty." If any of these memorable statements happened to be inscribed on the walls of the courtroom in which I was trying a case, as sometimes happened, so much the better, of course.

A number of others occur to me that have stood me in good stead through the years. One of the most impressive is by Richard Hooker, the noted English theologian and contemporary of Shakespeare:

"The voice of the law is the harmony of the world."

No less awe-inspiring is the reminder by Sir Francis Bacon, the sixteenth-century English philosopher and statesman, that "the place of justice is a hallowed place"—a pertinent rebuke to levity or other unseemly behavior on the part of one's adversary or the witnesses for the other side. I like, too, a saying attributed to Josiah Gilbert Holland, the nineteenth-century editor of the *Century Magazine,* who wrote under the nom de plume of Timothy Titcomb: "Laws are the very bulwark of liberty."

Finally, to bring this catalogue of useful quotations to an end, I may cite Samuel Butler, the nineteenth-century English author, who characterized truth as "precious and divine."

Naturally, if quotations like these are to serve their purpose in summation, they must be used with discretion—sparingly and relevantly. As Isaac D'Israeli said, "The art of quotation requires delicacy." Whether quotations are employed to reinforce an argument or as a text to be elaborated upon and expounded, they must, in either case, be chosen for their fitness to the occasion and particularly their appropriateness to the point that counsel is seeking to make.

Sometimes, too, a quotation or a story may be utilized in the light of what counsel knows about the jurors' backgrounds from questioning them during the *voir dire*. But if such considerations play a role in his choice of a proverb, a fable, or an illustration, he should be very careful to avoid being explicit about which juror or jurors he has particularly in mind. For example, it would be improper for him to single out one or two jurors and refer to them in his summation by name, nationality, sex, occupation, etc. Thus, if a lawyer would like to tell the jury a tale having its source in ancient Hebraic lore or to quote a saying from the Talmud, it would be in exceedingly bad taste for him to preface it by saying, "Mr. Cohen and Mr. Goldberg will, I am sure, appreciate this."

For the same reason, counsel has to exercise tact whenever he makes an allusion that he thinks some jurors, because of their particular background, will understand better than the others. If, for example, the case hinges on a situation with which women are likely to be better acquainted than men, it would be too flagrantly an attempt to curry favor with a few members of the panel for counsel to address himself exclusively to the female jurors and state, "The ladies on this jury will, I have no doubt, readily understand what I mean when I say . . ." Similarly, if the case involves calculations of profit and loss, it would be most injudicious for an attorney to look toward the one accountant on the jury and say, "I am confident that you, sir [pointing to him], will grasp the figures with ease."

No doubt the jurors selected for special mention may feel flattered at being set apart from and above their colleagues, but the other members of the panel are likely to resent this obvious discrimination. It is wiser to address them all as a body, even when one's remarks are really intended primarily for the ears of one or two who appear to be better informed or qualified to understand.

To be sure, the lawyer who wishes to enrich his summation with sententious quotations from the great philosophers, jurists, and statesmen of the past need not confine himself to what he can find recorded on the walls of courtrooms or carved over the portals of courthouses. He can just as well draw his inspiration from his own reading of the classics of literature. Shakespeare, the Bible, Aesop's fables, Bacon's essays, and the great poems of the English language, to say nothing of the writings of sages like Plato, Kant, or Nietzsche, constitute an inestimably precious heritage of learning and wisdom that no advocate can afford to ignore. Whoever wishes to be successful as a pleader of cases would do well to acquire early the habit of wide reading outside the field of the law and of committing to memory apt phrases, striking passages, or even whole stories or poems that might prove useful to him in his work. These then become part of his forensic repertoire, as it were, like the roles learned by an actor or opera singer. Any effort which a lawyer makes in this respect will be amply repaid.

Most famous orators keep in their memory a large stock of such useful material, as we see from the following verses, whose author is unknown to me (and my research has not uncovered him):

> Consider how time's vasty corridors
> Ring with words of famous orators.
> Are their epigrams spontaneous,
> Off the cuff, extemporaneous?
> Or do they, while in the shower or while
>   shaving,
> Think up some brilliant phrase worth
>   saving,
> Then roll it on the tongue and smile,
> And store it away for future file?
> Not even the great Churchill, without notes,
> Could stand and deliver such golden quotes,
> Had he not learned from his earliest boyhood
>   days
> To store away many a brilliant phrase,
> And then when he stood up before the throng,
> He could draw upon a treasury of phrases all
>   day long.
> Eloquence, like any success, toils, works,
>   bleeds, and sweats;
> Eloquence never forgets.

After all, as Pierre Bayle, the seventeenth-century philosopher said,

"There is no less wit and invention in applying rightly a thought one finds in a book than in being the first author of that thought."

Percy Foreman, who is generally regarded as one of the outstanding trial lawyers of our day, does not hesitate to call upon his great knowledge of the Scriptures whenever he thinks he can thereby make a favorable impression on the jurors. As an ordained Baptist deacon, he can cite chapter and verse from memory. But he draws as well from Kipling or Confucius as the need arises.

As for Aesop's fables, they are a most useful source of analogies and can often be cited to introduce arguments. Because of their simplicity, interesting and telling points can be drawn from them. For example, a lawyer whose client is suing to recover for work or services performed for the defendant can tell, to good effect, the story of the wolf and the crane:

> A wolf hired a crane to remove a bone lodged in his throat. When it was done, the wolf refused to pay and said it was enough that he had not eaten the crane. (In serving the wicked, hope for no gain.)

Every lawyer should be familiar with a few of these fables. He is almost certain to find one that suits his purpose. They should be included in his scrapbook, along with literary gems, bon mots, epigrams, quotations from noted lawyers and judges of yesterday and today, and Biblical references. Faithfully kept and added to from year to year, such a collection can prove of inestimable value if reviewed periodically and especially before summation.

In an article entitled "O Tempora, O Mores!" which appeared in the *American Bar Association Journal* of November, 1965, Mr. B. Nathaniel Richter, himself a distinguished member of the legal profession, recalls that the trial lawyer of yesteryear was a man steeped in the Greek and Latin classics and well versed in the writings of Milton, Shelley, Wordsworth, Keats, Browning, De Quincey, Addison, Swift, and Tennyson:

> The trial lawyers up to the end of World War I . . . were resplendent in their references to this great heritage. . . . Their summations contained references to passages that paralleled the situation in their own cases. . . . They were familiar with the French, German, Spanish, and . . . Russian writers. . . . Using these scintillating passages as lines of embarkation upon a given issue, the quotations in parallel would dazzle the jury or kindle in it an understanding of the point in question. . . . Today the summation is regularly colorless, boring, without life, without quiver, and, what is most unforgivable, without grace.

The fact is that there is hardly a human predicament, conflict, or situation encountered in our courts today that does not have its literary counterpart or analogue in the writings of the great masters of prose and verse. They have plumbed the depths of the human heart and have expressed the whole range of man's emotions and sentiments in words that few lawyers are likely to match. The classics have a perennial freshness and a universal pertinence. If, through ignorance or laziness, a lawyer does not take advantage of their insight, if he does not, as it were, borrow the eyes of the authors of the classics for a deeper vision, and their words for greater eloquence, he fails to do full justice to his client's cause.

I am not suggesting, however, that an advocate write out, read, or memorize a summation. That would be most unwise. An address to the jury should be extemporaneous and reflect spontaneity. Although a correct use of the English language and appropriate allusions are indispensable, these are but means to a lawyer's primary end, which is to convince the jury that truth and justice are on his side of the case. Anything that might distract the jurors from this end should therefore be avoided.

When, for example, the jury begins to suspect that the quotations and proverbs are being cited chiefly to call attention to counsel's great learning, their whole effect is not only nullified but rendered negative. The summation is not an appropriate place for a lawyer to show off how much he knows. If the words he chooses are to have their maximum effect, they must be within the scope of the jurors' comprehension. He should not try to impress them with the range of his vocabulary or his knowledge of foreign languages. He may make a favorable impression on one or two jurors who happen to understand him, but he will very probably lose ground with the others, who may well conclude that he is putting on airs or trying to put up a smoke screen of big words to conceal the weakness of his arguments. A lawyer should at all times keep in mind that his case may be won or lost on the acceptance or rejection of his summation to the jury.

For similar reasons, it is a serious mistake for a lawyer to use his summation to parade before the jury his knowledge of the law, however extensive it may be. Young advocates fresh from law school are particularly prone to yield to this temptation. Laudable though their intentions may be, they forget that the sole task of the jury is to determine the facts from the credible evidence. It is not within their province to pass judgment on the law of the case. It is rather the function of the judge, by his rulings and his charge, to give the law to the jurors. For counsel to attempt to do so is to pre-empt the prerogative of the Court. If his transgression meets with objection from his adversary, counsel can expect to find himself on the wrong end of a judicial admonition to "refrain from resorting to such tactics during the rest of your summation." Moreover, in sustaining the objection, the Court will order the jury "to disregard the law as stated to you by counsel."

To be sure, an experienced trial lawyer knows how to make indirect references to the law in his summation. He can, as it were, skirt around the edges of forbidden territory without actually committing a trespass, or he can tell the jury that the judge will instruct them as to the law which counsel believes is applicable to his case. But it takes some proficiency to tread upon such ground without sinking into it over one's head, and it is better for the inexperienced advocate to tiptoe around it when speaking to the jury. In this way, he can avoid the public humiliation of an objection from his adversary sustained by the Court and a rebuke from the Bench.

If a summation is to serve its purpose, it must be clear and coherent. The jury should be able to follow the argument from point to point, from premise to conclusion, with ease and understanding. The order in which the essential ideas are presented should be logical and readily comprehensible.

Since there is no appreciable time within which counsel can prepare his summation at the close of the trial, it is important that he be ready, in a sense, long before the last witness leaves the stand. To this end, he should come to court with a fairly well-organized outline of his remarks and should have readily available, at the counsel table, accurate, legible records, clear notes of the testimony—especially of those witnesses who said anything damaging to counsel's case—and all exhibits received in evidence. Then, when he stands before the jury to address them in summation, he should have these materials so arranged that he can lay his hands immediately on anything he needs. He should be able to pick up a card, an exhibit, or a file without having to stop and ask the indulgence of judge and jury as he fumbles through a mass of disorganized papers in a frantic effort to locate some elusive document. He should be so well organized before he starts to speak that he can maintain a flow of discourse uninterrupted by such disconcerting and distracting evidences of ineptitude. If he wants to quote a passage from a document, it should be instantly available, and the desired passage should be clearly marked off to catch his eye, so that he does not have to keep everybody waiting as he runs his finger down the page searching for it, mumbling all the while to himself.

Naturally, in planning his summation, a lawyer has to take into account the amount of time he will have at his disposal. He is permitted, at the Court's discretion, to address the jury for a reasonable time. The prevailing practice is for the presiding judge to call counsel for both sides to the bench and ask them to agree on the length of time each will need. Rarely does a lawyer require a full hour to sum up his case. But whatever length of time is agreed on, even if it is no more than half an hour, counsel would do well, if he is to speak last, to keep a close watch on the members of the jury while his adversary is addressing them. He can then take his cue from their apparent reaction. If they seem pained, exhausted, or inattentive, this is a sign that opposing counsel has spoken too long. Under these circumstances, rather than add to their misery, an astute advocate may score a point by announcing at the outset, as he rises to address the jury, "I shall try to conclude my remarks in about ten or fifteen minutes. I don't think more time than that is needed."

In this way, he alerts the members of the jury to the fact that the end of the case is in sight, and he can be confident that in the next ten or fifteen minutes they will pay attention to what he has to say. If he can possibly conclude in less time than he promised, he should try to do so. But under no circumstances should he allow himself to speak even a second overtime, unless he has forgotten something exceptionally important. In that event, he must tell the jury that he will need an additional two or three minutes, and he should beg their indulgence.

Of course, a lawyer has to be careful how he phrases his promise to the jury as he opens his summation. Otherwise he may say something like the advocate who, whether absent-mindedly or in an attempt to derogate opposing counsel, began like this:

> Gentlemen of the jury, you have just heard my adversary speak for an hour. All you heard during that time was a lot of nonsense. Now it's my turn, but I'll do it in ten or fifteen minutes.

He kept his promise, too, with nonsense and double-talk galore!

Unfortunately, many lawyers have a great capacity for verbalizing but have nothing to say. They speak at length, but to no avail. Apparently they believe that they must match their adversary in the amount of time consumed in summation. They are insistent on consuming "equal time." If opposing counsel spoke for forty minutes, they speak for at least as long and sometimes a little longer, as if using more words proved that they had the better of the argument.

If a lawyer is to avoid talking overtime, he must learn to pace himself mentally as he speaks. A particularly bad habit into which some trial lawyers fall is that of promising to conclude and then forgetting to stop. "With this statement I shall conclude," they say, and the jury perks up and looks relieved, only to be let down a few minutes later as it becomes all too evident that counsel has got his second wind and is continuing on and on. It is better to leave the members of the jury wanting more than to overstuff them with a superabundance of verbiage. For after a certain point they lose interest or become fatigued and cease to follow counsel's train of thought. The average person's span of attention, even when he is listening to something wholly absorbing, is, after all, limited. Once the jurors' minds begin to wander, they may resent counsel's constant chatter and wish he would sit down and be quiet.

Sometimes, in fact, a juror may show his impatience with a long-winded lawyer in an unmistakable way. In a mail fraud case in which there were several defendants, one was represented by a very successful attorney in his seventies. When it came time for the old gentleman to sum up, he proved to be interminable. He kept on going far beyond his allotted time, and when the Court called him to task, he announced to the jury that he would need "just a little more time." At this point, one of the jurors, a well-educated and cultivated man, had evidently heard about as much as he could take. "Don't you think," he asked the old windbag, "you would be better off to finish right now?"

I recall once, at the conclusion of a trial, the judge asked the defendant's attorney how much time he would need for summation. Counsel requested fifty minutes. Then, looking at the attorney for the plaintiff, the judge said, "I'll allow you twenty minutes. A lawyer does nothing but fan the air after that."

I am reminded, too, of the story told of Winston Churchill's reaction as he sat listening to a long-winded speaker in the House of Commons. All day long, while the business of Parliament remained paralyzed, the marathon monologue dragged on. Finally someone asked Churchill about the schedule: "What follows the speaker?"

"Wednesday," he replied.

In this connection, I commend to all trial lawyers the advice given by Lenore Eversole Fisher in her "Ode to a Public Speaker":

> Just get to the speech
> Instead of preluding,
> And finish it fast,
> Including concluding.

On the same theme is a little quatrain whose author is unknown to me but with whose sentiment I fully concur:

> I love a finished speaker;
> Oh, yes, indeed, I do.
> I don't mean one who's polished;
> I just mean one who's through.

Once a lawyer has decided to bring his summation to an end, he should do so gracefully. He should keep in mind that this is his final opportunity to make a good lasting impression upon the jurors before they retire to deliberate upon their verdict. It is always appropriate and in good taste, in concluding, to thank the trial judge for his fairness, patience, and understanding, and it is only courteous for counsel also to acknowledge his appreciation of the jurors' service as public-spirited citizens in assisting in the administration of justice. Finally, counsel should express his faith in the wisdom and fairness of their verdict in such terms as these:

> And now, as we come to the end of this trial, I feel sure that, in leaving this case with you for your verdict, I can count on you to consider the issues strictly on their merits, to be free of all bias and prejudice, to be fair in every respect, and to do justice in accordance with your solemn oath as jurors. And so I await with confidence "the moment of truth," when, I have no doubt, you will return a verdict in favor of my client. Thank you.

21

Cold Facts and Fiery Words

No doubt each lawyer must feel free to decide for himself which style of summation best suits his needs. Certainly advocates can be found using successfully almost every imaginable variety of oratorical and histrionic technique in their efforts to win a verdict. But, from my position on the bench as well as from my experience as a practicing trial lawyer, I have observed that certain modes of address are likely to be more effective with juries than others. Without wishing to lay down a hard-and-fast rule in regard to a matter that obviously admits of a broad range of legitimate possibilities, I would say that, by and large, the best approach to take is one characterized by earnestness, frankness, and directness.

In this age of talking to the jury "straight from the shoulder," no lawyer can afford to waste any precious minutes with meaningless flights of oratory. To be sure, there is a proper place in summation for impassioned eloquence or stirring appeals to sentiment. No doubt, too, a good effect can often be achieved, as we have seen, by the judicious use of appropriate rhetorical devices, such as striking figures of speech, analogies, literary allusions, and quotations, as long as they serve their purpose. But the average jury today, composed mainly of sensible, practical men and women in all walks of life, is not likely to be dazzled by a display of erudition or oratorical power. Although it is certainly important for a lawyer to know how to express himself, in summing up the successful advocate must put the primary emphasis on the justice of his cause, the logic of his argument, and the truth of the testimony on his side.

Indeed, in summation, as throughout the trial, adherence to truth, justice, and logic will add immeasurably to a lawyer's professional standing. To his fellow attorneys, to the judges before whom he appears, and to the community at large, he becomes known as a man of integrity. He commands respect. When he speaks, men listen; when he exhorts, they respond; when he argues, they reflect; and when he pleads, they yield.

His candor and honesty bring credit not only to himself but also to the bar as an institution for the improvement of the administration of justice and the preservation of our democratic system of government.

Doubtless on occasion a so-called "great trial lawyer" may temporarily attain prominence without concerning himself much with justice, truth, logic, or candor. For a while he may even seem to succeed in building a reputation on evasion, trickery, or untruth. In fact, he may continue for some time with apparent impunity to twist facts, wrongfully exaggerate trivial details, "hoodwink" judges, and "pull the wool over the eyes" of juries as he sacrifices his honor for a quick dollar. But the truth has a way, sooner or later, of coming out and making itself known, and justice, sometimes long overdue, ultimately triumphs. The shoddy tricks and the shabby deceptions no longer suffice. Then comes the day of the fall—perhaps even the crash—from the lofty heights of counsel's undeserved eminence to the lowest depths of shame, possibly including disciplinary proceedings against him.

In the long run, truth is the only tool that needs to be employed by trial lawyers who seek to win lasting success and respect in the profession. If the art of rhetoric is not the handmaiden of logic, if eloquence is not the sword of justice, then these accomplishments are altogether meretricious. This is what Publilius Syrus meant when he said, "He is eloquent enough who has the accent of truth."

The dedicated lawyer, convinced of the justice of his cause, does not need to resort to tricks or dodges. He will not be found among those who thump the table, beat on the rail, raise their voices, parade back and forth in front of the jury, or buzz about like a darning needle in an attempt to sting the jurors into attention. More often he will be seen addressing them in earnest tones, succinctly summarizing the essential facts, drawing logical conclusions, and reasoning with the members of the jury in order to show them where the truth lies.

A concrete example may help to illustrate how trial counsel can weave the thread of truth into the finished fabric of his summation and induce the jury to look favorably on his side of the case. The attorney for the defendant in a negligence action, in summing up, launched into a vitriolic attack on the plaintiff, impugning his integrity and veracity. Moreover, an important witness—let us call him Mr. Carter—called to corroborate the plaintiff's testimony, was subjected to equally merciless treatment under cross-examination. Counsel for the plaintiff, realizing that his summation was his last opportunity to communicate with the jury and to convince them of the sincerity and truthfulness of the plaintiff, addressed them substantially as follows:

Ladies and gentlemen of the jury, you heard my client, the plaintiff in this case, tell you, to the best of his recollection, what happened on the night when he was struck by the defendant's vehicle and sustained the severe bodily injuries which he described in detail. You also saw and heard the witness, Mr. Carter, corroborate the plaintiff's account of how the accident occurred. Now I'd like you to ask yourselves these questions:

Did this witness, in telling his story on direct examination, or during the lengthy and searching cross-examination conducted by my adversary, hesitate or falter even once?

Was the witness contradicted in a single fact to which he had testified?

Did he not convince you that the plaintiff, before he started to cross the intersection, took the precaution of looking to his right and to his left; that he walked carefully almost three-quarters of the way across the thoroughfare with the traffic light green and in his favor, again looking in one direction and then in the other; and that when he was only about eight feet away from the curb, he was hit and knocked down by the defendant's automobile, which had turned into the street being traversed by the plaintiff?

And did not this witness, Mr. Carter, impress you most favorably with his corroboration of the plaintiff's testimony?

Did not Mr. Carter explain his presence at the scene of the accident by showing you that he was standing in front of the shoe store which is on the corner of the intersection where the accident happened?

Did he not tell you that he owns the store and has conducted his shoe business at that corner for the past nine years?

Did he not further explain that he had just closed his store for the evening?

Do you recall he said that when he was approaching the nearest curb and was crossing the intersection about twenty feet behind the plaintiff, he saw the plaintiff walking with the traffic light in his favor?

You also remember, I am sure, that he said he saw the plaintiff, before crossing the street, look to the left and to the right, and that the plaintiff was only about eight to ten feet from the far curb when he was hit by the defendant's car, which had swung into the intersection, striking the plaintiff and throwing him to the ground?

Do you believe that this tradesman, the witness, Mr. Carter, who has served as president of the local businessmen's association, and who is a total stranger to the plaintiff, would tell anything but the truth to you regarding the plaintiff's accident?

Do you believe that a man of his position and standing in our community would color the facts to aid the plaintiff or harm the defendant?

Did he not unequivocally impress you as an upright and honorable gentleman, whose only motive was to tell the truth and relate the facts as he actually saw and remembered them of his own knowledge? What motive would he have for not telling the truth?

Here, the only art used was a climactic series of pointed rhetorical questions. These were designed to refresh the jurors' recollection of the significant parts of the testimony and to provide them with justifiable grounds for believing it. What counsel relied on substantially was the cumulative impact of the facts. Once having marshaled them, he allowed them to speak for themselves and to point unerringly to the only conclusion they could support.

From this we can see, too, that a good summation is selective. Here counsel chose to concentrate on the strong points in his own case. Under other circumstances, he might have picked out the chief weaknesses in his adversary's case—gaps in the evidence, illogical inferences, implausible hypotheses, indications of exaggeration, inconsistencies, suspicious suggestions of fraud, dubious claims, etc.—and he could have hit hard at them in an effort to bolster his case. In any event, whether he is representing the plaintiff or the defendant, counsel's primary task is to select his targets carefully and strike his blows where they will do the most damage.

However, what may appear to be the most vulnerable point in the position of the other side does not always constitute the most appropriate target of a summation. There are times when considerations of tact make it advisable for counsel to resist the temptation to take advantage of what seems like an inviting opportunity to destroy his adversary's case. This is exactly the dilemma that faced defense counsel in a negligence action brought against his client by an injured chauffeur. On cross-examination the plaintiff testified that he was suffering from a certain physical disability and that he knew he had this disability when he filled out his application to the motor vehicle authorities for the renewal of his chauffeur's license. Defense counsel then confronted him with a certified copy of the application, signed by him, in which he stated under oath that he had no disability.

With this kind of ammunition, some lawyers, in summation, might have sought to destroy the plaintiff's credibility by hammering away at the disparity between his sworn statement to the Bureau of Motor Vehicles and his testimony at the trial regarding his disability. What trust, they might have asked, is to be placed in the word of a man who so lightly disregards his solemn oath to tell the truth?

However, defense counsel took a far more moderate and sensible approach. He realized that the average juror tends to be sympathetic toward the "underdog" and is inclined to be indulgent toward a man in the plaintiff's position. After all, nobody likes to lose his right to operate a motor vehicle, especially when he needs his chauffeur's license to earn a living for himself and his family. A harsh condemnation of the plaintiff under these circumstances could be self-defeating. The jurors might regard an attack on the plaintiff on these grounds as a foul blow and might even begin to take his side.

Consequently, in order to use the plaintiff's testimony to best advantage, defense counsel said something like this in his summation:

> Ladies and gentlemen of the jury, I don't blame the plaintiff, and I wouldn't want you to blame him, for having denied his disability when he filed his application for the renewal of his chauffeur's license. We all realize that he has to drive a car to support his family. It certainly is difficult to give up a license. It's only normal to try to keep it. The sole reason why I brought out this fact in my cross-examination of the plaintiff was to show the end he had in mind and to point out that in everything a man does he has a purpose in view. You can certainly see here the extent to which some people will go to attain their ends. In this case, to attain his end, the plaintiff has exaggerated his claimed injuries. His purpose is to obtain from you a substantial verdict. Please keep that in mind.

Of course, I am not suggesting that there is no place for emotion in a summation. For an attorney to be reasonable and factual in his approach, it is not necessary that he also be cold and detached.

Many modern lawyers, in their eagerness to avoid emotionalism and empty bombast, go to the other extreme entirely. Their summations are little more than a dreary series of statistics and computations. Certainly the essential facts—medical, financial, and scientific—pertinent to the issues should be brought to the jury's attention in summation, and if they can be made more easily understandable by means of visual aids—charts, diagrams, blueprints, drawings, or medical models —these have their place too. On the other hand, if a display of emotion is well founded, a jury never resents it and may often be swept away by it.

Suppose, for example, that a witness testifies that a car was going ninety miles an hour and then came to a full stop in five feet. One lawyer might simply say, "Isn't that ridiculous?" Yet another, with equally good logic but far more passion, might cry, "Gentlemen, in the name of all that is reasonable, in the name of all that is logical, how dare my distinguished adversary present this witness to you? Does he take us all for a pack of fools? Does he think we are devoid of reason?"

In deciding whether and to what extent he should appeal to the jury's emotions, a lawyer has only to keep in mind a very simple rule: Be emotional only over a fact or a logical conclusion. Naturally, the emotion expressed in summation should be sincere. It should really be felt by the lawyer who is summing up. He cannot simply "act" or "emote." In fact, if a lawyer can properly be said to be an actor at all, it is only in the sense in which that term is applied to a disciple of the Stanislavsky school of acting; that is, he must follow the advice of the great Russian stage director and actually "live the part."

But to do that calls for something more than a clear, logical mind. A man has to have a heart, too. He must have a spontaneous and sincere feeling for humanity and a touch of imagination. I recall, for example, how a friend of mine, a distinguished trial lawyer, summed up in a negligence case in which he represented the plaintiff, a single woman of twenty, who had lost an eye in an automobile accident. He said to the jury:

> A young man will take her for a walk. He will sit with her in the park, as young people have done from time immemorial. He will gaze into her eyes—

Here counsel paused for a significant moment. Then, raising his voice dramatically, he continued:

> —and what eyes will he look into! One will be of *glass!*

In conveying to a jury the pain suffered by an injured plaintiff, counsel in a negligence case can, in his summation, demonstrate not only a responsible concern with the facts but also an intuitive sympathy with suffering. The problem he faces becomes especially acute if his client does not show any external evidence of injury—no broken bones, no missing teeth, no scarred or sutured skin, no facial disfigurement— nothing, in fact, that could be seen by an examining physician. Under these circumstances, defense counsel, in summing up, may tend to make light of the plaintiff's claims and to minimize her injuries. Counsel may even go so far as to speak slightingly of the plaintiff's suffering: "So she had to take a few doses of aspirin" or "She makes a big fuss over a twinge of pain in her back."

When it is the turn of the attorney for the plaintiff to sum up, his primary goal should be to make the pain suffered by his client as real as possible to the jurors. But how does one describe pain? How can a lawyer convey to the jury the suffering endured by the plaintiff? He can do so if he combines scientific knowledge with human sympathy and an imaginative identification with all who have suffered. If he is to paint for the jury a vivid and memorable picture of his client's pain, in order to obtain fair and reasonable compensation, he has to help them to appreciate its human side.

To this end, he must begin preparing early—long before the case comes to trial. First, he will have to ask his client a number of questions about the nature, extent, seriousness, and consequences of the pain. For example, he will want to know whether it was an intense stab of sharp, sticking pain, or a continuing dull pain, or a throbbing, intermittent pain, waxing and waning, but always felt, at every moment of the day and night. How long did each paroxysm last? How severe were the pains immediately after the accident? How many weeks or months went by before the pains lessened in severity?

And what effect did the pain have on the plaintiff's life? In the beginning, was the plaintiff able to dress himself, or did the pain require someone to assist him? Was the pain so severe that the tightening of a belt made it uncomfortable for him to wear clothes? Was the plaintiff able to get even one night's sleep for more than a month or two after the accident? How long was it after the accident until the plaintiff was able to go back to work? How did it feel when the plaintiff walked up a flight of subway steps? How long was it before he could get into an automobile without intense pain? If he was able to get to his place of employment, was he able to lift even a light carton of merchandise or operate even a business machine or do any manual labor at all without feeling such severe pain that he had to stop work entirely? If the plaintiff is a professional person or an executive, was the pain so excruciating that he could not concentrate on business details for more than a half hour at a time? How long did this inability to perform his normal business or professional duties continue after the accident?

Counsel will also want to inquire whether there was a time when the pain subsided, so that the plaintiff thought it had finally gone, only to find that as the weather changed, the pain returned with the same or even greater intensity, extent, and duration. Did he again have to give up his business or professional pursuits? How long did the recurrence keep him away from his work? Did the pain prevent him from enjoying the companionship of his family and friends? Did it change his entire mode of life?

The answers to these and similar questions, given in the words of the plaintiff on direct examination, should provide the jury with a comprehensive picture of the cost of his pain in human, nonmonetary terms. This information, buttressed by facts and figures concerning doctors' bills and earnings lost, needs only to be reinforced with relevant scientific data gleaned from medical books. There counsel will learn, for example, that pain is connected with the sense of touch, and that, curiously enough, though there are 500,000 organs of touch in the human body, there are 4,000,000 organs of pain in the skin.

Counsel is now ready to weave the fabric of a moving summation that will leave the jury with an unforgettable impression of the anguish endured by his client. He can begin by describing to the jury every muscle, every joint, every part of the body in which his client felt pain. Then he can proceed to describe how he felt when the pain came on—perhaps suddenly and frighteningly in the midst of a period of comparative relief. Next he can remind the jury of his client's answers to all the questions he asked him about his pain—its description, duration, and effect on his family, social, and business or professional life.

Thus, if the pains were accompanied by muscle spasms, instead of just mentioning this fact, and assuming that the jury knows what he is talking about, counsel should familiarize them with the medical meaning of the term. They should be made to realize that when a muscle develops a spasm, it cuts off its own blood supply, and a reaction, which doctors call "referred pain," may be felt some distance from its source. The severe shooting pain in the lower back suffered by counsel's client may actually have been set off by a muscle spasm in a limb. Every time the limb was raised above a certain point, the result was an excruciating pain in the sacrolumbar area.

Now, if counsel goes on to explain that the use of that limb is important in his client's routine operation of some machine in his daily work, he should be able to make it clear that it was pain—recurring pain, continuing pain, intense pain, day in and day out over a long period of time—that prevented him from performing his work, with a resultant loss of earnings. If the medical testimony elicited from the doctor called to testify on the plaintiff's behalf indicates that the painful condition will persist and even get worse in time, counsel should dwell on the permanent nature of the injury sustained by his client. In short, in developing his summation, he should keep the emphasis at all times on his client's pain and all its attendant and resultant evils—emotional, social, and financial—and he should not stop until he can detect from the expressions on the jurors' faces that they have thoroughly appreciated what his client meant when he said that he still "writhes in pain."

The basic principle underlying such a summation has been aptly formulated by Joseph P. Miller of the Nebraska Bar in an article in *The Practical Lawyer* published in October, 1964:

> In arguing pain and suffering, take the approach that has been described as the "whole-man" concept.
>
> That is, when a part of a man has been injured, or when a part of him aches and pains, he cannot divorce or separate that part from the whole man. When a man has a pounding headache, it is not just his head that is affected, but his entire personality, his entire enjoyment of living. Although his arms and legs suffered no injury and function as well as ever, he doesn't feel up to using them to bowl or golf or engage in other physical activities when his head hurts. He does not want to wrestle with his children or take them to the park. He is impatient with his wife. He is irritable with his fellow employees and perhaps even with the customers, thus affecting his ability to perform his job. In such a manner, a man's entire personality and mode of living has been changed by reason of pain and suffering, and it is not just an ache or pain confined to a small area of the body.

However emotional a lawyer may become in delivering his summation, he should never do or say anything that demeans him or his profession in the eyes of the jury. As a lawyer, he holds a position of distinction, dignity, and honor which it is his duty to maintain. His manner and mode of address in summation—and indeed throughout the trial—should be in keeping with his status as an officer of the court. He should never belittle himself as one lawyer did before me recently when he summed up substantially as follows:

> After hearing my adversary, I know that you must realize that he is an extremely able man. This is an important case to the defendants. Our claim is very substantial, and naturally the defendants have hired an experienced and articulate advocate. I may not be the best lawyer in the business, and my client may have been "cockeyed" to retain me to try this case, but I've done the best I could, to the best of my ability, to present my side of the case. I repeat: If you think I'm a "lousy" lawyer, don't hold it against my client. After all, we (and I refer to the other lawyer and myself) are only actors, and we're acting out our parts—I, on behalf of my client, and the other lawyer for his client. He has said a good many things, and now I'll just talk about the things I think you should think about. But let me tell you this. Don't believe me if you don't want to believe me. After all, I'm not George Wash-

ington. My name is John Jones. But I must tell you right now that the witness, Paul Smith, who was the last witness on yesterday, you know the fellow I mean—well, he, gentlemen of the jury, I swear to God, he was a ringer.

Of course, at this point I had to interrupt him and admonish him not to use such language in speaking to the jury. It was, besides, extremely prejudicial.

He continued in this disjointed and incoherent fashion, and I could see the amazement on the jurors' faces. After a while he actually took a cigarette out of his pocket and held it between his fingers. When I saw him put his other hand into his coat pocket, I thought he was going to take out matches and light up. Once again I interrupted him. "Mr. Jones," I said, "please put the cigarette away. May I remind you that no smoking is permitted in the courtroom."

"Judge," he replied, "I'm only holding it because I'm nervous."

It has been said—and there is possibly some truth in the assertion—that every advocate is an actor, but that does not mean that counsel should say so in addressing the jury. Just as an actor must be careful to play his part and keep within his role, so a lawyer must be judicious in his choice of words. If, for reasons of his own, he wants the jury to believe that he is less experienced, less polished, less learned, or generally less accomplished than his adversary, he can convey this message to them in a more dignified and seemly way than by referring to himself as a "lousy lawyer."

For the same reason that counsel should avoid denigrating himself, he should refrain from making derogatory remarks to the jury about his adversary. A lawyer's task is to try his case, not his opponent. Jurors do not like an attorney who disparages his adversary and often will vent their resentment on the offending lawyer's client. In this respect, they react very much in the same way as the electorate does to a candidate for public office who indulges in mud-slinging. I recall one in particular who used to begin his campaign speeches by saying, "One thing I promise you. I am not going to indulge in smears. I refuse to get down into the gutter with my cynical, dishonest, and moronic opponent." This candidate lost by a landslide.

Moreover, by casting slurs on the motives and character of opposing counsel in an attempt to prejudice the jury against him, an advocate not only reflects dishonor on his profession but may expose himself to deserved retribution. As Benjamin Franklin sagely observed, "If you say what you should not, you must hear what you would not."

If a lawyer finds that his client, his witnesses, or even his own manner of conducting his case is made the object of ridicule or derogation in his adversary's summation, the best policy is to ignore the offensive remarks or to refer to them briefly and address the jury in some such fashion as the following:

> Sometimes, you know, in the excitement of trying a case, lawyers say things that they do not really mean. Frankly, I do not want you to judge this case on the basis of some intemperate remark or unfortunate lapse in good taste on the part of my adversary. I would much prefer that you dismiss it entirely from your minds and attribute it rather to a slip of the tongue made in the heat of the argument. My client and I would like you, instead, to consider and weigh the testimony as you heard it from the lips of the litigants and their witnesses.

There is no need to match insult with insult. Yet there are times when a lawyer can be fairly beaten with the very club he has used against his adversary. I recall an experience I had when I was the Democratic leader of an assembly district and a State Senator from a district then known as the "Fighting Sixth" because of the ferocity of its annual primary contests. At the same time I was actively practicing law, using a good part of my income to pay for primary and election campaign expenses. One morning at about ten-thirty, one of my club workers came to my office and told me that a relative of his was in the Supreme Court awaiting trial in a case in which he was the plaintiff. His lawyer had just quit the case, and my friend wanted me to go to court immediately to represent the plaintiff.

Ordinarily I would have turned down such a request. However, I could not afford to lose the services of so valuable a doorbell ringer, especially at a time when another primary fight was in the offing. Therefore, I rushed over to the court with the intention of applying for an adjournment. By the time I met my newly acquired client, the case had already been called and sent to a trial part for the selection of a jury. My application for an adjournment was promptly denied, but the Court suggested that counsel for the defendant grant me half an hour to read the file and talk to my client.

When my thirty minutes were up, I questioned the jurors for about twenty-five minutes. My adversary then arose, and the first question he put to them was more or less as follows:

Q. Would you be inclined to go along with this plaintiff because his laywer is a district leader and State Senator? Would you take money out of the City's treasury and give it to the plaintiff because his lawyer is Senator Heller?

I was too stunned to make an objection. I said nothing about the incident. When it came time for my adversary to sum up, he started in the following vein:

When I agreed to accept you gentlemen as jurors, you all promised that you would not be swayed in the plaintiff's favor because his lawyer is a district leader and a State Senator. I expect you to keep your promise. The City of New York should not have to pay money to a claimant just because his lawyer is steeped in politics and holds high public office.

Now my ire was really aroused, but I did not show it to the judge or the jury. I could hardly wait for my turn to speak. When it came, I addressed the jury in somewhat the following terms:

My learned adversary has asked you not to award a verdict to the plaintiff because his lawyer is a district leader and a State Senator. He has pointed out that we should not be permitted to dip our hands into the public till for purely political purposes. Well, I agree with him, of course. But I am not here as a politician. I am here as a lawyer, proud of my profession, and trying to make a living and also to earn some money to pay for election expenses incurred in primary contests to maintain my position as district leader, which pays absolutely no salary. It is a party position of honor and gives me an opportunity to be helpful to people like you and my client here.

Why my adversary brought politics into this case is entirely incomprehensible to me. I would hate to suspect that he has an ulterior motive, since I have always considered him one of my friends. It appears to me that my learned adversary was trying to prejudice you against me and, through me, against my client, who has suffered serious injuries because of the defendant's negligence.

But why didn't my adversary show you the other side of the coin? In a moment I shall make him show it to you. The rules governing a trial say that my adversary cannot answer any arguments I now advance during my summation, after I have finished speaking. He has already explained this to you in his closing remarks. Therefore, I am going to ask my adversary a simple question which he can answer without saying a word. If the answer is yes, I would suggest that he remain in his seat; if it is no, let him rise. There's no rule against that.

And now, as I put my question to him, I want the reporter to take it down. Here's the question, Mr. Adversary.

At this point I turned toward him and, looking him straight in the eye, I asked:

Q. Did you not obtain your appointment as Assistant Corporation Counsel to represent the City of New York on the recommendation of Mr. X, your own district leader, and one of my valued friends?

My adversary remained seated. He was too honorable to deny it. I then continued:

Now that the score is even, let's get on with the case.

The plaintiff won.

The lawyer in this case was the only one in my twenty-seven years of active trial practice with whom I was angry at the end of a trial. In fact, we did not talk to each other for years, until one day he appeared before me when I sat as a justice in the Court of Special Sessions. I then called him to the bench and said, "Let's be friends again." We shook hands and made up. After we renewed our friendship, he was manly enough to admit that he had blundered badly. At the time of the incident he was, and remained until his death, one of the ablest trial lawyers in New York State. Even an excellent lawyer can err. Indeed, he keeps on making mistakes throughout his career—but not, let us hope, the same ones.

Any lawyer who underestimates his adversary's capabilities is leaving himself wide open for a possibly devastating blow. This is a mistake often made by seasoned attorneys on finding themselves opposed by advocates who look young and inexperienced. The overconfident veteran is easily tempted into saying something in his summation that he would hesitate to include if he thought better of his adversary's learning, ability, or experience in the ways of the law courts. But the riposte can sometimes prove an unpleasant surprise.

I am reminded of a trial that took place in one of the rural communities along the Red River in the southern part of Oklahoma. A railroad train was alleged to have struck and killed a cow. After the evidence had been presented, the attorney for the railroad company arose and said to the jury, "This is a simple case. It is, in fact, just a plain case of *damnum absque injuria.*" He then proceeded to expound the significance of this Latin maxim of ancient Roman law, which means loss or harm without injury in the legal sense, that is, a loss which does not give the harmed person the right to sue the person causing it. For such damage there is, of course, no legal remedy.

When defense counsel had concluded his summation, the young lawyer for the plaintiff addressed the jury in this fashion:

I am not skilled in the classics like my distinguished and learned adversary. I understand that he knows a great number of languages. He translates from Latin into English, and from English into Latin. I do not know very much Latin. As a schoolboy I attended Wapanucka High School, and there I had one term of elementary Latin. But I will give you my translation of the phrase *damnum absque injuria*. Translated from Latin into plain English, *damnum absque injuria* means nothing more nor less than: "It's a damn poor railroad that will kill a cow and won't pay for it."

He needed to say nothing further. He won his case.

Underestimating the intelligence of the jury can be quite as grave an error as assuming that one's adversary is less knowledgeable or capable than he really is. I recall a civil assault case tried before me in which the plaintiff was a refugee. He drove around in a dilapidated old car peddling from three to six dozen eggs to neighborhood grocery stores. During an altercation with one of his customers over the price of six dozen eggs, the grocer stabbed him, inflicting a serious wound that required twenty-five stitches. The peddler instituted an action to recover damages for the injuries he had sustained as a result of the incident. A man of limited education, he testified in broken English that he was hospitalized for four weeks and was unable to carry on his business for nine weeks. The amount the egg-peddler asked for his loss of earnings during this period was insignificant and would have made little difference in the total amount of the award for injuries as grave as he had suffered.

On cross-examination the defendant's attorney asked the plaintiff whether he had any books or records showing his daily sales, his profits, and his expenses. The peddler, who made a pitiable spectacle on the witness stand, pulled out of his pocket a dog-eared little ten-cent notebook and handed it to the lawyer. Defense counsel riffled through its pages, scowled, and asked the witness, "Don't you have a ledger book?"

Of course, the peddler did not know what the lawyer was talking about.

"How many dozen eggs did you sell on each of the ten days preceding the one on which you say you were assaulted?"

The witness took back his notebook and pointed to a number of plus and minus signs in front of a column of figures. He tried to explain that the plus signs indicated profits and the minus signs meant losses. It was his own "do-it-yourself" method of bookkeeping and entirely foreign to accepted accounting practices, but the peddler could no doubt have explained it to anyone willing to exercise a little patience. Defense counsel, however, professed to find the witness' explanations very confusing and kept trying to elicit from him definite figures for each day's receipts, expenditures, sales, etc., in accordance with conventional bookkeeping procedures. Realizing after a while that he was getting nowhere with this line of interrogation, counsel, in evident disgust, offered the notebook in evidence.

On summation, he said something like the following:

> Members of the jury, this man's veracity as to the events occurring on the day he says he was assaulted can be judged by what you saw this morning when I asked him to show me his accounts. I have offered in evidence the notebook he produced. I want you to take it into the jury room with you. Examine it. See if you understand the figures he has written in it. If you do, you're a better man than I am.

The jury did just that. They showed him they were better than he. In less than fifteen minutes they returned with a substantial verdict in favor of the plaintiff. It was reported to me that after the jury was discharged, the defendant's lawyer asked the foreman, "How did the jury decide this case so fast?"

The foreman replied, "We accepted your challenge to prove to you that we are better than you."

A similar mistake was made in summation by the attorney for the plaintiff in an action brought against an insurance company to recover for losses from a theft. The company refused to pay on the ground that the theft was not covered under the terms of the policy because the premises had not been broken into.

In his appeal to the jury, counsel for the plaintiff laid great stress on the "fine print" and the alleged technicality of the language in the insurance policy. In fact, he said that even he, as a lawyer trained in interpreting legal jargon, was unable to understand the involved and obscure provisions of the policy on the crucial point at issue in the case, though he had read it several times. It was so ambiguous, so confusing, so utterly incomprehensible, such a frightful example of legalistic equivocation and hair-splitting, as not to be in any way binding on the plaintiff. Finally, as the climax of his summation, counsel challenged "anyone on the jury who can understand the provision" to make sense of it, and he thereupon quoted it in full from the insurance policy.

As soon as he had finished reading, one of the members of the jury raised his hand and said, "I can understand it."

Lapses like these on the part of a lawyer are generally attributable to an excess of emotion. If it is a fault to deliver a summation without any feeling at all, whether of indignation or compassion, it is just as foolish for counsel to go to the opposite extreme and become over-emotional in his summation. Once an attorney allows himself to be carried away by his feelings, he may say or do things he will later regret. A trial lawyer must have himself under full control at all times.

For example, a serious mistake that I have seen often made is for counsel to become so infuriated with a party or a witness that he will make statements during his summation which outrage the jury's sense of fair play. If a lawyer decides to question the motives or the credibility of the adverse party or of any of the witnesses for the other side, he should be careful to confine himself strictly to the testimony and the inferences that logically follow from it. He must avoid making a single assertion that cannot withstand this test. For once he lets down his guard in this respect and allows himself greater latitude than fairness justifies, an alert adversary can take him to task and make capital of his exaggeration or distortion. For counsel to attempt to create the impression that all the opposition's witnesses are a pack of knaves and perjurers is just as unwise as to try to convince the jury that his own client and all his witnesses are saintly and infallible, incapable of making any error or committing any fault, whether deliberate or not.

Far too many lawyers, on summation, are in the habit of calling their adversary's witnesses "incorrigible liars." The use of such epithets and other words of scorn like "unprincipled," "conscienceless," "shameless," "heartless," "rogue," "scoundrel," and "unscrupulous," in referring to those on the other side, unless fully justified by incontrovertible evidence, certainly tends to heat up the atmosphere, but it contributes little or nothing toward illuminating the issues or convincing the jurors. On the contrary, the lawyer who indulges in such language is very likely to leave them with the impression that he is resorting to vituperation and invective for lack of any substantial arguments to support his case. In any event, personal abuse or vilification is offensive and unseemly.

There is another, more tactful way of calling the jury's attention to bad motives, bias, or unethical conduct on the part of an adverse witness. For example, if I wished to bring a witness' credibility into question, I would refer to him in some such way as the following:

> The witness, Mr. X, has made certain statements which, frankly, strain credulity. He is evidently so eager to be of help to his friend, the defendant, that he has become reckless and has distorted the facts. It is for you to search for the truth and, in your quest, to consider

whether his testimony gives a colored or exaggerated representation of what actually occurred.

To be sure, not all the angry or abusive statements made by a lawyer on summation are necessarily spontaneous outbursts. They may be the result of deliberate planning. However, preparation of this kind is directed, in my opinion, along dangerous lines.

By way of illustration, I may cite a negligence action brought some years ago by the victim of an accident which occurred while he was driving his automobile in an area where some construction work was in progress. Some pieces of concrete showered down from a scaffold, came through an open window of his car, and injured him so severely that one of his eyes had to be removed.

Counsel for the defendant began his summation—obviously prepared with much care—with a quotation from the Bible: "Blessed is the man who is without blemish and who seeketh not gold." He then went on to elaborate in great detail the full story of Susanna and the Elders, as told in the Apocrypha. The narrative concerns the unsuccessful effort of two evil-minded elders to take advantage of a virtuous woman by falsely accusing her of adultery and giving perjured testimony.

Once again, at the close of his summation, counsel quoted the passage with which he had begun: "Blessed is the man who is without blemish and who seeketh not gold."

The jury found for the defendant. Thereupon, the attorney for the plaintiff moved that the verdict be set aside. In granting the motion, in the interests of justice, the Court described defense counsel's summation as an "unfair trial practice":

> Although most adroitly and cleverly woven into the summation by the defendant's counsel, it was readily apparent that what counsel was attempting to do by innuendo was to compare the defendant in the present case to Susanna, while at the same time comparing the plaintiff and his witnesses to the elders who had formed a conspiracy to which reference has already been made. In the light of the attendant circumstances and the complexion of the jury, the appeal to prejudice appears to have had its desired effect, particularly when the strength of the plaintiff's evidence in this case is taken into consideration. Especially is this so when at the end of his summation, counsel again repeated his supposedly Biblical admonition, "Blessed is the man who is without blemish and who seeketh not gold." It could have left the jury with only the feeling that any verdict for the plaintiff which would deprive the defendant of "gold" would be contrary to their own Biblical teachings.

On appeal, however, the lower Court's order to set aside the jury's verdict was reversed on other grounds and the jury's verdict was reinstated. Subsequently, the Court of Appeals, with one judge dissenting, affirmed the Appellate Division of the New York State Supreme Court. In neither decision of the appellate courts was any mention made of defense counsel's summation. I cannot venture to predict what these courts would have said about this summation if it had been squarely presented to them for adjudication. I can only say that in my opinion it would be dangerous for a lawyer to count on having a similar summation sustained, and I would certainly not attempt to deliver one in the same vein.

Any appeal to prejudice not only is open to legal objection but may evoke an unfavorable reaction from the jurors as well. During the last war, when feeling against the German people was running high, a garage attendant, a man of German descent, was the plaintiff in a negligence action growing out of an accident at his place of employment, where he was struck by a car as it backed up to a gasoline pump. Defense counsel, during his summation, picked up the hospital record which the plaintiff had placed in evidence and began to read it. Everyone naturally expected him to read the notations regarding the plaintiff's injuries and to comment on them. But no, he read only the plaintiff's name—obviously Germanic—his age, and then, with exaggerated emphasis, the words, "born in Germany." Thereupon, counsel closed the record book and sat down.

Evidently this performance was intended to have a stunning impact on the jury. It was, however, the reverse of what defense counsel had expected. The verdict was many times the value of the injuries, and the amount awarded was paid without appeal.

But self-defeating appeals to prejudice, ill-will, envious resentment, or the baser passions are less often the result of miscalculation than of yielding to a rash, momentary impulse springing up in a sudden rush of emotion as counsel warms to his point. Sometimes, indeed, it takes only a few words uttered in the heat of excitement to spell defeat for the lawyer who used them.

This is exactly what happened to defense counsel in a case in which a widow sued an insurance company that had issued a $50,000 life insurance policy on her husband. Within two years of its issuance, her husband committed suicide by jumping from a Manhattan office building. The sole point in dispute during the ten-day trial was whether her husband was sane or insane when he took his own life. If he was insane, the widow would get the full $50,000; but if he was sane, she could recover, under the terms of the policy, only the premiums paid by her husband.

In his summation, defense counsel accused the widow of dishonoring the sacred memory of her husband for "a few lousy bucks."

Taking his cue from these four words, the attorney for the plaintiff, in his summation, effectively pointed out that $50,000 was hardly "a few lousy bucks" to the widow, but if $50,000 was just "a few lousy bucks" to the insurance company, it should have paid the widow rather than subject her to the mental anguish of prosecuting the action, reliving the whole horrible experience, and incurring the expense of the lawsuit.

The plaintiff prevailed.

If anger is a bad counsellor, maudlin sentiment is even worse. A lawyer's attitude toward his client should be marked by something like the professional objectivity of a doctor's relation to his patient. While we expect a surgeon to feel concerned about the fate of the person he is operating on, we would not want him to become so much involved emotionally as to impair his ability to think and act calmly and rationally. In the same way, a lawyer, especially if he consents to try a case for a relative or a dear friend, must beware of becoming too easily and too much affected by pity. If he finds his heart filled to overflowing at the spectacle of his client's plight, or if he becomes overwrought on learning of the grievous wrong he is called upon to right, it is better for counsel not to try the case himself, but to retain one of his colleagues who would handle it objectively.

A negligence case was tried before me in which the plaintiff sought to recover damages for serious injuries sustained in an automobile accident. Hurled through the windshield, he had required at least a hundred stitches on and around his face. In summing up his case, the plaintiff's lawyer, when he came to describe his client's injuries, suddenly turned away from the jury, looked toward the plaintiff seated in the front row of the courtroom, pointed to him, and said substantially:

Members of the jury, look at the plaintiff. How ugly he looks! Take into the jury room with you the picture, received in evidence, that shows how he looked before the accident, and then think of that face as you see it now, all scarred and sutured and seamed, all misshapen and monstrous and misproportioned. Compare the face that you see in this photograph, with its handsome, regular features, smooth skin, and finely chiseled profile, with this twisted and deformed caricature of a human physiognomy!

At this point, the lawyer, turning back toward the jury, hesitated for a few moments, too choked up with emotion to proceed, and finally burst into tears. Through his sobs he managed to convey the rest of his message to the jury:

> I am crying because he is my friend. Before the accident we used to go to parties and have good times together. He was my best friend, but now he won't go out with anyone—not even with me. He does not want people to see him. He has shut himself off from the world, hibernating in his solitude.

Copious tears continued to flow down the lawyer's cheeks. As he cried, he wiped away his tears with his handkerchief and kept on repeating, "He's so ugly! He's so ugly!" And then counsel could speak no more. Still sobbing, he shook his head sadly and sat down.

I could see that the jury was deeply moved. I too felt stunned and shocked. I had intended to charge the jury that afternoon, but I just could not bring myself to do so, and I adjourned court.

The next morning, when I charged the jury, I dwelt at great length on this incident, pointing out that appeals to sympathy, whether real or feigned, have no place in a trial. The jury must have borne these remarks in mind, for it leaned over backward and awarded the plaintiff much less than, under ordinary circumstances, it would have agreed on. Both lawyers concurred with me in this opinion.

At the other extreme from blubbering sentimentality, but in equally deplorable taste, is unseemly levity. There are some trial lawyers who consider it an absolute necessity that they inject into their summations at least one humorous story. They turn each summation into a comic performance, and they will go to any lengths for a laugh, evidently on the theory that it is a good idea to leave the jury in a happy frame of mind.

The function of summation is to convince the jurors, not to convulse them. To leave them impressed with the force of a cogent argument is not the same as to send them away laughing, nor is persuading them of the justice of one's cause a form of light entertainment. A trial is a serious affair and should be conducted with the decorum befitting its importance to the litigants.

However, if a lawyer has the opportunity and the wit to add an occasional light touch deftly and discreetly to his summation, he should, of course, do so without hesitation, as long as he can thereby bring out a point or strengthen his argument. I recall a negligence case in which counsel for the plaintiff did exactly this. Throughout the trial, his adversary placed heavy emphasis upon the fact that the doctor produced by the defendant was an "expert" in neurology, whereas the physician called by the plaintiff was only a general practitioner. Since the medical witnesses contradicted each other, defense counsel sought to persuade the jury that greater weight should be given to the judgment of the "expert" because he presumably knew more about medicine than an ordinary doctor.

The plaintiff's attorney, in his summation, handled this situation with great skill. He expressed himself in the following terms:

> I called to the stand the plaintiff's family doctor. He was the doctor who took care of my client at the time of the accident, and he is still doing so at the present time. He is, as the testimony shows, a general practitioner of long standing and excellent reputation in our community. I never made any pretense that he is an expert in the field of neurology or, for that matter, in any other branch of medicine. He is, however, a graduate of a well-known medical school. He has been licensed by our State to practice medicine and has been doing so successfully for over twenty-five years. He is affiliated with three of the best-known hospitals in this city. During his years of practice, he has diagnosed and treated hundreds, if not thousands, of head injuries. He certainly is well qualified to diagnose the head injury sustained by the plaintiff.
>
> Now, to contradict his testimony, the defendant's attorney brought in a doctor who represented himself as an "expert" in neurology. I am not going to quarrel with that. If he wants to earn his livelihood going around testifying as an "expert," that's his business. But, ladies and gentlemen, please remember this: the doctor who testified for the defendant had the same schooling as the family doctor called by me. They both passed the same State Board medical examinations and had to meet the same licensing requirements. Please keep in mind, too, that the defendant's doctor did not personally examine my client. As he himself admitted, he had not seen the plaintiff until the other day. He was therefore able to answer only hypothetical questions put to him by the learned counsel for the defendant.
>
> Ladies and gentlemen, would you accept answers of this kind from a doctor who never personally examined the plaintiff in preference to the answers given by my client's doctor, which are based on his personal examination and observation of the patient? I am sure you are not going to do any such thing.
>
> And now, in this connection, another thought comes to my mind which I should like to present for your consideration. On cross-

examination of my client's doctor, the defendant's lawyer asked whether this family physician had ever read certain books written by experts in neurology. The plaintiff's doctor truthfully answered that he had not. Well, this reminds me of a news item which I came across not so long ago. It told the story of a man who headed a company that offered expert advice on the stock market. He enjoyed a wide reputation as an expert in this field and wrote and published a widely acclaimed book entitled *How to Build a Fortune and Save Taxes*. The news item I saw was a report that this financial expert, who was constantly being quoted as an authority on the stock market, filed a petition in bankruptcy in which he listed liabilities of almost $56,000 and assets of about $2000.

Ladies and gentlemen, you can see that sometimes a self-proclaimed expert is not really an expert at all.

Sometimes, in his excitement or enthusiasm, a lawyer, in summing up, will make an embarrassing slip, as the defense counsel did in a recent criminal case. He waxed so eloquent in his summation that he was swept away by his own rhetoric and fairly shouted in conclusion, "My client is *guilty*."

The judge promptly interjected, "You don't mean that, do you?"

Confused and floundering, the lawyer blurted out, "Oh, no. I called it wrong. I reverse it."

"You can't do that," the judge replied. "You can't reverse your call, except in a phone booth, and then only with the consent of the party at the other end."

This lawyer was lucky that the judge possessed a good sense of humor and was able to dispel the tension counsel's excitement had created.

Even a seasoned trial lawyer can allow his emotions to run away with him, and he may unwittingly say something in summation that can be seriously detrimental to his client's cause. A man who is often acclaimed—and justly so, I think—as one of the nation's great advocates once made this mistake. He was representing one of several codefendants under indictment for having illegally paid a sum of money to an officer of a labor union. The defendants interposed three defenses: first, that the money they had passed was a bona fide loan; second, that venue was not proper, that is, that the alleged transaction took place outside the jurisdiction of the court; and third, that so much time had elapsed since the occurrence of the transaction that prosecution was legally barred under what is called the "statute of limitations."

The lawyer in question was last to sum up. He made an eloquent plea, dwelling at some length on the excellent character and impeccable respectability of his client. Then, in a surge of emotion, he said the following:

I am going to skip over venue and statute of limitations within two minutes. . . .

There is no venue . . . but I am not going to ask you to throw it out on that ground because we want vindication on the merits. . . .

For the same reason I want to dispose of the statute of limitations.

Even if you find that this is invalid on the ground of the statute of limitations, that it is stale and too old to assert, I am not asking you for my client to throw it out on that ground. If we are guilty on the merits here, I don't want to get out on the ground of the statute of limitations or venue. So I will skip it even though those are perfect defenses and meritorious morally. . . .

The trial judge, having taken careful note of these words, recessed the proceedings and called counsel for all the defendants to the bench. "Am I to understand that the defendants are withdrawing from consideration by the jury the questions of fact relating to venue and the statute of limitations?" he asked.

When the other defense lawyers emphatically replied in the negative, the lawyer whose summation had been interrupted was obliged to go back and assure the jury that they should consider the issues pertaining to venue and the statute of limitations after all.

Occasionally, it takes only a few words of sarcasm or a lame attempt at humor at the expense of the other side to alienate a jury. Recently three lawyers were trying a case before me, one for the plaintiff and two for the defendants. In summing up to the jury, after each of the defendants' attorneys had spoken, the plaintiff's lawyer referred to them scornfully as "the Ev and Charley outfit." At around that time, it seems, the Republican Party had designated Senator Everett Dirksen and Congressman Charles Halleck to speak against the programs of the Kennedy Administration, and newspaper columnists were calling them "the Ev and Charley show."

After eight hours of deliberation, the jury was deadlocked, three jurors holding out for a verdict for the defendant. Later, one member of the panel who was bitter at the deadlock disclosed that two of the jurors were staunch Republicans and had deeply resented what they conceived to be a sneer at their party's spokesmen.

A lawyer should bear in mind that, for the same reason he may not question a venireman about his politics, he should avoid injecting this subject into his summation in a manner that could be detrimental to his client. The minute I heard the plaintiff's attorney compare his adversaries to "Ev and Charley," I knew he had made a very serious error.

Indeed, there are times when even a single word spoken in summation can turn a case one way or the other. One of the first assignments undertaken by a young attorney after being admitted to the bar was the trial of a negligence case in behalf of the plaintiff in an area heavily populated at the time by immigrants. In his enthusiasm for his client's cause, he conducted his cross-examination with zest and perhaps in a tone louder than the circumstances warranted. The attorney for the defendant was a much older, more experienced, and more imposing lawyer. In his summation, he urged the jury not to be persuaded by the "bombastic" tactics of his younger adversary.

Because of doubtful liability, plaintiff's counsel expected that a verdict in his client's favor, if one was returned at all, would be at most for a modest amount. To his surprise, the jury awarded the maximum amount allowable. Puzzled, he later inquired of some of the jurors what had prompted such generosity.

"It's a shame," he was told, with some indignation, "that a nice young man like you should be called a 'bombastic.' "

Evidently the jurors thought the term cast aspersions on the young attorney's legitimacy!

I had a similar experience with a single word used by my adversary in his summation. Early in my career I represented a woman who, while a passenger in a taxicab, sustained a minimal fracture in her lower back. The defendant's counsel, during a summation which lasted only fifteen minutes, ridiculed the injury by hitting hard at the word "minimal":

> The plaintiff is exaggerating her injuries. I watched her throughout the trial as she sat here in court, and I'm sure you too observed her closely on the witness stand. Did she appear to be in any pain? Didn't she look completely relaxed? Was she wincing or writhing in pain, as her lawyer would have you believe? Didn't she appear perfectly normal and free from any of the injuries she said she had sustained?
> And, after all, why not? All she suffered was a *minimal* fracture.

He pronounced the word slowly, with emphasis on the first syllable: "*min'*-i-mal."

> You know what "*min'*-i-mal" means. The dictionary defines it as "small, infinitesimal, inconsequential, of no moment, insignificant." Yes, "*min'*-i-mal" is the word you must bear in mind when you start your deliberations. "Small" is the word you must bear in mind when

you start your deliberations. "Infinitesimal" is the word you must bear in mind when you start your deliberations. "Inconsequential" is the word you must bear in mind as you start your deliberations. "Of no moment" are the words you must bear in mind as you start your deliberations. "Insignificant" is the word you must bear in mind as you start your deliberations. All these words mean "*min'*-i-mal," "*min'*-i-mal," "*min'*-i-mal." Take that word and its definition with you into the jury room, and if you must award her a verdict, let it be a *min'*-i-mal one.

I replied substantially in this vein:

Of course, there is no question as to the defendant's liability, since the plaintiff was a passenger. Defense counsel has suggested, however, that her fracture was characterized by her own doctor as "minimal." That's true. It's right here in the bill of particulars. But "minimal" is a relative word. I'm sure every one of you has, at some time in his life, had a speck of dust or a slight cinder invade one of his eyes. Do you remember how much pain it gave you? Do you recall how you winced and writhed and made desperate efforts to wash the speck from your eye? You tried to remove it in order to get rid of the pain. Do you remember how you were incapacitated and couldn't think of anything else as long as you felt the constant irritation of that speck in your eye? Well, that speck too was *min'*-i-mal.

(I pronounced the word the way my adversary had.)

Yes, it was small. It was inconsequential. It was of no moment. It was insignificant. It was infinitesimal. And, when you finally saw it after it was removed, I'm sure you wondered how such a *min'*-i-mal, small, inconsequential, and insignificant speck could cause so much pain and suffering.

Members of the jury, I repeat, a minimal fracture is a relative term, and if the minimal fracture is in the lower back, as is the case here, you may not feel pain as you're sitting on a bench in the courtroom or on the witness stand, but when you bend to put on your shoes and stockings or to retrieve a coin you drop as you are about to deposit it in a subway coin box, or if you sneeze or cough, it may still be called "*mini'*-i-mal," but it is excruciatingly painful, no matter how much a smart lawyer may seek to *min'*-i-mize it.

The jury rendered such a large verdict for the plaintiff that the Court, without protest on my part, had to reduce it substantially.

I had a similar "one word" experience in one of the very first criminal cases I tried. The man I was defending was charged with a serious crime. The prosecutor concluded his selection of the jury by making the following statement:

Your duty, as you now understand it, is to find the defendant guilty
or not guilty. Do you promise that in your deliberations you will not
concern yourselves with the defendant's durance if you should decide
he is guilty?

The jurors looked as bewildered as I did, but they all solemnly assured him that they would not concern themselves with any such matter. At this juncture I asked the reporter to take down the question
and answer and to furnish me with a transcript.

During the recess I looked up the word "durance" and learned that
it means "imprisonment." Later, in my summation, I read to the jurors
the prosecutor's last question from the stenographer's minutes, and,
when I came to the word "durance," I defined it for the jury and asked:

Why didn't the District Attorney tell you in plain English what he
meant? Why was he covering up the fact that by your verdict this
man's family, consisting of his wife and four young children, may lose
him—husband and father and sole breadwinner—for a minimum of
seven and a half years and a maximum of fifteen years?

My argument must have had some effect. The jury could not agree
on a verdict. On the second trial I was fortunate in obtaining a plea
to a misdemeanor, and the defendant received a very light sentence.

Incidentally, the prosecutor made no objection to my statement, but
the judge, in his charge, properly instructed the jurors that the problem of sentence was not within their province. At this time I cannot
really say whether, when I raised the issue of sentence, I knew that
what I was doing was improper. Maybe I did not know any better. I
do remember, however, that this incident happened early in my career
when I was still as green as a new dollar bill.

In general, then, a summation, to be convincing, needs to be concise
and to the point. It should present the essential facts of the case clearly
and coherently, but it should also stir the jurors' noblest feelings by its
emotional force and its appeal to their sense of justice. It must be precise without being pedantic, logical without being cold, moving without
being mawkish, and dignified without being stiff. Its language should
be easily understandable and vigorous, and its tone tasteful and ingratiating. Both adversary and jurors should be treated with respect.
The whole speech should be marked by a scrupulous regard for the
truth.

But how does a trial lawyer apply these rather general principles to
the concrete case he is trying? Is there not a significant difference be-

tween a summation for the plaintiff and one for the defendant, or between the closing remarks of counsel in a civil suit and those in a criminal action? Does a lawyer sum up in quite the same way when he has a weak case as when he has a strong case? Are there not other special circumstances that may make a difference in the style, as well as the substance, of a summation?

The best way to learn the answers to these questions is to take every opportunity to visit our law courts and to observe the ablest members of the legal profession in action before the jury. The courtroom is, after all, "where the action is." There the spectator can see for himself what distinguishes the great masters of the American bar from the general run of lawyers.

Meanwhile, in the absence of an opportunity to watch directly the outstanding practitioners of this art, let us content ourselves with the vicarious observation of a number of lawyers as they sum up in different types of cases, while I comment on their strengths and weaknesses.

22

Suiting the Words to the Action

As we have seen, in legal parlance a lawsuit is called an "action." So—if I may give Hamlet's famous words of advice to the players a new twist—it would not be too much to say that a lawyer's task in framing his summation is to suit his words to the action.

This is not really difficult to do if he keeps in mind that, after all, the action itself consists mostly of words—the opening statements of both sides, the testimony given by the witnesses, questions asked by the attorneys and perhaps the judge, and, if counsel speaks last, his adversary's summation. Somewhere in this mass of words, which form the trial record, he should be able to find many that he can use for at least part of his closing remarks to the jury.

In a sense, then, counsel should be laying the groundwork for his summation throughout the trial by making note of whatever significant words or phrases give promise of being useful to his purpose. He should be particularly alert to every word uttered by his adversary, especially in summing up. Too often an attorney is so busy thinking about what he is going to say when his turn comes to speak that he loses whatever opportunity may arise to pounce upon some instance of loose thinking, invalid reasoning, or gross error in his adversary's summation.

One of the most brilliant examples of the technique of seizing upon the words of one's adversary and using them for one's own ends occurred during the dramatic debate at the United Nations between the late Adlai Stevenson and Valerian Zorin at the time of the Cuban missile crisis. A bitter exchange of charges and countercharges took place between these accomplished advocates. Stevenson accused the Soviet Union of having surreptitiously installed offensive missile bases in Cuba. In part of his reply, Zorin said:

> In its essence, the argument of the Soviet Union is that it was not the Soviet Union which created this threat to peace by secretly installing these [nuclear] weapons in Cuba, but that it was the United States which created this crisis by discovering and reporting these installations.

Whereupon Stevenson retorted:

> This is the first time, I confess, that I have ever heard it said that
> the crime is not the burglary but the discovery of the burglary, and
> that the threat is not the clandestine missiles in Cuba but their discov-
> ery and the limited measures taken to quarantine further infection.

This brilliant rebuttal was possible, of course, only because Stevenson *listened* to what his adversary was saying.

When I was the attorney for the plaintiff, I would take careful notes
of the statements made in my adversary's summation. I learned in
time to discern when he was about to bring it to a close. Then, picking
out the last or the next-to-the-last sentence of his peroration, I would
borrow it and use it as my own text. My summation would begin in
somewhat the following manner:

> Mr. Foreman, ladies, and gentlemen of the jury, I am glad that my
> adversary has implored you—and I quote—"to weigh the evidence care-
> fully, to treat as evidence in this case only the facts stated by the
> witnesses according to your best recollection, and to do what is right
> according to the dictates of your conscience."
> For the first time during this trial I find myself in perfect agreement
> with my adversary. I shall not only accept his suggestion, but I shall
> go further: I shall use it as my text in summation.

Thereupon, without any flights of oratory, I would immediately get
down to the business at hand by reviewing the evidence and shaping
it in a way which would be most favorable to my client.

To this end, I would not hesitate to rely on the record of the trial
itself by quoting pertinent passages from the transcript of the testimony. Generally I would begin by stressing the strong points in my
client's favor. Thus, I might proceed in this manner:

> Let us now weigh the evidence in order to see where the truth lies.
> You have seen the plaintiff, and you have heard him testify. He told
> his story, I'm sure you will agree, in a straightforward, honest way. You
> observed, too, how well the plaintiff answered the questions put to
> him on cross-examination by my adversary, a lawyer of high repute
> and great ability, whose skill in cross-examination is recognized in our
> profession as that of an expert.

I would then proceed with my assessment of the testimony.

However, my attention, during my adversary's summation, would be
directed toward not only the substance of his speech, but its tone as
well. For this too could be used as a basis for constructing an effective
reply. For example, if he proved to be an accomplished orator, capa-

ble of dazzling a jury with a brilliant display of wit, learning, and rhetoric, I might begin my summation in the following way:

> You have just heard a remarkably persuasive summation. Only a
> man possessed of the great talents and accomplishments of my dis-
> tinguished adversary, the attorney for the defendant, could have pro-
> duced such a masterpiece of forensic eloquence as you were just now
> privileged to hear.
>
> However, I must point out to you that the speech he delivered is not
> based on the facts in this case as evidenced by the testimony. When
> people lack proof, they sometimes seek to win by resorting to seductive
> eloquence. In this case we have been treated to a fine example of it.
> Because of a lack of proof, my adversary has artfully shifted your atten-
> tion to matters entirely foreign to the issues. It is an old device called
> "switching an argument."
>
> Let me point out one or two illustrations.

I would then proceed to call the jury's attention to discrepancies,
admissions, testimony, and exhibits damaging to my adversary's argument.

Sometimes counsel may find that his adversary will interrupt him
in the midst of his summation to interpose an objection to a perfectly
legitimate statement of fact or inference and inject a supposedly clever
remark designed to divert the jurors' attention or break their train of
thought. In such circumstances, the lawyer who is summing up should,
if he can possibly do so, seize upon opposing counsel's objection and
make capital of it by immediately turning it around and thrusting it
right back at him. This technique is very effective with juries.

Indeed, it was used successfully by Senator Albert Gore of Tennessee
in the debate in the United States Senate on the bill to provide health
insurance for the aged under Social Security. Senator Long of Louisi-
ana, who was opposed to the bill, offered an amendment containing
certain provisions which would have had the effect of emasculating it.
With the adoption of the Administration's proposal, every provision of
the Long amendment was eliminated, but it still bore his name. Thereupon Senator Long jumped to his feet and asked unanimous consent to
have his name dropped from the amendment and to substitute that of
the sponsor of the Administration measure, Senator Gore.

"I just want the Senator from Tennessee to step up here and claim
his baby," said Senator Long, grinning.

"Mr. President," Senator Gore immediately responded, "I'm proud
of it. I'll take it home and cuddle it the rest of its life."

Openings like this should be watched for and seized upon whenever they are offered. By the same token, counsel must beware of letting his guard down and giving his adversary similar opportunities for a retort that hits the mark.

Here, for example, is the way an alert trial lawyer, now my distinguished colleague, Justice Matthew Levy of New York County, made the most of such an opportunity in a situation in which his adversary sought to take advantage of the known financial irresponsibility of individual codefendants to help a defendant who was financially responsible. The plaintiff, a passenger in a streetcar, was hit by a stray bullet fired by one of three policemen in pursuit of two fugitives. The officers of the law were named as codefendants. During summation the Corporation Counsel based his argument on the fact that the police officers were only performing their duty, and he contended that it would be oppressive to charge them with negligence and make these poor men pay a heavy damage bill out of their small salaries.

Thereupon the plaintiff's attorney addressed the Court as follows: "In view of the statements made by the Corporation Counsel, I wish to discontinue against these poor policemen and let the case go to the jury only against the City of New York."

A substantial verdict was rendered for the plaintiff.

It is, in fact, by no means uncommon for a financially irresponsible defendant to be joined with a responsible codefendant. Counsel for the plaintiff, in such cases, faces a peculiar problem, even though he may have abundant evidence to prove the negligence of all the defendants. For there is always the possibility that the jury may find only against the defendant who is least able to pay.

Here is how one skillful trial lawyer handled this delicate situation. An uninsured woman brought suit against a bus company to recover for injuries she sustained when the automobile she was driving collided with one of its buses. At the same time, the bus passengers who were injured in the accident brought suit, in the same county, against both the bus company and the woman. This action came to trial first. The injured passengers all testified that both the bus driver and the woman had been negligent. The bus driver likewise blamed the woman. There were no other witnesses to the accident.

Thus, the woman's lone testimony was pitted against the overwhelming testimony of the passengers and the bus driver. Counsel for the passengers therefore feared that a verdict might be rendered against the uninsured woman, and not against the bus company. Accordingly, he decided on a bold move. In his summation, he told the jury he was so deeply impressed with the candor of the woman's testimony and her demeanor on the witness stand that, if he had known how honest she was, he would never have sued her.

The verdict was in favor of the plaintiffs against the bus company alone, and the woman was held to be not liable to either the company or the passengers.

If counsel represents the accused in a criminal case, he must, as we have seen, be especially cautious in phrasing his summation because the prosecutor speaks last. Unless he is effectively forestalled, he can do irreparable damage to the defense. However, even when laboring under this handicap, an astute advocate can, in his summation, turn the prosecutor's words to his own advantage. It was my practice, when I tried a criminal case, from the moment it began, to take copious notes of what the prosecutor, in his opening remarks, said he was going to prove. Depending on the facts and circumstances, I would order from the reporter a transcript of the prosecutor's opening statement. I would check every assertion he made against the evidence adduced at the trial. Significant words and phrases and any failure to provide the proof he promised would then constitute valuable material for a summation molded more or less according to the following pattern:

> When the District Attorney, in his opening statement, told you he would prove the defendant guilty of the crime of _____ [rape, burglary, robbery, forgery, arson, or whatever the charge], he, in effect, signed a promissory note to establish that all the elements constituting that crime were present in this case. The judge will later explain to you what these elements are. In the absence of such proof, the defendant must be acquitted.
>
> Now, when the District Attorney assured you that he would establish the defendant's guilt, he had to make good on that promise by presenting legal proof beyond a reasonable doubt. Let us, then, look at what he calls the evidence. Does it prove intent? No!

I would now raise as many legal doubts as possible on this score and stress the failure of the prosecution to adduce evidence to resolve these doubts. Then I would continue in the following vein:

> Now let us look at the element of corroboration [in a rape case, for example, where it is essential]. Did the District Attorney prove it? No!

(This failure too would be pointed out in detail.)

These are essential elements of the crime which the prosecution must establish, and which it has failed to establish. I respectfully submit that the District Attorney has failed to make good on his promissory note. Instead of honoring it by proving his case, as he said he would, he is in default. Like a bad check which bounces back with "Insufficient Funds" stamped across its face, his note should be stamped by you "Insufficient Evidence."

But this is not the only promissory note on which the District Attorney has defaulted in this trial.

I would then point to other deficiencies and shortcomings in the case presented against my client. Wherever necessary, I would read to the jury selected passages from the transcript. At all times I held the prosecutor strictly to the proof he promised to elicit. This kind of framework needs only to be filled in with supporting details drawn from the trial record to render a defense summation firmly resistant to virtually any attack that the prosecutor may subsequently make upon it.

Since the prosecution has the last word in a criminal case, it is very important for defense counsel to pay close attention to his adversary's summation. For even though it cannot be answered, it should be objected to if it contains prejudicial statements. If he refers to evidence not in the record or says anything else that is objectionable, defense counsel should promptly interrupt him, point out the offending passages to the Court and the jury, and move for the withdrawal of a juror and the declaration of a mistrial. The objection should be made in terms like the following:

The statements made by the prosecutor not only were prejudicial but also deprived the defendant of a fair and impartial trial, in violation of the "due process" clause of the Fourteenth Amendment of the United States Constitution.

In using this language, the defense will be raising a Federal constitutional question. This gives the defendant, after he has exhausted his remedies in the State courts, a possible chance to have his case adjudicated by the United States Supreme Court.

But the words of opposing counsel, whether spoken in opening to the jury or in summation, are not the only source of material for a lawyer's closing remarks. He may also find it necessary, as we have seen, to quote from the testimony of the witnesses, his own as well as those called by the other side.

For the purposes of summation, counsel may find it helpful to divide the testimony contained in the trial record into five possible categories.

First, there are statements of background detail or irrelevant trivialities that can be disregarded. Then, there is the evidence in support of counsel's case. Next, there is testimony that appears, on the surface, to be damaging to his client's position. There may also be some matter in the record that seems to give positive support to the other side, and some that clearly undermines it. To be sure, not all of these five categories may be represented to any significant extent in the testimony of every trial, and there may be a certain amount of overlapping, but it is still a good idea for counsel to keep them in mind in reviewing the record before summing up.

But first he must have the record to review. This means that he needs to take accurate, legible notes, at the counsel table, during the course of the trial, especially of testimony by adverse witnesses that appears to be damaging to his own case. For counsel can be sure that his adversary will call the jury's attention to such testimony in summation.

I always found it beneficial to take very full notes of adverse testimony. Being careful to write clearly, so that I could refer to my notations when necessary, I tried to get the actual language, and especially the key words, used by the witness. Of course, the fact that I had such extensive notes did not mean that, in summation, I spoke on every point included in them. It was my practice, before summing up, to analyze my notes and select for discussion only those that seemed likely to strengthen my case or weaken my adversary's.

Certainly testimony that appeared to be damaging to my client would not be ignored. If the witness who gave it enjoyed a good reputation, if he testified in a straightforward manner, and if he seemed to be honest in his recital of the facts as he recalled them, I felt that I could not afford to allow his testimony to stand without some appropriate comment. On occasion I would refer to it in this manner:

> I believe that this witness is a decent, honorable man. I do not think he would or did willfully try to relate to you any facts in contradiction of my client's testimony. I simply say to you that this witness' memory cannot possibly be so good as to enable him to recall in detail all the events which he related on the stand. He certainly has made an honest error.
>
> Let us look carefully into his testimony. The transaction about which he testified in such great detail took place over three years ago. Think of it! More than a thousand days and nights had come and gone from the time of the original transaction to the day he testified with such assurance and particularity about it! Now, we all know, from our own

experience in everyday life, the frailty of the human mind in this respect. We know how difficult it is to recall as minutely as did this
witness the details and circumstances of events and conversations
that took place even a few months or weeks ago.

Add to this the fact that the witness is not even a party to this
action, but only a bystander who happened to be present at the time
of the transaction. As he himself said, he is without any interest, one
way or the other, in the outcome of this case.

"Memory," said Ben Jonson, the great contemporary of Shakespeare,
"of all powers of the mind is the most delicate and frail." To see how
true this is, let me, for a moment, test your memory, members of the
jury. Do you sir, or do you, madam—and please do not answer me
except mentally—do you remember with whom you talked last week at
this time? Can you recall what the conversation was about? Can you
remember what you had for dinner two weeks ago, or what you and
your family discussed last Sunday at 3:30 P.M.?

"The memory of man," as an old Latin proverb says, "is apt to
slip." Surely the witness in this case, even with the best of intentions,
could not possibly have remembered accurately all those particulars
about an event which occurred, not last week or last month or even
last year, but more than three full years ago—a transaction, moreover,
at which he says he was present for about a half hour!

The fallibility of a witness' memory, as a matter of fact, makes a good
subject for discussion during summation, especially if opposing counsel
has sought to capitalize on relatively trifling discrepancies, slips, and
instances of inexactitude in the testimony of one's client and witnesses.
This is a common tactic, more generally used by counsel for the defendant in a negligence case. He will hammer away relentlessly, on cross-
examination, with an endless number of questions designed to test the
witnesses' recollection of exact distances, measurements, colors, words
used in conversations, and other insignificant minutiae. He will keep
pressing and pounding away at these trivialities until he catches the
witness in some small error or shows an inconsequential discrepancy
between the recollection of two or more witnesses.

I never objected to this line of questioning when I was trying cases.
Indeed, I only hoped that the judge would not lose patience with it
and order my adversary to bring his cross-examination on these points
to an end. Boring as such questions were, I was delighted to hear them.
In a case in which they constituted a particularly lengthy part of my
adversary's cross-examination, I made, in my summation, substantially
the following statement, by way of a humorous approach to a serious
problem:

After listening to my adversary's cross-examination, inquiring into such matters as exact sizes, shapes, dimensions, distances, colors, words, and other minute details which he considered so important, I felt very grateful to him. I learned something from him that will prove very useful to me in the future. I am going to send out notices to all my clients that before they get involved in any litigation, they should be fully equipped with a camera, a "walkie-talkie," a dictaphone machine, a tape recorder, measuring tape, and a colorimeter, as well as a thermometer, a scale, a pedometer, a barometer, and an anemometer. For how else could any witness ever satisfy my adversary and give him accurate answers to the kind of questions he propounds?

But even this equipment will not suffice. For it has been estimated that the average accident happens in a matter of seconds. It is all over in a flash. The fact is that it is humanly impossible, in that time, to observe with any degree of accuracy all the details he inquired about. And also consider, members of the jury, that the shock, the fright, and the pain which generally accompany any accident likewise militate against accuracy of observation at such a time. These emotional effects, to say nothing of others, make it extremely difficult for one who has undergone a traumatic experience to know the precise answers to the questions my adversary put to my client.

I read recently that a group of Air Force officers and enlisted men were asked to observe a moving vehicle for the purpose of estimating its speed. Their estimates ranged from ten miles to fifty miles an hour, although the car was actually going at twelve miles an hour. Now, I submit that it would be still more difficult to be accurate with respect to higher speeds. Why? Because the accuracy of observation under such conditions varies with the witness' age, vision, height, and many other factors.

I hope you will take these facts into account when you evaluate the answers given by my client and his witnesses to the questions asked by my adversary.

From time to time counsel may also have to explain to the jury conflicting versions of the facts as given in the testimony of his own witnesses even on direct examination. They may have differed among themselves as to what they observed or heard—the speed of a car as it traveled along the highway, the contents of an apartment, or the words of a conversation. Opposing counsel may be in a position to exploit these discrepancies by bringing them into such sharp focus in his summation as to convince the jury that the testimony is unreliable, biased, or untruthful.

I have encountered this situation and many others like it in both civil and criminal cases more times than I can remember. If I represented the accused in a criminal case, and I had to sum up first, I would face the issue squarely and bring it to the jury's attention at the earliest opportuntiy. There is nothing like beating one's opponent to the punch. The jury is impressed with the sincerity of an attorney who frankly faces the challenge presented by a conflict of testimony on the part of his own witnesses.

On the other hand, when I was trying a civil case and spoke last, I would usually take my cue from my adversary. If he failed to make capital of the discrepancies in the testimony on behalf of the plaintiff, I generally did not bother to discuss them either, depending upon their seriousness. But if my adversary seized upon them in his summation and sought to make an issue of them, I would reply along somewhat the following lines:

> Yes, members of the jury, there have been conflicts in the testimony of my witnesses. But this does not mean that they have not, to the best of their ability, told you the truth. Honest witnesses can and do differ. It is very unusual for two or more people to see or hear the same thing and give identical accounts of what they saw and heard, even shortly after the event, much less months or years later. Indeed, if all my witnesses had said exactly the same thing in regard to every point touched on in their testimony, if they had all given identical answers to the same questions, then I would be truly concerned and suspicious, and I know you would have every reason to be so too.
>
> I submit that the witnesses who have been so severely and unjustifiably attacked by my adversary were doing their level best to recall accurately what they had seen and heard. These witnesses are reliable and truthful.
>
> Now, gentlemen of the jury, just to show you what I mean, I'd like you to join me in a little experiment.

At this point I would pick up a legal folder from the counsel table and hold it up against my chest, completely covering my tie, and continue as follows:

> I've been before you all day, and I've been talking to you, face to face, for almost thirty minutes. How many of you, I wonder, can at this moment take the witness stand and swear to the color of my tie? After all, you've been looking at me standing in front of you for some time. You've had ample opportunity to make the observation.
>
> Please reflect on this point. I would like to suggest that when you get into the jury room, you poll each juror to see how many of you good, honest people knew the correct color of my tie. Just make a mental note now of what you say its color is as I stand before you covering it.
>
> And now, as I take the folder away, you can all observe that it's maroon. Gentlemen, if you make this simple test, you will better understand why honest men differ in describing what they observed. I am

sure my adversary will not argue that the members of this jury, whom he helped to select, are unreliable or dishonest just because they could not agree on their recollection of the color of my tie.

Members of the jury, this little demonstration is no trick on my part. It is a lesson in experimental psychology and invaluable to anyone interested in the administration of justice. This science teaches us how frail human memory is and how variable and uncertain our observation is likely to be. But such human weaknesses should not be equated with untruthfulness, bias, or falsification.

In this connection, I would suggest that every lawyer add to his library a volume entitled *On the Witness Stand* (Clark Boardman Co., Ltd., New York, N.Y.) by Hugo Munsterberg. I count myself indeed fortunate to have acquired a copy of this excellent book a short time after I was admitted to the bar. I have read it and reread it dozens of times and ascribe the success of many of my most effective summations to the fact that I related parts of it to jurors. Written almost sixty years ago, when the author was a professor of psychology at Harvard University, it is a collection of a series of magazine articles which he had previously published. I fully concur with the statement of former Governor Charles W. Whitman, in its Foreword, that ". . . they have lost none of their timeliness, interest, or helpfulness."

Two chapters of the book in particular bear upon the points I have been discussing—the fallibility of memory and the unreliability of observation. In a chapter entitled "The Memory of the Witness," the author describes his own experience as a witness in testifying about a burglary of his home that occurred one summer while he and his family were away at the seashore. The police caught the culprit with a part of the booty, and Professor Munsterberg was summoned to give an account of the discovery of the theft and missing articles when he returned home. Here is how he describes his testimony:

> I reported under oath that the burglars had entered through a cellar window, and then described what rooms they had visited. To prove, in answer to a direct question, that they had been there at night, I told that I had found drops of candle wax on the second floor. To show that they intended to return, I reported that they had left a large mantel clock, packed in wrapping paper, on the dining-room table. Finally, as to the amount of clothes which they had taken, I asserted that the burglars did not get more than a specified list which I had given the police.

Yet only a few days later he learned, to his surprise, that every one of these statements was wrong! Although he kept referring, in his statement under oath, to two burglars, he did not know, in fact, whether there was more than one. Moreover, entry had been made not through the window, but by breaking the lock of the cellar door. Nor had the clock been packed by the thief in wrapping paper, but in a tablecloth. And the candle droppings were found to be not on the second floor, but in the attic. Finally, the list of lost garments he gave the authorities was seven pieces short.

As a scientific psychologist, Professor Munsterberg was naturally curious to know how all these mistakes could have occurred. He eliminated at once the possibility that he suffered from a poor memory. During the previous eighteen years he had delivered about three thousand lectures without having needed even once to consult a single written or printed line or any notes while on the platform, nor had he needed to stop for so much as a moment to recall a name or to pull his thoughts together. Nor did he feel any prejudice against the defendant. Consequently, Professor Munsterberg was astonished to see how many illusions had made their way into his mind. His explanation is worth quoting:

> Of course, I had not made any careful examination of the house. I had rushed in from the seashore as soon as the police notified me, in the fear that valuable contents of the house might have been destroyed or plundered. When I saw that they had treated me mildly, inasmuch as they had started in the wine cellar and had forgotten under its genial influence, on the whole, what they had come for, I had taken only a superficial survey. That a clock was lying on the table, packed ready to be taken away, had impressed itself clearly on my memory; but that it was packed in a tablecloth had made evidently too slight an impression on my consciousness. My imagination gradually substituted the more usual method of packing with wrapping paper, and I was ready to take an oath on it until I went back later, at the end of the summer vacation. In the same way I got a vivid image of the candle droppings on the floor, but as, at the moment of perception, no interest was attached to the peculiar place where I saw them, I slowly substituted in my memory the second floor for the attic, knowing surely from strewn papers and other disorder that they had ransacked both places. As to the clothes, I had simply forgotten that I had put several suits in a remote wardrobe; only later did I find it empty.
>
> My other two blunders clearly arose under the influence of suggestion. The police and everyone about the house had always taken as a matter of course that the entrance was made by a cellar window, as it would have been much more difficult to use the locked doors. I had thus never examined the other hypothesis, and yet it was found later that they did succeed in removing the lock of a door. And finally, my

whole story under oath referred to two burglars, without any doubt at the moment. The fact is, they had caught the gentleman in question when he, a few days later, plundered another house. He then shot a policeman, but was arrested, and in his room they found a jacket with my name written in it by the tailor. That alone gave a hint that my house also had been entered; but from the first moment he had insisted that there had been two in this burglary, and that the other man had the remainder of the booty. The other has not been found, and he probably still wears my badges; but I never heard any doubt as to his existence, and thus, in mere imitation, I never doubted that there was a companion, in spite of the fact that every part of the performance might just as well have been carried out by one man alone; and, after all, it is not impossible that he should lie as well as shoot and steal.

Thus, in spite of his best intentions and an excellent memory, he had yielded to misleading suggestions, drawn erroneous conclusions, confused his perceptions, forgotten details, and been deluded by misconceptions. To be sure, in this case not one of his mistakes was of the slightest consequence. But the lesson he drew from this experience has a broad application:

My only consolation is the fact that in a thousand courts at a thousand places all over the world, witnesses every day affirm by oath in exactly the same way much worse mixtures of truth and untruth, combinations of memory and of illusion, of knowledge and of suggestion, of experience and wrong conclusions. . . . Every day errors creep into the work of justice through wrong evidence which has the outer marks of truth and trustworthiness. Of course, judge and jury and, later, the newspaper reader try their best to weigh the evidence. Not every sworn statement is accepted as absolute reality. Contradictions between witnesses are too familiar. But the instinctive doubt refers primarily to veracity. The public in the main suspects that the witness lies, while taking for granted that if he is normal and conscious of responsibility he may forget a thing, but it would not believe that he could remember the wrong thing. The confidence in the reliability of memory is so general that the suspicion of memory illusions evidently plays a small role in the mind of the juryman, and even the cross-examining lawyer is mostly dominated by the idea that a false statement is the product of intentional falsehood.

All this is a popular illusion against which modern psychology must seriously protest. Justice would less often miscarry if all who are to weigh evidence were more conscious of the treachery of human memory.

I think that the administration of justice would be enormously improved if only this wisdom could be imparted to every trial lawyer and every juror. Certainly, wherever appropriate, the point made by Professor Munsterberg should be included in counsel's summation.

Elsewhere in the same book, the author describes in detail an experiment performed in the classroom of a noted professor of criminology at the University of Berlin in order to study the exactitude of observation and recollection. Unknown to the rest of the class, three students, under the professor's direction, carefully rehearsed a little scene of violence, lasting less than a minute, which they later suddenly acted out before their astonished classmates in the midst of a lecture: a brief, heated exchange of words, a threat, the drawing of a revolver, an attempt to restrain the hothead, and, in the midst of a general uproar, the firing of the weapon.

After the professor had restored order and explained the purpose of the little drama he had written, he asked a part of the class to write at once an exact account of all that had occurred. Other students were to write their reports the next day or, in some cases, a week later. Still others were to give oral depositions under cross-examination.

The actual performance, consisting of both words and actions, was divided, for the purpose of the experiment, into fourteen parts. Any deviation from these—whether an alteration or addition or omission —in a student's report was counted as a mistake. The results proved to be most instructive. In regard to the words spoken during the incident, even the most accurate report was twenty-six per cent mistaken, with the poorest account running as high as eighty per cent in error.

> The reports with reference to the second half of the performance, which was more strongly emotional, gave an average of fifteen per cent more mistakes than those of the first half. Words were put into the mouths of men who had been silent spectators during the whole short episode; actions were attributed to the chief participants of which not the slightest trace existed; and essential parts of the tragicomedy were completely eliminated from the memory of a number of witnesses.

A series of similar tests later performed elsewhere in an effort to improve the conditions essentially substantiated the findings of the first experiment. Professor Munsterberg describes in particular one that took place in Göttingen at a meeting of jurists, psychologists, and physicians —"all, therefore, men well trained in careful observation."

> Somewhere in the same street there was that evening a public festivity of the carnival. Suddenly, in the midst of the scholarly meeting, the doors open, a clown in highly colored costume rushes in in mad excitement, and a Negro with a revolver in hand follows him. In the middle of the hall first the one, then the other, shouts wild phrases; then the

one falls to the ground, the other jumps on him; then a shot, and suddenly both are out of the room.

The whole affair took less than twenty seconds. All were completely taken by surprise, and no one, with the exception of the president, had the slightest idea that every word and action had been rehearsed beforehand, or that photographs had been taken of the scene. It seemed most natural that the president should beg the members to write down individually an exact report, inasmuch as he felt sure that the matter would come before the courts.

Of the forty reports handed in, there was only one whose omissions were calculated as amounting to less than twenty per cent . . . ; fourteen had twenty to forty per cent of the facts omitted; twelve omitted forty to fifty per cent, and thirteen still more than fifty per cent. But besides the omissions there were only six among the forty which did not contain positively wrong statements; in twenty-four papers up to ten per cent of the statements were free inventions, and in ten answers—that is, in one-fourth of the papers—more than ten per cent of the statements were absolutely false, in spite of the fact that they all came from scientifically trained observers. Only four persons, for instance, among forty, noticed that the Negro had nothing on his head; the others gave him a derby or a high hat, and so on. In addition to this, a red suit, a brown one, a striped one, a coffee-colored jacket, shirt sleeves, and similar costumes were invented for him. He wore in reality white trousers and a black jacket with a large red necktie.

The scientific commission which reported the details of the inquiry came to the general conclusion that the majority of the observers omitted or falsified about half of the processes which occurred completely in their field of vision. As was to be expected, the judgment as to the time duration of the act varied between a few seconds and several minutes.

I hope I have quoted enough from this fascinating and informative book to whet the reader's appetite for more, and to stimulate him to dip into its pages. He will find its perusal a richly rewarding experience.

On the other hand, apparent lapses of memory on the part of an adverse witness under cross-examination can be dealt with quite differently in summation, especially if the same witness seemed to have a good memory about the identical incident in giving direct testimony. Counsel may notice that a key witness for the other side answered questions on direct examination quickly, with hardly a moment's pause for reflection, but that on cross-examination he hesitated, dawdled, and frequently looked to opposing counsel for some guidance or clue before replying. Often his only answer, on cross-examination, was "I don't remember" or "I can't say for sure."

Of course, such a disparity should be called to the attention of the jury in summation. But counsel should not content himself with a relatively meaningless general statement to the effect that the witness was quick to answer questions on direct examination but hesitant on cross-examination. To achieve maximum effect, it is a good idea to obtain a transcript of the questions put to the witness and his answers and to read this to the jury. As counsel does so, he can interject remarks like, "You recall how this witness rapped out staccato answers without a moment's pause for thought, as if he had them ready on the tip of his tongue, when he was questioned on direct examination." Then, after reading to the jury a number of questions put to the witness on cross-examination, counsel can show how in each instance the witness hesitated, equivocated, or fell back on "I don't remember" and "I can't recall." By thus specifically illustrating the contrast between the witness' keen memory on direct examination and his shilly-shallying or lack of memory on cross-examination, counsel will be able to expose him as a person unworthy of belief.

Listening attentively to an adverse witness' direct testimony can also sometimes supply defense counsel with valuable material for his closing remarks. In a negligence case that I tried some years ago, a single sentence uttered by a witness for the other side in giving his direct testimony provided me with a lead for my summation. The plaintiff, whom I was representing, had been seriously injured in a collision between his car and that of the defendant. My client had entered, by a side road, a State highway along which the defendant was driving. The only eyewitness, a truck driver who was proceeding on the opposite side of the road, was called by the defendant. Neither this witness' name nor that of any other witness was entered on the police blotter.

On direct examination, this witness placed the blame directly on the plaintiff. He alleged, among other things, that he was driving his truck, with his helper sitting beside him in the front, when the accident happened.

While he was testifying, I looked around the courtroom to see whether the helper was present. Only the parties were in court. But, of course, the helper might have been waiting in the corridor. I hastily dispatched my assistant to take a quick look. He returned and reported that he saw no one outside.

On cross-examination I tried to show how difficult it would have been for the witness to see what happened from his position on the opposite side of the road. Would not the wide island separating the northbound and southbound traffic lanes and the distance between the witness and the scene of the accident have made it hard for him to see clearly what was going on, especially as he had to give attention to his own driving? Were not the lighting conditions of the road too poor for him to make an accurate observation under these circumstances?

However, this line of inquiry met with little success. He was a stalwart witness.

Since his name was not listed on the police blotter, I tried another tack:

Q. Did you give your name and address to the police?
A. No, I left before the police arrived. I was on my way to a railroad station to deliver perishable food to a freight train, and I didn't have enough time to wait around, so I jumped off the truck, wrote my name and address and my helper's name and address on a piece of paper, and gave it to the defendant.

At this point I realized that I was making no progress, since he was an excellent witness, and I dropped him. I did not ask him, "Is the helper in court? Why not?" I had no idea what his answer would be, and I quickly decided that if the helper did not testify, I would use this circumstance, if not satisfactorily explained, in my summation.

The helper was not called, nor was any reason given for his absence. This is substantially what I said in summation:

Members of the jury, with respect to the only alleged eyewitness called, the truck driver, I hope you noticed that I asked very few questions of him. Why? Because I doubted that he could possibly have seen what happened before the impact. He was busy driving his truck. He had to keep his eyes on his side of the road. At least thirty-five feet separated him from the cars that were involved in the accident. The lighting conditions were certainly not good enough for him to have had a clear view of the other lane. I was expecting the helper to testify, since the witness said—and I quote directly from his testimony—"I was driving my truck, and my helper was sitting next to me in front." You will also recall that he said he gave his helper's name and address to the defendant.

Members of the jury, I was prepared to conduct a vigorous cross-examination of the helper when he took the stand. To have done so with the driver would have put me in the position of letting the helper know in advance my line of inquiry and would have given him a chance to prepare for it. But the helper, as you know, was not called. And I think I know why, and I hope you will consider the reason in your deliberations. The helper was, of course, in a much better position to observe the accident than the driver. May I suggest that when you go into the jury room you try to figure out why the helper was not called to testify. The defendant's counsel is too shrewd not to have called him if my adversary thought the testimony of the helper could possibly strengthen the defense. Members of the jury, keep this important point in mind during your deliberations.

I am sure that the Court will charge you on the significance to be attached to the failure of a party to call a witness available to him, and I am further confident that you will follow the judge's charge in this respect. If you do, you will just have to discount what the truck driver said and discredit his testimony.

I believe this statement to the jury cast doubt on the witness' testimony, because the verdict was for the plaintiff.

After the trial, I asked the defendant's attorney why the helper had not been called.

"He was asleep when it happened," defense counsel explained.

Had the truck driver mentioned this fact in his direct testimony, the outcome might have been entirely different. Similarly, if I had asked the truck driver, on cross-examination, "Why isn't the helper here to testify?" and he had explained the reason, I would, in effect, have deprived myself of an opportunity to win the case on summation.

The value of listening closely to an adverse witness' testimony is likewise illustrated by an incident that occurred in a trial held before me some years ago. The plaintiff's "ace in the hole" was a witness who testified that he had never seen the plaintiff, Robert Reed, before or since the accident and did not know him. Defense counsel noted, however, that, in answering one question, the witness referred to the plaintiff not as Mr. Reed or as Robert Reed, but as "Bob" and then later as "Bobby."

In his summation, the defendant's lawyer pointed these references out to the jury, even though they were isolated remarks.

Ladies and gentlemen of the jury, you saw and heard the plaintiff's witness tell you that he did not know the plaintiff, that he had never seen the plaintiff before the accident, that he lived in the same neighborhood as the plaintiff, but that he never knew the plaintiff's name until he heard it in Court the other day. Yet you heard this same witness, on the stand, distinctly, audibly, voluntarily, and unhesitatingly refer to the plaintiff, not as Mr. Reed or Robert Reed, but as "Bob" and "Bobby." Now I ask you to use your good common sense and your experience in life, and tell me whether you ladies and gentlemen really believe that the witness did not know the plaintiff before the accident. I know what I think about that, and I am hopeful you will arrive at the same conclusion.

Another source of material for summation, and one that is often overlooked even by experienced trial lawyers, is to be found in the questions asked by the judge. If any of these are helpful to counsel's case, he should be sure to keep a record of them and of the answers they elicited. Indeed, it is a good idea to have the reporter immediately transcribe them. If they can possibly be used in summation, they carry much weight. The jury is very likely to be impressed if counsel says something like this:

> I think the most important questions asked during this trial were those put by the learned Court when he interrogated Mr. X—and I quote from the record: . . .

After reading the questions and answers, counsel can proceed along lines like the following:

> Members of the jury, I wanted the verbatim questions and answers, so I had the reporter transcribe them for me. The learned judge certainly highlighted the real issue in this case and put his finger on the true situation as it existed at the time of the controversy. In the light of these questions and answers, I am confident that you will be guided to a verdict in favor of my client.

These are but a few examples of the way in which a resourceful lawyer can find in the words of the trial record itself a veritable arsenal of weapons and ammunition for use in his final skirmish with his adversary. Among them, as we have seen, may very well be all that he needs to assure ultimate victory. Of course, in the actual trial, the very echo of these words quoted from the transcript, as they are heard by the jury in counsel's summation, after having been heard earlier when they were originally spoken by opposing counsel, witnesses, or the judge, has a psychological effect which it is impossible to reproduce in cold print. It is for this reason that I have so often stressed the desirability of young lawyers visiting our courts of law and observing our leading advocates in action in order to appreciate fully the effectiveness of the techniques I have described. There is much to be learned from watching a master at work. As the nearest approximation to firsthand experiences of this kind, I now invite the reader to accompany me, as before, on an imaginary round of such visits, this time to observe how the experts suit the words of their summation to the action they are trying.

23

"All's Well That Ends Well"

No matter how weak a case may appear up to the point at which counsel begins his summation, he still has one last chance of salvaging it if he can only find the right words for his closing remarks to the jury. Since his object in pleading his cause is to win a favorable verdict for his client, a summation that succeeds in doing so is all that is needed to cancel out the effect of a whole series of blunders and lapses in the earlier part of the trial. The idea, then, that should animate an advocate as he rises to address the jury for the last time is to end well, however poorly he may have begun. If a miss is as good as a mile, then, by the same token, a hit on the bull's-eye with the last bullet is as good as a whole fusillade landing right on target. In any case, the battle is not over until the last shot has been fired.

Yet, as we have observed, the summation is not an altogether independent element of the trial. Whether it makes use of the words of one's adversary, of the witnesses, or of the judge, or whether it weaves all three strands into its fabric, it must bear a close relation to what preceded it. For this reason, if we come to court as observers, just to hear and evaluate counsel's closing remarks, without a knowledge of the opening statements, testimony, objections, and exhibits to which they refer, we may find it difficult to judge their adequacy or even to understand them at all. Ideally, the words of each summation ought to be so well suited to the particular action of which it is a part as to be virtually inseparable from it. This fact must be kept in mind as we watch and comment on lawyers at work in closing to the jury.

Let us begin with an ordinary negligence case in which defense counsel realizes that on the question of liability his client's position is extremely weak. The situation is a common one. After reviewing the defendant's version of the facts and summarizing the evidence in support of it, he says the following:

> I would also like to explain to you why I now propose to discuss the plaintiff's claim for damages. I want you to understand that my doing

so does not mean that I believe that the plaintiff is entitled to the compensation he seeks. I do not concede that point to him. I discuss this question, however, solely as a guide to you in case you should conclude that my client is obliged to pay damages. I am sure that the Court will instruct you not to consider the question of damages in your deliberations if you should find that, as my client contends, there is no liability on his part.

Nor do we need any special knowledge of what went on earlier in the trial in order to appreciate the appropriateness of the following remarks, included in the summation of a lawyer representing the accused in a criminal action, to which we next turn our attention:

> This is the last opportunity I shall have to speak to you. Since the prosecution has the burden of proving the defendant guilty beyond a reasonable doubt, as I am confident the Court will instruct you, the rules governing a criminal trial give the prosecutor the privilege of opening and closing the case. Therefore, when I am finished with my remarks, I shall not be permitted to reply to anything that my learned adversary may say or ask in his speech. The reason for the rule, you see, is that a trial must come to an end. And, of course, this rule must be obeyed.

Somewhere along the line some such remarks should likewise be included, with appropriate modifications, in the summation of defense counsel in a civil action. In this type of trial, of course, the plaintiff has the burden of proving his case by "a fair preponderance of the credible evidence."

It may also be instructive for us to observe how, in trying a negligence case for the plaintiff, I dealt in summation with the adverse testimony of a doctor called on behalf of the defendant. Here too, only a minimum of background information, clearly inferable from the text of the summation itself, is needed to appreciate the technique employed. This is the way I handled the situation:

> Let me now address myself to the testimony given by Dr. X on behalf of the defendant. I only wish that the doctor had been more candid and cooperative in supplying you with the information I sought to bring to your attention when I cross-examined him. Undoubtedly Dr. X is a very busy man. He must be, since he has testified that he runs around from one law office to another examining many claimants every day. Yes, I said "law offices," not hospitals or homes of the sick. If he calls that practicing medicine, that's his privilege. I dare say that on the day he examined my client, he had a number of similar examinations to make. Unfortunately, as you heard, he wasn't very precise about just how many claimants he did examine on that particular day.

If he had produced his appointment book, I could have proved to you how short a time he was able to devote to my client. But from the doctor's testimony under cross-examination you could see, I am sure, that he had so many appointments bunched together on that day that he could not possibly have devoted more than a few minutes to examining the plaintiff. At most, his examination was a cursory and superficial one—far too hasty to be worth anything at all.

There is another fact, too, about the doctor that I think you might find it advisable to take into consideration when you evaluate his testimony. You noticed that he admitted being a neurologist. Yet the claimed injuries in this case involve orthopedics. Why was not an orthopedist sent to examine the plaintiff? This is a question that I am confident you will want to ask yourselves and discuss during your deliberations.

Here we may pause for a moment to note that I made my point by suggesting, rather than demanding, that the jury take account of the significant facts brought out in my summation. Naturally, if the doctor had testified that he was a general practitioner or a specialist in any branch of medicine other than orthopedics, I could have made the same point with appropriate modifications of language.

Here is how I continued:

Please bear in mind, also, that the doctor made this cursory and superficial examination without benefit of the hospital record. You heard him admit that on cross-examination. He never took the trouble to look at the hospital record of the plaintiff, although he could easily have done so. Now, members of the jury, would you call this doctor's examination thorough? Ask yourselves, how can any doctor possibly make a proper and intelligent examination without looking at the hospital charts? They reveal so much. They are, in fact, necessary for a full and adequate diagnosis. Is this the way medicine is practiced today? Suppose a lawyer neglected to examine all the papers and records pertaining to a client's lawsuit. What would you think of such a lawyer? In your business, what would you think of a job that was only half-done?

Of course, if the doctor had testified that he saw the hospital records a few minutes before he took the stand or when he came to court on the day he testified, but not at the time he made his physical examination of the plaintiff, I could still have argued along these lines, since the diagnosis was made *before* the hospital record was reviewed and without benefit of the information it contained.

But let us see how this summation continued:

Let me now point out a number of other problems I suggest you consider.

You will recall that the doctor testified that he found no evidence of pain or injury. The plaintiff's complaints, as he put it, were subjective. Yet you will also recall that the doctor admitted under cross-examination that a person may have pain without any objective evidence of it. To put the matter quite bluntly, what the doctor wanted you to believe was that my client really had no injuries. Well, if the plaintiff is feigning or imagining or exaggerating his injuries, why didn't the doctor indicate this on his report and say in so many words, "This patient is a malingerer"? Please take with you into the jury room the record he produced and look it over carefully. See whether any such statement is in it.

One more suggestion, and then I'll turn to some other phase of the case. It was not until I prodded and pressed him that the doctor finally admitted what percentage of his entire practice consists of cases like this. You heard him say that between fifteen and twenty per cent of his time is devoted to making examinations of this kind and testifying in court. He has evidently been making a career—or a good part of his career—out of running around to law offices and courtrooms, hastening from an examination to the witness stand and then rushing off to another examination, all in the course of a busy day's work.

Now, you can place this witness in any category you wish. In considering the weight to be given to his testimony, and even its credibility, ask yourselves whether he told you everything. Has he hired himself out as a biased witness? I am confident that if you weigh his testimony carefully, you will realize that this doctor earns close to forty per cent of his income as an itinerant physician and witness, and not really as a practicing physician like your doctor or mine, and is more interested in helping defendants and their lawyers than in shedding light on the real nature of the injury in this case. As I see it, his objective is to be able, if the defense prevails, to say to the lawyer who hired him: "I'm sure the jury held for the defendant because of my testimony. I trust you will hire me again."

In this summation, as we can see, inference plays an important role, as it does in many others. I recall hearing an excellent lawyer in my court recently conclude his summation in a death action with a particularly memorable and striking appeal to the jury's ability to draw the appropriate inferences from the evidence:

The deceased had her tragic rendezvous with death at the intersection of these streets. As a result of the defendant's carelessness and negligence, death laid its icy fingers on her brow and reft her brusquely from her family and loved ones.

We have had a silent witness here. I refer to the skid marks left by the tires of the defendant's automobile. They show clearly that he failed to operate his vehicle under proper control. As jurors, you must look for every thread of evidence. In these telltale skid marks you see a thread of the truth. They are your clue to where the truth lies in this case. They are mute but incontestable evidence whose hallmark is truth.

Sometimes counsel may have to try a case which depends entirely on inference. In other words, his proof, if it could be adduced, could be established only in the way we see it presented on television, namely, by the confession of a suddenly conscience-stricken adverse party or witness. Yet even under such apparently unfavorable conditions, it may be possible for a lawyer, in his summation, to marshal the circumstantial evidence so convincingly as to leave the jurors with no logical alternative but to draw the necessary inference from the facts presented. But, of course, he must have planned his whole strategy, including his direct examination and his cross-examination, with this in mind.

I once defended a woman in a divorce proceeding brought against her by her husband. A jury of twelve men had before it specifically only one issue: Did the defendant commit adultery in her apartment on a certain date? The contrast in the appearance of the litigants could not have been more striking. The plaintiff was a tall, handsome, dapper man. My client, on the contrary . . . well, let's just say in regard to her endowments that she left much to be desired.

The plaintiff's case was simple. When he and his witnesses broke into the defendant's apartment, they found her lying in bed with a man snugly ensconced in her embrace. The defense was that the corespondent had taken the defendant to a Chinese restaurant, where he put "certain drops" into her tea. The drops, she said, made her drowsy. The last thing she said she remembered at the restaurant was asking the gentleman to take her home, and the next thing after that which she could recall was being awakened by the breaking down of the door to her apartment and, to her surprise, finding a man in bed with her.

The defendant told me that after the plaintiff had become affluent, he separated from her, asked her for a divorce, and admitted to her that he had fallen in love with his secretary, whom she described as "young and beautiful."

I had him followed by an investigator, who reported that over a period of several weeks he had seen the plaintiff and his secretary on two or three occasions have dinner together after 6 P.M. at various restaurants. On each occasion they spent about two hours in the restaurant, after which the secretary would hail a cab and go to her home, while the plaintiff would get into his car and drive to his own apartment.

On cross-examination, the plaintiff readily admitted taking his secretary to dinner. He explained that she was bringing him up to date on matters pertaining to his business. Thus, I had no evidence to substantiate my client's contention that her husband was in love with his secretary and had "framed" the defendant on the night of her alleged adultery.

Of course, the secretary did not appear at the trial. However, when I was ready to proceed with my defense, I subpoenaed her and called her as a witness immediately after my client had left the stand. All I asked the young lady, after she gave her name, address, and occupation, was whether she had had dinner with the plaintiff on each of several occasions that I enumerated. When she admitted that she had, I excused her.

My summation concluded in somewhat the following fashion:

Gentlemen of the jury, the defendant contends that she was the victim of a "frame-up" contrived by her husband with the purpose of incriminating her on false evidence so that he could be free to marry his secretary. I realize how difficult it is to prove this kind of defense. Yet I hope you will take it seriously in the light of the circumstances that have come to your attention in this trial. In a case like this we just cannot get confessions or admissions, either from the principal or the other parties to the conspiracy. I am no district attorney, and I have no means of uncovering the maneuverings of the plaintiff before he instituted this action. Whatever he and others did will remain a secret which they will no doubt take with them to their graves.

But you must use your good common sense and figure things out for yourselves. Here is a man who has become affluent. Surrounded by wealthy and influential people in his huge and growing business, and accustomed to being catered to by everybody, he finds that his wife has not kept up with him. You observed her in court and had a chance to watch her closely on the witness stand when she testified. I am sorry to have to say this in her presence, but it is the truth, and there's no getting away from it. The fact is, as you can see for yourselves, she is quite homely. She is short and very ugly and certainly adds nothing to her husband's prestige in the circles in which he now moves.

In the early days of his career, when he was still on the way up, before he became well-to-do and rubbed shoulders with the wealthy, he would go home to his wife every night after work. Now he must entertain at night and be out with his customers, buyers, and associates practically every evening. In his newly acquired status as a tycoon, he just cannot take this graceless, inelegant, and ugly wife of his along with him. He is now fed up with her and would like nothing better than to be rid of her.

But, though he has rejected her, she still loves him and has refused to give him up. She wants to maintain their home and keep the family together. She wants her child to have a father.

Now, you remember seeing the secretary in court. I am sure you will agree with me that she is an exquisitely beautiful young lady—the kind of woman a man would be proud to be seen with in any company. Do you believe that the plaintiff and she have dinner from time to time only to discuss his business or rather to discuss their "mutual business"? Is it something new that a man, after some years, tires of his wife— whether beautiful or ugly—and wants to discard her for another woman, younger and more desirable? Men have committed the most heinous crimes to rid themselves of unwanted wives. You know that. Both litera- ture and law abound in such cases. Is it completely beyond the pale of reason that this rich businessman would, in order to rid himself of his wife, instigate or conspire to perpetrate an offense against her of the kind you heard described here in her testimony? Think about it! I am confident that you will not, by your verdict, help this plaintiff in his nefarious scheme. I am sure you will not allow him to emblazon on the guiltless heart of the defendant the infamous word "adulter- ess" and bring shame and misery to their innocent daughter, who still has her whole life before her.

This summation, of course, formed part of a total plan, of which my cross-examination of the secretary was an essential part. I deliberately asked her only a few harmless questions and did not directly accuse her of being the plaintiff's mistress. I did not abuse her. My chief purpose in calling her to the stand was to enable the jury to get a good look at her and to form in their minds an indelible picture of a ravishingly beautiful creature. I hoped that when they retired to the jury room, they would keep this lovely vision of her before them and compare it with that of the unattractive witness who preceded her.

Some trial lawyers acquire the reputation of putting on a show for the jury every time they sum up a case. After a while word gets around that a new performance is about to begin, and, as counsel starts his summation, the courtroom soon fills with curious spectators and col- leagues who have come to be entertained. These lawyers have no hesita- tion in making a spectacle of themselves, too often at the expense of their clients.

Let us join the throng in observing one advocate in particular who is rather proud of his forensic ability. Today he is supremely confident. This time, he indicates, he has something really special to present by way of summation. Somewhere, it seems, he read that it is a good idea, in closing to the jury, to use as one's text some famous quotation, preferably one that the jurors can see inscribed on the walls of the courtroom. He has decided to try this new idea, but he has gone even further. He has taken the trouble to do some research on the source of the quotation and proposes to make use of his findings in his address to the jury.

Here, then, is the way he begins:

> Gentlemen of the jury, I shall take as my text, in my closing remarks, the inspiring words you see inscribed on the wall of this courtroom behind the judge's bench. They read, "GREAT IS TRUTH, AND MIGHTY ABOVE ALL THINGS—ESDRAS."
>
> "Esdras," the Greek form of the name Ezra, is the title given to a collection of three ancient books, of which two have become part of the Bible as we know it today. The third, which forms a part of the Apocrypha, included in the Bible of the early Church, tells the delightful story of a public contest of wit and wisdom at the court of Darius, King of Persia, among three young soldiers of his bodyguard.

At this point counsel proceeds to narrate, in the exact words of the English translation, the full story from the Apocrypha, a lengthy narrative replete with circumstantial details and diffuse speeches. It may be summarized thus:

Three young members of Darius' bodyguard competed to see which one of them could best defend his choice of what he deemed the strongest thing in the world. The first, who declared that wine is the strongest, defended his assertion before the King and the assembled courtiers with a lengthy harangue celebrating the power of wine over men of all classes, including the King. The second, not to be outdone, launched into an equally wordy oration in defense of the thesis that the King is strongest, citing many instances of the King's power over armies and peoples. The third, who talked of the strength of women and of truth, first discoursed at great length on the power of women over men, including the King himself, but concluded with an eloquent and extended paean of praise to truth, the mightiest of all powers, above wine, women, and kings, enduring for ever and ever: "To her belong power and the royal dignity and authority and majesty in all the ages. Blessed be the God of truth!"

The story ends with the people shouting: "GREAT IS TRUTH AND MIGHTY ABOVE ALL THINGS. TRUTH IS GREAT AND SUPREMELY STRONG."

After narrating this tale in full to the jury, counsel proceeds as follows:

I feel supremely confident and strong in the belief that you, gentlemen of the jury, like the people who shouted the words you see inscribed on that wall, will take those words with you into the jury room and search for the truth—the mightiest of all things on earth—in this case.

This protracted introduction was presumably intended as the part of the summation which the jury was supposed to admire. It is typical of a certain type of courtroom oratory that is not much in fashion nowadays. What do we think of it?

Certainly the story held the jurors' interest. Apparently they had never heard it before, and they were enthralled as much by the language in which it was narrated as by the charm of the tale itself. Counsel did a good job of presenting it. But to what end? One speaks of the tail wagging the dog, but here it would seem more appropriate to say that the preamble swallowed up the text. Fascinating though it was, it usurped the rightful place to be accorded to a discussion of the substantive issues of the case, and its disproportionate length left little time for attention to the real problem facing the jury, namely, that of separating truth from falsehood. It was most successful as a diversion, in both senses of the word; that is, as a form of entertainment and as a distraction from the serious business at hand. Indeed, after such a lofty prologue, anything counsel may say about such mundane matters as the facts or the testimony or the evidence must seem like an anticlimax.

Moreover, counsel could not hope to match, in the later parts of his summation, the language and tone of this story, which he apparently memorized and delivered word for word as it is found in some translation of the Apocrypha. A remarkable feat, to be sure, all the more so as counsel never faltered in his delivery. As an actor, he no doubt rates high. But it is questionable whether he used good judgment as a trial lawyer. For how could he be sure that none of the jurors was familiar with the story? What if one or more of them already knew it? It is difficult to say what their reaction might have been to this long recital of a well-known tale. Perhaps it would be one of pleasure at hearing it again in the words of the text. But we cannot be sure of this, and for that very reason, I think, it is risky for a lawyer to embark on such a pretentious excursion.

Of course, I realize that this is a question of taste on which reasonable men might disagree. Yet it seems to me that the very possibility of a disagreement, of diverse reactions among the members of the jury, depending on their background and degree of sophistication, makes any such venture dangerous. I believe counsel would have done better either to have confined himself exclusively to the quotation, applying it directly to the circumstances of the case, or to have told the story briefly, in his own words, and in summary fashion.

To be sure, an effective summation need not consist only of words. If, in his closing remarks, counsel can show the jury, by some visual demonstration, that a witness' testimony is or is not worthy of belief, he will be presenting one of the most convincing of possible arguments. Juries like to see concrete evidence, in the form of a photograph, a document, or an actual object, corroborating or discrediting a witness' word, and they will respond quickly in favor of any lawyer who can give them something they can see and feel to support his case.

In order to serve their purpose in summation, visual aids do not have to be elaborate. In fact, complex charts, diagrams, tables, or models that require extensive explanation on counsel's part sometimes do more harm than good, because they may confuse or distract the jurors. Often all that is needed is a quite simple demonstration, such as was used by counsel for the defendant, a pastry cook who was accused of stabbing his employer with a paring knife during a heated argument in the kitchen over the apples to be used in apple pies. The complainant's brother brought the knife to court as evidence. On cross-examination he testified that he had obtained it "by fishing it out of the water from the back window of the restaurant," which, specializing in sea food, looked out on the waters of a bay.

Q. How did you do the fishing?
A. With a fish net that had a long handle, right from the window.
Q. Where was the knife?
A. It was lying at the bottom of the bay. I fished it up into the net.

During his summation, defense counsel asked for a bucket of water, and, as the jury watched, threw the knife into it. Since the handle, which made up half its length, was of wood, the knife floated.

The defendant was acquitted.

However, a lawyer must be careful not to take any unnecessary chances in making demonstrations of this kind. Unless he is positive that he knows exactly what he is doing, from having experimented in advance with the object involved, he runs the risk of sabotaging his whole case. This happened recently in an action brought against the City of New York on behalf of a child injured allegedly while using a swing in one of the City's parks. The contention of the plaintiff was that while the child was sitting on the swing, its chainlike support broke as the swing started to move, and the child, in being thrown to the ground, broke her arm.

During the trial the Corporation Counsel had a Park Department swing brought to court, and the child identified it as of the type she had been using at the time of the accident. The swing was accordingly received in evidence. It was the contention of the City that the supports had not broken and, indeed, were so constructed that this was an impossibility. The defense further maintained that the child must have been standing on the swing, lost her balance, and fallen off.

In the course of his summation, the Corporation Counsel placed great emphasis on these points. As he concluded his remarks, he picked up the swing and asked the jurors to take it into the jury room with them and inspect it closely. In fact, he said, with rising vehemence, "I don't care if you bang it on the floor, like this." With that, he suited his action to his words and forcefully threw the swing to the floor. It shattered.

Short of sitting through an entire trial and listening to every word spoken by each side, we may best appreciate the fine points of the art of summation by a careful perusal of this part of the trial record in a case in which it played a crucial role. Since, as we have seen, a summation necessarily makes reference to what preceded it, we may also have to familiarize ourselves with other pertinent parts of the transcript. In this way, we can see just how the techniques I have discussed are actually employed. Let us, therefore, take a case in point—a murder trial in which I represented the defendant—and see what we can learn from a study of the full text of my closing remarks to the jury.

24

A Case in Point

As is customary in a criminal action, the prosecutor, after the jury had been duly empaneled, selected, and sworn, presented in his opening remarks the People's case against the accused. Following my usual practice, I listened attentively and took careful note, as he spoke, of the chief points he proposed to prove. Later I underlined them in my copy of the transcript I received from the reporter. Each of the italicized expressions in the following slightly abridged and modified copy of the prosecutor's opening statement represents a commitment to the jury that he was bound to honor, and I was determined to hold him strictly to his word in every instance.

(Prosecutor's Opening for the People)

If the Court pleases, Mr. Foreman, and gentlemen of the jury, as I have said to you in my brief examination to qualify you as jurors, the Grand Jury of this county has indicted the defendant, Samuel Lang, for the crime of murder in the first degree, charging that on or about April 2, 1945, in the County of Kings, he *willfully* and feloniously and *with malice aforethought* stabbed and killed Ronald L. Green with a knife.

The State will show that on April 2, 1945, Ronald Green, in company with a man named Benson and two young ladies, had visited at Marcy Avenue here in this county, and that about eleven o'clock had taken the Gates Avenue bus on Fulton Street and Gates Avenue to proceed toward Borough Hall. These two *couples*, while seated in the bus as passengers, heard a girl remonstrate with this defendant and ask him to leave her alone. *She said he was annoying her and asked the passengers in the bus to help her.*

Ronald L. Green asked the defendant to please desist from annoying this young lady. When he was thus spoken to, the defendant took affront and objected. *He said he was not annoying the young lady.* However, after they had proceeded for a period of fifteen minutes or thereabouts, this defendant, *chafing, as it were, under a bit,* considered it an insult on the part of Ronald L. Green, and when the bus reached the corner of Rockwell Place, along Fulton Street, where

Bickford's restaurant is, and as he went out there, *he invited Ronald L. Green to come out there, and he used these words, "I will fix you."* Well, *Ronald L. Green and his friends were getting off at that place anyhow*, and, as he got off, this defendant did fix him. This is what we intend to prove.

This defendant is an ambidextrous fellow. In one arm he carried a package containing some goods manufactured in the place where he is employed, and *with his left hand he struck with a big knife at the throat of Ronald L. Green*, severing an artery, and then Ronald L. Green literally bled to death. His blood was all over Fulton Street. He never regained consciousness from the moment that he was struck in the throat. He was removed to the Cumberland Hospital and died there on the operating table about eleven-fifty o'clock.

The State is going to prove to you that immediately after the defendant struck the deceased, he proceeded towards Borough Hall, to the corner of Hudson Avenue, turned left, along Flatbush Avenue, and *started to run, pursued by Benson*, the male friend and companion in this party, at a fast clip. There was a patrolman on Flatbush Avenue and Livingston Street, and when Benson called the attention of the police officer to the reason for this man's flight, the *policeman pursued him*. The defendant then ran another block, along Flatbush Avenue, until he came to the corner of Third Avenue, Schermerhorn Street, and Flatbush Avenue. Then he turned right down Schermerhorn Street and threw the knife, still covered with blood, behind a car, and also threw away the package, likewise covered with blood. He ran down to the right until he came to Nevins Street. Then he turned left again, and when he got to the corner, he was still in sight of the policeman, who, with his pistol drawn, did not dare to shoot because of the traffic there. There was also a policeman standing at the corner, and the two of them never lost sight of the defendant as he was running.

The defendant then ran right on Nevins Street and was cornered by these two policemen in the middle of the block between Nevins and Bond Streets. He was then brought back to the scene, where he was identified by Benson and his two *lady* companions.

The police then brought the defendant to the Cumberland Hospital, where Ronald L. Green had already died, and they confronted him and asked him whether he had ever seen that man before, and *he denied ever seeing him*, although he said he was on the bus. The police officers asked him why he had run, and *he said he thought someone was chasing him and that they were going to cut his throat*.

We are going to prove to you that *there was sufficient premeditation, that this man said he was going to "fix" Ronald L. Green, that he was waiting to get Green*. That is why we say that there was premeditation. And when we prove all these facts, and we will prove them beyond a reasonable doubt and *beyond the shadow of a doubt*, we will ask your verdict of guilty as charged.

The opening statement for the defense was presented by one of my associates, Mr. Harry Serper, later a distinguished judge of the Criminal Court of New York City, who recently died. It was designed to effect a general denial without being at all specific. This cautious strategy avoided commitment to any assertion that could possibly be used against the defendant.

(Mr. Serper's Opening for the Defense)

If it please the Court, and Mr. Foreman and gentlemen of the jury: You have been picked to sit here at this trial because, as a special panel of the blue ribbon jury, you have a higher degree of intelligence than the average juror. Anything that the District Attorney may say at this time or anything that we of the defense may say should in no way influence you until after you hear the facts. Therefore, with your kind permission and that of the Court, we will waive our opening until the trial proceeds.

Now let us pass on to my closing remarks to the jury, since my summation contains the pertinent passages, slightly modified and abridged, from the testimony given during the trial. From time to time I shall comment on the strategy I was following in order to point out my use of particular techniques.

When the Court asked how much time I would need to sum up, I avoided any commitment by saying, "I have no idea, Your Honor. I think I should take anywhere from an hour to an hour and a half."

(Mr. Heller's Summation for the Defense)

May it please Your Honor, Mr. Foreman, and gentlemen of the jury: Now that we have come to the end of the case, in so far as the testimony is concerned, it is my solemn duty, on behalf of my colleagues and myself, to sum it up from the evidence adduced, as we of the defense see it, and to try to present to you logical reasons why you should find the defendant not guilty of the crime as charged. When I am finished, the District Attorney will follow me, and he will sum up the case as he sees it and give you his understanding of the facts. Then, when he is finished, His Honor will charge you on the law. After that, it will be your duty to go out and deliberate and bring in a verdict.

The reason I mention this procedure is that I want you to keep in mind that after I am finished speaking, whether I take an hour or an hour and a half, I cannot say anything further in this case. When the District Attorney follows me and sums up the case, he says what he feels he should say, and I have no opportunity, under the law, to answer him. That is the procedure. So that, if during the course of his summation, he should ask me any questions or imply that I could answer them, please bear in mind that once I have finished speaking, I can say nothing further, except to make certain motions, if necessary.

Next, I lost no time in charging that the prosecutor had failed to prove his case. I thus laid the basis for raising a number of reasonable doubts in the minds of the jurors.

> Gentlemen, I shall try to analyze the testimony to prove to you the utter failure of the District Attorney to prove Lang guilty of murder in the first degree, as charged in the indictment, and as the District Attorney stated in his opening that he would prove to you. As I am sure the Court will explain to you, the law defines murder in the first degree as the killing of a human being—unless it is excusable or justifiable—when committed from a deliberate and premeditated design to effect the death of the person killed.
>
> I charge the District Attorney's office with failing to prove a single element of the crime as defined by the penal law of this State. If there was a killing here, and if in some way Lang had anything to do with it—and there was no credible testimony showing or proving that he killed Green—such a homicide, whether he committed it or someone else committed it in a fight, was excusable and justifiable. There never was any intent on the part of Lang to commit murder. He was not going out to rob anybody or to do anything wrong. There was no motive. He was going home to his wife and five children. He got off the bus at the spot where he had to change in order to get to his home. There was no premeditation. There was no deliberation, and so there was no murder.

My reference to the defendant's wife and five children was intended to dispose the jurors favorably toward my client. At the same time, I sought to exploit the prosecutor's opening statement to the defendant's maximum advantage. Following up on the last point, I proceeded:

> Was Lang angry at Green? Was the accused, as the District Attorney stated in his opening, "chafing at the bit"—I believe those were the prosecutor's words—waiting in the bus until Green got off in order to follow him around in the dark of night, corner him in some dark spot, and put a knife through him, as the District Attorney would have you believe? Was Lang the aggressor? Did he plan the killing in the manner in which I have just described? If that is the way it happened, then, I agree, it was a premeditated homicide, a murder. But you know what the facts are, and I intend to go over with you every bit of the important testimony to show you the total failure of the District Attorney to prove a charge of murder against my client.
>
> Now, this defendant is charged with murder in the first degree. I say to you, he is either guilty of murder in the first degree, or not. If

he is not, you should acquit him. Gentlemen, I do not want any compromise verdict in this case. The District Attorney of this county saw fit, on the evidence he gathered with the police and detective force at his command, to bring a charge of murder in the first degree against this defendant, and so I say to you, from the facts, you either convict him of murder in the first degree, or you acquit him. We seek no compromise. The only thing that I ask you gentlemen to do in following me as I analyze the testimony is to put yourselves in the position of this defendant. Put yourselves in the position of Lang as he sits in the bus, all alone, on his way home, and then ask yourselves whether, under these circumstances, he had any idea or thought in his mind that he would be charged with murder and soon be within the shadow of the electric chair.

My remarks about a compromise verdict were an attempt to plant a seed in the jurors' minds. This was exactly what I was hoping for. My job was to save Lang from the electric chair. At the same time that I disclaimed the acceptability of a compromise verdict, I was indirectly suggesting it as a possibility in this case. I continued as follows:

I say to you that but for the grace of God it could have been any of you or the District Attorney or I in the bus where Lang sat. All of a sudden, Benson and Green started this foul talk about "mother-fucker" and began saying, "You are the man I saw." They thought they had identified a certain man with whom they might have had an encounter before boarding the bus, but they were mistaken. They had the wrong man. Suppose that had happened to you or to me. Ask yourselves, if you had been in that position, what you would have done under the circumstances. Would you, as a reasonable man, have acted in the same manner as Lang did? From what you know about life, from your own experience, would you not have acted the same way he did?

At this point I turned to key passages from the prosecutor's opening statement that I believed could be made to boomerang against his case:

Gentlemen, let us see what happened during this trial. The District Attorney said in his opening statement—and I quote from page 3 of the minutes: "This defendant, chafing, as it were, under a bit, considered it an insult on the part of Ronald L. Green, and when he reached the corner of Rockwell Place, along Fulton Street, where Bickford's restaurant is, and as he went out there, he invited Ronald L. Green to come outside there, and he used these words, 'I will fix you!'"

Now, why did the District Attorney bring these words, "I will fix you," into this case? You will recall that Benson could not remember offhand hearing these words, "I will fix you." Only after he was prodded did he say something about "get," but he could not remember hearing the words, "I will fix you." Why, then, are these words in this trial? I will tell you why. Because in order to prove murder in the first degree, the District Attorney must establish deliberation and premeditation. So, if he can establish that Lang, before getting off the bus, said, "I will fix you," the prosecutor can then imply that there was premeditation and deliberation, because Lang was deliberating and planning on "fixing" Green. That is all very neat, indeed. But, gentlemen, *those words were never used.* If they were uttered, how is it that Benson didn't hear them? Why didn't Benson say he heard them? Oh, to be sure, Benson says he heard something about "get." His conscience would not let him say, "I heard Lang say, 'I will fix you!'" He felt guilty about being mixed up in this fight—and who knows but that it was Benson's knife that inflicted the fatal blow?

Benson was one of the three key witnesses for the prosecution. This question raised one source of reasonable doubt. My objective at this point was to intimate the possible unreliability of Benson's testimony without directly accusing him of perjury. He had acknowledged involvement in an altercation in which he dropped his knife. He thereby provided the defense with an opportunity to employ the technique of shifting responsibility to him and thus furthering the jurors' doubts about the defendant's guilt. Here is how I exploited this opportunity:

You heard something from the District Attorney about a knife. It was supposed to have a little button that would open and close it automatically. Maybe that is the knife that Benson had. Look at this knife, the one that has been received in evidence. You cannot open it. It does not spring open. There is no way to spring this blade up. The only way to do it is to pull it open. And believe me, you have to try very hard to open it. You need at least two tries to get it open.

What, then, did the District Attorney mean when he told you about that springing blade? Whose knife was it? Maybe there's a little guilt on Mr. Benson's conscience, so when he took the witness stand, he did not testify that he heard Lang say, "I will fix you." Oh, no. That was left to the two coy and coquettish ladies, those modest girls, who testified for the prosecution. We will get to their testimony in a few minutes.

You see, Benson played end on a football team, and so did Green. Two smart boys. Two strong boys. Two fast boys. And the girls are just as smart. Oh, yes, these were clever witnesses—as clever as any I have ever seen in a court of law. Benson was not going to carry the ball and be the one to testify, "I heard Lang say, 'I will fix you!'" So the girls carried the ball. They were the halfbacks who carried the ball for Benson and ran around the ends and through the middle. At least, that is what they think they did. But when you analyze the testimony, you discover that they cannot and should not be believed. On the testimony of such people it would be a miscarriage of justice to find this defendant guilty as charged by the District Attorney.

And so, gentlemen, the words, "I will fix you," were injected into this case for the sake of bolstering up the charge of premeditation, which they knew they could not prove, to support the accusation of murder in the first degree.

Let us see for ourselves. I am reading from page 21 of the minutes, Benson's testimony on direct examination:

Q. Now, when the defendant got off the bus, did you hear him say anything to Ronald L. Green?
A. He said something, but I did not hear it.
Q. What?
A. He said something, but I don't remember exactly what he said.

Here you see Benson's guilty conscience at work. It is bothering him, but at the same time he knows that the two ladies are going to say that they heard Lang say, "I will fix you," so he vacillates. He wants to appear honest; so he says of Lang, "He said something, but I don't know what." When the learned Court asked Benson at this point, "What is your recollection?" there was no answer. When the prosecutor asked him, "What is your best recollection?" his answer was, "I don't know. He said something about 'get.'" I am quoting from the trial record:

Q. Get?
A. I don't know what else he said.

Doesn't that prove what I've been saying? Do you believe that Lang said, "I will fix you," and Benson did not hear it or would not have heard it or remembered it? I leave that question with you.

But now let us see what Benson said on cross-examination. I asked him:

Q. What did Lang do?
A. Just as the door opened, he struck Green, and he stepped off the bus. He said something, but I don't remember what he said.

When the prosecutor asked Benson what Lang said, he did not remember. When the judge asked him, he could not remember. And when the prosecutor came back and asked, "What did Lang say? What is your best recollection?" he said Lang said the word "get." Then, when I asked him, he said, "I don't remember what he said." The truth is, gentlemen, Lang said nothing whatever.

But then, of course, you have Miss Dotson coming in and playing quarterback. She knows just what to say, and she supplies the testimony. "Yes, I heard Lang say, 'I will fix you.'" That is not true. She never heard it, because it was never said. And the only reason those words were brought into this trial is to establish premeditation and deliberation, because this is necessary to convict Lang of murder in the first degree.

And what does Miss Brand have to say to all this? That sweet, coy, coquettish young lady who could not say a dirty word. It was vulgar. It was very vulgar. You remember her testimony. When she was asked by the prosecutor what Samuel Lang said to Ronald Green in the bus, she repeatedly refused to use the words, and it was not until the judge insisted on her telling the Court and jury what they were that she whispered them to him and counsel privately at the bench, and the judge put them on the record. She testified that Lang said, "I will fix you."

Now, if Miss Dotson heard it, and Miss Brand heard it—the girl who could not bring herself to say a dirty word—why didn't Benson hear it? Just keep that question in mind, please. It is very important. Remember, you said you would not convict this defendant unless you found him guilty beyond a reasonable doubt. Are you convinced beyond a reasonable doubt that Lang said, "I will fix you"? I am confident you will know what to think about that when you sit down together to deliberate upon your verdict in this case.

Then, too, when Benson testified on direct examination, did he say then that Lang had called Green a "mother-fucker"? No. He did not say so. Did Miss Dotson say that she heard Lang call Green a "mother-fucker"? Yes. And Miss Brand says that she heard it too. Now get the psychology of this case. Benson is a little worried. He is on the spot. He knows something about these knives. After all, he is testifying in a case in which a man's life is at stake, and he is worried. He cannot lie about certain things because he has enough to do to try to hang Lang. He does not say anything about calling him a name like "black mother-fucker," and I will tell you why. Because Benson is the one who called Lang, as Lang testified, a "black mother-fucker"!

Yes, Benson is the one that started this whole thing—that suave, fine-looking gentleman, who struts in here and takes the witness stand with such assurance, and knows all the answers and reads the testimony with the detectives and played end on a football team. Smart? Yes, he's pretty smart, but not smart enough to fool you. If Lang called Green a "mother-fucker," how is it that Benson didn't tell you about it? The answer is, you have to realize the fear in Benson's subconscious mind and the feeling on his part, which is just like that of a football player who says to himself, "I don't have to worry about blocking this guy. My teammate behind me, who's carrying the ball, has a pretty stiff arm. He's a fine halfback, and he'll go right down for a touchdown." And so he figured on these two girls carrying the ball for him and going down the field for the touchdown by perjuring themselves and lying in this court of justice and pinning it on Lang. That is the answer, gentlemen.

My comments on Benson's behavior in court—his strutting about and admitting that he had read testimony with the detectives—were designed to paint him as a "smart aleck" trying to "hoodwink" the jurors.

Next, I turned the jury's attention to signs that Miss Brand was putting on an act on the witness stand. When the prosecutor asked her what she had heard, she refused to say because the words were "vulgar" and she would not "say a dirty word." The remarks that follow were all intended to cast doubt on her integrity and veracity:

So let us have a look at quarterback Brand, that charming girl who cannot say a dirty word because it is too vulgar. The mother of two children, and separated from her husband, this young lady who cannot say a dirty word leaves her children with her mother and goes out with these men. She is Benson's girl friend and will carry the ball for him a little further than Miss Dotson. She knows that the day before she took the stand the trial was not going very well for the prosecution. So she throws in a bombshell. When she was asked what the girl sitting next to Lang said, Miss Dotson testified that the girl said she wanted Lang not to annoy her and that Lang had a knife. You remember that? Did Benson say anything about that girl saying Lang had a knife? No. Why not? Because it was never said. Did Miss Dotson say anything about it? No. Why not? Because it was never said. Why, then, does Brand say it? Why? Because Benson is her boy friend. She does not know how far she has to go in testifying to protect him. Maybe she thinks that Benson is on trial, that he is the defendant. And so she testifies that the girl said Lang had a knife. Do you believe it? Does it sound credible? Does it sound logical?

Now, just suppose that the girl did say that Lang had a knife and was annoying her. Why did these two men, such fine, upstanding, law-abiding citizens, get off the bus and follow Lang around the corner? To get some ice cream? We'll come back to that ice cream incident later. The answer is, gentlemen, no such statement was made by the girl, and Lang made no statement about "fixing" anybody. All these witnesses are carrying a little bit of this ball to get over the goal of sending this defendant to the electric chair. But they won't get away with it, because I am confident that you members of the jury will weigh the facts in this case intelligently and come to the inevitable conclusion that this defendant is not guilty.

At this point, I made further efforts to raise doubts by analyzing conflicting testimony and directing my ridicule against one of the chief witnesses for the prosecution:

Gentlemen, you will remember I asked Miss Brand whether she was married. You remember her answer. It is at page 156 of the minutes. On cross-examination she gave her name as "Miss" Brand. I quote from the record:

Q. Are you married?
A. No.
Q. Have you ever been married?
A. Yes.
Q. How many times were you married?
A. One.
Q. And were you divorced?
A. No.
Q. Are you now separated from your husband?
A. Yes.
Q. How long have you been separated?
A. (No answer.)
Q. How long have you been separated?
A. Since 1939.
Q. 1939?
A. Yes.
Q. And have you any children?
A. Yes.
Q. How many?
A. Two.
Q. How old are they, please?

Now she begins to stall, and I ask her:

Q. Yes?
A. Six and eight—six and seven.
Q. And where do these children live?
A. With my mother.

Now, gentlemen, did you notice that when I asked her, "Are you married?" she answered, "No"? But when I went over to my briefcase and took out a piece of paper that had nothing to do with this case, and I asked her again, holding the paper in my hand, "Have you ever been married?" she thought I had the record of her marriage on this piece of paper, and then her answer was, "Yes." I wonder how many of you recollect that incident. That is what happened. That is when I got her to admit that she was married. Would you believe that kind of witness? Yet it is on the testimony of this type of witness that the District Attorney wants you to find Lang guilty of murder in the first degree beyond a reasonable doubt! Would you take the testimony of such a witness and say, "Yes, Lang, the prosecutor is right: there isn't, as he said in his opening statement, the shadow of a doubt that you are guilty of murder in the first degree"? I don't believe you would say that.

Now, let us get back to the incident of the young lady suddenly walking from the back of the bus, where Lang is sitting, and saying, "Lang is annoying me," or words to that effect, and then adding, according to the testimony of the modest Miss Brand, "He has a knife." You remember that I asked one of the witnesses whether the young lady who allegedly complained about Lang was excited when she came down to the front of the bus. "Yes," said the witness. Gentlemen, if that incident happened, why wasn't the lady who was in the bus called as a witness? Now, I know what the District Attorney is going to say to that. "How could we get her? We don't know who she is."

Well, I will tell you how he could have produced her. All the witnesses were very exact. They knew the time they had left Miss Dotson's home, when they picked up Miss Brand, when they took the bus, how long they were riding in it, and what time it was in each case: nine-forty and ten-twenty and eleven-sixteen. They knew there were just seven or eight people in the bus. They knew all the answers. If they were telling the truth, then they knew what time the bus stopped at Bickford's. And they know the route along which the bus went. The District Attorney has at his disposal and command in this county one of the finest police forces in the United States and every resource needed to put this case into the hands of the finest sleuths and investigators. Why did not the District Attorney, the following day, put a detective in the bus from seven or eight o'clock on, and have him ask everybody in the bus, up to midnight or after, whether such an incident took place and what—if anything—they knew about it? They could have found the woman, because the testimony is that she said she was going to Borough Hall. If she was going to Borough Hall to work, she would have to go to work the next night or the next, and even if she was sick for a week, she would have to go eventually. There could have been some testimony, too, that an attempt was made to find this woman. Where is that? Who is this mysterious girl who suddenly looms up in the bus and asks for help?

The answer is, gentlemen, that no such girl was on the bus, and no such incident happened. But I am going to excuse the District Attorney for not producing the girl. He would probably argue, "We could not locate her. We did not know who she was. There was no way of telling who she was. All that we knew about her was that she worked in the Borough Hall section." But, Mr. District Attorney, she had to come on the bus eventually, the next day or even perhaps five weeks later. I will further say that in a murder case they should have worked every day in the week to try to locate her and get the facts. But I am going to exonerate the District Attorney. Maybe he could not have produced the girl. Maybe he has an excuse in her case. But there was somebody else that he could surely have produced, and if we had that witness in court, you would know the truth, and you would know that Lang is telling the truth. I'm not going to excuse the District Attorney for not producing that witness, because as to this witness there is no excuse. You know, what counts in a case is not the number of witnesses in court—in this case I think the State had about ten or twelve, and I had only the defendant and his wife. You see, the law does not look to quantity. What the law respects is quality. And so, gentlemen, I cannot excuse the District Attorney for not producing the witness that should have appeared here, and then you would have known the truth.

That witness was, of course, the bus driver. Where was he? Why wasn't he called to the stand? You cannot say that they did not know who the bus driver was. They know precisely when this bus stopped in front of Bickford's restaurant. And if another bus stopped there two or three minutes before or after that, they could have produced two or three or four bus drivers. There are records. Each bus driver must keep a record of the time, from the point where he starts to the point where he ends his run, and those records are on file. If two bus drivers got there at about the same time, as sometimes happens, both of them could have been questioned, and one of them would have said, "No, I'm not the one," and the other would have said, "Yes, I drove that bus."

Gentlemen, if that bus driver had been produced, he would have given the lie to the prosecutor's star witnesses. If Lang, in getting off the bus, with a package under his right arm, had struck Green, who was sitting behind Benson, as they say he did, either with an upward or a sidewise movement, like this or like this [demonstrating with my left arm], and then had run off the bus, the bus driver would have known that. And he certainly would have recalled any young lady coming to the front of the bus to complain about being annoyed by a man with a knife sitting at the back of the bus. Why wasn't the driver produced? Because neither of these incidents ever happened.

In fact, it was physically impossible for the alleged attack on Green to have occurred as it was described in the testimony. Did you see me, a moment ago, make that striking motion with my left hand, as if I had something under my right arm and could not use it to strike a blow? Did you notice how I had to turn in this direction [demonstrating]? Why, if Lang had done that and then run out, he would have had to turn around and pass young Benson, in order to get out of the bus, and that crack football player and fast runner would have jumped up and tackled Lang and killed him right there in the bus. That is why the bus driver was not produced. Yes, the driver would have given the lie to their testimony, to the words they say were uttered and the alleged blow struck by Lang, none of which ever happened.

In fact, not only did none of this happen, but the facts of the situation make it physically impossible for the blow to have been struck as described in their testimony. Lang could not strike Green in any way but from the side, like this [again demonstrating with my left hand], and, by the operation of the force of gravity, he would have had to bring the swing of his arm and his body around towards the bus and then turn around and jump off the bus. By that time, I repeat, the athletic young Benson would have tripped him or tackled him and killed him right in the bus.

Gentlemen, the whole thing never happened. It's all part of the act, part of the attempt to pin guilt on an innocent man.

Having thus capitalized on the failure of the prosecution to produce crucial witnesses, I next turned to the task of discrediting Benson, the People's star witness, especially in the eyes of the "family men" on the jury:

> Now let me review some of the testimony of Benson. As you will recall, he testified that he and Green were fast friends. Benson admitted being married, but said that he had left his wife and children in Virginia to come to New York. But he did not come here to try to make a living for them. He testified that he had left his wife down there working and taking care of the children.
>
> Let us look at the testimony of this fine, chivalrous gentleman, who alleged that he wanted to protect a woman who complained that Lang had a knife and was annoying her. I quote from page 36 of the minutes, containing part of my cross-examination of Benson:
>
> Q. Are you separated from your wife?
> A. No.
> Q. You just left her there?
> A. Yes.
>
> Well, I was a little surprised. How does he know Miss Dotson? He said he had met her at Virginia Beach some summers before. Had he come up north with her? Oh, no. He did not come up with her. He sort of put me off the track there. You have to be pretty persistent to be able to get the truth from a fellow like that. You have to keep plugging and asking and prodding. And so, you recall, I asked him, "Which of you came up north first?"
>
> A. She came first.
> Q. Then what happened?
>
> Then he followed. Do you think he didn't know she was already up here? You remember his testimony. He knew exactly where to find her, and he has been meeting her up here and going out with her.
>
> And this is the type of man, gentlemen, that the District Attorney wants you to believe and rely upon in order to convict Lang of murder in the first degree! Of course, they tried to paint him as a lover of womanhood, a chivalrous gentleman who would commit murder if somebody insulted a woman. But would you consider him the type of man you would believe? Would you say he was a chivalrous gentleman—a man who would leave his wife and two children and come up here to be with Miss Dotson? Now, this is part of the testimony in this case, gentlemen, that you have to consider in your deliberations. You see, you have to look at a witness, as he testifies, and ask yourselves: "Is he the type of man that I am going to believe? Does he seem to be reliable? Is he an honorable man? Is he telling the truth, the whole truth, and nothing but the truth, as he swore to do?" Would you rely on this individual to do something for you that was important? Would you hesitate to trust him?

You have to be clear in your own mind that Benson is the type of man you would believe before you can find my client guilty. Because Benson's testimony and that of the girls is the basis on which you will have to find the defendant guilty or not guilty. That is why I call your attention to the type of individual he is. And I ask you to decide in advance, before you start your deliberations, whether Benson or Dotson or Brand are individuals worthy of your belief.

Warming to my attack on Benson, I now struck hard for a knockout blow by questioning his sobriety on the night of the killing:

Now, let us look closely at a certain incident that I think is very, very important. I asked Benson, "When you went out that night, how many drinks did you have?" Did you notice how cagey he was? He remembered that he had two drinks in one place—I think it was the Arlington—and then from there he went to another place, where he had two drinks more. So, according to Benson, they had only four drinks. Well, of course, we're not going to call a beer, which they used as a chaser, a drink. Of course, for me, a beer would count as a drink, but let us assume that in Benson's case, a beer is just like a glass of water. So we'll say that he had only four whiskies, the four which he testified to. We have only Benson's word on that, and you and I know already how much trust we can place in Benson's word. But he did not drink alone. Green was with him, and we do have a way of knowing how much alcohol Green had in him when he was killed. Do you believe that on Easter Monday, when this incident was supposed to have happened, Benson and Green were sitting in that bus with only four drinks apiece and four chasers of beer in them, half imbibed at one place and half at another? Do you believe that?

Well, I am going to prove to you that—if I may use street language —both of them were "cock-eyed drunk." Seated in that bus, they were both "loaded." No, I could not tell that from Benson's testimony, because he held on tight to those two drinks in each place—not counting, of course, the four chasers, which were not water, but beer. Smart boy? You have to have some brains to play football. He held me back with those "only four" drinks.

But when did we discover the truth? How did we find out? Why do I feel justified in saying that they were "soused"?

Let me read you the testimony of Dr. Madsen, called by the District Attorney, as it appears on page 173 of the minutes, when he was cross-examined.

Q. Doctor, will you please look at that report of the analysis of the organs of Green and read it for the record?

A. This is a report from the office of the Chief Medical Examiner of the City of New York, Division of Laboratories, in regard to the brain taken from the body of Ronald L. Green for the determination of the presence of alcohol.

He found what he termed "three plus" or more than three per cent alcohol concentration present in the brain of Green. He considered it a large amount. This report, signed by the Chief Medical Examiner of the City of New York, was offered and received in evidence and is part of the record in this case that you may want to examine. So, when I say that Green and Benson were drunk, it is not because of anything Benson said or I say now, but because this official report says so. And incidentally, when the amount of alcohol in the bloodstream is only ten one hundredths of one per cent, the law presumes a person to be drunk.

So now you have the picture. Now we have constructed it. I must confess it puzzled me for a while, but I think it is beginning to take shape now. Three plus!

I ask you to figure it out for yourselves in the jury room. If the witness by his testimony tried to show you that with four drinks he was not drunk, and the law says that if there is an alcohol concentration in your brain of ten one hundredths of one per cent you are presumed to be drunk, and the report of the medical examiner says that he found three plus in the dead man's blood, you must please figure out how many drinks these men had. Certainly, in my opinion, and I may be wrong, it is entirely up to your own finding, I would say certainly that each had more than four drinks—how much more they had, you will have to figure out for yourselves.

It is for you gentlemen to determine whether or not I am justified when I previously said that they were both "cock-eyed drunk."

Now let us look at the picture. Two good-looking girls come into the bus with Green and Benson, both of them stinking drunk. They're "big shots"—great athletes. They can take on anybody. They look around the bus and see this poor fellow—I'd call him a "mopey-looking" fellow and not overbright—come in, carrying a little bundle under his arm. He is minding his own business, going home to his wife and five children. And so these "big shots" swagger over to him and say, "I know you from somewhere." He looks at them in bewilderment. He doesn't know them. He has never seen them before. He can't tell what is on their minds. All he is thinking of is getting home to his family.

But these bullies see he's an easy mark. They start to become abusive. "Sure, you're the man I saw, you black mother-fucker!" shouts Benson. Lang begins to feel frightened. He sees he's no match for these two big drunken bruisers. So he says to them, "Forget it," as he gets off the bus.

You remember his testimony on this point. Did he get off at the wrong place? No. Did he get off at the place where he was supposed to get off at? Yes. Did he have any intention of doing anything special when he got off the bus? No. He got off first. He had no reason to believe that anyone would follow him, and he was going home. When he said, "Forget it," he meant it. As far as he was concerned, when he got off that bus, the whole incident was over and done with. Do you follow me? It is as clear as crystal in my mind. I think it is in yours too.

Then, when Green and Benson saw Lang get off that bus, the psychological effect of somebody talking back to them in the presence of their girls was just like what the District Attorney described, but in reverse: they were, as he aptly put it, chafing under the bit. They couldn't and wouldn't take that kind of stuff from a little pipsqueak like Lang. They were two big ends on a football team. So they got off after this poor fellow to teach him a lesson. Maybe they really did think he was somebody else who had done something they didn't like. I don't know about that. But everyone agrees that when Lang got off the bus and started to walk, Green followed him on one side, and Benson followed him on the other.

Do you believe their story, that they were all walking together across the street, sort of having a tête-à-tête, or do you believe Lang's story that, when he got off the bus and looked around and saw Green coming off, he started to run for his life, with the two of them in hot pursuit? Do you know what bears out Lang's testimony? The testimony of Benson, who said of Lang, "He had his head behind him." That is, Lang kept looking back at his pursuers as he ran. If he was just walking with them at his side, why should he look around? He was looking around because he was being followed, because he was being chased, and because Green was trying to catch him. So he ran across the street. Before he could reach the other side, Green had him, and the fight had begun.

Green had a knife, and so did Benson. They were going to go to work on Lang, but the great Architect let that knife fall out of the hands of Green. Then the fight continued, and amidst all those swinging arms, including Benson's, Green was killed. Did Lang do it? He said he does not know. He did not deny it because he did not know. Benson had a knife too. It could have been his knife that struck the fatal blow. Was it his knife? He said no.

Now, the District Attorney is well able to bring anyone he wants here to testify. He called to the stand a very learned blood-grouping expert, and he had the medical examiner testify. They examined everything—blood spots and all. They can analyze anything at all—hair, cloth, anything. How is it that they didn't have that knife tested for fingerprints? If Lang was the last one that had that knife, and the detectives picked it up, why didn't they have it analyzed for fingerprints? It would have been interesting to see whose fingerprints were on this knife. Maybe they were not Lang's. Maybe they were the fingerprints of Green. Weren't you entitled to see the fingerprints? Shouldn't the District Attorney do that when he comes into court and charges a man with murder in the first degree? Is that what you'd call establishing his guilt beyond a shadow of a doubt, as the District Attorney promised in his opening?

To clinch my point, I now proceeded to a visual demonstration with the knife that had been received in evidence:

Oh, they thought they would be able to link Lang to the knife in another way. They had a couple of halfbacks to rely on. Brand and Dotson were going to prove that this knife belonged to Lang and that he wielded it. What did these girls testify to? Well, they said the knife was "busted" on the side. Now, just take a good look at that knife, gentlemen. Just pass it around quickly, please [handing the knife to the jurors]. The girls testified that they were on the other side of the street during the fight. That is a distance of about thirty-five or forty feet—and I am standing now at that distance, more or less. Now according to the testimony of Brand and Dotson, when Green and Lang were on the other side of the street, Lang, as he reached the sidewalk, suddenly turned around and stabbed Green, without a fight or anything happening up to that point. They said Lang was walking slowly, with Green behind him, and all of a sudden, Lang turned around and stabbed Green. Do you believe that? Does it sound true? Is it credible? No man does that. He would have to be bereft of his senses, he would have to be insane, to do a thing like that, and I think that you can observe that my client is not insane.

But the significant part of it all is that, although they said they could not see where Lang got the knife from, they both said they observed that it was broken, that something was missing from it. You heard that testimony. Now, as I go across the room with the knife in my hand this way, can you, gentlemen, see enough of it to tell me whether any part of it is whole or broken? Can you even see the blade from where you are? Let us try it again, because this is the distance at which the girls were supposed to have been standing from Lang. Can you see it? Of course not. It was impossible to see it at that distance. And this happened in the dead of night, please remember. One policeman who was there testified that it was dark. They could not have seen this. They are not telling the truth. They had to identify the knife; so they gave this testimony. These girls are perjurers. They should be condemned by your verdict. It would be shameful to let such people get away with that kind of testimony. But that is what they came in here to tell you.

Oh, these girls are smart, and they are tough, too. In fact, if Green had really been hit by Lang as he got out of the bus, these two girls would have dived at him and killed him right then and there. Do you know why I say that? Not because I am guessing. No, as the testimony of the policemen shows, when they took Lang—I think they said to the hospital or to the scene of the crime—they had to take him in the car, because these girls wanted to go and get him. Yes, they are tough. They looked sweet and demure until they told us who they were, and you saw how they testified. Gentlemen, do not permit them to fool you.

And so, let's forget all this about a walk around the bus. It did not happen that way at all. Somebody—I don't know who it is; I wish I could put my hands on him—is planning and building up this case; but the perfect crime has not yet been "architected," if there is such a word, and the architect here is a little bit off on his blueprints. It's all just too perfect to be believable. I consider Benson, Dotson, and Brand as three of the smartest witnesses that I have ever cross-examined in any kind of trial that I have been engaged in, and, gentlemen, I've tried all kinds of cases. They knew all the answers. They had everything down pat. They knew just what to expect from me. They knew what I was trying to find out. They knew everything. But the architect was a little wrong in one respect. It was all too perfect.

Do you mean to tell me that they all remember there were seven or eight passengers in the bus? Why didn't any one of them say ten passengers? Why didn't somebody say what Lang said when he was on the stand: "I don't remember how many passengers there were in the bus"? And when the District Attorney asked him, "Don't you remember?" he said, "I don't remember." But the three of them knew there were seven or eight passengers in that bus. Splendid cooperation and corroboration, I must say! Fine field work! Excellent football playing. But what it all adds up to is perjury.

Then they remembered that they got off at Bickford's to go for some ice cream. Now I want to get to that matter of ice cream. You know, the prosecution has to prove premeditation. Besides, it has to be shown that Green was not the aggressor. So some sort of picture has to be painted for the jury, and that's where the ice cream comes in. I'll show you why it was brought into the picture. The girls were being taken home, they say, but the stop at Bickford's was not the place where they were supposed to get off to go home. They were supposed to ride on farther and get off a few stops beyond Bickford's. But to try to make you believe, or to attempt to fool you into thinking, that Green was not the aggressor, the District Attorney, when he opened this case, said, and I quote, "Ronald L. Green and his friends were getting off at that place anyhow." And later on he said and the testimony showed that they had to get off because they wanted ice cream. That is why the ice cream was brought into this case.

But the truth of the matter is that there never was any talk about ice cream, that they never intended to get off at that corner, and that the only reason they did get off there was that they went out to fight with Lang. But they had to give you some sort of excuse for Green's getting off at that corner when he had to continue on with the girls to take them home. That is why they brought the ice cream in. Another one of their falsehoods. Another lie designed to pin the guilt on the defendant.

They weren't going for ice cream. They were going to get Lang. If they were going for ice cream, why didn't they all get off and walk as couples should? You heard the District Attorney, in his opening statement, describe them as "two couples." Why, then, didn't Brand walk with Benson, and Dotson with Green? Why didn't they walk along the street and go into an ice cream parlor? No, they weren't going for ice cream. They were going for this man—they were brave lads, each armed with a knife and "loaded to the gills," the two of them. Even the four of them would have fought this man. That is how brave they were.

And do you believe Benson when he says he saw Lang stab Green? Why, they were all in such a fight, such a melee, that he did not know what happened himself, any more than Lang knew there had been a stabbing. All Lang knew was that a man with a knife in his hand was following him, chasing after him. Benson managed to get rid of his knife before the police arrived. The policeman who testified said he did not see Benson's knife, but he did testify that Benson said, "Let me at him!" In other words, Benson wanted to get at Lang. That is what the policeman testified to. What does that mean? That means that Lang is telling the truth. It corroborates Lang's testimony. That is what he said. That is why he did not stop running. He was scared. He did not know what was happening. And that is why he turned around. Benson was followed by the policemen. When Lang saw Benson running after him with a knife, he thought that if he stopped he would be caught by Benson. But when Lang saw the policeman behind Benson, he stopped. He felt safe. And he immediately said to the policeman and to the detectives as well that they had the wrong man. His mind, please remember, does not work so fast. He did not mean, when he said they had the wrong man, that he was not in the fight. He was in the fight, and he admitted it. What he was trying to say when he said, "They got the wrong man," was that his attackers were mistaken when they referred to him on the bus as some other person. What he was telling the police was, "I am not the man they were after. I don't know what happened." I am sure that the District Attorney in his summation will tell you that Lang did deny that he had ever seen Green before in his life or that he had had a fight with Green or that he had killed Green.

The detective who testified tried to intimate that. You remember he said he asked Lang, "Did you know the man?" and Lang said no. But deep down in his heart, the detective knew he was asking a question designed to trap an unwary witness. He knew that the proper question should have been, "Have you ever seen this man before tonight?" not "Did you see him?" That was a trick question. The detective is a "smart aleck" with an angle, and I think you are satisfied that I demonstrated this afternoon in my cross-examination of him that he is not altogether truthful. He has some interest in having this man convicted. It would be nice to have on his record the fact that he helped to convict a man accused of murder. Please don't let it get around, but sometimes this sort of work earns a promotion. I think the detective was angling for that rather than for the truth. Please remember he is the detective who read the minutes of the trial to Benson this afternoon. Do you believe that as he was reading the minutes, as he told you on the stand, Benson just came over, and he did not see Benson reading them? A fine detective, he is, if he cannot see what is going on right under his nose!

At this point, the Court interrupted to ask how much longer I would take. I said that I would speak for about twenty or thirty minutes longer. From this point on, having committed myself to a definite amount of time, I kept my eye on my watch as I spoke.

I think I have covered most of the important facts which I want to bring to your attention. I think you are satisfied that there was a fight. I am sorry for the man who was killed and his family, and I know we all are. But all I can say to you is that, under the law, I think, from all the circumstances, you will find that this defendant is not responsible for the unfortunate incident that occurred.

Now I want to touch briefly upon the testimony of the witnesses. I know I have trespassed upon the time of the Court. The judge has been very patient.

THE COURT: Take as much time as you wish, Senator. Don't mind about the time. This is an important case. Take as long as you wish.

Thank you, Your Honor.

The judge has been very patient throughout the entire trial, and I am going to try to conclude, because I feel that I have covered practically all the important issues in this case.

I next exploited an opportunity presented by certain questions which the Court asked witnesses during the course of their examination. My purpose was to give the jury the impression that the judge agreed with the reasoning of the defense.

You remember that Miss Dotson testified that Lang struck Green as Lang was getting off the bus or just before he did so. Well, I would like to call to your attention the questions asked by His Honor at that point, because, in my opinion, they are very significant. I think you will make up your own mind as to the credibility of her entire testimony after you hear these questions of the judge and Miss Dotson's answers read from the record. I quote from page 131 of the minutes:

(By the Court)

Q. Was not Green provoked when he was punched by the defendant?

A. What?

Q. Was not Green provoked by the punch, and didn't he defend himself and go back at him?

A. No, he did not do anything, only when he was talking to him.

Q. But when Lang hit Green, didn't Green attempt to hit back at him?
A. No.
Q. Didn't your friend Benson try to punch back at him?
A. No.
Q. You mean to say that Green did not say anything to the defendant at the time he was punched?
A. No, I did not hear him say anything.
Q. Did you say anything?
A. No.
Q. Did your girl friend say anything?
A. No, I did not hear her say anything.
Q. Did you say anything to Green or to Benson?
A. No.
Q. After you saw what Lang did to Green?
A. When I saw him across the street.

She is being "cute." She is trying to bring in some other part of the testimony. But the Judge straightened her out:

Q. I don't mean that. I mean in the bus, when this thing happened.
A. No.
Q. You mean to say that Green did not do anything at all about defending himself?
A. No.
Q. And neither did Benson do anything about it?
A. No.
Q. Green just took the punch, did he?
A. That is right.

That, in my opinion, is enough to show that you should disregard everything this witness said as unworthy of belief. It is palpably untrue. She is lying. She is carrying the ball just too far. You can see that from the pertinent questions the Court asked her and the answers she gave. Why, if Lang had struck Green in the bus, I think I have convinced you that Lang would have been the dead man in this case, and the other two fellows would have been the defendants. No such incident ever happened.

Gentlemen, the truth lies at pages 131 and 132 of the minutes. If no such incident happened, then what did happen was exactly what the defendant said happened. Benson and Green, with three-plus alcohol in their systems, put this defendant in imminent fear of losing his life.

And now, having struck several hard blows at the prosecution witnesses, I felt safe in showing the jury that I appreciated the candor of at least one witness for the prosecution whose testimony was not damaging to the defense.

I want to say a word, too, about the testimony of Officer Gilligan. His demeanor throughout was straightforward, and he appeared as a truthful and honest witness, and he deserves to be commended for his candor. He is the one, you recall, who ran after Lang, but he would not shoot because he was afraid he might hit somebody. Now, I am going to show you some of the missing links in this case. Officer Gilligan was asked by the District Attorney—I quote from page 184 of the minutes:

> Q. When you finally apprehended him, did you say anything to him?
> A. I asked him why he didn't stop when I yelled at him. He said, "Somebody was chasing me." I said, "I am a police officer. You should have stopped. I could have shot you." He said, "I don't know. Somebody was chasing me."

Is that any different from what Lang told you here on the witness stand? Doesn't that corroborate Lang's testimony? And so does the officer's answer to the next question of the District Attorney:

> Q. Was Benson along with you?
> A. Yes. Benson was running with me.

Is that any different from what Lang said? Didn't Lang also testify that Benson was running with the policeman? Benson wanted to finish the job he had started out to do with Green.

And what do we find on page 188 of the minutes? This part of the cross-examination of the police officer:

> Q. Well, officer, the question asked of the defendant was whether or not he knew the deceased before that night, is that correct?
> A. Yes.

The reason that question was asked was that the District Attorney was trying to give the impression that when Lang was apprehended, he said he did not know Green. That was not so. What Lang meant was that he had never seen Green before meeting him in the bus that night. Lang was telling the truth. It was not his fault that the detective could not or would not ask the right question. Continuing the cross-examination of the police officer, you will recall that he was asked:

> Q. And Lang denied knowing him before that night, is that right?
> A. Yes.

Of course! Lang had never seen Green until that night.

> Q. About what time did you get back to the scene with the defendant at Fulton and Hudson Streets?
> A. Well, it was between 11:30 and 11:45.
> Q. Wasn't it dark at that time?
> A. Oh, yes. It was dark.

And the other witnesses wanted you to believe that it was light there!

Q. About 11:30 it was pretty dark in that neighborhood, wasn't it?

A. Yes.

This officer told the truth.

I now proceeded to analyze and appraise the People's case, with the object of raising reasonable doubts, and, at the same time, I tried to put the defense testimony into perspective by conceding that the defendant may have been mistaken in some of his statements.

What kind of case has the District Attorney got here? Does he want you to believe that, with all the lights lit on Fulton Street, with people and automobiles passing by, Lang stood at the curb and in the presence of hundreds of passers-by, without any motive, stabbed to death an innocent man? Isn't that his case? That is what the State is trying to prove. They were all sure there was plenty of light. Why were they saying it was light on that street? Because they had to get a description of that knife into their testimony. They had to be able to describe this blade, which you were unable to see in this well-lit courtroom when I went over there and which you cannot see even now as I stand before you, until I call it to your attention, as I did before when I showed you where part of the knife, as these witnesses testified, is broken. That is why they thought they had to say it was light. But this honest officer says it was dark on that street.

Whose knife really went through Green's neck? What about that knife that opens on a spring? Does this knife open that way? Oh, our good friend Benson says he hasn't got a knife and did not have a knife. He says he never saw a knife. When I cross-examined him, I asked him, "You work in a tailor shop. Did you ever see a knife there?" He said no. Do you remember that testimony? He never saw a knife in the tailor shop! Do you believe that? Then I asked him, "What did you see there?" He said, "I only saw shears there and blades." He never saw a knife there! A lie. You see, my friends, how, as the ancient proverb says, "One lie begets another." Benson knew that I knew he had a knife. And that is why, the very following day, Miss Brand came in and said, "Not only did I hear him talk and hear that woman say that Lang was annoying her, but she also said Lang had a knife." Dotson, Brand, and Benson, you see, had had a little chat in the meantime, and that is the way it came out.

I think, too, that I demonstrated during my cross-examination and my recross-examination of the detective that he is not to be believed. He is the fellow, you remember, who asked those trick questions. Please bear in mind, as well, that he denied that Benson was reading the minutes of this case with him. As the detective in charge of this investigation, he may have some interest in this case. I believe I have already touched on that—you know, the promotion.

As for the testimony of the man from the ribbon company, well, in my opinion, it is just an attempt on the part of the District Attorney to say, "If I can't prove Lang guilty of murder in the first degree, then I can at least prove him guilty of petit larceny, of taking a piece of cloth or something else." You heard the testimony of the gentleman. He said he could not identify the cloth. He did not know anything about it. And assuming, for the sake of argument, that Lang did take it out of there, what has that got to do with this case? This is just an attempt to prejudice you against the defendant by suggesting that a fellow who would steal a piece of cloth would commit a murder. But Lang denied it.

Gentlemen, as I stand before you, I am holding this bag in my hand, People's Exhibit 5. Now, suppose any one of you had been in that bus. Would it be natural for you to look at the bag? I would say yes if the holder of the bag was close enough to you. But would it be natural for you to memorize the numbers on the bag? How many of you could take the stand right now and swear to your own automobile license-plate numbers? Do you believe Miss Brand noticed those numbers on the bag? She testified that she saw them. She saw everything! Nothing escaped her attention, apparently. But I am sure you will recall that when I asked her whether she remembered any other writing on the bag, she looked somewhat surprised. You see, that was not in her script. Now, gentlemen, if she saw those numbers, which you will notice are very small, as she said she did, she certainly would have seen at the top of the bag the words "Trojan, 1-8," the name of the maker of the bag. Maybe the scriptwriter did not notice them stamped there, or maybe he thought that if she knew both the numbers and the maker, that would be too much for the jury to swallow. If she noticed these numbers—and I defy any man on the jury to tell me he sees them— how is it that she missed the name? But, as I say, Miss Brand had to carry the ball. She was the halfback and the quarterback and everything else, because she was worried and is worried today about Benson.

And now, gentlemen, I come to the testimony of Mr. Lang. I will review it briefly and then conclude my remarks. I think you will find that on cross-examination Mr. Lang did not say one thing which he did not also tell you when I examined him. I think he told you an honest, straightforward story, which the District Attorney was unable to shake. I think he satisfied you that there was a fight and that he was involved in it, as he admitted. And when he said, in answer to the District Attorney's question, "Did you stab Green in the neck?" "I don't know," I think you believe him, as I believe him. When he said, "I don't know," he was telling the truth. And when the District Attorney asked, "Wouldn't you say you did it?" and he said, "I don't know; I won't say yes, and I won't say no," he showed that at least he is man enough not to say definitely that Benson did it. He does not know. He knows he was in the fight with Benson and Green and their two—shall I say "lady"?—friends. They say definitely, "Yes, he did it." This man is telling the truth: "I don't know."

And then, as you will recall, he said, on both direct examination and cross-examination, that after it happened, he ran away. He said he ran three-quarters of a mile. I think his distance is a little wrong. Gentlemen, if that thing had happened to me, I would have run thirty-four miles. If two fellows got off a bus and chased me with a knife, I would run the rest of my days. The first law of nature is self-preservation. That is exactly the situation that Lang found himself in. He had to protect himself. It was either his life or the other fellow's. Of course, he did not know when the fight started, that it would end in a killing, and he did not know even after it ended that anybody had been killed.

Gentlemen of the jury, when Lang said he tried to get away from Green, does that show he was the type of man who was looking for a fight—even up to the point where he saw Green standing in front of him with a knife? You remember that testimony. The District Attorney brought it out himself on cross-examination. Lang said, "When I saw them coming, I swung over. I started to get away." Is that the conduct of a murderer—trying to get away, in the light of all this imminent danger and the reasonable belief that his life was in danger? No. It is the act of any normal person who does not want to take a human life, who does not want to be involved in any trouble. Lang has never been in any trouble in his whole life. He has never been convicted of any crime. He has never been arrested. He has never had a "run-in" with the law. Why should he want to go out and commit murder? And why should he want to kill a man he had never seen before? He did not want to rob him. He did not want to take these girls away from him. Then what was his motive?

The answer is: There, but for the grace of God, sit a hundred or a thousand men to whom the same thing might have happened.

"What else were you doing?" the District Attorney asked him.

"I was dodging around," he answered.

Is that the act of a man bent on murder? "I was dodging around to get away from Green. I was dodging around to get away from Benson."

"And what else were you doing?"

"I was watching him."

Why, certainly he was watching him. Green had a knife. Lang had to watch him. Then the District Attorney asked, "What else did you do?"

"I backed up three or four steps."

Now, if Lang had wanted to kill Green, he could have let the package drop and really go to work on his assailant. Did he do that? No. He backed up. He retreated. He did not have to do that. Is that the act of an aggressor?

He may have backed up and picked up the knife the moment he saw Green trying to stab him and stabbed Green instantly. The law says that killing a man is murder in the first degree, unless it is excusable and justifiable. I maintain that if Lang killed Green, his act was excusable and justifiable. I would have done the same thing under those circumstances.

Then the District Attorney asked Lang how tall he is. Lang is shorter than Green was.

"What else happened?"

"Green was cutting at me."

"You're a pretty strong fellow," said the District Attorney to Lang.

Yes, perhaps if Green had been sober, and if Benson had been sober, and if they had taken a good look at this fellow and felt his muscles, maybe then they would not have started a fight with him. But you know how bullies are. They start fights because they think the other fellow is a weakling. In this case, Lang was perhaps the stronger.

"Did you see the cut on Green's neck?" asked the District Attorney.

"I would not say I did, and I would not say I didn't. I don't know." That was Lang's answer. Isn't that in line with his honest testimony in this case?

And then Lang was asked a lot of questions about his statements to the District Attorney after the crime. They bring Lang in after this horrible experience, and the District Attorney asks him a lot of questions. I want to read you just one question, to show you what was attempted in this case right from the beginning. Listen to this question. It's the only one I am going to read, because the answers to the rest of the questions absolutely bear out the defendant's story and his defense.

Q. Did you finish a bottle of wine before you got on the bus?
A. No, sir. I did not finish a bottle of wine. I had a glass of muscatel wine. That's all.

Where did the District Attorney get that question from? What prompted him to ask it? Where is there any evidence that Lang drank a bottle of wine? Who told that to the District Attorney? Who is trying to build up this case? Who is filling the ear of the District Attorney with these things? Was it the detective in charge of the investigation, the fellow who lied so brazenly here on the witness stand and who bore false witness against an innocent man standing in the shadow of the electric chair? Was it someone else? Where did the idea of Lang's finishing a bottle of wine come from? Did it come out of the air? They thought perhaps that in his dazed condition he might say, "I drank a bottle of wine." But no, his answer was, "I had a glass of wine." Do you know where that came from? Lang probably told it to the detective when he was asked, "Were you drunk?" So the detective walked over to the District Attorney and said, "Hey, he had a bottle of wine." That is how these things are done. And that is why we have juries to examine into all the evidence and to find out where the truth lies.

Finally I made an effort to appeal to the jurors' sense of justice and to their intelligence in evaluating the evidence:

Now, gentlemen, I know that you will remember the questions and answers I read to you, and that you will consider the facts in this case. I am concluding my summation now. I did not expect to take an hour and three-quarters; but, believe me, I could speak for another two hours, except that I feel I have sufficiently covered the major points in this case. I am confident that you will realize that the facts as presented by the District Attorney have been distorted.

If ever there was a case that cries for understanding and consideration, I think this is the case. I am not asking for mercy, gentlemen, though I have never known a person who did not need it. I am asking only for understanding. You do not have to be a criminologist or a District Attorney or a lawyer or a judge to understand this case. You just have to put yourselves in the position of Mr. Lang and ask yourselves whether, under the circumstances, you would not have done the same thing he did. Ask yourselves, too, whether it will do society any good or make your life or my life any safer or anybody's life safer if this defendant is convicted of murder in the first degree on the basis of the testimony you have heard in this case.

Gentlemen, on behalf of my colleagues and myself, I stand before you now, performing a most solemn duty. We have been assigned by the Court to defend this man. It makes no difference, under the law, who the man is, white or black. The eyes of the woman who holds the scales of justice are blindfolded. She does not want to know who is before her. All are weighed in the same balance. We have given this man the best defense we could. We have represented him as if he were the president of a railroad or of a bank and he was paying us a fabulous fee. We have tried honestly and conscientiously to do our duty as his attorneys. If, in the course of this trial, any one of us has said anything or done anything which you think you want to hold against the defendant, please do not do so. This defendant is not guilty of the crime as charged. We plead with you for his life. We ask you to have some understanding of his situation and consideration for him as you deliberate on your verdict.

You cannot find this defendant guilty. A verdict of guilty in this case would make a travesty of justice. I say to you, and I repeat, I want no compromise verdict. I want you either to find this defendant guilty as charged or to acquit him. I say to you, by every law of humanity, by every law of justice, it would be nothing short of monstrous to visit upon this defendant a verdict of guilty. I call upon you, on the basis of the facts in this case, to acquit this defendant and send him home in peace to his wife and his five children.

Thank you.

We are now in a position to appreciate, in retrospect, the overall plan and structure of this somewhat lengthy summation.

When a man's life is at stake, and the circumstances are as involved as they were in this case, defense counsel is justified, as the Court recognized here, in speaking to the jury at considerable length, as long as he sticks to the issues and avoids unnecessary digressions. There was, to be sure, a certain amount of repetition in this summation, but its purpose was to remind the jurors of the important points and to make sure that they were driven home. My intention was to keep planting in their minds seeds from which could spring justification for the jury to find reasonable doubts.

One must also realize, in reading the text of a summation, that when it was delivered it was accompanied by gestures, bodily movements, facial expressions, significant pauses, varying intonations, and visual demonstrations. Indeed, reading just the words of a lawyer's summation from the cold print of the trial record is like reading the text of a play without viewing it. One misses the actual drama as it was enacted—the changes of tempo and pitch, the contrast between logical reasoning and impassioned indignation, the transition from irony to biting sarcasm, the gradual shift from a tone of skeptical inquiry to one of open scorn, and the sudden leap from an imaginative reconstruction of a whole scene in the mind's eye to the visual inspection of a concrete object in the courtroom. All of these are essential elements of the total summation.

And so, expressions that may appear repetitious are nonetheless perfectly legitimate when summing up to the jury. When they deliberate, they may ask for parts of the testimony to refresh their recollection about disputed points. However, they are more likely to request further instructions from the judge or a reading back of parts of his charge. In any event, they are not entitled to have the summations reread to them. Therefore, if counsel's voice is to have any effect in the jury room, the jurors will have to rely on their memory of what they heard him say. If later they repeat his arguments in seeking to persuade one another, it will be because they were impressed with the force of his reasoning and the power of his words when he spoke to them. The summation is counsel's last opportunity to make his points stick in their minds. All the more reason, then, for a summation to be as memorable as possible.

We can understand now, better than we could at first, the full significance of the italicized passages in the text of the prosecutor's opening statement; that is, the words and phrases which I underlined in my copy of it because I intended to build a good part of my summation on them. Expressions like "willfully," "with malice aforethought," "couples," "chafing under a bit," "I will fix you," "getting off at that place anyhow," "with his left hand," "started to run, pursued by Benson," "denied ever seeing him," "beyond the shadow of a doubt," etc., which were used by the District Attorney in his opening to the jury, all obviously played an important—I may say even a crucial—role in the structure of my summation. I used the prosecutor's own words to confute him.

First, my plan called for an analysis of the crime charged. After breaking it down into its legal elements, I addressed myself to each in turn, showing that the facts did not support deliberation or premeditation, and that the homicide, if committed by the defendant at all, was excusable and justifiable in self-defense.

Next, I proceeded to raise doubts on points of fact bearing on premeditation by first questioning the credibility of testimony that clearly challenged common sense and then attacking the veracity of each of the star witnesses for the prosecution. Here I relied on the transcript of their testimony, which I had previously marked up and arranged in appropriate sequence. To this end, I used long slips of paper on which I wrote key words such as "ice cream," and which I inserted into the corresponding parts of the record for ready reference, so that I was able to proceed from one point to the next without any loss of time. We can see, too, that wherever I could, I supplemented the reading of parts of the transcript by calling to the jurors' attention the demeanor of the witnesses in evading or equivocating. Only after I felt that I had, in each case, thoroughly demolished the credibility of a witness did I change my tone to one of outright denunciation and call him or her a "liar" or a "perjurer."

Then I had to explain to the jury the motives of each witness who twisted the facts. Using consistently the image of football teamwork, because the chief male witness for the prosecution had testified that he and the deceased were football players, I led the jury to see why and how the prosecution's chief witnesses collaborated in giving false or misleading testimony, and I hinted at the possibility of collusion with the detective in charge of the investigation.

An important part of the logical structure of my argument depended also on the witnesses whom the prosecution could have called but failed to produce, and on what they might have said had they testified. In other words, I capitalized not only on the flagrant instances of unbelievable testimony, but also on the gaps which the prosecutor left in the evidence and which he could have filled in.

Having discredited the prosecution witnesses, I offered the jurors a plausible alternative account of what must have happened, pieced out from the testimony of the defendant, and corroborated, so far as possible, by that of the police officer whom I praised in my summation. The fact that the defendant's story was not significantly changed under cross-examination, but actually reinforced, was likewise called to the jury's attention and supported by appropriate quotations from the trial record.

As for the visual demonstrations and the reference to the judge's questions, these were used, I think to good effect, as additional weapons to weaken the prosecution's case and to strengthen the defense.

Finally, in the light of the facts, I exhorted the jurors to base their verdict on their sense of fair play, their understanding of the predicament in which the defendant had found himself.

Looking back at it now at a distance of some years, and reviewing it in the light of experience gained since then, I can see where I could have improved this summation. It is not perfect, and it is not offered here as an ideal model in every respect. Forged as it was in the heat of battle, it reflects something of the rough-and-tumble quality of a courtroom skirmish. If it is not as polished as it might be, one must remember that summations are not prepared in the cloistered leisure of a library. It was an extemporaneous speech, as all summations should be.

Yet hindsight and experience can be beneficial in improving even the ability to speak extemporaneously. I am convinced that self-criticism is an indispensable part of a lawyer's professional responsibility. If he is to grow in service to his clients and the community, if he is to refine and perfect his art, he must learn to profit from his own experience, whether successes or failures. To be dissatisfied with oneself, to refuse to settle into complacent stagnation, to be constantly looking for better ways—this is the road to progress in every enterprise, and especially in the work of the trial lawyer.

It was my habit to go over each trial, whatever its outcome, and ask myself: Where did I go wrong? What opportunities did I miss? What could I have done that I didn't do? What could I have done better? What can I learn from this experience that may help me the next time I try a case?

I found it challenging, stimulating, and useful to look back at my work in this spirit and to appraise it critically. After all, if a lawyer is to aspire to the role of an artist, he has to look upon his daily toil as part of a creative enterprise. This means recognizing and correcting mistakes, improving successful techniques, and pioneering along new-found avenues of approach.

How can this be done? How can a trial lawyer attain the degree of craftsmanship that will enable him to take his place among the elite ranks of the masters of his art? We still have these final questions to consider.

VIII

IMAGE OF A PROFESSION

25

Portrait of the Trial Lawyer as an Artist

Unfortunately, the image of the trial lawyer through the ages has been, for the most part, anything but flattering. As far back as we go, it seems, the members of our profession have been looked upon with hostility. A host of moralists, philosophers, essayists, novelists, poets, and dramatists of all nationalities and periods have attributed to lawyers every vice from meanness, deviousness, and rapacity to unscrupulousness and fraud.

Plato—to name one of the earliest in a lengthy tradition—quotes Socrates as calling lawyers "unrighteous," "crooked," "servile," "practiced in deception," and "warped." St. Luke denounced them for having "rejected God's counsel," "laden men with burdens," and "taken away the key of knowledge." Seneca speaks contemptuously of their "trafficking in mad wrangles" and "hiring out their anger and their speech" for a price. An old Italian proverb runs, "Better a mouse in the mouth of a cat than a man in the hands of a lawyer." According to an equally ancient Russian proverb, "When God wanted to punish man, He created lawyers." And in the English language, the pun on "lawyer" and "liar" has been part of the stock-in-trade of comedians for generations.

Goldsmith thought lawyers more ready to get a man into trouble than out of it, and Carl Sandburg asks,

> Why does a hearse horse snicker
> Hauling a lawyer away?

According to Oliver Wendell Holmes, Sr., "You can hire logic in the shape of a lawyer to prove anything you want to prove." Nor did his son, the great Justice Holmes of the United States Supreme Court, appear to have a much higher regard for the average run of lawyers, if we may judge from his disdainful reference to their "greedy watch for clients" and their "mannerless conflicts over often sordid interests."

Quotations to a similar effect could be multiplied indefinitely from the writings of Milton, Shakespeare, Jonson, Rabelais, Swift, Steele,

Lamb, Keats, and many others. And to their repellent literary image of the legal profession a visual dimension has been added by the hard, brutish faces of the lawyers depicted in the drawings and paintings of Daumier, Rouault, and other masters of the graphic arts.

One explanation for the low esteem in which lawyers have apparently been held is that in every case there is a loser as well as a winner; so that, as Francis Cowper points out in the *New York Law Journal* of July 18, 1966, "at least half of the customers are sure to go away critical and disappointed; while . . . the winners, convinced of the invincible validity of their case, will feel that the process of getting them their rights was too . . . dear and endlessly complicated by . . . the self-interested subtleties of their legal advisers."

To be sure, the members of the bar have had their defenders, too, and recently attempts have been made in our mass media to present a more balanced picture. But the weight of public opinion appears to have been favorably affected only to a limited extent. It is paradoxical that lawyers have pleaded everyone else's cause but somehow have been unable to refute centuries of slander directed against their own profession.

Actually, the trial lawyer serves an indispensable function as counsel, mediator, and advocate, and will continue to play a useful and necessary role in society as long as conflicts arise among men and an adversary system of resolving them is in operation. But it seems to me beyond question that there is room for improvement in the quality of the service that the trial lawyer renders. Progress in this regard is more likely to come from efforts on the part of individual lawyers to raise their own standards—technical, educational, cultural, and ethical —than from any institutional reforms or professional codes and canons, important as these no doubt are. If each lawyer would address himself to his own improvement in these respects, the reputation of our profession would take care of itself and would cease to be a matter of adverse comment.

Unfortunately, although such continual self-development is within the power of every lawyer, not enough take the necessary pains to perfect themselves in their art. Too many, once admitted to the bar, think their education has come to an end. In fact, however, this is the time when the most important and valuable lessons still remain to be learned. Every lawyer has an obligation to continue his education throughout his career, not only to increase his technical competence but also to qualify himself better to fulfill his responsibilities to his clients and the public. Especially at the beginning of his career, when he is likely to have more leisure than later, he should use it for self-improvement.

Many educational opportunities are open to him. He can take courses at a number of places, such as the Practicing Law Institute in New York. He can pursue further study on his own in the particular branch of the law in which he has a special interest. He can visit courtrooms to watch experienced trial lawyers at work, noting not only their strong points but also the mistakes that, as we have seen, even the ablest and most seasoned advocates make in the heat of battle. He can study records of trials in which specialists who have proved their success in particular fields of law display their techniques, and he can benefit vicariously from their priceless experience. He can keep abreast of current decisions, opinions, and trends by developing early the habit of carefully perusing the pages of his local law journal and reading as many legal periodicals as possible. He can become better familiar with basic medical terminology and more knowledgeable about recent advances in psychosomatic medicine and their legal implications. When he is not trying cases, he can keep himself in good practice—and, incidentally, before the public—by speaking at social, fraternal, charitable, and political clubs, at meetings of the local P.T.A. and civic organizations, or in panel discussions.

In short, just as a successful businessman concerns himself not only with making a sale today, but with building good will and improving his services to his customers, so a lawyer can keep a step ahead of his brethren by continually seizing opportunities to broaden his knowledge, sharpen his skills, and maintain close contact with the community.

When I was a young man, I used to visit the courts to watch such skilled and noted trial lawyers as Theodore Kiendl, Charles Tuttle, and Ferdinand Pecora, to mention just a few. I looked upon them worshipfully as men of genius and would ask myself nervously how I would ever be able to conduct a cross-examination as effectively as they did or sum up to a jury so convincingly. Later, however, with greater experience, I came to understand that steady application is the prime requisite to the mastery of the art of trying cases. I do not minimize the great talents of these distinguished trial lawyers when I say that they were not really men of genius. Rather, they had developed the habit of patient, painstaking, daily, drudging attention to their work, including its most commonplace details. They had followed the procedure of Charles Dickens, who said of himself:

I never could have done what I have done without the habits of punctuality, order, and diligence; without the determination to concentrate myself on one object at a time, no matter how quickly its successor should come upon its heels. . . . Whatever I have tried to do in life, I have tried with all my heart to do well; whatever I have devoted myself to, I have devoted myself to completely; in great aims and in small, I have always been thoroughly in earnest. I have never believed it possible that any natural or improved ability can claim immunity from the companionship of the steady, plain, hardworking qualities, and hope to gain its end.

Walter E. Craig, former President of the American Bar Association, put the matter succinctly in his address at its annual meeting in 1963:

Constant diligence, careful preparation, and continuous study do more to make a good and successful lawyer than native ability or genius.

At any rate, what we call "genius" is, as Thomas Edison reminds us, "one per cent inspiration and ninety-nine per cent perspiration."

If a lawyer's years of experience at the bar are to count for anything, he must learn to recognize his mistakes and to profit from them, so that he does not keep on repeating them. "The greatest of all faults," said Carlyle, "is to be conscious of none." A complacent optimism founded on winning a string of several cases is a costly luxury that no lawyer can long afford to indulge in. He must resist the temptation to become satisfied with his successes and to believe that he is invincible.

In the first place, "success" in winning cases is a relative matter. If more thorough preparation, a greater knowledge of the law, or more detailed information about the medical, technical, or other intricacies of a case could have resulted in a larger award for his client, counsel may have little to congratulate himself upon if all that he "wins" is a verdict of lesser amount. That kind of "success" ultimately comes very dear.

Moreover, if the truth were but known about many trial lawyers who have achieved a reputation for winning cases, we should find that often their accomplishment consisted in nothing more than making fewer mistakes than their opponents. How often, in a football game, for example, does the difference between victory and defeat turn on a fumbled or intercepted pass or a missed tackle! The same is true in any contest, including—if I may reverse a well-known phrase—"combat by trial." Many a case has been won only because the other side made a fatal blunder, missed an opportunity, or was guilty of a careless oversight. Some may say that there is injustice in a system that allows verdicts to depend on such accidents or human failings, but it is in the nature of adversary proceedings to place a heavy burden of responsibility on counsel for each side to make the best case he can for his client.

At any rate, these are reasons enough why a lawyer has to look at his successes with as critical an eye as he casts on his failures. Only thus can an advocate become aware, as he proceeds from case to case, of his own strengths and weaknesses.

Nor can a lawyer ever rest on his oars and just coast along on his own momentum. Each trial is a new race against fresh competitors and calls for the utmost in effort if he is to bring his client victory. Like an athlete, a lawyer must keep himself in top form at all times. He is always "in training," as it were. The sharp edge of his legal acumen has to be kept constantly honed and ready for use.

A young trial lawyer may at first find it difficult to know at what point he is succeeding or failing. He will need to win or lose many cases before he can see exactly where he is going and whether he is being successful. After a number of trials he may find himself coming to the fore, amid loud and fervent huzzahs from press and public, and everything will look rosy. But anyone who allows such adulation to go to his head and fails to work even harder is due for a rude awakening. He must continue to keep searching for new ideas and new ways of improving himself. A lawyer has to make a "hit" every time he "goes to bat" for his client. He gets no credit for good hitting and good batting in previous games.

Yet it is impossible to win every case. A lawyer must lose cases if he is to learn how to win them. Under no circumstances should he become discouraged if he loses. The most successful trial lawyers have taken many a beating and suffered many a setback during the course of their careers. After all, this should not be surprising. Just as the best surgeons are the ones who are asked to perform "hopeless" operations, so the cases showing the least promise of success generally find their way to the ablest lawyers. The problems become more difficult, the demands become more unreasonable, the closer one gets to the top, and to stay on top requires even harder work than to get there. Counsel will know he has become a really good trial lawyer if he receives plaudits even when he loses.

I am reminded, in this connection, of the scene in Lewis Carroll's *Through the Looking-Glass* in which Alice finds herself running as hard as she can to keep up with the Red Queen, but the trees and the landscape around them never seem to change. However fast they run, they never manage to pass anything, and when, at the end, Alice finally stops in exhaustion, she finds that they have been under the same tree all the time.

"In my country," Alice says, "you generally get somewhere if you run very fast."

"A poor sort of country that is!" snorts the Queen. "Here it takes all the running you can do just to keep in the same place. If you want to get somewhere else, you have to run twice as fast."

And that is the way it is in the legal profession too.

Actually, lost cases may eventually turn out to be blessings in disguise.

For years I tried cases for the Democratic Party in Brooklyn. One day the chief counsel for the party, Francis D. McGarey, later a Justice of the Supreme Court of the State of New York, handed me two files, saying, "Here, Lou, try these cases." They were due to be tried the following day, one in the morning and one in the afternoon, before two different judges. In each case my opponent was to be the chief counsel for the Republican Party, A. David Benjamin, now a Justice of the Appellate Division of the Supreme Court of the State of New York, Second Judicial District.

When I examined the first file, I discovered that the proceeding was to invalidate designating petitions in a primary election contest on the ground that they were permeated with fraud. However, in looking through the other file, I learned that in the afternoon my job was to oppose an attempt to invalidate designating petitions allegedly permeated with fraud. In other words, I was supposed to present opposite arguments on the same day in two cases of the same type.

"I hope you don't think I'm a magician," I said to Mr. McGarey.

I shall never forget his reply: "Lou, do the best you can."

The next day I tried the first case in the morning and lost it. In the afternoon, when I appeared in the second case, I promptly called to the judge's attention the Court's decision in the first case. Thereupon, he turned to my adversary and asked, "What do you say to that?"

Mr. Benjamin extricated himself by saying, "Your Honor, I find myself in the same position as Abraham Lincoln when he was a lawyer and was reminded by a judge one afternoon that he had earlier argued the other side of the question just as persuasively. You will, I am sure, recall his response. He said, 'This morning I thought I was right; this afternoon I know I am right.'"

I lost both cases. However, I did my best, and that is all that is expected of any lawyer.

If an attorney finds that he has made an erroneous statement in the course of the trial, he should not be afraid to admit it then and there in open court. The strongest and wisest are the first to acknowledge their mistakes. Rather than try to conceal or disguise an error, it is better to say to the judge, "Your Honor, I said a while ago . . . [repeating the erroneous statement]. I have just learned that I am in error. May I apologize to the Court, the jury, and my adversary, and assure you it was not intentional. In the interests of fair play, I respectfully withdraw my statement."

The courtesy, candor, and decency exemplified by such an admission of error are the hallmarks of a good trial lawyer. He is polite not only to the judge and the jury, but to his adversary as well. If, to cite another illustration, opposing counsel does not have his copy of the marked pleadings ready for the Court, the lawyer who is "on his toes" steps up to the bench and says, "Your Honor, perhaps I can be of help to my adversary in supplying the Court with a set of marked pleadings until my friend can find his, which I am sure he must have somewhere in his files."

Indeed, courtesy on the part of a trial lawyer is more than just a tactical means of giving the judge and the jury a good impression of his gentlemanly qualities. Good courtroom manners are one of the outward signs of the fact that a lawyer is an officer of the Court, clothed with its dignity, and bound by the canons of the bar to be fair and candid.

Thus, just as etiquette may be said to express, as Henry Hazlitt so aptly puts it, "the ethics of everyday life," so an advocate's politeness to his adversary, the Court, and the jury is merely an extension of a basic regard for the ethical principles of fairness and candor. The lawyer who keeps these principles in mind at all times will naturally conform his conduct to their requirements in all his contacts in the courtroom.

Certainly the trend today is strongly in the direction of frankness, fairness, and openness and away from deviousness and concealment. In an article in the *New York Law Journal* of August 31, 1966, Jacob Weinstein suggests that we may "have reached a stage in our legal development when more weight should be given to the attorney's position as an officer of the Court and less to his position as advocate waging a private fight using tactics dependent on the client's view of morality." As Drinker says in his *Legal Ethics*, ". . . the old idea that litigation is a game between the lawyers has been supplanted by the more modern view that the lawyer is a minister of justice." He adds, however, that "the theory of our system is still that justice is best accomplished by having all the facts and arguments on each side investigated and presented with maximum vigor by opposing counsel, for decision by the Court and jury."

As matters stand today, the prosecutor of a criminal case is under a duty to bring to the attention of the Court and the jury any and every bit of evidence in his possession which may tend to exonerate the accused. If he willfully conceals such evidence, he is not only being unfair to the defendant, but he is violating his oath of office and the law and is himself subject to prosecution.

Indeed, there is today a noticeable tendency, especially on the part of our Federal judiciary, to minimize the role of surprise by the prosecution in criminal cases and to grant the defense the right to know in advance of trial the results of blood tests, for example, or the content of documents to be placed in evidence. The theory underlying this trend has been well stated by United States Attorney Jon O. Newman. In a memorandum to his assistants in the Federal Judicial District of Connecticut he said, "The issue is whether a criminal trial is to be a game, with a premium on suspense, when you have the evidence, and bluff when you don't, or whether it will be a conscientious pursuit of the truth."

On the other hand, the defense lawyer in a criminal case has no duty whatever to let the judge or the jury know about any facts which may be detrimental to his client's case. For example, if his client is charged with burglary, and he knows it to be a fact that the accused was convicted of other felonies on a number of occasions, it is counsel's duty to conduct his defense in such a way that these convictions are not disclosed. And since the burden of proof is on the prosecution, the defense is not obliged to disclose anything in advance.

There is no doubt that judges do appreciate well-prepared, courteous, candid, and cooperative lawyers, and depend to a considerable extent on them. I am reminded of what Yogi Berra said when he was asked, on being named manager of the New York Yankees, "What makes a good manager?"

"A good ball club," he replied.

In the same way, if the question were asked, "What makes a good judge?" I would reply, "Good lawyers." Indeed, it would not be too much to say that a judge is as good as the lawyers who are trying a case or arguing a motion before him. If they have the facts and the law at their command, the judge will have little difficulty in making proper decisions. In fact, it takes amazingly little time for a judge to recognize the lawyer who works with him, rather than against him. Judges like to have good lawyers before them, especially if the issues involved are intricate, and they remember and appreciate the services performed by the really able attorneys.

On this point I can do no better than to quote a former Chief Justice of the Supreme Court of the United States, the Honorable Charles Evans Hughes:

> The highest reward that can come to a lawyer is the esteem of his professional brethren. That esteem is won in unique conditions and proceeds from an impartial judgment of professional rivals. It cannot be purchased. It cannot be artificially created. It cannot be gained by artifice or contrivance to attract public attention. It is not measured by pecuniary gains. It is an esteem which is born in sharp contests and thrives despite conflicting interests. It is an esteem commanded solely by integrity of character and by brains and skill in the honorable performance of professional duty. . . . In a world of imperfect humans, the faults of human clay are always manifest. The special temptations and tests of lawyers are obvious enough. But considering trial and error, success and defeat, the bar slowly makes its estimate, and the memory of the careers which it approves is at once its most precious heritage and an important safeguard of the interests of society so largely in the keeping of the profession of the law in its manifold services.

Needless to say, the same qualities that command the respect and admiration of a lawyer's peers in the profession win the esteem of the judges before whom he practices. A trial lawyer who deserved and won this kind of regard from his fellow advocates and the members of the judiciary was the renowned John W. Davis. Here is the tribute paid to him by one of his frequent adversaries, Beryl H. Levy, in his book *Corporation Lawyer: Saint or Sinner?*:

> He was a man of consummate graciousness. His soft-spoken manner . . . , his courtly manners, his absence of pretension: all were deeply impressive. . . . When colloquies were held at the judge's bench out of the hearing of the jury, or when conferences were held in the judge's chambers . . . , his quick, "No, we can't do that!" carried infinite weight and put an end to any further discussion on the subject. Throughout the trial he was on the most fraternal terms with us on

the other side. The reader will recall Shakespeare's observation that adversaries in law "strive mightily, but eat and drink as friends."

I once heard an argument before the bench in which one of the attorneys, without referring to any authorities, expounded on the law at some length. Then the Court turned to his adversary, who had earned the reputation of thoroughly researching the law in any case in which he appeared, and asked, "Is that what the courts have held?"

"No, Your Honor," counsel quietly answered. Then he opened one of the lawbooks he had with him, read a few paragraphs from a decision, and closed his argument by saying, "This is the law that applies, and my adversary's argument has never been accepted by the courts."

Whereupon the judge replied, "I knew you would have the right answer," and promptly decided the matter in favor of the "good lawyer."

Experiences like this show that success at the bar must ultimately be rooted in solid knowledge and integrity. Flamboyance, eloquence, and showmanship are no substitutes for these indispensable qualities. What counts in the long run is the way in which an attorney can bring to bear on any question before him all the relevant legal knowledge, factual information, and logical reasoning needed to achieve a resolution of the issue favorable to his client.

Proficiency in public speaking is, of course, a valuable asset to an advocate; but to be an accomplished trial lawyer, it is not necessary to be an orator or to have mastered the techniques of acting. The important requirement, in this respect, is that counsel have a good command of the English language and be skilled in the art of communication and persuasion. Having acquired the necessary background of knowledge, he must be able to choose the right words to be convincing, ingratiating, and informative, and attune his remarks to the tribunal before which he is appearing. He will not thereby expose himself to the rebuke described by Mr. Justice Hilbery in his book on *The Duty and Art in Advocacy*:

> A counsel much given to emotional rhetoric began to open a case before Mr. Justice Swift, who was sitting alone. He had not gone far before he was giving full rein to his oratory. Mr. Justice Swift tapped on his desk.
> "Mr. Blank," he said, "there is no jury."
> Then came the appropriate apology, and the counsel began again, and again was soon indulging in rolling periods and highly flowered dec-

lamation. For some time the judge suffered it. Then there came the tap of the pencil on the desk.

"Usher," he said, "switch on the light over the jury box. Mr. Blank does not believe me."

Whether counsel is speaking to the judge, the jury, or a witness, he should choose his words so as to convey precisely and easily the thought he wishes to express. A lawyer, after all, makes his living by the use of words. They are the tools of his profession, and their selection deserves the same careful consideration as a carpenter gives to the problem of deciding whether an adze, a plane, a chisel, or a file will best serve his purpose in a particular job. Unless he possesses some measure of competence in the use of words, a lawyer will not be able to transmit his message clearly and forcefully on behalf of his client.

Yet words are weapons as well as tools, and they can be dangerous to their user if they are ineptly wielded. A lawyer should remember that during any trial he will have many opportunities to keep his mouth shut. Often he will find that he can be more helpful to his client by being silent than by speaking. He must learn when to say nothing and try to curb any tendency to speak out of turn, to raise futile or self-defeating objections, or to let his tongue wag too freely.

On the other hand, when he does find it necessary to speak, he should do so clearly and forthrightly. Counsel should neither split his hearers' eardrums with stentorian blasts, as if seeking to drown out sense with sound, nor whisper in funereal accents, as if mourning for a dead or hopeless cause. Clarity and audibility are important not only for the sake of the judge and the jury, but also as a means of ensuring an accurate record of the proceedings by the court reporter.

This often neglected aspect of a lawyer's speech in the courtroom is discussed with the seriousness it deserves in a most enlightening article entitled "Are We Overlooking the Verbatim Record?" by Leonard J. Buckley in The Detroit Lawyer of October, 1965. The author, himself an official court reporter and former officer of the Michigan Court Reporters Association, deplores what he calls the "growing laxity" among members of the legal profession in their attitude toward the verbatim record of the proceedings. He complains that court reporters are finding it increasingly difficult to fulfill their responsibilities because lawyers, "perhaps unknowingly, and . . . certainly unintentionally," place obstacles in the way of taking down a verbatim record that may ultimately prove to be of vital importance to them.

Mr. Buckley asks: "Is there gradually passing from the courtroom scene the deliberate speaker, one who gives careful attention to choice of language and delivery, syntax, enunciation, continuity in presentation of proof, persuasive and succinct argument?"

One of the chief impediments to an accurate recording of counsel's remarks is, he says, "slurred or mumbled speech." He quotes a woman juror who said, "I was trying very hard to concentrate on the facts of the case, but I found it almost impossible because the trial attorney was difficult to hear and irritating to watch. He mumbled and dropped his voice. His movements were abrupt and jerky; he fiddled with his glasses, and he paced nervously. He distracted his audience."

In another case, the attorney, in his final argument, "strode across the courtroom away from the jury, and with his back to the Court, the jury, and the reporter, spoke . . . to a blank courtroom wall." Presumably he spoke with some histrionic purpose, but it misfired, because the jury rendered a verdict against his client for a very large sum of money, equivalent to "at least five hundred dollars per second while he was at the wall."

Mr. Buckley warns, too, against the common practice of stipulating with one's adversary out of hearing of the reporter, whose duty it is to make a record of the understanding reached between both sides. He also reminds lawyers of the need to clarify expressions like "here," "there," "this much," "that one," "he did like this," etc., which otherwise mean absolutely nothing in the transcript. The reporter, of course, is not authorized to insert into the record his own conclusions as to what they mean. Failure on the part of counsel to supply the necessary elucidation of such elliptical terms may render meaningless and useless what might otherwise have been an important part of the trial record.

Naturally, a good lawyer insists that witnesses likewise speak clearly, for the record, and slowly enough so that their testimony can be taken down accurately by the reporter. Nor does the courteous advocate speak at the same time as the judge, a witness, or opposing counsel is speaking. Instead, he allows the reporter to record each speaker's statement, including his own, in turn. Moreover, an alert attorney describes or identifies all exhibits in advance of offering them in evidence and refers to them by exhibit number at all times, so that the record always shows what he is talking about. Finally, the considerate lawyer takes pains to provide the reporter, in advance, with a glossary of technical terms to be used in the trial—e.g., "methylene," "fermeture," "occipito-mastoid," etc., as a precautionary measure to avoid errors and needless interruptions. After all, a court reporter, however knowledgeable, cannot reasonably be expected to be familiar with the specialized vocabulary of expert witnesses or with all the new terms that have come into use as a result of recent advances in medicine, electronics, chemistry, physics, and the other sciences.

Summing up his conclusions on this important but often overlooked aspect of a trial lawyer's work, Mr. Buckley writes:

> In my years of reporting I have made one particular observation— that the good lawyers . . . the ones who are held in highest esteem by their associates, the ones who are considered "the" practitioners, who are a delight to behold as they practice their art . . . are the lawyers who consistently and emphatically speak TO the record.

There should be no guesswork about what a lawyer is saying, and if there is the slightest doubt about what a witness may have said, counsel should ask him to repeat his words. The lawyer who is at all times record-conscious is a joy not only to the court reporter but, more often than not, to the judge, the jury, and his client as well.

If counsel has any doubts about himself on this score, he can easily test his clarity and audibility by listening to a tape recording of his own speech. This is the way actors improve their diction, and it is one that can be recommended also to lawyers.

Lord Birkett has stated as well as anyone the qualities that should become apparent in a lawyer's speech and demeanor in the courtroom:

> I like the advocate who speaks up so that he can be heard. I like the advocate who uses good English, who selects his words and becomes more effective because of that. I like the advocate who is not a sycophant, who will stand up to the Court. . . . It is essential that he should know his facts perfectly, and it is essential that he should know his law perfectly. But my belief has been and is that your advocate, to reach the heights, must be more than a man of law. He must be in some degree a man of letters.

Clearly, this is a portrait of the trial lawyer as a person who is more than just a master craftsman. The "man of letters" is a fully rounded human being, the heir to millennia of culture, to whom, in Terence's famous and oft-quoted phrase, "nothing human is alien."

We can best understand this larger, more inclusive, humanistic view by asking ourselves: What makes a trial lawyer? Is it only a knowledge of the law? Matthew Arnold said that no man could be a good Christian who knew only his Bible; and by the same token no man can be a trial lawyer who knows only his lawbooks. What makes a trial lawyer is every experience that helps him to understand the nature of the human condition and the thoughts and feelings of his fellow men. Bach, Beethoven, Schubert, Schumann, and Brahms help to make a trial lawyer. But so do Rodgers and Hammerstein and the composers of rock-'n'-roll. Dickens and Shakespeare and Milton make a trial lawyer. Kant's *Critique of Pure Reason* makes a trial lawyer. So does a detective story by Arthur Conan Doyle. Like literature, art, and philosophy, the cases that come to trial range over the entire gamut of human experience, and a trial lawyer is made by every aspect of human life. A trial lawyer is made by imagination, education, sensitivity, compassion, and understanding—all the fruits of a rich and varied experience, actual and vicarious.

I realize that this conception of the trial lawyer transcends the rather narrow view that many advocates tend to take of their professional responsibilities. They limit unduly the range of their vision and the sphere of their intellectual and cultural development. They are so much concerned with the acquisition of mere forensic technique, important and even essential though this is, that they fail to think of themselves as, at least potentially, creative artists, using imaginatively all the rich resources that an intimate familiarity with art, literature, philosophy, and science could place at their disposal.

As Nathaniel Richter reminds us in the article *The Decline of the Trial Lawyer* from which I earlier quoted:

> A good trial lawyer is neither one versed only in the arts nor one versed only in science. A good trial lawyer is a whole man—a man of the arts and sciences, a man of rhetoric and philosophy and devotion to justice.

Mr. Richter deplores the fact that so many modern trial lawyers have failed to take advantage of all that our fathers and forefathers—and indeed what the whole of mankind—have left as their greatest heritage: the literature of the world.

The trial lawyer must be a man of learning, not only in the law, but in everything that expresses and illuminates human life. Only then can he aspire to the status of an artist who makes use of the legacy of the past to build creatively in the present.

What does it mean, concretely, to speak of a trial lawyer as an "artist" rather than as a legal craftsman or technician? To be sure, this means, first of all, a mastery of his own field and of trial techniques. But the artist goes beyond this. He breaks away from outworn patterns; his vision extends over a wider view, and his insight, illuminated by education and reflection, penetrates more deeply. He dares to be imaginative and inventive, because he stands, as it were, on the shoulders of the giants of the past. It is in this sense, too, that we can understand the full significance of Francis Bacon's often misinterpreted dictum that "every man is a debtor to his profession."

Let me illustrate with a rather homely example how a trial lawyer who is resourceful, ingenious, and willing to discard the rules of the textbook can use a little applied psychology to good effect in a courtroom. The case was indeed a troublesome one. An elderly, peace-loving couple, the owners of a three-family house, were literally exhausted by fruitless litigation in their repeated efforts to oust a family of vexatious tenants, consisting of a father and mother, their five boisterous children—ranging in age from five to thirteen—and the maternal grandfather. Time and again the elderly couple brought the family to court, charging them with disorderly conduct, and each time the defendants would appear with a veteran neighborhood lawyer who argued, "It's no crime to have children," or "This childless old couple are seeking to vent their envious resentment on their tenants just for having children," and the case would invariably be dismissed.

What made matters worse was that, on arriving home, the tenants would take their victory in court as a license to encourage their unruly brood to indulge in new and wilder capers, such as dragging their bicycles up the hallway, tramping up and down the stairs, jumping and screaming at all hours of the day and night, and, in general, making life all but unbearable for the old couple.

Finally, in spite of their continued defeats, they decided to take one more chance. This time they instituted an action in a civil court to evict the tenants on the ground that they were creating a nuisance. Back went the defendants to the same neighborhood lawyer, who demanded a jury trial.

On the day of the trial, with the jury duly impaneled, the tenants and their five brats were jubilant. Their lawyer, in his opening to the jury, lost no time in launching his standard attack on the plaintiffs as envious villains who begrudged the defendants their children. In a burst of grandiloquence, he concluded by saying that children "are the hope for the future of our country."

Watching the faces of the jurors as they listened to his adversary's rhetoric, the landlords' counsel had a sickening feeling that his clients' cause was being lost even before the first witness was called to the stand. In desperation, he resorted to an unusual stratagem. He remembered that while the jury was being selected, the five children had been running up and down the aisles of the courtroom, screaming and bumping into spectators. They had knocked off their grandfather's hat and used it as a football, to the accompaniment of loud shrieks and much vigorous tussling. Reasoning that it would be to the best interests of the landlords' case to have these rampageous little demons in the courtroom during the trial, the attorney for the plaintiffs decided to apply some "reverse psychology." Keeping his fingers crossed, he asked the judge to *exclude* the children during the course of the trial "in order to avoid possible sympathy in the jury box."

Immediately defense counsel jumped to his feet and protested indignantly against any motion to exlude from the courtroom "the citizens of tomorrow" and "the future of American society." His plea was so fervent and stirring that permission was granted for the children to remain in court throughout the proceedings.

Needless to say, it was not long before they had reverted to their customary obstreperousness. Resuming their wild antics, they chased one another around the courtroom, emitting earsplitting war whoops, tugging at their grandfather's beard, and knocking over chairs at the counsel table. In fact, during a recess, while the members of the jury were standing in the hallway, some of them were almost bowled over by the jostling, tackling, and darting of these irrepressible imps, and one juror was actually struck in the face by a ball thrown by one of the rowdies to put his brother "out at the plate"—the plate being another juror.

It did not take the jury long to return with a verdict for the plaintiffs.

Although inventiveness cannot, by its very nature, be learned from a textbook or even from direct observation of creative lawyers at work, I am convinced that an attorney can cultivate the habit of mind that leads to the search for new solutions to old problems. He must face each case as a fresh challenge and seek in it the elements that make it unique. If he is to avoid stagnation and falling into a rut, he must beware of easy formulas, so-called short cuts, and routinism in his approach and be ready to strike out into untried paths, like a pioneer. There is, to be sure, some risk in breaking new ground, but there is also the exhilaration of discovery and professional growth. To the resourceful lawyer, precedent is not a straitjacket or a Procrustean bed, but a fertile source of ideas for adapting the decisions of the past to the needs of the present. The advice which André Gide gave to writers can certainly be extended to lawyers as well:

> Do not do what someone else could do as well as you. Do not say . . . what someone else could say . . . as well as you. Care for nothing in yourself but what you feel exists nowhere else—and out of yourself, create.

However, a unique individuality is not the only characteristic that distinguishes the achievement of the true artist. Just as a painter, a sculptor, or a composer aims, in each of his works, at a single, harmonious, unified effect, and chooses his materials accordingly; so the creative trial lawyer, precisely because he is himself a "whole man," strives to make everything he does or says in court contribute to the whole picture he is seeking to present of the case he is trying. His speech, his tone, his bearing, his choice of words, his pace—all add something to the total impact on the members of the jury.

For example, a tempo that is too slow can have a deadening, stupefying, and even somnolent effect on them. Some lawyers, especially those hired on a per diem basis, love to stay with a case indefinitely, nursing it along and permitting the trial to drag on and on. They seem to forget that the judge has other business to attend to and that the jury would also like to see the case brought to an end.

Malcolm Wilson, one of my former colleagues in the New York State Legislature and now Lieutenant Governor of New York State, once told me what happened to a very able trial lawyer whose leisurely pace unduly protracted the proceedings in an important action. After the case had lingered on for several tedious weeks, the laggard attorney, who never missed an opportunity to win the favor of the jury, remarked one morning, at the opening of the session, with one eye on the panel, "I trust Your Honor will take judicial notice of the fact that I have had a haircut since we adjourned yesterday."

The judge, who was noted for his quick wit, promptly responded, "The Court so notes, but also takes judicial notice of the fact that unless you move along more rapidly in the trial of this action than you have to date, you will need another haircut before we are finished."

The way a lawyer dresses also has a subtle effect on the jury, and, of course, this is especially important in the case of female counsel. On the subject of her attire I can do no better than defer to the opinion of an expert, Gladys M. Dorman, member of the Board of Higher Education of the City of New York and a very able lawyer:

If she dresses too well, some of the women on the jury may resent it, and if she wears very tailored clothes, the men might feel that she is aping the masculine sex. I don't know if I have solved the problem, but if the trial lasts at least two days, I usually start with a black or brown tailored suit, but with a feminine, frilly blouse, and on the second day, a tailored wool dress in a bright blue or lavender color.

The story is told of a celebrated trial lawyer whose exploits before juries made him a legendary figure. When he tried a case, the court-room was packed to capacity, for one never knew what was going to happen. He would enter the courtroom with only a scrap of paper in his hands, and wearing baggy, ill-fitting clothes somewhat the worse for wear. He had the baffled appearance of a country bumpkin suddenly pushed onto the center of the stage. Meanwhile, out of sight in the corridors stood aides with suitcases crammed with the documents he needed. It was not long before he had the jurors sympathetically help-ing him to try his case. But somehow he managed to win case after case.

Those days are gone forever. This technique simply will not work any longer. Jurors in this day and age are just too sophisticated to be "taken in" by this type of trial lawyer. He went out with the horse and buggy.

Yet appearances in this regard can often be deceiving. It would be a great mistake for a lawyer to underrate an adversary simply because he gives the impression of being unprepared, careless, or lax. The dangers involved in trying to take advantage of a seemingly inattentive oppo-nent are well illustrated by what happened in a case in which Harold H. Corbin, who has gained fame as one of the outstanding trial lawyers at the New York bar, represented the defendants. Opposing counsel, a noted and formidable adversary, was reading for the record page after page of a lengthy examination before trial. On and on he droned, hour after hour, in the same monotonous voice. The jury hardly needed any inducement to fall into a drowsy stupor.

This was the perfect setting for Mr. Corbin to display his talents. Slouching down in his chair, he extended his legs, placed his spectacles on his forehead, closed his eyes, and for the longest time feigned sleep. Both attorneys lulled the jury into somnolence.

Suddenly, however, as the efficient but undramatic counsel for the plaintiff was plodding on through the dry subject matter, thunder broke loose, in the form of the booming voice of Mr. Corbin: "Why," he roared, "didn't you read the *whole* thing? You deliberately left out part of the answer!" Whereupon, he unceremoniously snatched the minutes from the hands of his startled adversary and said, "Here, let me read it." He then proceeded to read the omitted part. The jury was now thoroughly alert, and a number of them nudged their neighbors, in open admiration, not only of Mr. Corbin's remarkable photographic memory but of the strikingly dramatic way in which he used his talents. Needless to say, Mr. Corbin won the case.

A trial lawyer should beware of traps like these and avoid the temptation to "slip one over" on an apparently heedless adversary.

Obviously, resourcefulness, imaginativeness, inventiveness, and what I have called "art," to say nothing of mere technical competence or craftsmanship, cannot be learned from a book or a course, nor can the presence of these qualities be ascertained to any significant extent in a written examination designed to determine a candidate's qualifications to practice law. Law school curricula prepare students only for the bar examination. They do not equip one to work in the courts. This is not the fault of the law schools or their teachers. The difficulty stems from the very nature of trial practice, which calls for aptitudes, skills, and talents that are best developed through the experience of actually trying cases in the courts. To establish his credentials as a trial lawyer, counsel must actively engage in the examination of veniremen and witnesses and in all the other practices that constitute the everyday work of a member of his profession. The true and proper regimen for the embryonic trial lawyer has been aptly stated by Presiding Justice Bernard Botein of the Appellate Division of the Supreme Court of the State of New York, First Department, in his excellent book, *Trial Judge:*

> I know of no child prodigies among trial lawyers. A certain seasoning of actual experience is a necessary ingredient in the development of the trial advocate. He can learn a good deal from books. He should, of course, have the rules of evidence at his fingertips and be well grounded in the law affecting his case. But, to develop beyond the point of adequacy, he must learn from his own mistakes and successes and from watching other lawyers in action.

Certainly there is a growing need for better-trained advocates. Far too many trial lawyers, both neophytes and veterans, while apparently proficient in legal theory, are patently deficient in the art of advocacy itself, that is, in the actual presentation of a case and the conduct of a trial. My own trial and judicial experience lead me to concur fully with the following remarks of the late Justice Robert Jackson of the United States Supreme Court:

> It seems to me that, while the scholarship of the bar has been improving, the art of advocacy has been declining. If the weakness of the apprentice system was to produce advocates without scholarship, the weakness of the law school system is to turn out scholars with no skill at advocacy.

Our law schools serve their function in equipping the young attorney with a basic knowledge of the rights and duties involved in a case and of the rules of practice and evidence employed in a trial to vindicate those rights and enforce those duties. In addition, the young lawyer interested in assuming the role of trial counsel will have been well served by his formal education if there has been inculcated in him a penchant for continued, lifelong self-education. But neither law school instruction nor subsequent reading, no matter how avid or extensive, will suffice to make one a skilled trial lawyer.

A duty thus devolves upon the experienced advocate to take novices under his tutelage, to entrust to the deserving student the trial of minor cases after he proves to be qualified, to offer constructive criticisms, and to watch over him with a kindly eye and a firm hand. Although primarily obligated to his own client for the attainment of successful results in pending litigation, the trial lawyer owes a further duty to society and his profession to stimulate other barristers to a higher standard of accomplishment in the courtroom for the purpose of enlarging the relatively small circle of highly qualified advocates who today constitute the ablest members of the bar.

With this end in view, my former colleague in the State Senate, the Honorable Daniel Gutman, dean of the New York Law School, suggested in the summer of 1960, after I had presided at a moot trial at the school, that I deliver a series of lectures to the senior class on how to try a case. At first I was reluctant to undertake what appeared like a formidable task, for I thought that a prerequisite to the presentation of such lectures would be intensive research in a vast number of compendiums and textbooks on trial techniques. A superabundance of literature, it seemed, was available to the students, and the law school professors appeared to be better qualified to impart the necessary information to them.

However, the distinguished dean insisted that in my lectures I draw upon my experiences as an active trial lawyer and as a judge in the criminal and civil courts. Such a course, he stated, particularly if the students were permitted to ask questions after each lecture, would be of great value to them. This proposal was an exciting challenge to me, and I decided to accept it.

I thought that I would need no more than four or five lectures to complete the course. In fact, I delivered approximately twenty; and, before I realized it, the semester had ended. I adopted the dean's suggestion that the students be permitted to ask questions. These proved to be most interesting and provocative and showed that during their years in law school the students had been seriously troubled by their apparent lack of knowledge of how to try a case. I believe I could have given many more lectures without in any way exhausting the subject. For how does one impart a lifetime of experience to others? No lawyer can possibly transmit to anyone else—and surely not by lecturing— the art he has developed through the years, bearing, as it does, the stamp of his uniqueness and reflecting the nuances of his individual personality.

At the conclusion of the course, many of the students wrote to me. Again and again their letters stressed the fact that the full value of the experiences I related to the class would have been better realized if only the course had been tied in with an actual courtroom trial. The analogy was drawn with the practical experience that a medical student gains from his required period of internship and clinical training. Only in this way could the gap be bridged between textbook or lecture theory and the concrete problems of litigation faced by the legal practitioner who has to apply what he has learned to pleading a case in court.

I realize well that this book, based as it is in good measure on the lectures I gave, cannot constitute more than a partial solution of the problem. The fact is that there are a great many trial lawyers who do not manifest in the remotest way a knowledge of how to ask questions during the *voir dire*, direct examination, or cross-examination, how to lay the foundations for offering an exhibit in evidence, how to request the Court to charge a jury, how to take exception to a charge, or how to make motions during or incidental to trial. Even if a book covered all these matters in the greatest detail, it still could not fill the gap completely between theory and practice.

With this object in view, in an article in the *New York Law Journal* of November 12, 1964, entitled "A Plan for Compulsory Court Certification of Trial Lawyers," I recommended the method with which I worked—and I mean *worked*—when I became a law clerk. I accompanied my employer to court and watched him "go to bat" in trial after trial. By the time I was admitted to the bar, I knew my way around, about, inside, and outside the courts. I studied the habits and techniques not only of my employer but of his adversaries as well. Likewise, I observed and learned much about the mannerisms of the judges. I made it my business to go from court to court, following and watching outstanding trial lawyers like Lloyd Stryker, Max D. Steuer, Samuel Untermeyer, and Francis L. Wellman, as well as those I have previously mentioned. From each of these distinguished lawyers and from many others, I acquired techniques which later stood me in good stead. I took copious notes while I observed these giants of the bar in action, and in later years I used my notes to great advantage.

Today, I think, there is need for a planned program, to be sponsored by our courts, making it *mandatory* for the lawyer who chooses trial work to go through an observation period of "on-the-scene" activities in open court before judges and juries. I favor such a system as a means of educating the beginner at the bar in courtroom advocacy and trial strategy. Lecture series, clinics, moot trials, courses in trial techniques, postgraduate seminars, and panel discussions among trial lawyers no doubt have their advantages, but they cannot take the place of the "live" experience of the trial itself. In my article I proposed that every newly admitted attorney who is desirous of becoming a trial lawyer be required by court rules, before he assumes his role as an advocate, to devote a minimum of three hundred hours—two hundred hours in civil trial work and one hundred in criminal cases—within a specified period of time, to observing the way experienced trial lawyers conduct themselves in court. Before being eligible to try his first case, he should be required to see trial practitioners of proven ability as they question a panel of veniremen, as they conduct direct examinations and cross-examinations, and as they argue motions and deliver summations.

The record of the prospective trial lawyer's hourly attendance at these observation sessions could be duly kept by a properly deputized clerk of the court, and credit would be granted for observing only those trial lawyers who had been certified by a selected panel of judges. In much the same way as student teachers, before being permitted to take over a class, are required for a specified period to sit in the classrooms of qualified and experienced pedagogues and observe their methods of inspiring, instructing, disciplining, and testing their pupils, fledgling trial lawyers can have their three hundred required hours of observation proportionately divided among the salient phases representative of a trial in its entirety. Perhaps fifty hours could be devoted to observing the selection of jurors, twenty-five to the opening statement, fifty to direct examination, seventy-five to cross-examination, twenty-five to trial motions, and seventy-five to summation.

A number of refinements of this plan suggest themselves. Even among seasoned trial lawyers there are often differences of opinion concerning the phase of a trial in which a particular advocate is recognized as being most proficient. I would take cognizance of this situation by having the panel of judges evaluate the skills of the trial lawyers under their observation in respect to each facet of the trial. Then the student could be assigned, in every instance, to those attorneys selected by the judges as being especially adept in the conduct of the particular phase of the trial to be studied. Only after he had satisfactorily concluded such a course of observation of trial techniques, under the supervision of qualified masters of the art of advocacy, for the allotted number of hours would the panel of judges issue a trial lawyer's certificate attesting to his eligibility to try cases.

Something like this very procedure is, in fact, followed and has proved its worth in allied fields of endeavor. For example, in Washington, D. C., where I had the honor, some years ago, of serving as Representative from a Brooklyn congressional district, teachers of government, in order to make their classroom instruction more meaningful, were given the opportunity of working with a congressman, assisting him in routine tasks, attending committee hearings, and being present to observe sessions of Congress. Similarly, district attorneys' offices arrange for deputies to be assigned, for a time, to assistants before being permitted to assume the full responsibility of trying a case on their own. And, of course, in many a large law firm, the beginner is required to observe veteran members in action until he is deemed to be qualified to represent the firm in court.

Besides medical students, other professional men, such as dentists, architects, surveyors, engineers, insurance underwriters, and many members of the clergy are required to serve periods of internship varying from one to three years before being accepted as fully qualified practitioners of their respective specialty. It seems to me to be manifestly unfair to the clients, to the courts, to the bar, and to society in general that a lawyer only a day or two removed from the classroom or the seminar should be allowed to become engaged in the prosecution or defense of a civil or criminal case and assume all the responsibility it entails.

The nearest approach to my plan that I know of is the pioneering project undertaken by the Michigan Law School for qualified seniors. There, in connection with a course in trial practice, a television closed circuit permits the students to view all the proceedings in both jury and nonjury trials. A similar technique for teaching trial practice was recently adopted by the University of Texas Law School in one criminal court and three civil courts.

To my mind, it is in this direction that the greatest promise lies of raising the standards and ultimately improving the image of our profession. Under my plan, the beginning attorney would be permitted to pace himself while practicing law, acquiring clients, coming to know and be known in the community, and deciding whether or not to become a trial lawyer. He could then look forward with greater assurance to the day when, having been duly certified, he could join the ranks of the select few. That will be a day of signal honor for him, and the bench and the bar will be better served, for the endless chain of trial lawyers will have been strengthened by the addition of another powerful link. Only then will the base of the bar be broadened by the knighting, as it were, of gallant, properly equipped lawyers, ready and able to do battle in the judicial arena.

If, as has been said, "a court is a battlefield where truth and falsehood are locked in mortal combat," then it is on that battlefield, and not in the cloistered confines of the classroom or the seminar, that the young, inexperienced lawyers must win or lose their spurs, have their mettle tested, and achieve forensic success.

In relation to that "trial by combat," a book such as this one on the art of advocacy can be considered no more than a kind of manual of arms. Yet it will have served its purpose if it helps in some measure to raise the sights of the combatants, to strengthen their resolve to "fight the good fight," and to pursue unflaggingly the goal of perfecting their art and bringing honor to our noble profession.

Index

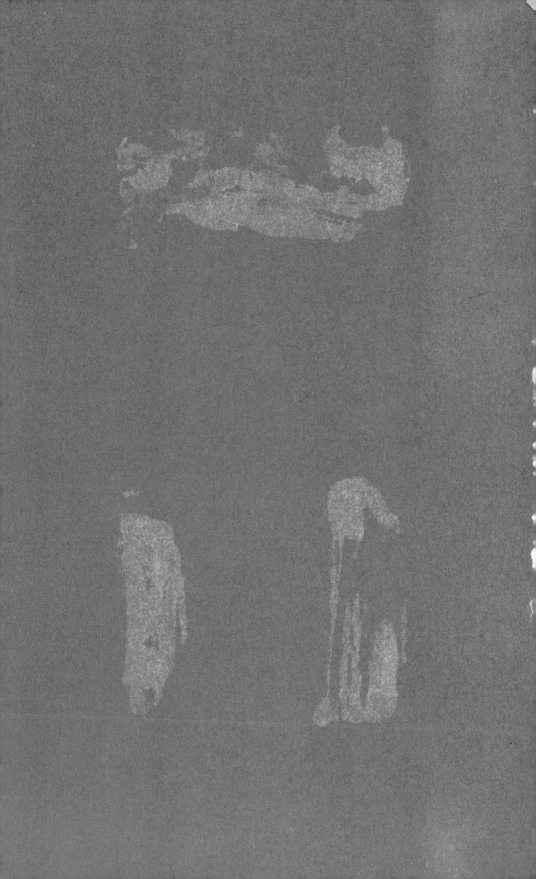